The Holocene Ev
of the London T

Archaeological Excavations (1991–1998)
for the London Underground Limited
Jubilee Line Extension Project

MoLAS Monograph Series

1 Excavations at the Priory and Hospital of St Mary Spital, London,
Christopher Thomas, Barney Sloane & Christopher Phillpotts
ISBN 1 901992 00 4

2 The National Roman Fabric Reference Collection: a handbook,
Roberta Tomber & John Dore
ISBN 1 901922 01 2

3 The Cross Bones Burial Ground, Redcross Way, Southwark,
London: archaeological excavations (1991–1998) for the London
Underground Limited Jubilee Line Extension Project, Megan
Brickley & Adrian Miles with Hilary Stainer
ISBN 1 901992 06 3

4 The Eastern Cemetery of Roman London: excavations 1983–1990,
Bruno Barber & David Bowsher
ISBN 1 901992 09 8

5 The Holocene Evolution of the London Thames: Archaeological
Excavations (1991–1998) for the London Underground Limited
Jubilee Line Extension Project, Jane Sidell, Keith Wilkinson, Robert
Scaife & Nigel Cameron
ISBN 1 901992 10 1

The Holocene Evolution
of the London Thames

Archaeological Excavations (1991–1998)

for the London Underground Limited

Jubilee Line Extension Project

MoLAS MONOGRAPH 5

Jane Sidell, Keith Wilkinson,
Robert Scaife & Nigel Cameron

MUSEUM OF LONDON ARCHAEOLOGY SERVICE

Published by the Museum of London Archaeology Service
Copyright © Museum of London 2000

Production and series design by Tracy Wellman
Typesetting and design by Jeannette van der Post
Edited by Monica Kendall
Reprographics by Andy Chopping

Printed by the Lavenham Press,
Lavenham, Suffolk CO10 9RN

*Front cover: face section monolith sampling; examining monolith
tins in the laboratory; electron micrograph of* Cocconeis placentula

*Back cover: Thorney Island in the prehistoric period (present day
buildings have been added to locate the view); augering on the
Thames foreshore at Hungerford bridge; electron micrograph of*
Cyclotella striata

CONTRIBUTORS

Principal authors   Jane Sidell – archaeology, sea-level analysis
                        and additional sedimentology
                        (Museum of London Archaeology
                        Service, 87 Queen Victoria Street,
                        London EC4V 4AB)
                        Keith Wilkinson – stratigraphy,
                        sedimentology and mollusc analysis
                        (Department of Archaeology, King
                        Alfred's College, Winchester SO22 4NR)
                        Robert Scaife – pollen analysis
                        (Quaternary Environmental Change
                        Research Centre, University of
                        Southampton, Southampton SO17 1BJ)
                        Nigel Cameron – diatom analysis
                        (Environmental Change Research
                        Centre, University College London,
                        26 Bedford Way, London WC1H 0AP)

Additional diatom   Simon Dobinson (Environmental Change
analysis   Research Centre)

Archaeology of
Westminster   Christopher Thomas

Production   Jeannette van der Post and
                        Tracy Wellman

Illustrations   Andy Chopping, Susan Banks, Jeannette
                        van der Post, Keith Wilkinson, Robert
                        Scaife, Nigel Cameron, Jane Sidell, Kate
                        Pollard, Sarah Jones, Kikar Singh

Project
management   Al Green, Mike Hutchinson, Jane Sidell

Editing   Monica Kendall, Richard Malt

Academic referee   Martin Bell (Department of Archaeology,
                        The University of Reading, Whiteknights,
                        Reading, Berkshire RG6 6AH)

CONTENTS

List of figures viii

List of tables ix

Foreword by Martin Bell xi

Abstract xii

Acknowledgements xiii

List of abbreviations xiv

PART 1 BACKGROUND AND METHODOLOGY

Introduction   1   The Jubilee Line Extension Project 1

History of the project 2

Objectives of the palaeoenvironmental project 2

This volume 4

Project methodology   2   Introduction 5

Fieldwork 5

Assessment 6

Analysis 7

The palaeoenvironmental context of the JLE project   3   Introduction 11

Late Quaternary geology and geomorphology of the Jubilee Line Extension 11

Late Devensian and Holocene vegetation and environmental change in London 18

PART 2 SITE STRATIGRAPHIC AND PALAEOENVIRONMENTAL DATA

Holocene environments in Westminster   4   Introduction 21

The archaeology of Thorney Island 21

Storey's Gate 25

Parliament Square 36

Palace Chambers South 37

Westminster Underground Station 47

St Stephen's East 49

Conclusions: the sedimentation and environment of Westminster 61

Middle and Late Holocene environments in west Southwark   5   Introduction 64

The archaeology of Southwark 64

Joan Street 66

Union Street 77

Conclusions: the sedimentation and environment of west Southwark 86

Holocene environments in Rotherhithe and Canning Town   6   Introduction 89

The archaeology of Rotherhithe and Canning Town 89

Culling Road 90

Canada Water 92

Canning Town (Station and Limmo sites) 99

Conclusions: the sedimentation and environment of

Rotherhithe and Canning Town 101

PART 3 CORRELATION, DISCUSSION AND CONCLUSIONS

Late Glacial and Holocene development of the London Thames   **7**   Introduction 103

Lithostratigraphic sequences: depositional environments,

chronology and diagenesis 104

The braided river of the Late Devensian 106

A meandering river of the Early and Middle Holocene . 107

Transition to a tidal river 109

The tidal river of the Late Holocene 110

Holocene vegetation development in London   **8**   Introduction: the natural vegetation 111

Influences of the Neolithic 112

The Bronze Age woodland 113

The Iron Age 115

Roman and post-Roman periods 115

The interaction of environmental change and human habitation   **9**   Introduction 118

Prehistoric site location, taphonomy and representation . 118

The influence of the changing river on human occupation 121

The Jubilee Line Extension and future palaeoenvironmental

studies of the London Thames 122

Appendix: Analytical methodologies   **10**   Introduction 125

Sedimentology 125

Biostratigraphy 127

Dating 128

Topographic modelling 129

French and German summaries   **11**   130

Bibliography   The Research Archive 132

Published works and other reports 133

Index 139

FIGURES

Fig 1 The line of the Jubilee Line Extension with the study areas highlighted 2

Fig 2 Excavation in advance of tunnelling 3

Fig 3 Westminster, Stratford Langthorne, Redcross Way and London Bridge 4

Fig 4 Example of face section monolith sampling 6

Fig 5 Augering (coring) on the southern foreshore as part of the JLE programme 6

Fig 6 Excavation of a late 14th-century canons' house at Palace Chambers South, Westminster 7

Fig 7 Chronological chart 12

Fig 8 Quaternary deposits present along the route of the JLE 15

Fig 9 Current age–altitude curve for relative sea-level fluctuations in the Thames estuary based on published data 16

Fig 10 Electron micrograph of *Cocconeis placentula* . . . 17

Fig 11 Parliament Square, Westminster 22

Fig 12 Map of the Westminster study area 23

Fig 13 Plan of Thorney Island, Westminster 24

Fig 14 Foundations of a late 13th-century inn abutted by the gatehouse to New Palace Yard, Westminster . 25

Fig 15 Lithological diagram from Storey's Gate, Westminster 27

Fig 16 Pollen diagram from Storey's Gate, Westminster . . 28

Fig 17 Diatom diagram from Storey's Gate, Westminster . . 32

Fig 18 Pollen diagram from Parliament Square, Westminster 38

Fig 19 Sections from Palace Chambers South, Westminster . 40

Fig 20 Particle-size distribution of samples from Palace Chambers South and St Stephen's East, Westminster . . 41

Fig 21 Lithological diagram from Palace Chambers South, Westminster 42

Fig 22 Pollen diagram from Palace Chambers South, Westminster 44

Fig 23 Lithological diagram from St Stephen's East, Westminster 51

Fig 24 Section drawing, St Stephen's East, Westminster . . 52

Fig 25 Mollusc (>1mm) frequency histogram from St Stephen's East, Westminster 53

Fig 26 Pollen diagram from St Stephen's East, Westminster . 54

Fig 27 Diatom diagram from St Stephen's East, Westminster . 58

Fig 28 Reconstruction of dry-land topography and the Thames and the Tyburn at Westminster in the Mesolithic, Neolithic and Late Iron Age 62

Fig 29 Map of Southwark 65

Fig 30 Lithological diagram from Joan Street, west Southwark 67, 68

Fig 31 Pollen diagram from Joan Street, west Southwark . 70

Fig 32 Diatom diagram from Joan Street, west Southwark . 74

Fig 33 Lithological diagram from Union Street, west Southwark 78

Fig 34 Pollen diagram from Union Street, west Southwark . 80

Fig 35 Diatom diagram from Union Street, west Southwark . 84

Fig 36 Electron micrograph of *Cyclotella striata* 88

Fig 37 North Greenwich Station and the Millennium Dome 90

Fig 38 Map of Rotherhithe and Canning Town 91

Fig 39 Lithological diagram from Canada Water, Rotherhithe 94

Fig 40 Pollen diagram from Canada Water, Rotherhithe . . 96

Fig 41 Electron micrograph of *Fragilaria brevistriata* . . . 99

Fig 42 Representation of the stratigraphy recorded at the Canning Town Limmo 100

Fig 43 Aerial view of the JLE eastern section 103

Fig 44 Facies of the JLE sites plotted against altitude and chronology 105

Fig 45 Topographic model of 'Mesolithic' period river systems in central London 108

Fig 46 Minimum age by which in-channel sand strata have ceased accreting, plotted on a west–east axis . . 108

Fig 47 Current age–altitude curve for relative sea-level fluctuations in the Thames estuary based on published data with five additional points from JLE sites . . 110

Fig 48 Sample production chart 126

TABLES

Table 1 Sites and samples submitted for assessment . . . 7

Table 2 Diatom halobian groups 10

Table 3 Pleistocene strata of the London Thames –
conflicting views 13

Table 4 Chronology and altitude variants of the Thames
lithofacies 16

Table 5 Beds of the Westminster member 63

Table 6 Facies of the Jubilee Line Extension 104

Table 7 Particle-size samples examined during the project 127

Table 8 ¹⁴C dates obtained from the sites 129

FOREWORD

Dr Martin Bell
Department of Archaeology
University of Reading

The Jubilee Line Extension Project represents a major piece of transport infrastructure development which has been richly productive of archaeology. The interim results of the project as a whole have already been made available to a wider public through an attractively produced booklet (Drummond-Murray *et al* 1998). Now we have a promptly produced final report on that part of the project which looks at the evidence for the past environment of the Thames Valley concentrating on the Holocene, the last 10,000 years. Jubilee Line project results are integrated with those of earlier work on the London Thames making this a most useful synthesis of the present state of knowledge.

Unusually for Britain the emphasis is explicitly geoarchaeological; the sedimentary context of the archaeological and biological evidence is foregrounded in a way which has for much longer been current in the United States or the Netherlands. The increasing prominence of geoarchaeology in Britain has come about partly as a result of major infrastructure projects. Planning aspects of the Jubilee Line Extension were under an enabling Act of Parliament, but developer-funded assessments and excavations now constitute the greater part of archaeological activity in Britain with the implementation of Planning Policy Guidance Note 16. Increasingly archaeologists are called on to assess deep

sediment sequences and their archaeological content in order to inform the planning process. That requires a real understanding of how sediments formed and how they relate to the history of human activity. The importance of such an approach was particularly apparent in the case of the Jubilee Line Extension; its entire route runs through areas with later Quaternary sediments, although the tunnel itself is generally deeper within Tertiary deposits.

Developer-funded assessments are focused on planning rather than academic objectives and are often small scale. Many do not get published in the conventional way and there are concerns about how the results will be integrated within wider archaeological syntheses. This monograph helps to identify a way forward by demonstrating what can be achieved from the seemingly unpromising circumstance of numerous, often quite small holes, such as ventilation shafts, scattered within four main study areas over a distance of 12km between Westminster and Canning Town. Through developing an understanding of the overall sedimentary sequence, broader-scale synthesis becomes possible. This involved, for instance, investigating some sites with very little archaeology but considerable interest from the perspective of understanding past human environments. What can be achieved from integration of data derived from many sites and palaeoenvironmental sources is illustrated by the remarkable series of maps showing the changing topography of Westminster from the Mesolithic to the Iron Age.

The hallmarks of this volume are an emphasis on Holocene geoarchaeology, a demonstration of the potential of that approach for the synthesis of data from many scattered holes and the way in which the results are integrated with earlier work in the environments of London and the Thames. The success of this broad synthetic approach reflects the imaginative vision of London Underground Limited and the archaeological organisations with which they have worked.

xi

ABSTRACT

This book is based on the Jubilee Line Palaeoenvironmental Project. This was established in order to provide a geoarchaeological context for the overall Jubilee Line archaeological project which led to major research in Westminster, Southwark and Stratford. The aims were to characterise the sedimentary sequences uncovered along the line of the new extension and recreate the change and development of the Thames floodplain in central London. This could then be used as a biophysical framework upon which to develop interpretations of the human societies using this area of London during the Holocene.

The project has focused on four main study areas: Thorney Island, west Southwark, Rotherhithe and Canning Town. In all these areas, models of sedimentation, riverine change and the developing vegetation have been examined. The individual accounts are presented in detail and are supported by extensive diagrammatic representation of the data. These examinations have shown local trends at the individual sites. However, from these, it has been possible to draw overall conclusions relating to the whole of the study area: a 12km stretch throughout some of the richest archaeological zones in England.

A three-stage model for the development of the Thames throughout the Holocene has been proposed. An initial post-glacial braided river traversing a wide floodplain was followed by a single-channel meandering course. This was finally followed by the upstream progression of the tidal head bringing the study area into the catchment of the Thames estuary. This event took place in the Late Bronze Age and naturally would have affected the occupants of the floodplain, evidence for whom is gradually becoming more extensive.

ACKNOWLEDGEMENTS

The analysis and publication of this volume has been entirely funded by London Underground Limited (LUL), Jubilee Line Extension Project (JLEP), to whom the authors, on behalf of MoLAS, would like to extend their grateful thanks. Particular thanks should go to Paul Chapman and Marcus Karakashian of the Jubilee Line Extension Project who have worked closely with and supported MoLAS throughout the archaeological project.

This project was first considered and designed by James Rackham and John Dillon and then developed by the authors, with the assistance of Peter Hinton. The project was managed with the assistance of Mike Hutchinson and Al Green, the overall archaeology project managers for the JLE archaeological project, with Barney Sloane and Gordon Malcolm, post-excavation programme managers.

The authors would like to express their thanks for the assistance rendered during the fieldwork, assessment and analysis by many individuals; in particular, James Rackham, Peter Hinton, John Naylor, Simon Dobinson, Jerry Lee, Russell Wynn, Dan Bird, Ewan Shilland, Julian Bowsher, Robert Cowie, James Drummond-Murray, Simon Mason, Christopher Thomas and Marek Ziebart.

The publication has been designed by Tracy Wellman and Jeannette van der Post with photographs by Andy Chopping and illustrations produced by Susan Banks, Sarah Jones, Kate Pollard, Kikar Singh and all principal authors, and edited by Monica Kendall aided by Katie Frederick. The authors are particularly grateful to Martin Bell for his guidance as academic referee, while additional peer review was provided by Antony Long and Richard Malt who are both thanked for their comments.

ABBREVIATIONS

AMS	accelerator mass spectrometry
BAR	British Archaeological Reports
BGS	British Geological Survey
BP	Before Present (1950)
^{14}C	radiocarbon
cal.	calibrated
CAW	Canada Water (also CW)
CBA	Council for British Archaeology
CECQR	(former) Centre for Environmental Change and Quaternary Research
CUG	Culling Road
CW	Canada Water (also CAW)
DGLA	Department of Greater London Archaeology
DUA	Department of Urban Archaeology
ECRC	Environmental Change Research Centre
ERL	Environmental Resources Limited
GIS	Geographic Information System
GLEAS	Greater London Environmental Archaeology Service
GLSMR	Greater London Sites and Monuments Record
GSF	Geoarchaeological Service Facility
IRSL	infra-red stimulated luminescence
JLE	Jubilee Line Extension
JLEP	Jubilee Line Extension Project
JOA	Joan Street
LBE	London Bridge
LOI	loss-on-ignition
lpaz	local pollen-assemblage zone
LUL	London Underground Limited
MAP2	*Management of archaeological projects* (English Heritage 1991)
MHWST	mean high water of spring tides
MoL	Museum of London
MoLAS	Museum of London Archaeology Service
MS	magnetic susceptibility
MSL	mean sea level
OAU	Oxford Archaeological Unit
OD	Ordnance Datum
OIS	oxygen isotope stage
OSL	optically stimulated luminescence
pasz	pollen-assemblage sub-zone
PPG16	Planning Policy Guidance Note 16
PSA	particle-size analysis
PSQ	Parliament Square
QECRC	Quaternary Environmental Change Research Centre
RSL	relative sea level
SGT	Storey's Gate (also ST)
SLAEC	Southwark and Lambeth Archaeological Excavation Committee
SSE	St Stephen's East
ST	Storey's Gate (also SGT)
tdlp	total dry-land pollen
TL	thermoluminescence
UNION	Union Street (also UNS)
UNS	Union Street (also UNION)
UPD	updated project design
WSS	Palace Chambers South
WUS	Westminster Underground Station

Part I:
Background and
methodology

1

Introduction

Jane Sidell

The Jubilee Line Extension Project

(Fig 1)

The £2.8 billion extension to London Underground's Jubilee Line is the first new addition to the London Underground for over two decades. It was the largest civil engineering project of its time in Europe and included a substantial archaeological fieldwork component designed to coordinate with construction work. The project took place after a considerable time on the drawing board; following the Second World War, plans were laid for new underground lines linking the south and east of London to the centre of the City. The regeneration of Docklands and the new Canary Wharf development gave these plans the necessary impetus and, as a result, the Jubilee Line Extension Project (JLEP) was conceived. In August 1989 an 'archaeological impact assessment' of the route was commissioned (Environmental Resources Ltd 1990) and as a result of this, the impact of cutting a swathe through some of the most archaeologically sensitive parts of central London was fully realised; the line in fact terminates above the remains of a medieval Cistercian abbey. In order to do justice to the archaeology that would be destroyed by building the shallower components such as ticket halls, escalator shafts and air vents, archaeological excavations were proposed for these areas (Fig 2). The train tracks themselves are mainly located in tunnels bored through the London Clay, which was laid down in the Eocene (part of the Cainozoic Era) roughly 55 million years ago (Ellison & Zalasiewicz 1996, 94). Therefore, these deposits were laid down significantly before human occupation and as such are of little interest to archaeologists. It is mainly with the last 10,000 years that archaeologists working on the JLEP are concerned.

The archaeological excavations were centred on three main areas of known historic and archaeological interest – Westminster, Southwark and Stratford, which between them cover roughly the last 7000 years of human development in London (Fig 3). Many of the individual sites were located in extremely archaeologically sensitive areas, the excavation of which generated a whole new data set relating to an important range of themes. These include evidence of early farming in Neolithic Westminster, the growth of the Roman suburbs south of the River Thames, the death rates of Cistercian monks in medieval Stratford and the burial and disease incidence of prostitutes in 18th-century Southwark.

Conventional archaeological publication has tended towards stratigraphic narratives of individual sites. Rather than pursuing this approach, the research of over 50 archaeologists on the JLEP excavations has led to a series of thematic publications. These cover the Roman occupation of Southwark (Drummond-Murray *et al* in prep), the archaeological development of Westminster (Thomas *et al* in prep), the Cistercian Abbey of St Mary, Stratford Langthorne (Barber *et al* in prep) and the post-medieval Cross Bones burial ground at Redcross Way, Southwark (Brickley *et al* 1999). In addition to these texts, popular works and leaflets were prepared to inform the public about the archaeology in their local area, for instance *The big dig* (Drummond-Murray *et al* 1998).

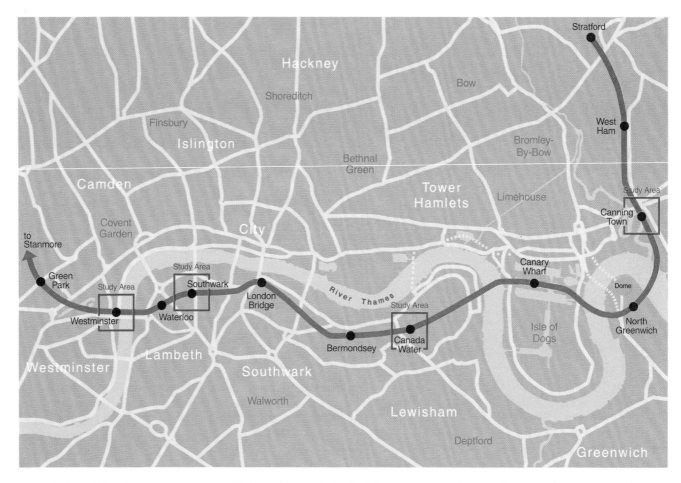

Fig 1 *The line of the Jubilee Line Extension with the study areas highlighted © Crown copyright. All rights reserved. Corporation of London LA 087254/00/12*

The project which led to this book was entitled the Jubilee Line Extension Palaeoenvironmental Research Project (henceforward 'the project'). It was designed to complement the other research projects and create an overarching environmental and topographic context in which to frame the new data arising from all the Jubilee Line excavations. Without a thorough knowledge of the landforms, vegetation and sedimentary processes operating within a zone of human habitation (particularly in the prehistoric period), it is extremely difficult to propose models of how societies behaved and developed. This project was the first of its kind in London and marks an important step forward in the contextualisation of 'traditional' archaeological interpretation within a topographic and ecological framework.

a site by site basis. These discussions led to a proposal for a fully integrated project to complement the other themed projects, particularly that centred upon Westminster (Thomas *et al* in prep). A number of problems were associated with the construction of the line, causing a subsequent halt to the archaeological project. These were resolved in 1994, and the sampling, which had begun in 1991, was continued. The sampling did in fact continue into 1998; however, the bulk of the excavations were completed by the end of 1995. Owing to the tight timetable for completion of both the line and the overall archaeological project, it was decided to undertake a review of the project in the summer of 1995; details of this are given in chapter 2.

History of the project

The project was devised initially by James Rackham (formerly of the Greater London Environmental Archaeology Service) (GLEAS) and John Dillon (formerly of the London Borough of Southwark) to examine sedimentary and ecological sequences from sites excavated along the route. Initially, negotiations took place with London Underground Limited (LUL) for analysis on

Objectives of the palaeoenvironmental project

The overriding objective of this project is to consider the lithological and ecological history of the area along the route of the Jubilee Line Extension. This was to be undertaken using a suite of bioarchaeological and geoarchaeological techniques with dating control provided by radiometric and typological methods. The research is central to MoLAS's research agenda for

Fig 2 Excavation in advance of tunnelling

London, in view of the need to better understand human interaction within the dynamic topographic systems of the Greater London area. A series of more detailed objectives were drawn up in the Project Design (Sidell 1995) and were maintained following the formal assessment and review of research objectives in 1997 (Sidell 1997). These are as follows:

- To examine the sedimentary sequences as exposed along the line of the extension.
- To understand the nature and development of the local and regional vegetation in the Holocene.
- To establish a dating framework for selected sites and events.
- To analyse the causes and events leading to deposition and accumulation of the sedimentary units and develop a facies model of deposition.
- To consider the possible origins of the sediments and therefore influences acting upon the Thames system by tributaries and terrestrial processes.
- To correlate and link sites by these approaches.
- To map the subsurface topography, *ie* the surface of the Pleistocene gravels and Holocene peats, and consider the influences of this on site formation processes.
- To consider the influence of tidal factors within the temporal and geographic boundaries.
- To propose and test models of sedimentation along the route.

The parameters governing this project were such that it was not necessary to be confined to sites with a demonstrable human presence, as is commonly the case with archaeological investigations carried out as part of the planning process. The archaeology of the Jubilee Line project was not regulated under Planning Policy Guidance Note 16 (PPG16) which was issued subsequent to the initiation of the Jubilee Line excavations. Instead, the archaeological programme was regulated under an enabling Act of Parliament. The initial Parliamentary bill was deposited in November 1989. This covered the details of constructing the line, acquiring land, planning permission and incidental matters such as temporary road closure. A further bill was deposited in 1990 to reflect modifications to the scheme. Both bills were opposed but finally, in March 1992, royal assent was granted and the parliamentary Act was passed (London Underground Act 1992) (Willis 1997). The project was proposed as research to place the archaeology of the line into a wider palaeoecological context; therefore, sedimentary sequences in areas undisturbed by human impact were the optimum sources. Consequently, a number of sites used in this project and discussed in this volume do not appear in the other published volumes of the JLE archaeological projects. These include the Southwark sites of Joan Street (JOA90), Union Street (UNS91), Culling Road (CUG93) and Canada Water (CAW91). In addition the Canning Town sites are mentioned in this text. Several of these sites produced exceptional palaeoecological sequences while being almost entirely devoid of archaeological features or artefacts. A notable exception are the two butchered red deer antlers recovered from Canada Water and Joan Street.

This volume

The text is divided into three parts. The first of these, Background and Methodology, outlines how and why the JLE archaeological project came into being, and what part is played by the palaeoenvironmental project. It also examines research objectives, data collection and the analytical methodologies employed by this project. The rationale behind these methodologies and their preference over others is the emphasis of this part. The actual detail of the methods, from fieldwork to laboratory techniques, may be found in the Appendix. Part 2, Site Stratigraphic and Palaeoenvironmental Data, outlines the results of the litho- and biostratigraphical analysis from each site examined within the chronological framework of the Holocene. These are grouped by three geographical areas: Westminster, west Southwark, and Rotherhithe and Canning Town. Conclusions are presented for the geomorphological and ecological development of each area. Part 3, Correlation, Discussion and Conclusions, reviews what has been learnt about the main areas under study: the history of the Thames, the development of vegetation and the geomorphology of the central London region. The book is concluded with a brief examination of the way forward for palaeoenvironmental research in the capital. It should be noted that several parts of the monograph have been produced by partial use of unpublished excavation, evaluation and assessment reports (so-called 'client' or 'developer' reports), which are not in the public domain but available in the Museum of London Archive. These reports will, in many cases, not be published beyond what is used in this account. However, to facilitate access for interested researchers, those used in preparing this text have been separately listed at the beginning of the bibliography.

Fig 3 Major projects: from top, Westminster, Stratford Langthorne, Redcross Way and London Bridge

2

Project methodology

Jane Sidell and Keith Wilkinson

Introduction

By virtue of this project being devised as an examination of the geomorphological and ecological development of a given study area, it was decided to adopt a geoarchaeological approach (*sensu* Butzer 1982, 35–42; Rapp & Hill 1998, 1–5) comprising the study of lithostratigraphy, biostratigraphy and chronostratigraphy. The detailed methodologies employed throughout this project are described in the Appendix; this chapter outlines why specific approaches were favoured. Alongside this is an account of how the project progressed from initial sample collection to publication. The fieldwork is examined, followed by the mid-project review (MAP2 assessment (English Heritage 1991)). The chapter then examines the way in which the laboratory analyses were conducted and concludes by discussing the presentation of the data and the generation of a synthetic discussion

Fieldwork

Generally samples were collected from trench sections during conventional archaeological evaluation and excavation. On occasion, sampling was undertaken directly from the construction sites: for instance, the second phase of sampling undertaken at Joan Street took place during the sinking of grouting shafts. The sedimentary sequences were sampled using stainless steel monolith tins (500mm x 50mm x 50mm) which were hammered into cleaned and recorded sections, selected on site as representative locations (Fig 4). They were taken, in the main, by Jane Sidell, although several of the earlier sites were sampled by senior archaeologists of the Department of Greater London Archaeology (DGLA). The use of monolith sampling from trench faces rather than coring (Fig 5) was determined by two main reasons. Firstly, the archaeological work on the JLEP was driven by trench excavation, and therefore it was logistically appropriate to work within the archaeological project wherever possible and collect samples from available sites. Secondly, trench sampling has a number of advantages over coring: generally a large exposure is available from which to carefully select the sample location and avoid anomalies which cannot be viewed through coring. Additionally, these sections may be recorded in detail to assist with the sedimentary description of characteristics such as bedding and dip – again, aspects which it is often impossible to record accurately during coring owing to the narrow samples retrieved. Furthermore, some types of coring often lead to compression of sediment, causing problems of assigning 'correct' Ordnance Datum (OD) levels. (Although the sediment has almost certainly undergone significant compression since it was laid down, coring may add a further error of up to roughly 10%.) Additionally, coring may be done at an angle away from true vertical, which again will affect calculation of OD heights.

Fig 4 Example of face section monolith sampling

Samples were retrieved through coring at one site only, the Canning Town Limmo (chapter 6). This was a result of the large scale of construction which was such that the whole area could not be easily examined through trench excavation.

The combination of monolith tins and bulk samples was used in order to generate two distinct groups of samples which could then be used for a variety of analytical techniques. Monolith samples are used for high-resolution sedimentary analysis, initially to describe the facies sequence (in conjunction with field observations) then subsampled on a fine scale (in this case at 1 or 2cm intervals) for other techniques such as biostratigraphic analyses. Bulk samples collected adjacent to sample columns are used for associated research requiring larger volumes of sediment, such as mollusc analysis or occasionally ^{14}C assay (these generally are split from the monoliths). All samples are directly related through stratigraphic links defined by context numbers.

Assessment

Following the completion of most of the fieldwork, a MAP2 (English Heritage 1991) style assessment was undertaken on the sediments, pollen and diatoms. Three subsequent sites (all in Westminster) have been assessed individually and two were not thought to be of high enough potential to contribute directly to this volume. One site – Palace Chambers South – was sampled during three separate interventions (Fig 6) and all samples collected have been analysed in tandem.

Fig 5 Augering (coring) on the southern foreshore as part of the JLE programme associated with strengthening the tube tunnels under the Thames at the Hungerford rail bridge

The assessment was undertaken in order to establish the preservation and diversity of biological groups, define the potential for analysis of the assemblage of samples, and re-evaluate the original research objectives. To this end, all the monolith samples collected throughout the project were examined and subsamples were split and submitted to Robert Scaife for assessment of the pollen content. Further samples were submitted to Nigel Cameron for assessment of diatom valves. At this stage, the sites in question were as shown in Table 1.

In addition to these sites, samples from Culling Road, Rotherhithe (CUG93) (Wilkinson 1994) and Redcross Way, Southwark (REW92) (Wilkinson 1996b) had been previously assessed and were not recommended for detailed analysis. Two sites excavated by the Oxford Archaeological Unit (OAU) had also been assessed outside the palaeoenvironmental project. Environmental reports from these were considered during the assessment stage of this project, for instance the Canning Town Limmo (Bates et al 1994). However, it was not possible to undertake any detailed analysis.

Table 1 Sites and samples submitted for assessment

Name	Location	Site code
Canada Water	East Southwark	CAW91
London Bridge	Central Southwark	LBE95
206 Union Street	West Southwark	UNS91
Joan Street	West Southwark	JOA90
St Stephen's East	Westminster	SSE94
Westminster Underground Station	Westminster	WUS90
Palace Chambers South	Westminster	WSS94
Parliament Square	Westminster	PSQ94
Storey's Gate	Westminster	SGT94

Furthermore, several sites were abandoned which were scheduled for excavation and were in known areas of palaeoenvironmental interest with important sedimentary sequences and prehistoric archaeology. This was owing to excessive soil contamination, for instance at North Greenwich and Canary Wharf stations and Durands Wharf, Rotherhithe.

Assessment of the stratigraphy, sedimentology and biostratigraphy at each site led to the identification of a series of sites that had high potential for detailed analysis. These were discussed at a meeting of the authors in the context of their relative locations and initial chronostratigraphy. A number were selected for further work, namely Palace Chambers South, St Stephen's East, Storey's Gate (all in Westminster), Union Street and Joan Street (in west Southwark) and Canada Water in Rotherhithe. In conjunction with the assessment, an updated project design (UPD) was prepared (Sidell 1997) to focus the analysis of all specialists to address specific questions relating to site formation, vegetation and sea-level development. It also detailed methods for analysis, a preliminary publication synopsis, and a programme of work and costs.

Fig 6 Excavation of a late 14th-century canons' house at Palace Chambers South, Westminster

Analysis

Lithostratigraphy and sedimentology

The main source of data for lithological interpretation has unsurprisingly been morphological and structural description of the sedimentary beds encountered at the JLE sites. These were made both in the field by the archaeologists excavating the site, who produced both a written (*ie* context descriptions) and a drawn record (*ie* section drawings), and subsequently by geoarchaeologists working on the monolith samples in the laboratory. Unfortunately there was no opportunity for geoarchaeological description of sequences in the field. Having access to both sources of description has been vitally important as both have inherent advantages and disadvantages. The archaeological site record in the case of the DGLA and later MoLAS has in most cases been made to standard criteria (Spence 1990) and later criteria (Westman 1994). For several

of the sites large areas have been examined, allowing some assessment to be made of spatial variation in deposits, inter-deposit relationships and basic structures. However, the suitability of archaeological recording methods for interpreting non-cultural (*ie* 'natural') stratigraphic sequences of the type often encountered on the JLE has been questioned by geologists and geoarchaeologists (Farrand 1984; Collcutt 1987; Stein 1987; Barham 1995). The argument put forward by these authors is that by placing emphasis on relationships between different 'contexts' by use of Harris Matrices (Harris 1979a; 1979b; 1989), archaeologists are diverted from recording and interpreting the deposits themselves. Indeed, although most archaeological site manuals are based on standard sedimentary (Spence 1990; Westman 1994) or pedological criteria (Wessex Archaeology 1994a), there is little provision in these documents for recording bed structures such as cross-bedding, normal and reversed bedding, lamination, or different types of bedding planes.

Using laboratory description of monolith samples for interpretation is of course not without its problems. Despite the fact that a very detailed record can be made of individual strata and the nature of contacts between sediment bodies under controlled, unchanging conditions, it is still the case that the sample window is small. Thus it is impossible to define structural properties at scales greater than laminations. It is often debatable as to how typical the sample is of the site stratigraphy as such samples are most often taken in areas of the most complex bedding. In this project, description of monolith samples was undertaken according to standard sedimentological criteria (eg Tucker 1982) to categorise the strata, and in particular address the issue of recording contacts, while assessment of the drawn and photographic record has enabled bed structure to be reconstructed. Therefore although no one source of descriptive data was ideal, by using a combination of these sources an interpretation of the stratigraphy at each site may be made, suggesting how beds formed, over what sort of time span and where in the sequence unconformities occur.

Laboratory analytical data have played a supporting role to that of description. Hypotheses generated from morphological data discussed above were examined using a series of sedimentary tests made on closely spaced subsamples from the monoliths. Magnetic susceptibility measurements (high and low frequency) were uniformly made on the subsamples using the methodology of Gale and Hoare (1991, 221–6), while the samples were subsequently combusted at 550°C to determine organic carbon content. Magnetic susceptibility is perhaps best known in archaeology as a technique for prospecting for archaeological sites (Clark 1996); however, it has a longer history in the study of sequence stratigraphy. For example various magnetic criteria have been used for lithostratigraphic correlation, particularly of loess sequences (eg Kukla et al 1988; Chen et al 1995), in provenance studies of fluviatile (Oldfield et al 1979) and till deposits (Vonder Haar & Johnson 1973) and in tracking weathering and pedogenesis. However, magnetic susceptibility is also a useful indicator of human activity as many anthropogenic activities such as burning and pottery manufacture lead to magnetic enhancement (Thompson & Oldfield 1986). In this study magnetic susceptibility data have been used to determine the presence or absence of human activity and impact during sediment accumulation, and also as an aid in reconstructing weathering surfaces.

Organic carbon content of present-day soils has, in a similar way to magnetic susceptibility, been used as a criterion in prospecting for archaeological sites (Aston et al 1998), but is more familiar in stratigraphic studies of lake, intertidal or alluvial sediments (eg Thomas & Rackham 1996; Wilkinson et al 2000). Such measurements are particularly useful in examining sites where peats and largely inorganic muds are found interbedded, since closely spaced measurements can indicate the degree of conformity in sedimentary contacts and provide evidence of short-lived flood or stand-still events that are not visible in the lithological record. In sites where archaeological activity is suspected, the data can be used alongside magnetic susceptibility measurements to determine whether humans were present as anthropogenic activities are commonly a net producer of organic matter.

Particle-size analysis has also been carried out using sieve (Gale & Hoare 1991, 86–7) and Sedigraph techniques on samples from four sites, but at coarser intervals than the sedimentary tests detailed above. Particle-size analysis is perhaps the most important technique used in modern sedimentology and is an essential component of lithological characterisation (Gale & Hoare 1991, 56) as well as being a natural stepping stone to analysis of particle shape and mineralogy (Canti 1995). The samples submitted for particle-size analysis are together representative of the stratigraphy found on all the sites of the JLE examined in this project, and have thus allowed this basic categorisation to be made. The results of particle-size analysis have been combined with the morphological data to produce more detailed and informed description. Particle-size distribution has also been taken to be indicative of the environment of deposition, sediment provenance and weathering histories. For the purposes of this project the interest is in the nature of the fluvial environment represented by sample particle-size distribution. Criteria for the size distribution of fluvial sediments have been modelled by Folk and Ward (1957), Sengupta (1975; 1979) and Middleton (1976) among others, and it is these that have been used in interpreting the JLE particle-size data.

Interpretation of lithostratigraphic and sedimentological data in the context of the JLE has not been a straightforward process. Information has been collected from a number of different sources, but has been integrated in the text that follows, rather than simply presenting the data under technique-based sub-headings. It is hoped that in this way the reader will better understand how the different categories of sedimentary information interrelate and together allow a comprehensive interpretation of the mechanisms of sediment accretion at each of the study sites.

Biostratigraphy

Palynology

The analysis of sub-fossil pollen and spores recovered from Holocene sediments was for a long time regarded primarily as a dating technique. With the advent of ^{14}C measurements allowing absolute dating of environmental events, pollen analysis is regarded as an essential tool for reconstructing past vegetation and environments. Pollen grains and spores can be preserved in a wide range of soils, sediments and archaeological contexts. Peat deposits are especially suitable for analysis having accumulated through time under waterlogged anaerobic conditions which are favourable for pollen preservation. Pollen preserved in such conditions may be used to examine temporal changes in the vegetation environment brought about by natural climatic and plant biological factors and the effects of human interference on these habitats. The advantage of pollen is that, unlike plant macrofossils (largely seeds), representation of both the local and regional vegetation and the environment can be gained. Seeds in such deposits tend to come only from the peat-forming vegetation with little representation of the dry-land habitats.

The interpretation of pollen extracted from such contexts is complicated by a wide range of taphonomic factors. These comprise the essentials of pollination ecology such as entomophily or anemophily which produces very substantial differences in pollen production and area of dispersal. Typically, in the latter, tree taxa such as birch and pine produce very substantial numbers of pollen grains which may be wind disseminated over great distances. In contrast are taxa such as lime/lindens which being insect-pollinated produce far smaller numbers of grains. Other taxa such as beech although wind pollinated have heavier pollen grains which along with insect-pollinated types also do not travel great distances from their source. The overall result of these variations in pollen productivity and dispersion is the differential representation of tree, shrub and herb pollen at sites within a pollen catchment. Depositional factors may also give rise to pollen assemblages skewed in favour of pollen types which have robust pollen walls (the exine) whereas weaker grains may have been destroyed in adverse conditions. Thus, when examining pollen diagrams in this volume, the reader should be aware that the percentages or size of the pollen record of each taxon is not a reliable measure of the importance of a plant type. For example, only a few grains of beech (*Fagus*), ash (*Fraxinus*) and lime (*Tilia*) can be regarded as significant whereas even quite high percentages of birch (*Betula*), pine (*Pinus*) or hazel (*Corylus avellana*) may be less significant, representing wind-blown pollen from a wider pollen catchment. For more detailed explanations of palaeoecological techniques used see especially Bell and Walker (1993), Lowe and Walker (1997) and Moore *et al* (1991).

In spite of the complexity of pollen recovery and interpretation, valuable information can be gained on the vegetation communities which relate to the on-site (autochthonous) peat-forming communities as well as, predominantly, the nearby dry-land vegetation. During the construction of the Jubilee Line Extension, extensive thick peats and organic muds were found underlying the floodplain silts of the River Thames. The analysis of these has enabled detailed studies of the past vegetation of the central London region for the past 6000 years. Pollen analysis has provided information on the biostratigraphy and on-site depositional environments which relate to the lithostratigraphy, sedimentological and diatom analyses which have also been carried out. Due to the broader footprint of the pollen signal, data on the character and development of the late prehistoric and historic vegetation of central London have been gained. These data are presented on a site by site basis using standard pollen diagrams.

Diatom analysis

Diatoms (Bacillariophyceae) are a class of algae abundant in all moist and aquatic habitats in freshwater, brackish and marine environments. Diatom communities are usually diverse and occupy a range of habitats including open water (*plankton*), attached to or associated with inorganic materials such as sand (*epipsammon*), mud (*epipelon*), rock (*epilithon*) and attached to the submerged surfaces of macrophytes (*epiphyton*).

Diatoms are distinct from other algae in having a silica cell wall composed of two overlapping valves linked together by girdle bands and their taxonomy has developed based largely on the valve features (Round *et al* 1990). This has allowed palaeoecologists working on fossil diatoms to use the same approach to taxonomy as diatomists working with modern material. Fossil diatom assemblages preserved in lake, river, coastal or ocean sediments provide records of the species composition, habitats and productivity of former diatom communities. As a result of their sensitivity to specific characteristics – for example acidity, nutrient content and salinity – diatoms can also be used to reconstruct aspects of past water chemistry and related environmental parameters.

The use of diatoms in palaeoecological studies increased in the 1990s and their potential as palaeoecological indicators is clear. However, there remain a number of difficulties in applying diatom analysis in estuarine and intertidal archaeology. These problems include the following:

• The quality of preservation varies in different contexts and, despite the presence of aquatic sediments, diatoms are not always preserved.
• The taxonomy and ecology of many diatoms, particularly those of coastal and estuarine habitats, are poorly understood.
• Interpretation of diatom assemblages, again particularly in estuarine contexts, must take into account a number of taphonomic factors such as the transport of species beyond their lifetime ranges and the differential preservation of taxa.

Where these difficulties can be overcome and there are strong environmental gradients, such as salinity, to which the diatom taxa respond, these algae are able to provide high-quality, species-rich palaeoenvironmental data which are available from few, if any, other groups of aquatic organisms.

Diatoms were selected as the most appropriate group of aquatic organisms to analyse from the sedimentary sequences selected for the JLE Palaeoenvironmental Project. Diatoms are the primary producers at the base of many aquatic ecosystems and form species-rich communities, which are highly sensitive to water quality and, under suitable preserving conditions, form diverse fossil assemblages. Of particular importance in estuarine habitats is the strong relationship of diatom species composition to salinity gradients. Based on the assessment stage of the project, which showed that at a number of sites diatoms were well preserved in alluvial sediments and at the contacts with organic sediments, sections were selected for more detailed diatom analysis (Cameron 1995).

In this project, diatom species have been ascribed to halobian groups (after Hustedt 1953; 1957). These have optimal growth in water with salinity equivalent to the ranges shown in Table 2.

Table 2 Diatom halobian groups

Halobian group	Salinity preference
polyhalobian	>30g l⁻¹
mesohalobian	0.2–30g l⁻¹
oligohalobian halophilous	optimum in slightly brackish water
oligohalobian indifferent	optimum in fresh water but tolerant of slightly brackish water; unknown, taxa with unknown salinity optima
oligohalobian halophobous	restricted to freshwater environments and intolerant of brackish and marine waters

Chronostratigraphy

Generally, the strata encountered on archaeological sites are dated by applying established artefactual chronologies to the contexts which artefacts are derived from. This method (relative dating) is generally reliable and acceptable so long as certain problems such as residuality (reworked material) are taken into account. However, in order for such methods to apply, there need to be archaeological features and strata present on the site. In the sites selected for this project, there were very few of these present. Therefore, it was necessary to find a different method for constructing chronologies for each site. Arguably one of the more reliable forms of absolute dating is ^{14}C (radiocarbon) which relies on measuring the ratio between the unstable (^{14}C) and stable (^{12}C and ^{13}C) carbon isotopes and by measuring this ratio against the known half-life of ^{14}C and establishing when the organism died. The procedure is based on several fundamental assumptions which have been questioned in recent years (see review in Lowe & Walker 1997, 240). However, the method is generally accepted as valid and continues to be the most widely applied absolute dating method for Holocene sediments. In the text ^{14}C dates are quoted in radiocarbon years as supplied by the laboratory, followed by calibrated age ranges (2σ) in parenthesis. Where chronology is discussed without reference to ^{14}C dates, dates are quoted in calibrated years BP. Calibration was carried out using the curve of Stuiver *et al* (1998) for dates postdating 18,000 BP.

The ^{14}C method was selected as the preferred method for several reasons. Primarily, it was selected because it was the technique most consistent with the stratigraphy encountered on these sites, which almost always contained some organic deposits. There was insufficient timber to use the most accurate absolute method, dendrochronology. This relies on the availability of wood samples (generally oak, *Quercus* sp) containing at least 50 rings, preferably with bark edge, or at least sapwood.

Many archaeological sites in London, for instance Thames Court (Ayre *et al* 1996), have had chronologies of remarkable accuracy constructed using this method. Unfortunately, the sites selected for this project contain very few large pieces of wood. Although suitable samples might have been expected from within peat horizons, this is in fact rarely the case. A few dendrochronology samples have been dated from the historic levels of several of the archaeological sites (notably at Westminster) and as such have assisted in establishing the chronologies for those sites.

Topographic modelling

In order to consider the data generated by the combined analyses within a three-dimensional context, it was decided early on to attempt terrain modelling of the subsurface topography in key areas along the line of the route. Initially, discussions were held with the LOCUS team (London Computerised Underground and Surface Project) of the British Geological Survey (BGS) and the engineers on the JLEP. As a result of this, geotechnical data were collected from previous site investigations along the route, from the BGS library and from archaeological trench data. Additionally, the entire JLEP database was made available. The data were used to construct models of the surface of Pleistocene gravels and the Holocene sands and peat horizons using three-dimensional point-data for contacts between major facies types. In the case of Westminster, point-data were gathered from trenches and the modelling was substantially refined by consideration of the location of archaeological features and artefacts. Most of this was undertaken by Christopher Thomas who coordinated and undertook the majority of archaeological work for the Westminster project.

There are a number of problems with this type of modelling, and this should be taken into account when examining the products which are proposed as tentative plots to be modified in the light of future study. These difficulties include limitations of the data, for example boreholes are rarely drilled consistently across a geographical zone; also the quality of descriptions and detail tends to vary between drillers: one driller could record a single facies as 'alluvium', while another could record the same as 'fine silt/clay, fining up with occasional sand laminae and local organic flecks'. There are also limitations with software, most notably the problems of satisfactorily extrapolating between points. All these problems have been encountered with this project. However, if the results are treated as generalisations of actual subsurface topography, then they may be seen as useful graphic tools.

3

The palaeoenvironmental context of the JLE project

Keith Wilkinson, Robert Scaife, Jane Sidell and Nigel Cameron

Introduction

This chapter reviews the current state of knowledge of topographic and environmental change in the London basin during the Late Quaternary (*ie* the end of the Devensian and the Holocene), (Fig 7). This must of necessity be a summary chapter. However, comprehensive references are included for readers wishing to pursue any of the topics further. The purpose of this chapter is to provide a context for the research undertaken during this project.

An account of the geomorphology and topography of the region opens this review, and includes a summary of the geology, hydrology and changes induced by relative sea-level (RSL) change. The first section of the chapter is then concluded by a review of the development of vegetation and environment across the region. These three sections cover major aspects of the landscape and environment of the lower Thames Valley which would have had a major effect upon populations living and passing through the area.

Late Quaternary geology and geomorphology of the Jubilee Line Extension

Introduction

Any map detailing the course of the Jubilee Line Extension will show how the route follows the River Thames, always remaining within half a mile of it (except to the west of Westminster and north of Canning Town) (see Fig 1), while the line crosses the Thames four times. However, looking at a geology map it is immediately obvious that the entire Jubilee Line Extension has been built beneath deposits relating to an earlier Thames river system dating from the later Quaternary period (see Fig 8). Indeed, in the last 400,000 years, processes associated with migration, downcutting and accretion of the Thames have been the single largest factor influencing the geomorphology of not only the route of the Jubilee Line Extension, but the whole of Greater London. Thus when the project was formulated it was realised that most of the stratigraphy with which it would be dealing would be of fluvial origin, relating to previous courses and floodplains of the Thames. These deposits have ranged from gravel terraces of the later Pleistocene, through sands deposited within river channels of the Early to Middle Holocene, to peats of the Neolithic, Bronze and Iron Ages and estuarine clays of the historic period. In comparison few fully terrestrial deposits have been investigated, these consisting solely of occasional samples almost invariably from the medieval

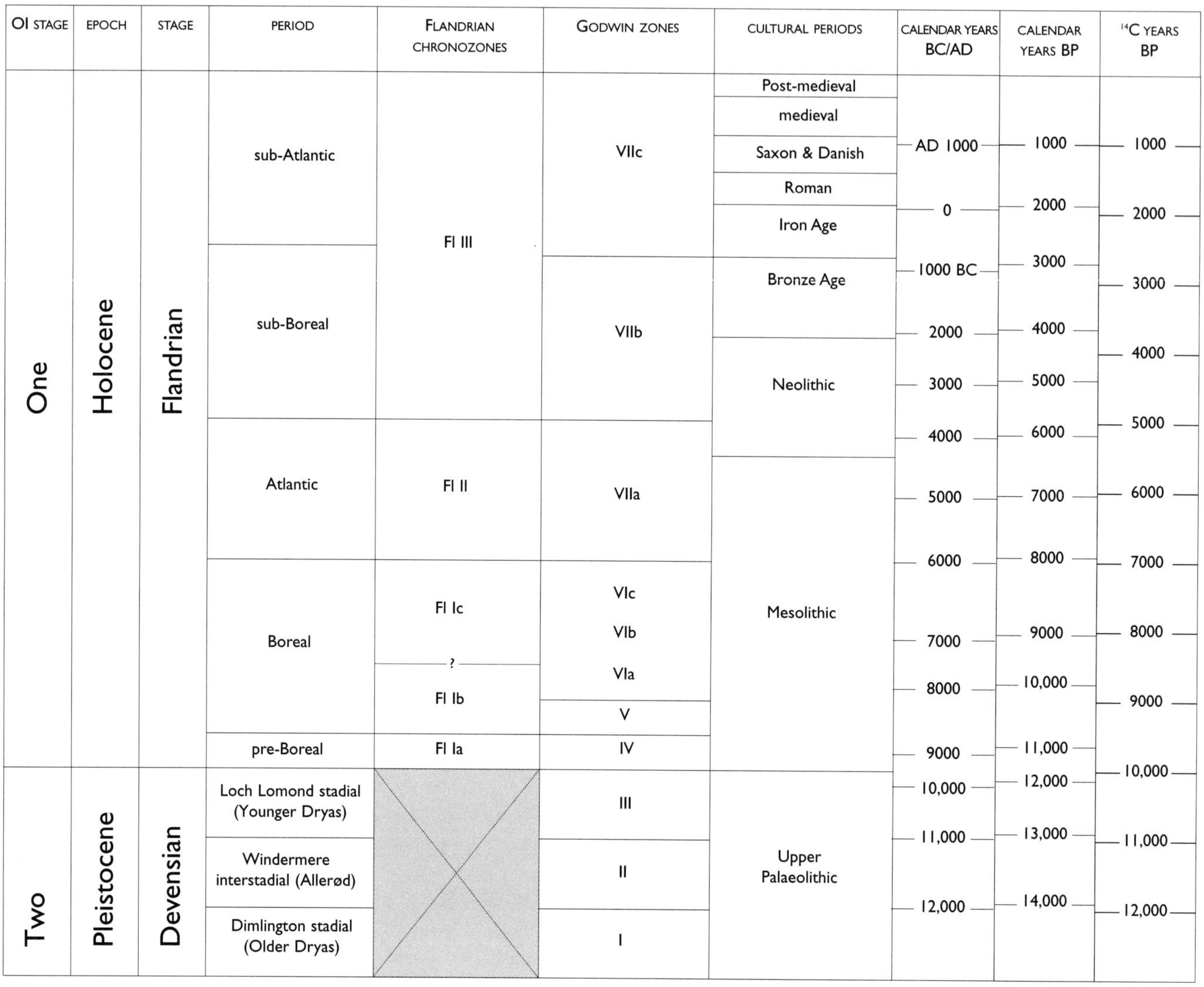

OI STAGE	EPOCH	STAGE	PERIOD	FLANDRIAN CHRONOZONES	GODWIN ZONES	CULTURAL PERIODS	CALENDAR YEARS BC/AD	CALENDAR YEARS BP	^{14}C YEARS BP
One	Holocene	Flandrian	sub-Atlantic	Fl III	VIIc	Post-medieval			
						medieval		1000	1000
						Saxon & Danish	AD 1000		
						Roman		2000	2000
						Iron Age	0		
			sub-Boreal		VIIb	Bronze Age	1000 BC	3000	3000
							2000	4000	4000
						Neolithic	3000	5000	
							4000	6000	5000
			Atlantic	Fl II	VIIa		5000	7000	6000
							6000	8000	7000
			Boreal	Fl Ic	VIc	Mesolithic		9000	8000
					VIb		7000		
					VIa		8000	10,000	9000
				Fl Ib	V		9000	11,000	10,000
			pre-Boreal	Fl Ia	IV		10,000	12,000	
Two	Pleistocene	Devensian	Loch Lomond stadial (Younger Dryas)		III		11,000	13,000	11,000
			Windermere interstadial (Allerød)		II	Upper Palaeolithic	12,000	14,000	12,000
			Dimlington stadial (Older Dryas)		I				

Fig 7 Chronological chart

and post-medieval periods, and from the very tops of sequences such as at Union Street and some of the Westminster sites.

While the river has constantly changed its patterns of flow in response to climatic fluctuations, environments in the London region have altered as a result of the self-same processes. Changes in vegetation have been particularly rapid during the Holocene period as a response to climatic amelioration and later due to human forest clearance and agriculture. In recent years the sheer scale of development in Greater London has enabled the study of these vegetation changes and it is therefore possible to produce a detailed model of landscape evolution from the end of the Devensian Late Glacial to the present post-industrial times. Thus in this section current views of the evolution of the Thames through the later Quaternary period and Holocene vegetation change are reviewed using data from recent, non-JLE projects in the London area. With this information at hand the reader will be readily able to understand how the data from the project fit into a wider chronological framework of landscape and vegetation change.

Gravel terraces and associated Pleistocene stratigraphy

(Table 3)

The subject of the Pleistocene development of the Thames has been covered in detail in a number of recent texts (Gibbard 1985; Bridgland 1994; 1995; Bridgland et al 1995), which detail, often with conflicting interpretations, the evolution of the Thames fluvial system from oxygen isotope stage (OIS) 15 (Cromerian complex) to 2 (Devensian Late Glacial) (see Fig 7). As the deposits investigated as part of this project date from after 18,000 BP (Before Present, ie 1950) (21,000 cal. BP), events predating this are not of great importance as far as this study is concerned, except for the fact that they moulded the landscape in which later sedimentation took place. Therefore, discussion of the period prior to 18,000 BP (21,000 cal. BP) is limited in this account and readers wanting to obtain further details are referred to the references given above. Traditionally the Pleistocene succession of the Thames has been split geographically with areas to the west of the 'Goring gap' being termed the upper Thames, those to the east of the Goring gap, but west of central London the middle Thames, and those to the east the lower Thames. In addition there are separate sequences for Middle Pleistocene sequences of the Thames in both Essex and East Anglia. As the JLE passes through both central and eastern London, its route lies in both the middle and lower Thames zones, and therefore two systems of nomenclature apply (that used in the following text is for the lower Thames, with middle Thames equivalents, Gibbard 1985, in parenthesis). Correlation between deposits in the two zones is largely agreed for all except the latest period of the Pleistocene, although there is still intense debate as to the taxonomic status that should be given to certain gravel strata (Gibbard 1985; Bridgland 1994; Gibbard 1994; Bridgland 1995; Gibbard 1995).

The Thames adopted what is approximately its present course through London sometime during OIS 12 (Anglian). Prior to OIS 13 (Cromerian complex) it had run north-westwards from west of Maidenhead, through the Vale of St Albans, into East Anglia and exiting into the North Sea via the north Norfolk coast. Over time the East Anglian part of this route, characterised by the Kesgrave Sands and Gravels (Rose *et al* 1976), moved progressively southwards, so that by OIS 12 the Thames ran from the Vale of St Albans eastwards to Chelmsford and exited into the North Sea east of modern Colchester (Bridgland 1988). The southward movement of glacier ice during OIS 12 deflected the Thames southwards to a course similar to that of the present day, although at Southend-on-Sea it flowed northwards, again to exit into the North Sea near Colchester. Within this new channel a series of gravel strata were deposited late in OIS 12 (the lower Thames Dartford Heath Gravel (Gibbard 1994) and the middle Thames Black Park Gravel), after which there appears to have been a period of incision, perhaps by as much as 14m, coinciding with the very end of OIS 12 (Gibbard 1994). Accumulation of a further gravel (the Swanscombe Lower Gravel bed) took

place in the channel produced by the incision event during the end of OIS 12 and into OIS 11 (Hoxnian *sensu* Swanscombe). During the latter period energy flows were reduced through increased water depth in an ameliorating climate and fine-grained in-channel and later floodplain deposits were produced (Swanscombe Lower Loam). This was followed by a further period of firstly high-energy, gravel-producing flows (Swanscombe Lower Middle and Upper Middle Gravels) in a deteriorating climate. During this period it would seem that the Thames was confluent with the Dutch river Scheldt (Kerney 1971; Gibbard 1994) for the first time. These later Swanscombe Gravels fined upwards into a fine-grained deposit (Swanscombe Upper Loam) containing the famous Swanscombe skull and are thought to have formed within a periglacial environment, which can probably be correlated with OIS 10 (Early Saalian *sensu* Bridgland 1994, or Wolstonian *sensu* Mitchell *et al* 1973; Gibbard 1985; 1994).

Further downcutting occurred later in OIS 10 as climates deteriorated, followed by accretion of the lower Thames Orsett Heath Gravel (= middle Thames Boyn Hill Gravel) under high-energy, braided channel flow, followed by the Corbets Tey Gravel in similar conditions, which continued to accumulate until OIS 8 (mid Saalian/Wolstonian), punctuated by interglacial low-energy deposits of OIS 9 (Hoxnian *sensu* Hoxne) at Ilford (Cauliflower Pit), Purfleet and Grays according to Bridgland (1994). Throughout this period of accumulation and during previous phases the Thames had flowed on a slightly more northerly course than at the present day east of the City of London, but during deposition of the subsequent OIS 8–6 (mid–late Saalian/Wolstonian) lower Thames Mucking Gravel (= middle Thames Taplow Gravel), its course moved progressively southwards. According to Bridgland (1994) accretion of the Mucking Gravel was interrupted by accumulation of interglacial deposits in OIS 7 (Intra-Saalian temperate episode – 'Ilfordian'), typified by sites such as

Table 3 Pleistocene strata of the London Thames – conflicting views

| OIS | (Bridgland 1994; 1995) | | (Gibbard 1985; 1994; 1995) | |
	middle Thames	lower Thames	middle Thames	lower Thames
1	Floodplain alluvium	Estuarine deposits	Floodplain alluvium	Estuarine deposits
2	Shepperton Gravel	Submerged	Shepperton Gravel	Submerged
5a, 5c, 3	Kensington, Sunbury, Isleworth	Submerged	Kensington, Sunbury, Isleworth	Submerged
5d-2	Kempton Park Gravel	Tilbury Marshes Gravel	Kempton Park Gravel	Tilbury Marshes Gravel
5e	Trafalgar Square and Brentford	Below floodplain	Trafalgar Square, Brentford	Aveley, Crayford, Ilford, Grays Thurrock, Purfleet, Northfleet
6	Kempton Park Gravel/Taplow Gravel	Mucking Gravel	Kempton Park Gravel/Taplow Gravel/ Lynch Hill Gravel	Mucking Gravel/Taplow Gravel/Corbets Tey Gravel
7	None in London	Aveley, West Thurrock, Crayford, Northfleet		
8	Taplow/Lynch Hill Gravel	Mucking Gravel/Corbetts Tey Gravel	↓	↓
9	None in London	Purfleet, Grays		
10	Lynch Hill Gravel/Boyn Hill Gravel	Corbetts Tey/Orsett Heath Gravels		
11	None in London	Swanscombe deposits	None in London	Swanscombe deposits
12	Boyn Hill/Black Park Gravel	Orsett Heath Gravel	Black Park Gravel	Orsett Heath Gravel

text on white background is gravel strata, while text on grey background represents temperate episodes of mainly fine-grained or terrestrial accretion.

Ilford (Uphall Pit), West Thurrock, Crayford and Northfleet. As can be seen, the exact chronology of these gravel-accumulation events is a matter for some debate, primarily because of the complexity of deposition during the post-OIS 10, pre-OIS 5e (Ipswichian) periods, and the consequent lack of sites with clear stratigraphic relationships. All interglacial sites listed by Bridgland (1994) as being of OIS 9 or 7 date based on vertebrate assemblage and amino acid dates, Gibbard (1994; 1995) attributes to OIS 5e (see below) on the basis of stratigraphy and palynology. Nevertheless the one indisputable fact for this period is that fossil material within the gravels, which appear (taking the Bridgland view) to have formed over a longer period of time than the interglacial deposits, is indicative solely of periglacial environments and would therefore appear to suggest that for the majority of time, accretion was in cold climates.

OIS 5e interglacial deposits are well represented in London, consisting mostly of fine-grained channel fill and floodplain sediments, particularly in areas around Hackney, Highbury, Shacklewell, Clapton, Stoke Newington (Hackney Downs Organic Deposits) and, most famously, Trafalgar Square (Franks et al 1958; Franks 1960; Preece 1999). Sites to the east of the JLE – including Grays Thurrock, Sandy Lane, Aveley, Purfleet and the Crayford to Erith 'brickearth spread' – on the other hand, include sedimentological, molluscan and ostracod evidence for the deposition of intertidal sediments (Hollin 1977; Holyoak 1983; Gibbard 1994), although, as has already been discussed, these deposits are attributed to earlier interglacial episodes by Bridgland (1994; 1995). If the Gibbard model is accepted, these data suggest that the mid OIS 5e marine transgression (reaching 10.6m OD at Purfleet) probably did not reach as far as central London, or indeed the easternmost point of the JLE, although in what is now central London water levels did increase as a result. Towards the end of OIS 5e there was a fall in RSL, probably as a result of eustatic changes, but possibly also caused by enhanced sediment accretion in the estuary and tributaries (Gibbard 1994). Nevertheless the result was a progradation of fine-grained freshwater sediments eastwards.

Following the return to cooler conditions in the subsequent OIS 5d–4 (Early Devensian) and the consequent fall in eustatic sea levels, a period of river downcutting occurred. Within this new channel renewed gravel aggradation, of firstly the lower Thames West Thurrock Gravel and then the Tilbury Marshes Gravel (= middle Thames Kempton Park Gravel), took place in a braided river environment. The Tilbury Marsh Gravel is partially capped by the Langley Silt Complex – a series of fine-grained sediments of mixed colluvial and aeolian origin, reworked by fluvial processes. These sediments are generally thicker in west London and thin to the east, and have been luminescence-dated to 17,000 years BP (Gibbard et al 1987), in other words the end of OIS 3 (Middle Devensian). Below these deposits are found localised temperate climate deposits in the form of organic channel fills, which have been correlated with OIS 5a (Cassington interstadial: Maddy et al 1998), 5c (Chelford interstadial: Coope 1959; Rendell et al 1991) and/or 3 (Upton Warren interstadial: Coope et al in prep) by Bridgland (1994), notably at the South Kensington Ismaili Centre

(Coope et al in press), Kempton Park (Gibbard et al 1982) and Isleworth (Coope & Angus 1975; Kerney et al 1982). A further period of downcutting occurred during OIS 3 leading to the formation of a buried channel, beneath the modern river, followed by accumulation of the Shepperton Gravel, which at the present day is 1–2m below river level. During the OIS 2 (Devensian Late Glacial), climatic amelioration of the Windermere interstadial (c 15,000–13,000 cal. BP) and the consequent reduction in sediment supply seem to have led to a hiatus in deposition. Many of the braided channels in the Shepperton Gravel were abandoned (Wilkinson et al 2000) and within them organic sediments accumulated during the Windermere interstadial, the Loch Lomond stadial (c 13,000–11,500 cal. BP) and into the Early Holocene, including sites such as Masthouse Terrace, Isle of Dogs (K N Wilkinson unpublished data), Silvertown (Wilkinson et al 2000) and West Drayton (Gibbard & Hall 1982). Some of these abandoned channels appear to have been relatively large, and in one of them, Bramcote Green in Bermondsey, distinctive lacustrine sediments accumulated from before 13,000 cal. BP until the Early Holocene (Thomas & Rackham 1996). Other than the channel fills, little other sedimentation seems to have taken place in the Thames floodplain during OIS 2, although solifluction sequences are known from areas on chalk geology to the south. It is notable that there is no conclusive evidence of gravel accretion in OIS 2 in London, although sand aggradation is noted elsewhere in the Thames catchment (Gibbard 1985; Collins et al 1996).

Plotting the course of the JLE against the Pleistocene fluvial geomorphology indicates that it underlies three units: the Taplow/Mucking Gravel, the Kempton Park Gravel and the Shepperton Gravel (itself underlying Holocene 'alluvium') (Fig 8).

Freshwater fluvial systems of the Late Glacial and Early Holocene

Despite the fact that the Pleistocene development of the Thames has been extensively studied and is now well published, its Holocene evolution has not been similarly discussed with anywhere near the same intensity. The landmark work of Devoy (1979) in relation to sea-level change is still the only extensive work on the subject, but only covers the Thames in eastern London, Kent and Essex; an area well to the east of the route of the JLE.

By the beginning of the Holocene, at around 11,500 cal. BP, the Thames floodplain seems to have been incised by a number of channels, with localised accretion of organic sediments in examples that had been abandoned by the river. Beyond the floodplain it is unclear what depositional environments were present due to the absence of terrestrial deposits dating to the Early Holocene. However, pollen data from the former suggest that soils were developing beyond the floodplain margins and were supporting pine and to a lesser extent birch woodland (Thomas & Rackham 1996; Wilkinson et al 2000). The channels abandoned in the Devensian Late Glacial seem to have become entirely filled by about 10,000 cal. BP (accretion into the former Bramcote Green lake continued a little later: Thomas & Rackham 1996). Thereafter there are extremely few sites to the west of Tilbury, where deposits dating to the period *c* 10,000 cal. BP to 6850 cal. BP have been encountered.

To the east of Tilbury, Devoy recognised two marine transgressive (Thames I and II) and a single regressive cycle (Tilbury II) from this period (Devoy 1979), but no evidence for these has been found from the JLE area. A model has recently been put forward by Wilkinson *et al* (2000) that goes some way to explain this apparent hiatus. As discussed above, from the Windermere interstadial the Thames was already abandoning many of its former braided channels. Thus by the end of the Late Glacial or the very beginning of the Holocene the Thames had, as a result of climatic amelioration causing a reduction in maximum flow energy, adopted a meandering bedform with the main channel in a similar location to that of the present day. It is notable that similar changes are recognised in a number of continental rivers including the Maas and the Vistula (Collins *et al* 1996). Due to reductions in sediment supply from the floodplain as a result of the stabilising influence of vegetation on the contemporary soils and reduced erosion through the absence of spring ice melt, this system seems to have been stable for several millennia. Because of this stability it is unlikely that significant sediment sequences would have formed on the floodplain, while most soils from this period developing on the floodplain appear to have been eroded by later agriculture. However, within the Thames channel widespread accretion continued, but changed in calibre from predominantly gravel-sized material characteristic of the high-energy braided Devensian river, to sand, as a result of falls in peak discharge energy. The sand is likely to have been reworked in substantial quantities from existing Pleistocene and perhaps even Tertiary strata as the river channel migrated across its floodplain, initially during the Loch Lomond stadial and then in the Early Holocene. This sand has been found extensively in areas of London west of the City during the JLE investigations and appears to have formed large cross-bedded, dune-like structures. Examples of such sand systems have also been recently found at Erith (Sidell *et al* 1997) and Silvertown, east of the City of London (Wilkinson *et al* 2000), but here and elsewhere in the east strata are less extensive probably as a result of subsequent tidal scour. In sand-accreting systems few biological remains survive, so direct dating is difficult, but based on ^{14}C results from peats above the sands, the dune systems at the above sites can be dated to before *c* 6400 cal. BP, while ^{14}C dates from organic muds stratigraphically older than the sands indicate that they formed after *c* 12,000 cal. BP (Wilkinson *et al* 2000).

Middle to later Holocene sea-level change in London

(Table 4)

Research has been undertaken on Middle to later Holocene Thames sediments and archaeology with reference to the development of the river and estuary for over a hundred years (*eg* Spurrell 1889). Later studies led to the development of models of sedimentation and river-level/sea-level change

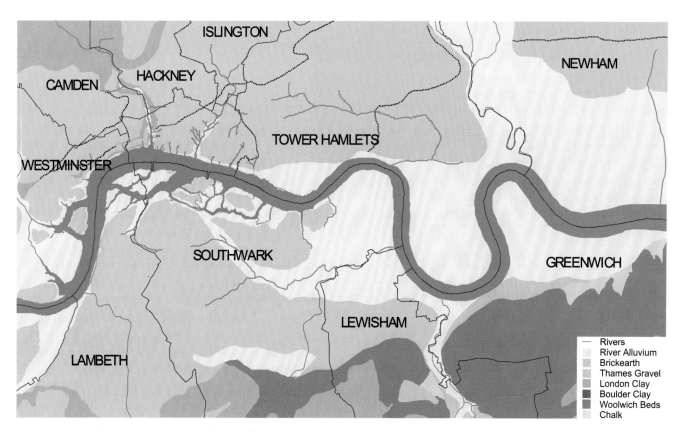

Fig 8 Quaternary deposits present along the route of the JLE © Crown copyright. All rights reserved. Corporation of London LA 087254/00/12

(King & Oakley 1936; Greensmith & Tucker 1976; Devoy 1979). Recent work in the inner Thames estuary (Wilkinson *et al* 2000; Sidell submitted) indicates that these models may be oversimplistic. This is based on detailed comparisons of the stratigraphy and chronological sequences between sites which exhibit marked differences in sedimentation.

As mentioned above, the most comprehensive and most extensively referenced model was proposed by Devoy (1979), with a study area covering the Isle of Grain to Crossness. A sequence was constructed using facies-based modelling and ecological reconstruction. The now-familiar 'Thames-Tilbury' model has since been regarded as the seminal work in this area (Haggart 1995). Interdigitating peat and estuarine clay/silts were identified throughout the study area, characterised in terms of lithology and biostratigraphy, and classified as 'Tilbury' (organic) and 'Thames' (minerogenic) units. The latter were considered to be equivalent to periods of RSL rise, and the former to periods of drop in RSL or decrease in the rate of sea-level rise. The model commences with the initial rapid rise in RSL following the retreat of the ice sheet. This saw an increase in RSL of over 15m between the end of the Devensian (*c* 11,500 cal. BP) and *c* 6850 cal. BP, which is paralleled in south-eastern England as a whole (Long & Tooley 1995). This would have had a significant effect upon any people occupying the outer and mid estuary floodplain which would have been rapidly encroached upon by tidal waters. Settlement areas along the river margins progressively moved to higher ground as the land below was overtaken by the rising water levels.

Devoy constructed two age–altitude curves of relative sea-level movement: one for Tilbury (mid estuary) and one using data from Crossness, Dartford and Broadness (inner estuary) (Fig 9). These data suggest that river levels have oscillated, but indicate a general rise through time. Initially, at the beginning of the Holocene, this rise is thought to be rapid, and compares with data from adjacent geographical areas, such as the Netherlands (Jelgersma 1961) and northern Britain (Tooley 1976). This rise tails off towards *c* 6850 cal. BP and from then river levels increase more slowly. A recent model suggested by Long *et al* (submitted), discusses the changing rates of river level in the Thames estuary (along with the Severn estuary and Southampton Water). This proposes a three-stage model of estuary development with the initial Early Holocene rapid rise in RSL mentioned above, followed by a contraction in the

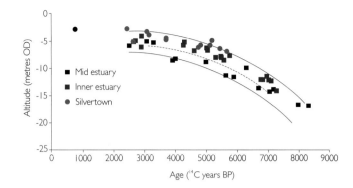

Fig 9 Current age–altitude curve for relative sea-level fluctuations (MSL) in the Thames estuary based on published data (after Devoy 1979; Long 1995; Wilkinson et al 2000)

estuary between roughly 6850 cal. BP and 3200 cal. BP. This is shown by a seaward expansion of substantial tracts of semi-terrestrial marsh deposits along the river margins and in the tributary valleys. This is likely to have been caused by a drop in the *rate* of sea-level rise (not necessarily a drop in relative sea level itself) leading to peat forming at a greater altitude than the rising tide levels. The final stage of the model proposes a subsequent rise in the rate of sea-level rise, continuing to the present day, presenting itself as a series of estuarine clays which submerged the earlier marshes as the estuary expanded once more.

Therefore, although Devoy's (1979; 1980) model is the most detailed that exists, several problems have been identified (Haggart 1995), for instance the need for two distinct curves, which suggests that it cannot necessarily be applied to the whole of the Thames estuary. Although this was never proposed in the original study, the model has been applied widely throughout the Thames estuary by archaeological researchers in the absence of more detailed models in their own study areas. Recent research indicates, however, that the model is not always applicable outside the original study area, both in terms of lithology and age/altitude analysis. Sea-level index points from the mid Holocene levels at West Silvertown Urban Village (Wilkinson *et al* 2000) are comparable with the trends indicated by Devoy for the inner estuary and serve to strengthen the trends of river movement proposed for this zone of the estuary. A series of excavations in the wetlands both north and south of the river, for example Dagenham (Meddens 1996) and Thamesmead (Sidell 1998), suggest that the lithostratigraphy of these sites is not easily comparable with that recorded at the type site of Tilbury (Devoy 1979). Rather, the Thames floodplain during the Holocene was a complex environment of peat-forming communities, migrating channels and sand eyots (Sidell 1998).

Data and models presented by palaeoecologists and geomorphologists tend to cease at approximately the beginning of the historic period, primarily owing to a lack of easily dated and fossiliferous organic sediments dating to periods after 1950 cal. BP. However, archaeologists have produced a detailed database for the changing levels of the Thames in the historic period. This has been achieved through analysis of archaeological structures and horizons

Table 4 Chronology and altitude variants of the Thames lithofacies (after Devoy 1980; 1982)

Event	Commencement	Cessation
Thames V	c 1600 cal. BP (-0.75 – +0.44m OD)	no data
Thames IV	2750 cal. BP (-1.8 – 0.8m OD)	no data (-0.9 – +0.4m OD)
Thames III	4250 cal. BP (-6.7 – 1.9m OD)	2900 cal. BP (-2.0 – 1.0m OD)
Thames II	7550 cal. BP (-12.3 – 6.8m OD)	5700 cal. BP (-6.9 – 3.0m OD)
Thames I	9200 cal. BP (-25.5 – 13.2m OD)	7800 cal. BP (-12.5 – 8.0m OD)

and their relationship to the height of the river (Milne & Milne 1982; Milne 1985; Brigham 1990). Such research has generally been confined to the Roman and later periods, for which more substantial archaeological evidence exists, which almost perfectly extends from the models of palaeoecologists/geomorphologists such as Devoy and Long. A review of the evidence for river levels in central London (Milne *et al* 1983) concludes that the Thames was tidal to approximately London Bridge in the 1st century AD, with high tide at *c* +1.25m OD. The rising water levels also widened the river to nearly a kilometre at high tide, creating a number of tidal islands and mudflats (Graham 1978; Milne *et al* 1983). At the end of the 1st century, the southward and downward progression of the Roman quays from sites such as Regis House at London Bridge (Brigham *et al* 1996) indicates that water levels dropped. This trend appears to have continued through to the 4th century, falling by as much as 1.5m. This change seems to have reversed during the Saxon period, but current research from Thames Court (slightly to the west of London Bridge) indicates a trend similar (southward and downward progression of riverside revetments) to that from the Roman period, with river levels dropping between the mid 10th and late 12th century (Sidell 1998; Wilkinson in prep). Evidence from both Thames Court (Sidell submitted) and Westminster (Thomas *et al* in prep) indicates that the river levels began increasing again from 1181 (obtained through dendrochronology): the date of a revetment from Thames Court which indicates the first rise of the river for several hundred years. This would appear to be partly a result of the construction of the first stone version of London Bridge, with the substantial stone piers causing a damming effect (Watson & Brigham in prep). However, in medieval levels there is evidence for a gradual but continual rise in relative river levels (Milne 1985) which continues to the present day.

Previous diatom studies of Holocene environments in central London and the River Thames

Integrally linked with sea-level studies is the analysis of diatoms. The contemporary diatom communities of the River Thames, their taxonomy and ecology, have been studied since the mid 19th century (Roper 1854; Belcher & Swale 1986). The marked response of diatom communities to environmental change, and in particular to changes in salinity and nutrient concentrations, has led to the application of diatom analysis in palaeoecological studies of the river, its tributaries and at waterfront archaeological sites. Devoy's study of Holocene sea-level changes in the lower Thames estuary (Devoy 1979; 1980) employed diatom analysis, along with lithostratigraphic, pollen and ^{14}C analyses, as a means of identifying sea-level rise and fall. The background of Devoy's sea-level study is discussed above, but his successful use of diatom analysis in this context was followed by the application of diatom analysis as an environmental archaeological technique in the River Thames (Milne *et al* 1983; Battarbee 1988).

Debate about the effect of the tectonic subsidence of south-east England and the London basin on the tidal head of the Thames led to the suggestion that during the Roman period the river was not tidal above Dagenham and Crossness (Akeroyd 1972). Devoy's study was restricted to sites below Crossness. Diatom analysis of securely dated archaeological contexts associated with waterfront archaeological sites provided a means of testing this hypothesis. At Pudding Lane, excavation of early Roman quays revealed foreshore sediments dating from AD 70 to approximately AD 100 (Milne *et al* 1983). The most common single species in all the samples collected from the foreshore sediments was *Cyclotella striata,* a brackish-water species common today in the plankton of the Thames and other European river estuaries. Both the dominance and excellent state of preservation of this species led to the conclusion that this dominant component of the diatom assemblage was derived from the adjacent river. Halophilous, freshwater diatoms such as *Fragilaria pinnata* and *Cocconeis placentula* (Fig 10) were also abundant. These non-planktonic forms are tolerant of slightly saline conditions and therefore it was suggested that they may either have grown close to the site of deposition or may have been carried downstream from less saline habitats. A small number of exclusively marine diatoms was also present in the samples, including *Cymatosira belgica, Rhaphoneis surirella, Rhaphoneis amphiceros* and *Cocconeis scutellum.* The presence of polyhalobous diatoms results from their transport upstream on flood tides. The mixture of diatom species associated with salinities from marine to fresh water exemplifies the problem of post-mortem transport in estuarine and coastal environments. However, despite the taphonomic problems of these diatom assemblages, Battarbee's analysis showed unequivocally that the Thames was tidal in the City during the Roman period.

Following Battarbee's work, Juggins (1988; 1992) addressed some of the ecological and taphonomic problems of diatom-based salinity reconstruction in the River Thames. Contemporary source diatom communities and surface sediment death assemblages were surveyed and their species distributions were used to derive a quantitative relationship

Fig 10 Electron micrograph of Cocconeis placentula

or 'transfer function', relating diatom composition to salinity. The value of individual diatom species as palaeosalinity indicators was assessed and, for example, a number of planktonic diatoms, transported significantly outside their lifetime ranges, were removed from the fossil diatom counting sum. The transfer function was applied to diatom assemblages sampled from waterfront archaeological sites in the City of London, dating from about AD 50 to the mid 17th century. Reconstructed salinities varied from a minimum of 107mg l^{-1} during the mid 1st century to a maximum of 400mg l^{-1} during the 13th century. However, it was suggested that samples from earlier periods and from archaeological sites above the City would add to the tentative conclusions based on a limited number of samples (Juggins 1992).

During the 1980s and 1990s, largely as a result of construction work exposing waterlain sediments, diatom assessments and analyses were carried out at more than 20 archaeological sites associated with the Thames in and around London (N G Cameron unpublished data). The primary concern of most of this and of earlier environmental archaeological diatom studies has been the qualitative evaluation of salinity. For example, Ross (1976) analysed 16th-century foreshore deposits from Abbey Precinct, Westminster, and Boyd (1981a; 1981b) has assessed early 14th-century material from the mouth of the River Fleet at Tudor Street and late 2nd-century sediments from New Fresh Wharf. Qualitative data from these sites appear to show similar estuarine diatom assemblages to those described for Pudding Lane above. However, at a number of sites, as well as salinity changes, nutrient enrichment has been apparent from the composition of diatom assemblages (N G Cameron unpublished data). Boyd (1981a) has also concluded, from diatom and other microfossil data, that there was evidence for severe organic pollution in the River Fleet during the 14th century.

The future role of diatom analysis in elucidating the environmental history of Thames archaeological sites appears to lie not only in refining the knowledge of sea-level, salinity and other tidal-related factors, but also in the quantitative investigation of the timing and degree of aquatic pollution in brackish and fresh water (see *eg* Bennion 1994).

Late Devensian and Holocene vegetation and environmental change in London

During the 1990s, urban renewal in the City and East End of London provided the opportunity to study the palaeoecology of Thames floodplain peat and alluvial sediments in detail. Prior to this, palynological data were few, with only *ad hoc* sites examined where suitable sediments were encountered, and thus, relatively little was known of London's Holocene vegetation history. Clear knowledge of Holocene vegetation

and environment change in London relied on a few studies including those of Hampstead Heath (Girling & Greig 1977; Greig 1989; 1992) and Runnymede Bridge (Greig 1991, 234). A number of smaller palynological studies relating to Romano-British and later soils, peats and sediments including the Temple of Mithras (Scaife 1982b), Copthall Avenue (Maloney & De Moulins 1990, 102) and late medieval–Tudor deposits at Broad Sanctuary, Westminster (Mills 1982) have also been carried out. Palynological data have also accrued from the studies of sea-level change undertaken by Devoy in the lower Thames (Devoy 1977; 1979; 1982); at Mar Dyke, Essex (Scaife 1988b, 109) and at Southwark (Tyers 1988).

In recent years, major developments in the City of London and the research excavations at Runnymede Bridge have resulted in a substantial increase in the knowledge of Holocene vegetation and changes across the London region. Of the total number of sites for which pollen data are available, the majority of these have yet to be published or are at assessment stage only. Those that have been published include Bramcote Green (Thomas & Rackham 1996), Uxbridge (Lewis *et al* 1992), Enfield Lock (Chambers *et al* 1996), Bryan Road, Rotherhithe (Sidell *et al* 1995) and Silvertown (Wilkinson *et al* 2000). From these somewhat geographically disparate sequences, there is now a broad understanding of the Late Devensian and Holocene vegetation chronology. However, only Runnymede Bridge has afforded detailed analysis of the larger part of the Holocene through multiple pollen analyses of the Thames alluvium and peat (Greig 1992; Scaife in prep). Additional analyses across London are now indicating local differences in ecology and environment, illustrating the value of new pollen analyses spanning the same time period from geographically different sites.

Sites dating to the Late Devensian cold stage illustrate the openness of vegetation and harshness of the environment during the period from 18,000 to 11,500 cal. BP. Data come from the Lower Colne at West Drayton Marshes (Kerney *et al* 1982), Kempton Park, Sunbury (Gibbard & Hall 1982) and from Bramcote Green (Thomas & Rackham 1996). The latter is of importance, demonstrating the presence of the Windermere interstadial phase of birch and pine colonisation prior to the return of harsh stadial conditions from *c* 12,800 to 11,500 cal. BP. Sites which are transitional from the cold, Devensian stage into the present Holocene interglacial at *c* 11,500 cal. BP are also present and have been analysed from Bramcote Green (Thomas & Rackham 1996), Point Pleasant, Wandsworth (Scaife *et al* in prep), Three Ways Wharf, Uxbridge (Lewis *et al* 1992) and Enfield Lock (Chambers *et al* 1996). Sites recently or currently under investigation include the Elizabeth Fry School, Newham dated to 9900–9500 cal. BP (Davis *et al* 1995), Silvertown (Wilkinson *et al* 2000) and Strathville Road (Wilkinson *et al* in prep), all demonstrating further the local dominance of pine woodland in the Early Holocene (Boreal period).

The migration and establishment of pioneer woodland in the Early Holocene in Britain from their glacial refugia is becoming increasingly understood in terms of regional variations through the use of ^{14}C dating and plotting of isopollen maps (Birks 1989; Huntley & Birks 1983). It is clear, however, that there are substantial gaps in this picture, especially from southern England. It is anticipated that several sites, now available in London, will remove these gaps. Flandrian Chronozone I sites (*ie* pre-Boreal and Boreal) show clearly the dominant phase of birch and pine woodland and a later ousting of these by oak and elm woodland. These sites include Peninsula House, City of London (Scaife 1983), Enfield Lock (Chambers *et al* 1996), Three Ways Wharf, Uxbridge (Lewis *et al* 1992) and Bramcote Green, Bermondsey (Thomas & Rackham 1996). As yet unpublished sites include Strathville Road (Wilkinson *et al* in prep) dated to 9270±60 BP (10,668–10,241 cal. BP) (Beta 76897), Meridian Point (Sidell *et al* in prep b) and Point Pleasant, Wandsworth (Scaife *et al* in prep); the latter dating to 9410±160 BP (11,173–10,224 cal. BP) (Beta 98138) and 9620±80 BP (11,196–10,689 cal. BP) (Beta 98137).

Data for the Middle Holocene (Flandrian II) are available which show the importance of woodland in many areas which was dominated by lime with oak (*Quercus*), elm (*Ulmus*), hazel and alder (*Alnus*). This is in accordance with other regional pollen studies carried out in the 1970s to 1990s (Moore 1977; Scaife 1980; Greig 1982b; Scaife 1987). In London this is evidenced from Hampstead Heath (Girling & Greig 1977; Greig 1989; 1992), Runnymede Bridge (Scaife in prep) and Silvertown (Wilkinson *et al* 2000). The preceding sites, while associated with the periods of the earlier and Late Mesolithic, do not show conclusive evidence for human impact on the vegetation and environment of this time. This is not unexpected given that these peoples were assumed to have been largely ephemeral groups of hunters and foragers utilising the environment but not in sufficient numbers to have caused any impact. It is from *c* 6300 cal. BP, the Late Holocene, that the earliest impact on the natural vegetation (wildwoods) has been evidenced in the region. This is initially manifested by the often discussed 'elm decline', Neolithic clearance and agricultural activities.

By far the majority of recently analysed sites span the late prehistoric period, in many cases with peat accumulation starting at or just after the primary elm decline at *c* 5750–6300 cal. BP. These include Bryan Road, Rotherhithe (Sidell *et al* 1995) at 5040±80 BP (5932–5603 cal. BP) (Beta 68577); Ferndale Street at 4480±60 BP (5314–4871 cal. BP) (Beta 80895), and Beckton Alp, Nursery and Tollgate with dates ranging from *c* 4900 to 5450 cal. BP. Along with data from Hampstead Heath, these sites show the reduction in elm pollen at the 'primary elm decline' (Scaife 1987; 1988a) and increasing quantities of herb pollen including cultigens, ruderals and segetals which mark the start of significant changes in woodland structure and dominance and the associated expansion of herb communities.

Such changes initiated in the Neolithic become more pronounced with a number of sites showing more extensive Bronze Age clearance of existing woodland. Rainham Marshes (Scaife 1991) is especially important and is one of a number of sites which is associated with wooden trackways

(Meddens & Beasley 1990), providing access across the Thames floodplain/marshes. Such trackways have also been found at sites at Beckton and Silvertown and have produced pollen associated with the environment in which they were constructed (Scaife 1997; Wilkinson *et al* 2000). One of the principal features characterising the late prehistoric vegetation of southern and eastern England is the importance and dominance of *Tilia* over large areas. It is now recognised that this taxon, renowned for its under-representation in pollen spectra (Andersen 1970; 1973), was the dominant woodland taxon over large areas (Moore 1977; Scaife 1980; Greig 1982b). Its maintenance and ultimate decline during the late prehistoric period is one of the principal features which has come to light during analysis of the Jubilee Line profiles and as such is discussed further in Parts 2 and 3 below. Its demise, which was once associated with climatic deterioration from the sub-Boreal to the sub-Atlantic at *c* 800 BC (Godwin 1940; 1956; 1975a), is now attributed to human activity (Turner 1962) and pollen taphonomic effects (Waller 1994b). As such, this event is now recognised as being asynchronous across the region. There are now a significant number of sites available from London which exhibit this asynchroneity although the more common occurrence of the decline is thought to date to the Middle to Late Bronze Age. Apart from the Jubilee sites discussed here, sites from Beckton (Scaife 1997) and Rainham Marshes (Scaife 1991) serve to illustrate this point. Removal of this woodland not only illustrates the need for agricultural land at this time, and associated increased land pressure, but also removal of the last vestiges of natural woodland.

Subsequently, the Iron Age, Romano-British and historic periods are represented palynologically by a number of sites which are closely archaeologically related, or are data obtained from minerogenic floodplain deposits such as those obtained at a number of the Jubilee Line sites discussed in this volume. As might be expected, the majority of these sites are rich in herbs typical of human-disturbed habitats including waste ground, urban and agricultural activities and from domestic waste. Conversely, all show a treeless environment at least in the local region. Few major sites are as yet published but attention is drawn to the analysis of peats (Scaife 1982b) underlying the Temple of Mithras excavated by W F Grimes (Shepherd 1998) and comparable sequences at Copthall Avenue (Maloney & De Moulins 1990) and to New Palace Yard, Westminster (Greig 1992). The latter has produced a record of local vegetation spanning the Iron Age to Saxon periods. All of these are very rich in herbs of waste ground and cultivation although some trees remain. In the case of the Temple of Mithras this includes *Juglans* (walnut).

There are similarly few post-Roman sites which have been published although a number are currently under investigation. Broad Sanctuary, Westminster (Mills 1982) illustrates the foul state and squalor of the late medieval to Tudor period, with the stream site analysed, consisting of a running sewer containing human and animal ordure. A very diverse pollen assemblage comprising largely weeds of waste ground, cultivation and food passed through the gut (largely cereal) was found and typifies urban pollen assemblages (Greig 1981; 1982b).

Part 2:
Site stratigraphic and palaeoenvironmental data

4

Holocene environments in Westminster

Keith Wilkinson, Robert Scaife, Nigel Cameron, Jane Sidell and Christopher Thomas

Introduction

(Figs 11 and 12)

The archaeological analysis associated with the development of Westminster Underground Station required the most complex investigative programme of the overall JLE archaeological project. The logistics of station development combined with the need to do justice to the extremely important and complicated archaeological stratigraphy led to a series of watching briefs, evaluations and excavations. These were undertaken between 1992 and 1998 and, in total, 16 discrete interventions took place, producing archaeological features and artefacts dating from the Mesolithic to the late post-medieval/modern period (Thomas 1997). The geographical location of the sites adds to the complexity of the archaeology: the central point of Thorney Island and the surrounding branches of the Tyburn stream and the Thames consist of terrestrial, semi-terrestrial and aquatic deposits. The movement (both laterally and vertically) of the Thames and the Tyburn throughout the Holocene deposited an extremely complex mesh of sediments across the study area, and while many trenches have been opened and investigated, it still proves difficult to fully understand the ways in which this landscape has developed.

The archaeology of Thorney Island

Christopher Thomas

Thorney Island (Fig 13) was defined by the River Thames and the River Tyburn. Mesolithic flints have been recovered from the Island and from the adjacent land suggesting some form of transient occupation on the site. Postholes, pits and ditches in association with Neolithic flints and Late Neolithic and Early Bronze Age pottery indicate settlement activity on the lowest-lying ground alongside the Thames. It is unclear what sort of activity was taking place on the highest ground as only limited excavation has occurred there. There is evidence of ard marks on the Island suggesting cultivation. These were found adjacent to a timber revetment built alongside an inlet from the Thames. A second revetment lay further from the river when river levels were presumably rising and had covered the ard marks. A series of pits, ditches and postholes behind the later revetment indicate continuing occupation. No dating was recovered from these features but their level (just below OD) suggests they date from a similar period, perhaps the Early Bronze Age.

Previous excavations at Westminster (Mills 1980) have suggested Iron Age activity on the Island but given the similarity in levels and in the deposits it may be that the occupation material there also dated to the Late Neolithic and Early Bronze Age. However, an Iron Age revetment from immediately to the north of the Island indicates definite activity in the area (Andrews & Merriman 1986) and a pit containing a single sherd of pottery, possibly of Early Iron Age date, was found under Parliament Square.

Fig 11 Parliament Square, Westminster

Only slight evidence of activity has been found on the Island from the Roman period. Substantial quantities of building material including tile, brick and *opus signinum* have been recovered from recent excavations and from beneath Westminster Abbey. A hypocaust pila, areas of floor and a masonry wall were found beneath the abbey in the 19th century, and a stone sarcophagus was recovered from immediately to the north of the abbey in 1866 (Westlake 1923; Poole 1870).

Little evidence of Middle Saxon occupation has been recovered although tradition asserts that the abbey was founded in the early 7th century. It was refounded in about AD 960 by Dunstan. The foundation of Westminster Palace has been traditionally attributed to Edward the Confessor (reigned 1042–66). New evidence indicates that a wide ditch was dug to define the palace and perhaps the abbey, possibly at an earlier date. It was revetted with timber posts and planks and a bridge was constructed across it into the palace site. [14]C dating indicates a date for the timber posts of AD 960–1050 (Beta 88695/6). Most sites on the Island have found evidence of a large flooding event which covered most of the Island and which appears to date to about 1050. This flooding sealed the bridge and revetment.

In 1097 William Rufus expanded the palace by building the Great Hall (Westminster Hall), the largest medieval hall in Europe.

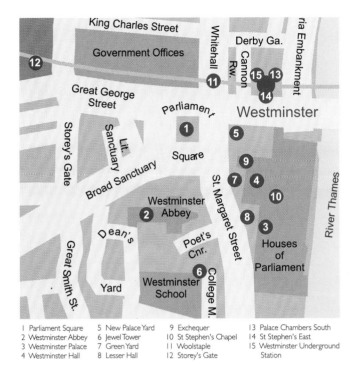

King Charles Street

Government Offices

Whitehall

Derby Ga.

Cannon Rw.

ria Embankment

12

11

15 13

14

Great George Street

Parliament

Westminster

Storey's Gate

Lit. Sanctuary

Broad Sanctuary

Square

1

5

9

7 4

10

Great Smith St.

Dean's

Poet's Cnr.

St Margaret Street

Westminster Abbey

2

8 3

River Thames

Yard

Westminster School

6

College M.

Houses of Parliament

1 Parliament Square	5 New Palace Yard	9 Exchequer	13 Palace Chambers South
2 Westminster Abbey	6 Jewel Tower	10 St Stephen's Chapel	14 St Stephen's East
3 Westminster Palace	7 Green Yard	11 Woolstaple	15 Westminster Underground
4 Westminster Hall	8 Lesser Hall	12 Storey's Gate	Station

Fig 12 Map of the Westminster study area © Crown copyright. All rights reserved. Corporation of London LA 087254/00/12

No evidence for the residential buildings within the palace to the south of the Great Hall from the 11th century, however, has been recovered.

During the reign of Henry II the palace both expanded and became better defined. A new river wall was built in 1179–80 (Colvin *et al* 1963, 493), and this probably relates to a large timber dock which was built on the north side of New Palace Yard. Rising river levels would have necessitated the new river wall and the dock appears to have functioned by allowing barges to float on to it at high tide and resting on its floor at low tide. The dock was at least 12.67m long and was probably in excess of 5m wide. The actual length of the dock may have been as much as 51m. To its west a stone building containing large stone ovens was constructed. It is likely that the precinct walls around Westminster Abbey were also built at this time. Integral with these was the great drain of Westminster Abbey which exited out on to the foreshore. A complete section of this was found beneath the garden of the Jewel Tower. A new timber wall was also built during this period to divide New Palace Yard from the Green Yard. Documentary evidence also indicates that a new chamber was built for Henry II and that the 'Lesser Hall' was rebuilt, possibly by adding a second storey.

During the 13th century the importance of the medieval palace grew as a result of Henry II's decision in the late 12th century to move the site of the Exchequer to Westminster. A new building was constructed to house the Exchequer by 1244 in the Green Yard which had its timber wall and gate replaced in stone. A fragment of a building to the south of this wall was found with a step or dais at one end and a floor of greensand slabs. This 'Green Yard' seems to have become the part of the palace designated for the carrying out of

government. A new gate was built to New Palace Yard in 1287 and this was found to abut a slightly earlier building which may have been an inn (Fig 14). Within this building was a timber-lined cesspit containing parts of barrels and a number of wooden vessels. Some of the timbers lining the cesspit had been reused from a Hanseatic type of ship known as a cog. In the mid 13th century a large stone building was built within the northern precinct of Westminster Abbey. It had painted plaster walls and was likely to have been one of the high-status houses of the merchants of the October Fair which was held in the abbey precincts every year.

Progressive reclamation of the land to the north of the palace took place during the 13th and 14th centuries resulting in a large block of land being available for use behind a new river wall by the mid 14th century. This land was used for the canons of St Stephen's Chapel's houses. Part of one of these with a large intact culvert was excavated. The chapel itself, within the precincts of the palace, was rebuilt from 1292 to 1363 (Colvin *et al* 1963, 522). It was a two-storey chapel with the upper chapel reserved for the king. It was constructed on large timber piles which were driven into the silts which had built up in a prehistoric channel or inlet from the Thames beneath.

The former gate to New Palace Yard was demolished in the late 14th century and a replacement was built outside the excavated area. Yard surfaces, mostly in gravel with stone chippings, were found inside New Palace Yard. In the south-west corner of the palace precincts a new tower, the Jewel Tower which still stands, was built for the king's personal plate and jewellery. This had its own moat and was built on land previously within the precincts of the abbey, presumably because space in the palace precinct had become so limited. By this time the merchant's house within the northern precinct of the abbey had been remodelled; the painted plaster was stripped from the walls and new partitions were inserted.

At the end of the 14th century, Richard II embarked upon the rebuilding of the Great Hall. The piers were removed, the walls heightened by 5ft and a new hammerbeam roof was constructed by Master Hugh Herland. Henry Yevele designed two new towers and a ceremonial entrance way at the north end of the hall and flying buttresses were built along the west side of the hall. Walls were built between the buttresses to form a range of buildings. Small areas of the town were also excavated. A ditch that lay between two properties on the west side of King Street had three phases. On either side were cesspits and refuse pits that were dug in the back gardens. An area to the east of King Street found a similar ditch that exited into the Thames. By the mid 14th century this area was laid out as a part of the Woolstaple (or wool market) which was set up by Edward III in 1353. A range of buildings surrounded a courtyard containing the Woolstaple. The back garden of one of those buildings was found with a wall and ditch behind. The garden contained refuse pits and a chalk well which was subsequently rebuilt in brick.

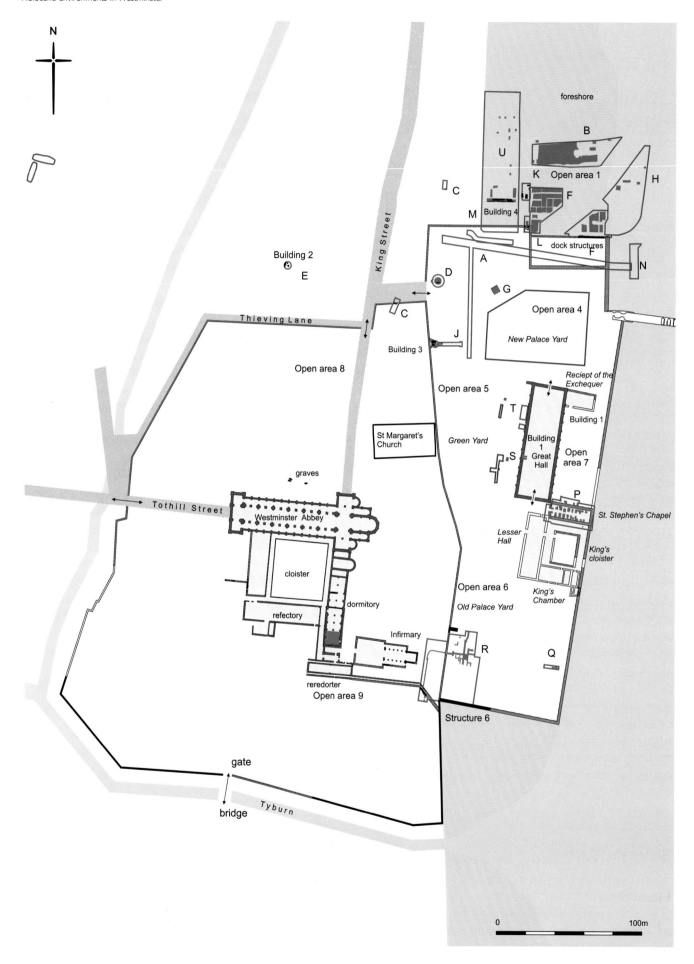

N

foreshore

B

U

K   Open area 1

C   H

F

M   Building 4

L   dock structures

F

N

King Street

Building 2

E

A   D

G

Open area 4

C   New Palace Yard

Thieving Lane

J

Building 3

Open area 8   Open area 5

Reciept of the
Exchequer

Green Yard   T   Building 1

St Margaret's
Church   S   Building
1
Great
Hall   Open
area 7

graves   P

Tothill Street   Westminster Abbey   St. Stephen's Chapel

Lesser
Hall   King's
cloister

cloister   King's
Chamber

dormitory   Open area 6

refectory   Old Palace Yard

Infirmary   R

Q

reredorter

Open area 9   Structure 6

gate

bridge   Tyburn

0   100m

Fig 13 Plan of Thorney Island, Westminster

Fig 14 Foundations of a late 13th-century inn abutted by the gatehouse to New Palace Yard, Westminster

While there is evidence of continued activity in the 16th century in those areas of the town that were excavated, there is considerably less evidence of activity within the palace at this time. The fire of 1512 effectively ended the use of the palace as a royal dwelling. The increase in activity seen in the 17th century may be a reflection of the rise in the importance of parliament. It was during this period that the formation of the current street pattern began. The gates to the palace and abbey were demolished allowing widening of the streets in the 18th century. New drains were inserted in New Palace Yard and a well was dug into the gatehouse between New Palace Yard and the Green Yard. This contained a complete delftware bottle dated to 1627.

The archaeological excavations at Westminster have revealed a well-preserved sequence of highly important archaeological material relating to the Late Saxon and medieval royal palace and abbey; the medieval and post-medieval town, and the post-medieval seat of parliament. There is also clear evidence of a prehistoric settlement and indications of some form of Roman settlement. There are still important archaeological questions relating to all phases of the occupation of the site which require answering but the most recent works have helped to define those questions and put them into context. These are laid out in the publication of the archaeological data for Westminster.

Storey's Gate

Introduction

Storey's Gate is located in the extreme south-east corner of St James's Park, adjacent to a 19th-century Royal Parks Constabulary Police lodge situated at the junction of Birdcage Walk and Horse Guards Road (see Fig 12). The site is named

after the keeper of James I's aviary, Edward Storey, who is thought to have lived in a house once located in the area. The land-use history of the site from the later medieval period is relatively well known, while prior to the 13th century the area appears to have been low-lying marshland associated with the Tyburn, which runs to the east of the site. The area to the west of the Tyburn seems to have been unoccupied until the early 1200s when the Maudit family, the hereditary chamberlains to the crown, moved to the area and thereby triggered its occupation, so that by 1300 tenements were in place along most of the 'Long Ditch' (the Tyburn). In the 1530s the whole area of what is now St James's Park was acquired by Henry VIII and was turned into a deer park complete with a retaining wall. This necessitated demolition of some of the existing dwellings, presumably culverting of the Tyburn and drainage of the whole area. This drainage may have been done in conjunction with culverting/diverting the Tyburn via a series of revetted drainage ditches. The area has remained as a park ever since, except for the construction of various buildings fronting Birdcage Walk in the 17th and 18th centuries, which have since been demolished.

Investigations were undertaken over a four-week period in February and March 1994 by Wessex Archaeology, as an escape shaft was to be built, emerging into the basement of the relocated police station. Two trenches, each measuring 8m x 3m were excavated over the site of the shaft and within the footprint of the basement. These were initially machine dug to 1.2m below ground surface after which excavation was by hand. Following the excavation of a further 1.2m in depth (the trench having been stepped in 1.5m from the original machine-dug outline), trench boxes were inserted and continuously lowered as investigations proceeded. This process was continued until archaeologically sterile sands were encountered at around 4.5m below ground surface. The stratigraphy revealed by the investigations was of both archaeological and palaeoenvironmental interest. The uppermost 1.4m of deposits, extending down to +2.0m OD, consisted of demolition debris, wall footings, service trenches and similar deposits. All are likely to date to the last 200 years, but contained large quantities of reworked artefacts from the early post-medieval and medieval periods. Much of the demolition debris is likely to relate to structures shown fronting Birdcage Walk in 17th- and 18th-century maps. At the base of these deposits was a 0.2–0.5m thick well-sorted silt/sand which is likely to be the pre-18th-century ground surface, and therefore may relate to Henry VIII's deer park. Between +1.10m OD and +1.66m OD were a complex series of structural remains, including stone walls, construction layers, postholes and pits. Associated with these were large quantities of artefacts ranging in date from the 13th/14th to 16th century, while distinctive building materials of both the medieval and post-medieval period were found. The building therefore appears to have been constructed in the later medieval period and rebuilt in early post-medieval times. It was built on redeposited fine-grained alluvial strata containing large quantities of reworked artefacts from periods spanning the Mesolithic to medieval, and was probably part of the 14th-century expansion on the western side of the Tyburn.

Deposits found below +1.0m OD are almost exclusively waterlain in origin and seem to be successive fills of a large palaeochannel with a maximum depth extending to −0.65m OD. The palaeochannel was cut into archaeologically sterile sands which range in elevation from −0.65m OD to +0.50m OD and therefore indicate that the channel was of no more than 1.15m in depth. Three phases of infilling seem to have occurred; the latest is the most complex and consists of a series of silt/clays and sands, filling both minor channels and as more general spreads. These fills are associated with artefacts dating to the 12th/13th centuries, although once more residual prehistoric flint and Romano-British tile was also found. Below these at +0.13m was a 0.40m thick highly humified organic mud or peat, containing no artefacts beyond worked and burnt flint. Beneath peat at −0.30m OD were a series of fine-grained mineral deposits with occasional parallel peat laminations, but which contained no artefacts, and below these the well-sorted sands discussed above. Sampling was concentrated on the palaeochannel sequence with four monolith tins being taken through the reworked silt/clays and the lower *in situ* deposits, although neither the base of these nor the underlying sands were sampled. The results of sedimentological, palynological and diatom investigations are presented in Figs 15, 16 and 17 respectively.

Lithostratigraphy and sedimentology

The base of the sequence consisted of sand deposits that due to the absence of archaeological material were not sampled. These sands are almost certainly of fluvial derivation and are likely to be comparable to those found elsewhere in Westminster, for example at St Stephen's East, Palace Chambers South and Westminster Underground Station (see below). A channel was cut into the sands, presumably from the Tyburn, and then seems to have filled with predominantly fine-grained material, which was partially sampled. The process of channel formation is suggestive of relatively high-energy flow, despite the fact that the sand is comparatively easily eroded, yet the initial fills are indicative of low-energy processes. It would therefore appear that following channel formation the new channel was rapidly abandoned by a process of avulsion allowing fine-grained material to accumulate during flood events. Unfortunately it cannot be determined when this occurred as no dating evidence was recovered from this part of the sequence, although evidence from elsewhere in Westminster suggests that channel formation and abandonment in the sandy substrates of Thorney Island was at times rapid. It would appear that over time the channel became increasingly marginalised from stream

flow and organic mud began to develop on top of the mineral deposits at 3300±70 BP (3691–3378 cal. BP) (Beta 127617). These organic muds outcrop between −0.50m OD and +0.19m OD and contain moderate quantities of wood fragments, but also roots, suggesting *in situ* plant growth, indicating extremely low water levels. Nevertheless, organic carbon contents within the organic muds are not especially high, averaging 20%, and suggest that input of mineral sediment in flood water was regular. Despite the fact that burnt flint was noted within the organic muds during the excavation, χ^{lf} (low frequency magnetic susceptibility) values are extremely low at 10^{-8} m^{3}kg^{-1}, suggesting that fires were not lit *in situ* and that the flint has therefore been transported. Indeed, there is no evidence for human activity on sedimentological grounds from either the organic muds or the underlying deposits.

Unconformably overlying the organic mud are a series of well-sorted mineral silt/clays of a black (7.5YR2.5/1) colour at the base, lightening progressively upwards to very dark greyish-brown (10YR3/2). Both organic contents and χ^{lf} values progressively decrease up through the sequence, although there are two isolated peaks of organic carbon of *c* 40% at around +0.30m OD. However, despite the presence of moderate quantities of artefacts recovered during the excavation of these strata, there is once again no sedimentological evidence for *in situ* human activity. Thus the artefacts deposited are almost certainly reworked, or were rather simply thrown into the watercourse. The whole sequence would appear to date to the 12th and 13th centuries on ceramic grounds, and thus there is a hiatus of *c* 2000 years between accumulation of the organic muds and the mineral alluvial deposits. Indeed it would appear that active erosion has occurred of the organic mud surface in the form of channel scour. Thus a major part of the later prehistoric and early historic sequence is missing as a result of channel formation in the medieval period. The fact that channels pass through the site in the 12th century indicates that the watercourse abandoned in later prehistory had been reactivated. However, stream velocities appear to have been slight, leading to deposition of silt/clays both within channels and as overbank spreads, although the latter were still confined to the boundaries of the original palaeochannel cut into the sand. Nevertheless, there is evidence for higher-energy events leading to localised scour, as can be seen for example in a fine sand outcropping between +0.73m OD and +0.69m OD. Within the upper 0.20m of the sequence there is evidence for increasingly dry conditions, while the presence of root channels indicates that the area was no longer permanently waterlogged. However, χ^{lf} values continue to decline suggesting that only limited pedogenesis occurred; in other words, flood frequency was sufficient to prevent the formation of a stable soil. Organic carbon contents increase to 35% in the very top of the waterlain silt/clays (+0.90m OD) and based on both this and site descriptive evidence it is possible that some sort of turf line once existed. This level also marks the top of the infilled channel sequence.

Deposition subsequent to the filling of the channel took place almost exclusively as a result of human or other terrestrial

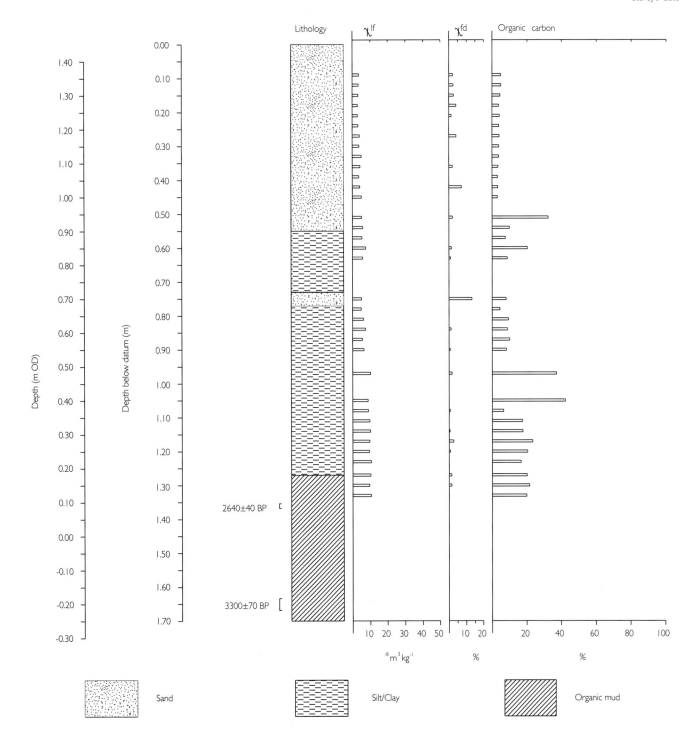

Fig 15 Lithological diagram from Storey's Gate, Westminster

processes. The top of the sampled sequence consists of poorly sorted sands and silt/clays containing large quantities of 13th-/14th-century ceramics. These are likely to be levelling horizons placed on the site to increase ground height relative to the water table, and are probably associated with construction of the structure outlined in the introduction above. Nevertheless, iron staining within the levelling horizon indicates that conditions were still damp, although complete inundation does not seem to have occurred. Given the fact that ceramic fragments were found both on the site and within the samples it is perhaps surprising that χ^{lf} values are the lowest of the entire sequence at 5^{-8} m³kg⁻¹. These data would appear to

show that little abrasion of the ceramics occurred once they had been incorporated within the deposits (*ie* few fragments of <2mm were generated) and therefore that fluvial processes played no part in the formation processes (Wilkinson in prep).

Pollen biostratigraphy

Pollen data have been obtained from the organic muds and overlying mineral deposits, from between −0.32m OD and +0.68m OD. This therefore encompasses the basal organic mud of Bronze Age date and overlying sediment units of medieval date and waterlain origin. Five local pollen assemblage zones

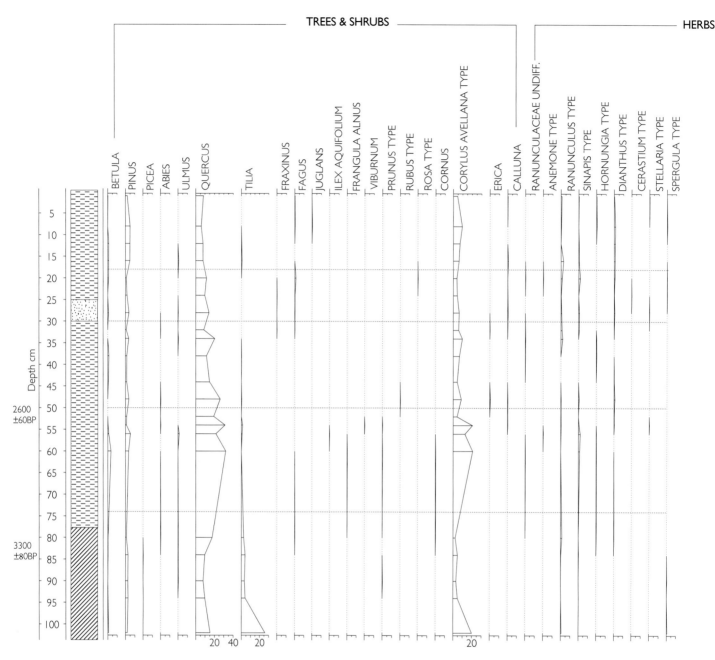

Fig 16 Pollen diagram from Storey's Gate, Westminster

have been recognised (see Fig 16) which delimit the principal changes in the on-site vegetation. These are characterised from the base of the profile upwards:

ST:1 -0.32 – -0.04m OD *Tilia-Quercus-Aster-*Poaceae

This corresponds with the lower part of the organic muds and top of the underlying sand (a possible palaeosol). *Tilia* is most important in this zone, especially in the lowest level at the top of the basal sand (26%). Other trees include *Quercus* (15%), *Corylus avellana* type (20%) and *Picea* (spruce) sporadically. Herbs are important (to 85%) dominated by Poaceae (grasses) (average 30%), *Aster* type (daisy family) (peak to 25%) and Cereal type (to 20%). Other taxa of note are Lamiaceae (mint family), *Plantago lanceolata* (ribwort plantain), *Bidens* type

(daisy types), Lactucae (dandelion family) and large (thin-walled) Poaceae. Marsh/aquatic taxa are dominated by Cyperaceae (sedges) (18%), *Typha angustifolia* (lesser reedmace) type (to 30%), *Alisma* type (water plantain) (6%) with a presence of *Typha latifolia* (greater reedmace), *Iris* and *Alnus*. There are high values of *Pteridium aquilinum* (bracken) (60%) with *Dryopteris* type (typical fern) and *Polypodium* ('polypody' fern) both of greater importance in the basal sand.

ST:2 -0.04 – +0.20m OD *Quercus-Corylus avellana* type-*Alnus*-Poaceae

There is a break in the sequence between 62cm and 80cm resulting in an unfortunate gap in the pollen profile. However, the zone demonstrates the decline of *Tilia* (to <5%) and the

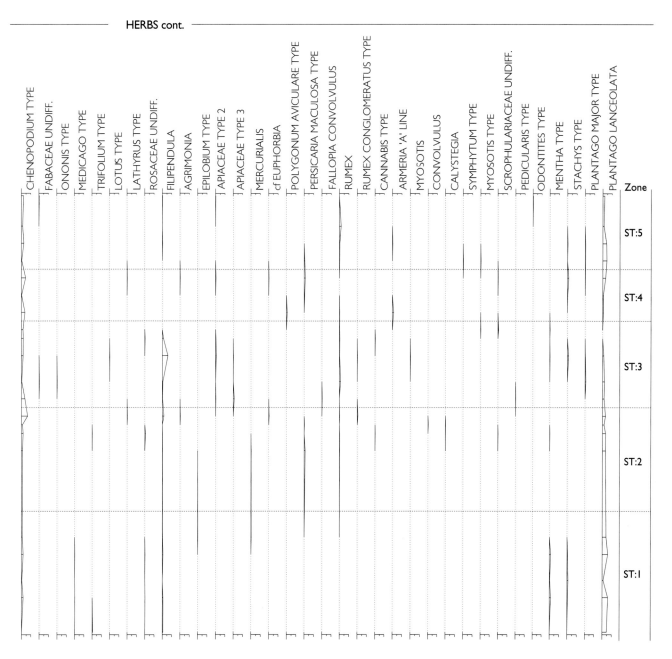

HERBS cont.

CHENOPODIUM TYPE
FABACEAE UNDIFF.
ONONIS TYPE
MEDICAGO TYPE
TRIFOLIUM TYPE
LOTUS TYPE
LATHYRUS TYPE
ROSACEAE UNDIFF.
FILIPENDULA
AGRIMONIA
EPILOBIUM TYPE
APIACEAE TYPE 2
APIACEAE TYPE 3
MERCURIALIS
cf EUPHORBIA
POLYGONUM AVICULARE TYPE
PERSICARIA MACULOSA TYPE
FALLOPIA CONVOLVULUS
RUMEX
RUMEX CONGLOMERATUS TYPE
CANNABIS TYPE
ARMERIA 'A' LINE
MYOSOTIS
CONVOLVULUS
CALYSTEGIA
SYMPHYTUM TYPE
MYOSOTIS TYPE
SCROPHULARIACEAE UNDIFF.
PEDICULARIS TYPE
ODONTITES TYPE
MENTHA TYPE
STACHYS TYPE
PLANTAGO MAJOR TYPE
PLANTAGO LANCEOLATA

Zone

ST:5

ST:4

ST:3

ST:2

ST:1

(Fig 16 cont)

greater importance of *Quercus* and *Corylus avellana* (35% and 25% respectively). There are, however, small numbers of *Abies* (fir), *Fagus*, *Ilex* (holly), *Frangula* (buckthorn/black dogwood), *Alnus* and *Cornus* (dogwood). Marsh elements show a marked expansion of *Alnus* (peak to 80%) with lesser values of Cyperaceae and *Typha angustifolia/Sparganium* (bur reed). Herbs in general remain similar to zone 1 with the occurrence of Poaceae (40%), Lactucae (8%) and *Plantago lanceolata* (5%). *Aster* type and cereal type of the preceding zone are markedly diminished

ST:3 +0.2 – +0.4m OD Poaceae-Cyperaceae

Alnus values of zone 2 are sharply reduced while Cyperaceae expand sharply to 90%. At the base of the zone there are peaks of

Typha angustifolia (23%) and *Typha latifolia* (10%). Trees and shrubs are subordinate to herbs with *Quercus* and *Corylus avellana* type remaining the principal taxa. *Tilia* reduces to low levels and absence. Non-marsh herbs are dominated by Poaceae (to 60%) with Lactucae (10%) and Cereal type (peak to 15%) showing increases.

ST:4 +0.4 – +0.52m OD Poaceae

Cyperaceae decline from zone 3 to 30% while Poaceae and Cereal type remain dominant (45% and 15% respectively). There are peaks of *Bidens* type, Asteraceae (10%) and *Chenopodium* type (goosefoot) (5%). *Armeria* (sea lavender and thrift) 'A' line is noted. Trees and shrubs comprise *Quercus* (15%) and *Corylus avellana* type (10%) with sporadic *Fraxinus*, *Fagus*, *Betula*, *Pinus* and *Ulmus*.

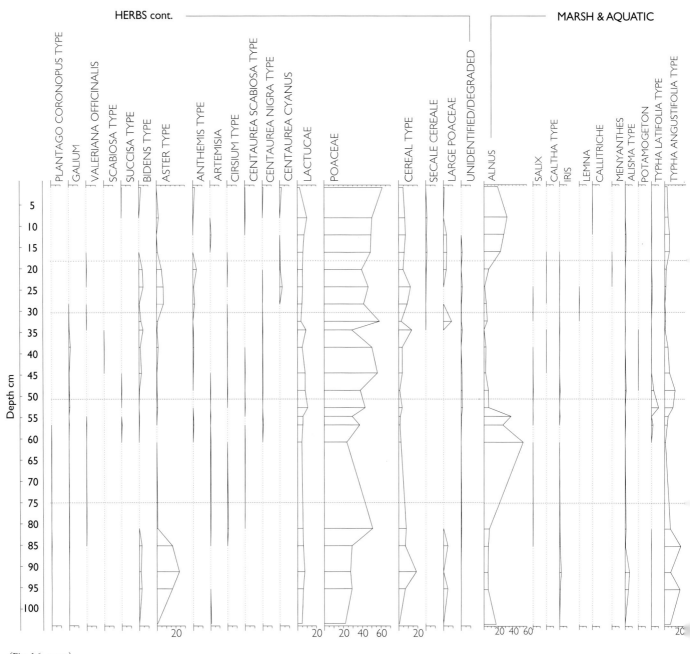

(Fig 16 cont)

ST:5 +0.52 – +0.68m OD Poaceae-*Alnus*-Cyperaceae-*Pteridium aquilinum*

This uppermost zone is delimited by peaks of *Alnus* (35%), *Pteridium aquilinum* (75%), *Typha angustifolia/Sparganium* (6%), *Plantago lanceolata* (5%), Lactucae (12%) and large Poaceae. There is also an expansion of *Pinus* (8%) with *Quercus* (10%) and *Corylus avellana* type (10%).

Diatom biostratigraphy

Initially, 13 samples were assessed for diatoms (Cameron 1995). Identifiable diatoms were absent from the base of the Bronze Age organic mud sequence, but samples analysed from upper levels of the organic mud contained both freshwater and estuarine type diatom assemblages. Diatoms

from the overlying minerogenic silt/clay and sand strata were preserved to varying degrees and contained a range of diatom salinity groups. Diatom analysis was therefore carried out on samples where the assessment indicated that there was potential for percentage counting and additional samples were prepared where further detail of the stratigraphy was required (see Fig 17).

Analysis of the diatom-bearing basal sample in the organic mud showed a diatom assemblage composed entirely of freshwater taxa; brackish water and marine taxa are absent. The dominant species include a range of oligohalobous indifferent diatoms, for example: *Fragilaria* spp, *Achnanthes lanceolata*, *Achnanthes minutissima*, *Amphora libyca* and *Amphora pediculus*. However, the upper sample from the same stratum does have very small percentages of

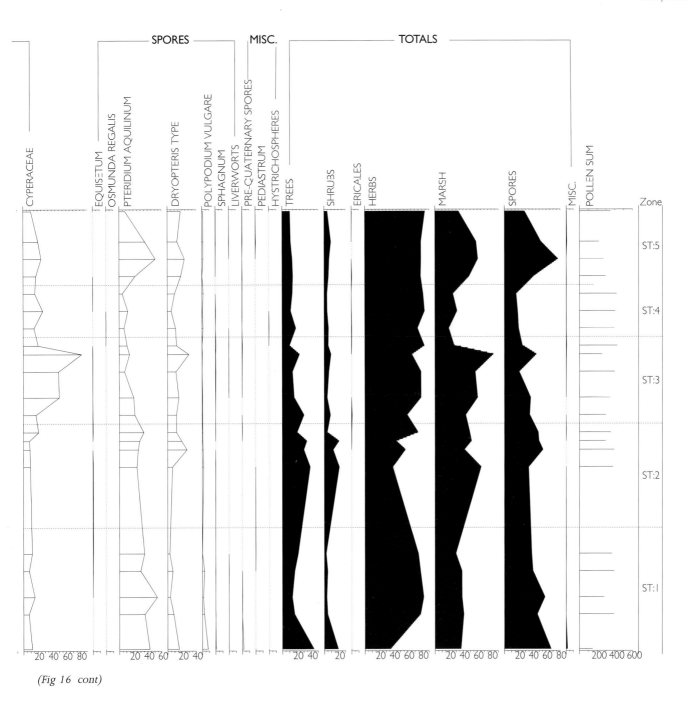

(Fig 16 cont)

halophilous, mesohalobous and possibly (a marine *Opephora* which is difficult to identify with certainty) marine diatoms. The dominant halobian group remains one of oligohalobous indifferent taxa, and their composition is similar to that of the lower organic mud sample. The suggestion is, therefore, either that there was a slight increase in salinity during accretion, occasional flooding from tidal reaches, or, perhaps more probable, that sediment mixing processes have introduced the component of brackish-water diatom assemblages from more recent sediments.

Samples from within the medieval mineral silt/clays between +0.42m OD and +0.46m OD have much reduced percentages of freshwater diatoms (<20%) and these are stress-tolerant *Fragilaria* spp only. There is clear evidence of increasing

tidal influence with mesohalobes and then marine diatoms becoming the dominant groups. In the lower of these samples the estuarine diatom *Cyclotella striata* is dominant, comprising over 30% of the assemblage, along with other mesohalobous and halophilous diatoms. Polyhalobous taxa (*Cymatosira belgica*, *Paralia sulcata* and *Thalassionema nitzschiodes*) reach a cumulative abundance of about 15%. At +0.46m OD, diatom preservation is poor, although the polyhalobous taxon *Cymatosira belgica* reaches an abundance of almost 40%.

Samples from the upper part of the silt/clays between +0.58m OD and +0.60m OD show a return to dominance of mesohalobous and oligohalobous indifferent taxa with a maximum percentage of mesohalobes of almost 40% at +0.60m OD. Polyhalobous taxa are present only in the sample from +0.60m OD (10%) and the percentage of freshwater diatoms

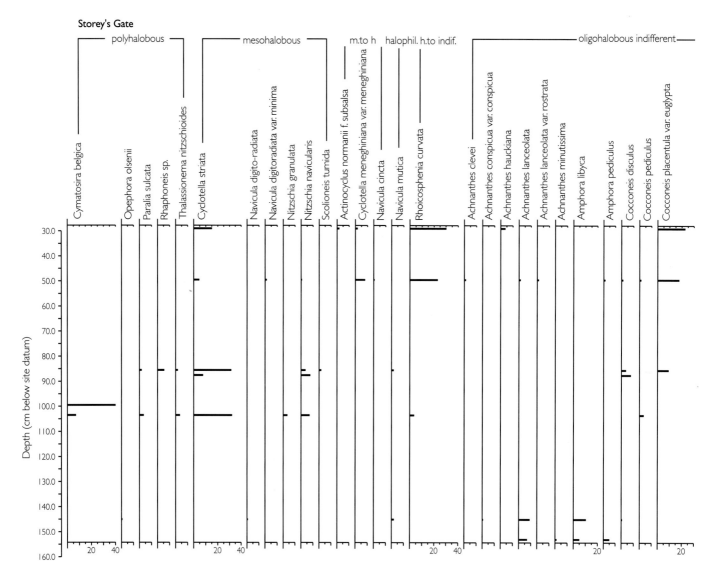

Fig 17 Diatom diagram from Storey's Gate, Westminster

is slightly reduced. These two samples indicate, therefore, that the environment was tidal and it appears that salinity was increasing as the percentage of brackish-water diatoms and outer estuary plankton increases in the upper sample. The following level analysed, at +0.62m OD, although poorly preserved, shows a return to freshwater conditions with no brackish or marine diatoms present. A high proportion of the species present could not be assigned to any halobian group as a result of the poor condition of valves and fragments (eg c 40% *Gyrosigma* sp, which probably represent epipelic diatoms growing in shallow fresh water), but about 25% of the diatoms were identified as oligohalobous indifferent taxa.

From above +0.62m OD to the top of the sequence, the two samples analysed show a trend of increasing salinity compared to the assemblage recorded at +0.62m OD, although not reaching the high salinities reached in the middle of the sequence but with more stability in the flora. Marine plankton is absent from the samples at +0.62m OD, +0.97m OD and +1.17m OD while mesohalobous taxa, dominated by the estuarine, planktonic

species *Cyclotella striata* (maximum 15% at +1.17m OD) absent at +0.62m OD, increase in abundance towards the top of the sequence. At the same time halophilous diatoms associated with epiphytic habitats have increasing percentages in this section of the sequence. These epiphytic taxa include *Rhoicosphaenia curvata* which reaches a maximum of 30% at the top of the profile, and the freshwater (brackish-water tolerant) taxon, *Cocconeis placentula* var. *euglypta*, which reaches an abundance of over 20% at the same level. The diatom assemblages in the upper section of the sequence indicate, therefore, that the channel was tidal, but has a diatom flora representing conditions towards the upper limit of the tidal range.

Discussion

The data collected from Storey's Gate indicate that this part of Westminster was dominated by a major palaeochannel, probably the northern branch of the Tyburn, for a substantial part of the prehistoric and then historic period. The channel cuts sand deposits which are thought to have been laid down

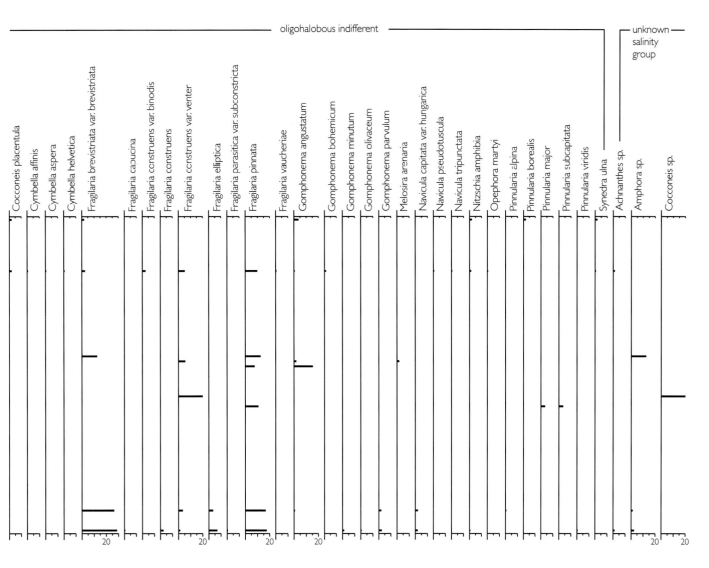

(Fig 17 cont)

over an extensive area of the Westminster region in the Late Glacial/early post-glacial period. These sands have been found at several other sites described by this project, for instance under Westminster Underground Station. The channel was probably first cut in the Early Holocene. However, the initial infilling sediment suggests a low-energy aquatic environment and it is possible that the channel did not accrete sediment in its earliest phases. Unfortunately, limited microfossils have been recovered from these basal fills, which could have helped to characterise the processes of sedimentation at this point. Sparse pollen is preserved from the interface of the sands and overlying organic muds, indicating the dominance of lime woodland. It seems possible that the channel may only have been relatively short-lived at this period, owing to the fact that the initial sediments suggest a low-energy environment and they are sealed by organic muds indicating that the energy of flow had dropped sufficiently to allow vegetation to take a hold. Fluvially derived sediment was still being deposited, however, indicating that the channel had not been totally cut off. Both pollen and diatom remains were recovered from the organic muds. The high pollen value of *Tilia* (25%) in the basal pollen level (see

Fig 16) is consistent with local growth on a basal palaeosol formed prior to waterlogging of the site and organic accumulation. Subsequently it declines within zone 1 to values of <10% during the time span represented by the organic accumulation. At *c* 3500 cal. BP there is a further decline to low levels and a further decline to absence from 2640±40 BP (2839–2737 cal. BP) (Beta 127739). This reflects a complex history of lime growth at this site. The high value in the basal level/palaeosol clearly represents on-, or very near, site growth and dominance of lime woodland on drier soils, a fact seen at the majority of sites examined along the JLE. Reduction in lime values during zone ST:1 is associated with a change to organic, wetter deposits which were less suited to the growth of this woodland, and a consequent reduction in pollen from on-site sources. However, there is also a clear association of this decline with a peak of cereal pollen (and Asteraceae). This also implies a human causation, that is, a typical lime decline seen at sites in London and across southern and eastern England as a whole. Lime declines have been largely dated to the Middle to Late Bronze Age but with earlier dates of Middle/Late Neolithic at Union and Joan Streets and much later in Epping Forest (Baker

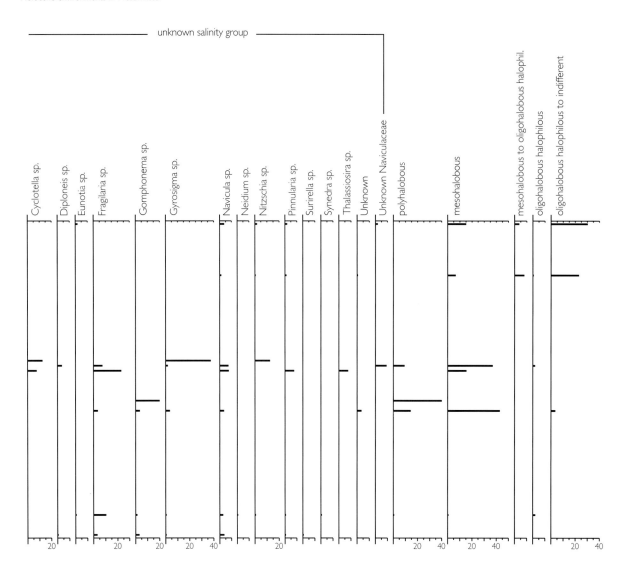

(Fig 17 cont)

et al 1978). The further decline at 2800 cal. BP may be due to taphonomic factors or due to final removal of native lime in this region during the Iron Age.

Characteristically, with removal of the *Tilia*, *Quercus* and *Corylus avellana* remained the dominant tree and shrub pollen taxa. Less well-represented pollen taxa include *Ulmus*, *Fagus* and *Ilex* which may have been growing locally although the possibility of fluviatile transport should be considered with regard to the minerogenic sediments from which the pollen was extracted. Of particular note are the sporadic records of *Picea* in zone 1 and *Abies* in zones 2–3. While there is the possibility that these pollen are derived from Tertiary sources, their overall preservation and staining was comparable/similar to the Holocene pollen. It is possible that these may derive from long-distance marine dissemination as these sediments were laid down under tidal conditions and saccate pollen is known to be over-represented in waterlain sediments. While Roman exotic introduction is a possibility at other sites, the Iron Age date here rules this out.

The diatom evidence from the base of the organic mud sequence indicates that the deposits were entirely freshwater –

there is no evidence for any estuarine species, although it should be borne in mind that the assemblages are poor ones. However, the upper levels of the organic mud, at *c* +0.19m OD, contain halophilous, mesohalobian and a possible polyhalobian species. This demonstrates that the upper levels of the organic mud were deposited under increasingly saline conditions. Although there is a possibility that this is a result of mixing at the sedimentary interface, it is also quite possible that this is the first indication of tidal migration to this point upstream in the Middle Bronze Age. It is extremely unfortunate that the subsequent reactivation of the channel led to erosional events and a hiatus in deposition at this very interesting point in the history of the site. The date of the later group of sediments has been attributed using ceramics found within the sediments and gives a 12th-/13th-century date. This indicates that there was a change at this time in the sedimentary regime influencing the depositional processes acting within the channel. However, it is not possible to date when the erosional processes started, as it cannot be stated with any certainty how much sediment was eroded, or whether there were any other periods when accretion rather than erosion took place.

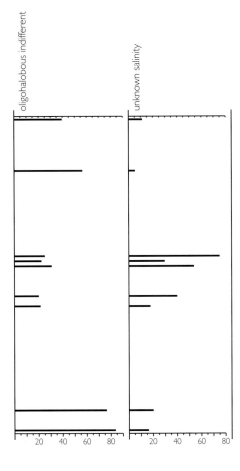

(Fig 17 cont)

The medieval silt/clays and sands may have been deposited as a result of human action in Westminster from the early medieval period. Changes to urban and agricultural land use may have altered the mechanics of channel flow and therefore led to the transition from an erosional to accreting regime. Microfossils were present within these deposits and indicate that the waterbody was certainly tidal. In fact, the sediments present at +0.46m OD show the strongest marine influence within the entire sequence, indicating that the Thames was probably strongly tidal to this point, leading to the tributaries and channels also being affected. This would doubtless have had an effect upon the local population in terms of river defences, water and waste management and obviously navigation. At a higher level within these medieval sediments, it would appear that the tidal influence drops, with the brackish-water species assuming dominance over the polyhalobian taxa. Potentially, this could be caused by several factors. It could be a straight reflection of events occurring in the main channel of the Thames; the tidal head could have migrated slightly downstream leading to a decrease in marine species relative

to the brackish-water species present in the sediments being deposited. However, the channel is peripheral to the Thames, and the decrease in tidal influence at this point may be a result of changes in the relative balance of water flow and sedimentation between the Thames and the Tyburn. With the increase of occupation and reclamation in this area, and the consequent increase in river levels (relative to the land) associated with the tidal head and tidal range, there may have been development of river defences. This could potentially have increased the proportions of fresh water (from the Tyburn) to salt water in the channel. Additionally, if the Tyburn channel was being used for water distribution and navigation, then construction of sluices etc at the mouth of the Tyburn may have led to reconfiguration of the Thames/Tyburn confluence, again altering slightly the patterns of sedimentation and balance of fresh to salt water further up the channel.

The uppermost fills of the channel suggest that salinity levels increase and that the tidal influence gets stronger. This probably relates to a reversal of the factors which led to the previous decrease in salinity; either relative river levels have increased with the progression of the tidal head further upstream, and/or tidal water is dominating the Tyburn channel to a greater extent than previously. However, the marine influence does not reach the levels encountered when the second phase of sedimentation began, at *c* +0.4m OD, and in fact the uppermost diatom assemblage suggests that the river at this location is probably at the uppermost limits of the tidal range. This is doubtless confused by the mixing taking place within the Tyburn. However, it is certainly significant that the river was more strongly tidal at this location in the earlier rather than the later medieval period.

The channel appears to have finally dried out in the late medieval/early post-medieval period, although it appears to have remained damp and probably boggy for some time. A possible turf line at *c* +0.9m OD would suggest that the area was reclaimed but not significantly used at this period. The deposits covering the infilled channel were levelling dumps used to fully reclaim the land and prepare it for the substantial construction work which regenerated the boggy area and took the form of houses, tenements and the deer park.

Conclusions

Three main phases of sedimentation have been identified, two of which are within the channel and the third is subsequent to the final filling of the channel. The latter may be identified with the reclamation of the area in the late medieval/early post-medieval period prior to development of houses and parkland. The presence of a basal palaeosol has been noted, on which lime with hazel woodland grew. Local waterlogging initiated colonisation of the site by grass-sedge dominated reed swamp with consequent peat accumulation. Subsequently, the change to inorganic sediments saw a reduction of these reed swamp elements and a marked expansion of *Alnus* with *Salix* (willow). The reed swamp was overtaken and destroyed through estuarine sedimentation. Further waterlogging caused a return to sedge/reed fen over extensive areas causing the demise of carr woodland. This resulted from rising regional base levels caused by late prehistoric positive eustatic changes.

Throughout the profile, there are strong indications of human activity with cereal pollen and associated arable weeds. Unfortunately, the two phases of channel sedimentation are separated by a major hiatus, leaving only late prehistoric and medieval sediments, and no certain date for the inception of erosion. The erosion was possibly caused by the encroachment of the tidal head upon this area, leading to a rise in relative river levels and a higher energy regime, causing erosion rather than accretion of sediment. Although there is a suggestion of tidal influence at the interface of the two sedimentary units within the channel, it is uncertain whether this marked the beginning of one constant rise in relative river levels, or, as appears to have happened in the City, further downstream, that there were a series of fluctuations, culminating in the medieval period, after approximately 1181 (Sidell submitted), with a rise which appears to have been continuous to the present day.

Parliament Square

Introduction

Archaeological investigation of Parliament Square took place during the construction of a 4.57m diameter grouting shaft located in Canning Green, on the western side of the square. Excavation was initially of a circle 5.5m in diameter, and was carried out entirely by machine, after which archaeological deposits were recorded by hand. After the archaeological excavation the grouting shaft was machine excavated to a depth of 35m. Despite the relatively small area investigated, a number of medieval features were found sealed beneath deliberately deposited material dating to the Tudor period. These medieval features included rubbish pits and a possible drainage ditch (possibly extending to the 'Long Ditch' or Tyburn), dating to the later 13th and early 14th centuries, overlying a further ditch and timber structure dating to the late 12th century. The earliest medieval layers consisted of surfaces of sand and granular clasts, overlying fine-grained sediments, again containing artefacts from the later 12th century. Fluvial sands containing struck flints were encountered at +0.60m OD.

Two monolith samples were taken from the 12th-century and earlier waterlain deposits during the investigations, but during the assessment phase these proved to be of relatively

low potential for further study and therefore no analytical work was carried out. The following text is a summary of the information gleaned at the initial stage of work which provides several useful indicators for the local processes operating in the area of Parliament Square.

Lithostratigraphy

The monolith samples were taken from fine-grained waterlain stratigraphy present between +0.20m OD and +1.12m OD. The lowest part of this sequence, between +0.20m OD and +0.33m OD, consisted of homogeneous olive-brown (2.5Y4/3) silt/clays, coarsening upwards to dark greyish-brown (2.5Y4/2) fine sands with a silt matrix. In the uppermost part of the deposit wavy parallel laminations were found, highlighted by iron stains. It is likely that these deposits formed within a channel, while the reversed bedding is an indication of increasing energy levels during accretion, possibly caused by channel migration towards the site, although a further possibility is the increasing effect of tidal processes. Overlying the mixed silt and sand deposits was a complex series of sands, with sharp bounding surfaces between individual strata suggesting frequent depositional events and erosional cycles. Although an unconformity exists between the sand deposits and the underlying silt/clays, it is likely that any hiatus is minimal as the sands represent a continuation of trends observed in the lower sediment. The sands are highly variable and range from olive-brown (2.5Y4/3) silt-rich fine sands with distinct wavy parallel lamination to pale yellow homogeneous medium to coarse sand. All are representative of accretion within a channel where energy levels were constantly altering, again due to channel migration or tidal processes, causing localised erosion of existing surfaces at the same time as deposition was occurring elsewhere in the channel. Indeed granular and pebble-sized flint and chert clasts were noted at the base of certain strata, and are probably representative of lag, where finer-grained material in the underlying deposit has been removed through fluvial erosion. These data indicate that accretion was not continuous, but was rather spasmodic and punctuated by localised erosional episodes. Iron stains present towards the tops of some of the fine-sand-dominated units, and particularly as part of the laminations in these sediments, suggest that water levels were on occasion so low that the surfaces of sand bars were exposed to subaerial weathering. Mollusc shell noted within the sands was of the genus *Bithynia*, which tends to prefer larger bodies of moving water, but is otherwise tolerant of a wide range of aquatic ecologies. Charcoal was noted at the very top of the sequence indicating human activity, but volume mineral magnetic studies carried out during the assessment do not suggest enhancement in any part of the sequence. Thus the charcoal has almost certainly been reworked from elsewhere, but nevertheless almost certainly relates to activity in the 12th century, when this area of Westminster was being rapidly colonised.

Pollen biostratigraphy

Pollen analysis was carried out to assessment level only on this sequence because of the lack of sound archaeological dating evidence for deposits underlying the 12th-century strata. Pollen samples were examined from the sands down into mineral silt/clays, that is spanning +1.0m OD to +0.20m OD. Of the eight samples analysed, seven contained well-preserved pollen and although only examined to assessment level, with smaller than normal pollen counts, the data were felt to be interesting enough to present in diagram form (Fig 18).

A total of 50 pollen taxa was recorded from the site. Generally, herbs are dominant throughout the sequence with higher values of Lactucae (50%) and Poaceae (to 60%) in the lowest and uppermost levels. In addition are a variety of ruderals including Brassicaceae (charlocks), Polygonaceae (knotweed) and other Asteraceae types, while cereal pollen is also present. These pollen spectra suggest waste ground and arable cultivated areas, but alternatively, in such medieval minerogenic sediments, the assemblages may have been of secondary derivation from crop processing, human and/or animal waste dumped into and transported by the river. Tree and shrub pollen comprise predominantly *Pinus* (to 16%), *Quercus* (to 30%), *Corylus avellana* type (to 20%) and *Alnus* (18%), with the latter particularly abundant in the mineral silt/clays. There are occasional/sporadic occurrences of *Tilia*, *Fagus* and *Ilex*. Also of interest and note are the small numbers of *Picea* and *Abies*. As with the other sites attributed to the historic period on the JLE, the consistent presence of *Quercus* and *Corylus avellana* pollen is evidence of the woodland which remained in the region as a whole following removal of *Tilia* in the late prehistoric period, and which apparently survived well into the medieval period. The depositional environment would appear to have been channel marginal – that is, marsh or floodplain – for the greater part of this sequence, with growth of fen taxa such as *Typha latifolia*, *Typha/Sparganium*, Cyperaceae and *Osmunda regalis* (royal fern) and algal *Pediastrum* cysts. These data seem to be indicative of a retrogressive hydrosere, replacing the drier conditions evidenced in the mineral silt/clays which supported sedge fen and some alder. In such sequences, the taphonomy of the pollen is complex and may result in representation of taxa eroded from earlier sediments and/or transported from extra-local sources. This may explain the presence of the *Abies* and *Picea* grains. However, preservation comparable with other Holocene stratigraphy, and the increasing number of such records of these taxa in sequences along the JLE, suggest that long-distance marine dissemination may be responsible for the occurrence of these non-native trees and the relatively large numbers of pine pollen. A further possibility is that they were introduced into the local area in the Roman or later period as ornamental, exotic trees, as has been suggested for a medieval flora from Silvertown (Wilkinson *et al* 2000).

Diatom biostratigraphy

Seven samples were assessed for diatoms from the Parliament Square sequence. Diatoms were absent from the basal samples and were poorly preserved in the overlying units. Further analysis was not, therefore, carried out. However, some useful palaeoenvironmental information was derived from the assessment. The absence of diatoms from the mineral clay/silts at the base of the sampled monoliths gives some support to the hypothesis that these silts were deposited at the margins of a channel, where, in shallow water deposits, processes such as drying of the sediment would be more likely to lead to breakage, dissolution and loss of the diatom record.

Diatoms preserved in the overlying sands and thin interbedded organic mud contained a mixture of brackish and freshwater taxa, and from +0.40m OD upwards a number of marine species were also present, including *Paralia sulcata*, which was relatively common at +0.45m OD. Brackish-water taxa such as *Cyclotella striata* and *Nitzschia navicularis* were the most common diatoms found throughout the sequence. These deposits therefore represent estuarine conditions and the diatom assemblages are consistent with deposition either within a channel or by flooding.

Conclusions

The sedimentary data from Parliament Square suggest that the sampled units all accumulated within an aquatic environment and most probably a river/stream channel. This channel appears to have undergone a complex history, with a series of accretion and erosional episodes and swings in energy level. Also, occasional exposure of previously submerged deposits is likely, which all suggests a variety of processes affecting this channel, presumably associated with links to the Tyburn and the Thames. The diatom evidence suggests that all sampled deposits were laid down in a brackish intertidal environment, while palynological data suggest the vegetation was open throughout, with evidence for declining base levels. The pollen data also provide evidence for the widespread impact of people on the surrounding vegetation, including the growing of cereals, and possibly the deliberate planting of firs and pine as ornamentation. All the sediments sampled occur above OD, but it is nevertheless impossible to correlate the sequence with the other Westminster sites without further dating evidence because of the local nature of factors leading to deposition.

Palace Chambers South

Introduction

(Fig 19)

In 1994–5, a series of excavations was carried out on the southern side of Westminster Station, beneath the former Palace Chambers. Four separate sites (Site 1 west, Site 1 east,

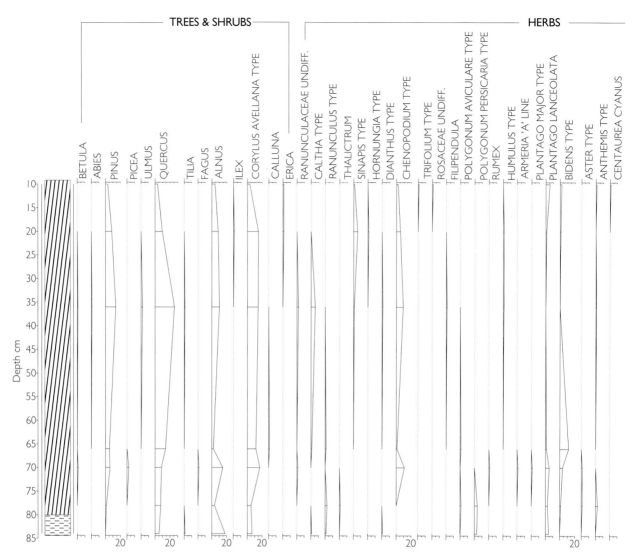

Fig 18 Pollen diagram from Parliament Square, Westminster

Site 2 and Site 6) were investigated and all were excavated down to prehistoric waterlain sediments. The stratigraphy was locally complex and cannot easily be correlated between sites. At Site 1 west, which was investigated in 1994, fine-grained sediments extending upwards from +0.20m OD, and containing ceramics from the 12th to the 14th century, overlay a series of fluvial sands. These contained prehistoric pottery, tentatively attributed to the Late Neolithic or Early Bronze Age, and a moderately large collection of struck flint, including a series of blades, and a fragment of a polished Neolithic axe. In turn the artefact-bearing sands overlay further fluvial sands, which extended down at least to −1.54m OD without gravel being encountered. Cutting into these deposits was a series of postholes and a single pit, which were associated with the Neolithic/Bronze Age artefact assemblage.

Sites 1 east and 2 were successively investigated in 1995 and broadly similar results were obtained from both. Above 2.0m OD was a series of post-medieval features, below which was a medieval building of 14th-century date, with associated drains, pits and material deliberately deposited on the foreshore. These lay on reclaimed land, covering a wall of 12th-century date that had once bounded the river, along with a timber dock. This series of

predominantly archaeological deposits sealed waterlain stratigraphy consisting of silt/clays, overlying organic muds, with further silt/clays and sands extending down to at least −2.00m OD. No artefacts were recovered from this stratigraphy, although three ^{14}C dates were obtained during the present analytical programme indicating accretion between 5200 cal. BP and 3200 cal. BP (see Table 8).

Monolith samples were taken from three of the four sites: Site 1 west, Site 1 east and Site 2. The first sampling was carried out on Site 1 west where three monolith samples were taken from the complete depth of the sequence in August 1994, followed by sampling of three vertical sections from Sites 1 east and 2 during 1995. One of the latter was entirely of archaeological stratigraphy, consisting of a complex of deliberately deposited sediments of medieval date which were of very little value for examining palaeoenvironment and are not considered further here. The remaining samples are from deposits that underlie the 12th-century river wall and which therefore both correlate with and also predate those taken in 1994. Together these samples represent a total of 3.7m of stratigraphy, dating from the Middle to later Neolithic and the medieval periods. Sedimentological data from all sites are presented as a histogram in Fig 21, while palynological results are presented in Fig 22.

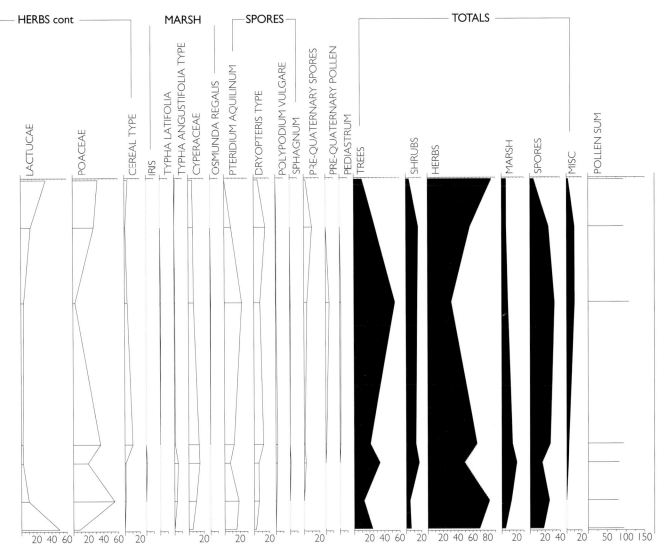

(Fig 18 cont)

Lithostratigraphy and sedimentology

At the base of the sampled sequence lies at least a metre of
laminated sands outcropping between −2.40m OD and −1.20m
OD. These sands are locally diverse, but typically consist of
uniform sequences of brownish-yellow (10YR6/6) medium
and fine sands with widely spaced wavy, parallel laminae of
olive-brown (2.5Y4/3) silt/clay. Wherever such laminae occur,
the sands immediately above are iron stained. Rounded and
sub-rounded, granular and pebble-sized flint occurs in distinct
bands, while all boundaries within the deposit are gradual,
suggesting that sedimentation was not punctuated by erosional
episodes. Particle-size analysis (Fig 20) indicates that the sands
are either moderately or well sorted (*sensu* Folk & Ward 1957)
and have near symmetrical distributions around the normal.
Indeed, given the inferred origin of the deposits it is surprising
how well sorted the sands are, and were it not for the relatively
coarse mean particle size (+1.58–2.28ϕ) the distribution would
appear to be more characteristic of an aeolian environment.
The graphic particle-size data combined with the fact that less
than 2% of material was of silt and clay grade suggest that the
sands formed in a non-changing sedimentary environment

(*ie* there appears to have been no alteration in energy levels
over the time span of accumulation), and little diagenesis has
occurred.

A single twig fragment was found in one of the silt/clay
laminae at −2.15m OD subsequently dated by AMS (accelerator
mass spectrometry) to 4300±60 BP (5032–4659 cal. BP) (Beta
122929), suggesting that the sand was accreting in the Middle
to later Neolithic. A conventional ^{14}C date of 3570±70 BP
(4085–3644 cal. BP) (Beta 119790) from the interface with
the overlying silt/clays suggests that accumulation of the sands
had ceased by the end of the Neolithic or Early Bronze Age,
when finer-grained sediment began to form. Throughout the
sands both organic carbon contents and χ^{lf} measurements are
extremely low, causing massive fluctuation in χ^{fd}. However,
above −1.50m OD, χ^{lf} and organic carbon both increase,
probably as a result of a minor fining upwards sequence that
can be seen in the particle-size distribution with slightly higher
proportions of silt and clay. It is also possible that some organic
rich material may have been worked downwards within root
channels, although this effect is likely to have been minor given
the minimal silt/clay content of the deposits. Nevertheless, such
channels were observed extending downwards from the

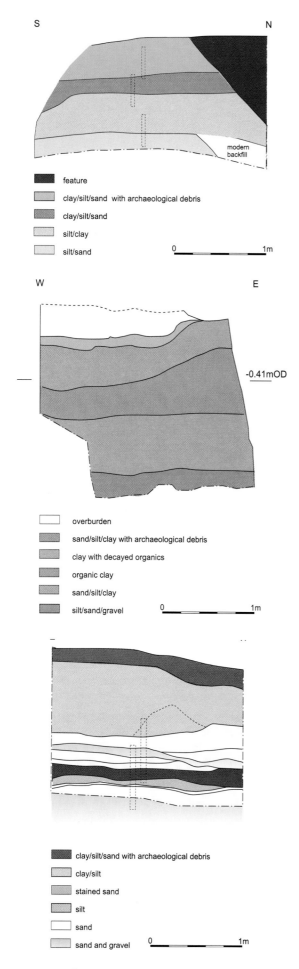

S   N

feature
clay/silt/sand with archaeological debris
clay/silt/sand
silt/clay
silt/sand

0   1m

W   E

-0.41mOD

overburden
sand/silt/clay with archaeological debris
clay with decayed organics
organic clay
sand/silt/clay
silt/sand/gravel

0   1m

clay/silt/sand with archaeological debris
clay/silt
stained sand
silt
sand
sand and gravel

0   1m

Fig 19 Sections from Palace Chambers South, Westminster

interface with the silt/clays found above the sands, and are undoubtedly the product of a stable ground surface on top of the sands that has subsequently been truncated.

On the basis of the morphological and analytical data, the sand deposits are likely to have formed semi-continuously within a moderately high-energy river that was continuously changing course. The data are also suggestive of a high sediment supply and an unchanging environment prior to *c* 4000 cal. BP. The fining upwards above −1.50m OD is a product of decreasing flow energies, caused either through channel migration away from the sample site, channel abandonment or increase in water depth. The latter is less likely given the fact that iron staining and indications of a terrestrial surface are found, indicating that the channel bed/margins were exposed to subaerial processes. Thus, all indications are that reduction in energy was the result of a decrease in water depth. Within such an environment the silt/clay laminae are indicative of accretion in very slow flowing or still water.

Unconformably overlying the sand strata at −1.20m OD, and dated to between 3570±70 BP (4085–3644 cal. BP) and 3110±60 BP (3467–3085 cal. BP) (Beta 119780), are a series of dark greyish-brown silt/clays. These would appear to have formed following an erosional event, presumably of fluvial cause, which had removed a terrestrial surface developing on the top of the sands. The length of any hiatus between the silt/clays and the sands cannot unfortunately be determined, although the former were accreting in the later Neolithic/Early Bronze Age into the Middle to later Bronze Age. The clay/silts are largely homogeneous, but do contain occasional fine wavy laminations of organic mud (two of which were sampled to obtain the ^{14}C dates quoted above), indicating periods of extremely low energy accretion, in a semi-terrestrial environment. Indeed, energy levels throughout sedimentation would appear to be low and given the likelihood that a terrestrial surface existed prior to accretion are likely to be as a result of fallout from suspension following overbank flooding. Within the fine-grained sediments are found moderate quantities of charcoal, indicating human activity within the floodplain. However, although mineral magnetic values are higher than in the underlying sands (*c* 20^{-8} m³kg^{-1} compared to 5^{-8} m³kg^{-1} in the sands), they are not of sufficient magnitude to indicate *in situ* human activity and probably merely reflect a decrease in average particle size. Organic carbon content remains at about 20% throughout much of the silt/clays and then rapidly increases in the top of the deposit to around 40% with an associated fall in χ^{lf} values. These sedimentological properties are indicative of an increasing influence of terrestrial processes on sedimentation, and therefore suggest an increasing relative height of the sample site above river level, or situation within a channel which had been cut off from the main river except during flood events.

Organic carbon content increases still further to 50% in the black (2.5Y2.5/1) organic mud that conformably overlies the silt/clays discussed above at −0.58m OD, suggesting that accretion of such a deposit was merely a culmination of a process that began earlier. The organic mud is parallel laminated throughout suggesting episodic accretion, while a single thicker lamina at −0.56m OD is of light yellowish-brown (2.5Y6/3) medium to fine sand, which is likely to have formed during a single high-energy event such as a storm. Sand is otherwise found throughout the deposit in low proportions, while charcoal occurs more frequently. Once again the latter is almost certainly not a product of *in situ* human activity as χ_{lf} values are low throughout, and therefore the charcoal particles must have been washed in. Although there is no direct dating, it is certain that the organic muds and later fine-grained deposits are from later than 3110±60 BP (3467–3085 cal. BP), and thus are almost certainly of later Bronze and Iron Age date. Conformably overlying these organic muds are further parallel laminated very dark grey (2.5Y3/1) silt/clays, marking a return to conditions found prior to the accretion of the organic muds. Within this deposit, organic carbon contents decline to around 30%, which is probably mostly concentrated within individual organic laminae. These latter may be produced by algal blooming which occurs following periods of high spring tides in the present Thames estuary (R Malt pers comm; Wilkinson in prep). There is certainly no morphological evidence for rooting, which may be indicative of a terrestrial surface.

Accretion of the lower silt/clays and deposits above possibly occurred more or less continuously in a floodplain environment, with individual depositional episodes marked by laminations occurring during individual flood events. If such a mechanism for deposition is accepted it would indicate that a major change in depositional environment occurred at around 3800 cal. BP, following accumulation of the sands, which certainly took place in freshwater conditions. The overlying (lower) silt/clays are the

first manifestation of low-energy floodplain deposition. The organic muds mark a subtle change in the depositing environment and are most likely to have accumulated as a result of accretion heightening the sample site in relation to the adjacent river, which reduced the frequency and duration of flood events. The overlying silt/clays may have accumulated in a similar depositional environment to those lower down, but could also have formed in an estuarine environment, and may thus be indicative of rising RSL. Also notable within the upper silt/clays is the quantity of charcoal present, which was not found in the underlying sands. While mineral magnetic measurements demonstrate that the charcoal is not the product of *in situ* human activity, the sheer quantity of material present would appear to indicate widespread human activity in the wider environment. It may be suggested from these data that the upper silt/clays relate to the medieval period when human activity in the Westminster area is known to have increased. If this is the case a substantial period of hiatus is possible between the organic muds and the upper silt/clays, although as has already been observed there is no morphological evidence for a disconformity.

Unconformably overlying the intertidal and sand sequence between −0.15m OD and +0.20m OD are archaeological deposits relating to the 12th-century river wall. These consist of very dark greyish-brown (10YR3/2) poorly sorted sandy silts containing moderate quantities of flint granules and pebbles, with ceramic and charcoal fragments. These deposits represent material deliberately deposited on the foreshore to raise levels above that of the adjacent river, probably as part of the process of construction for the retaining wall and associated with the use of the dock. However, the material used to do this

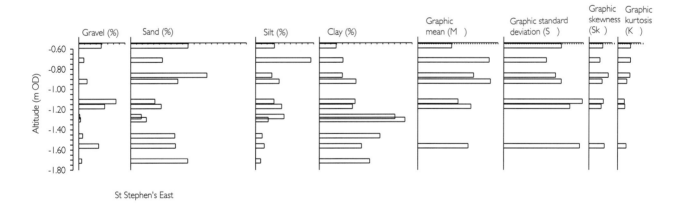

St Stephen's East

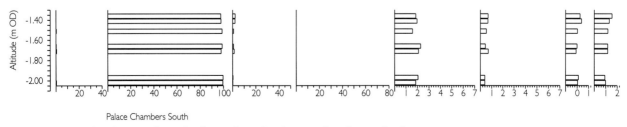

Palace Chambers South

Fig 20 *Particle-size distribution of samples from Palace Chambers South and St Stephen's East, Westminster*

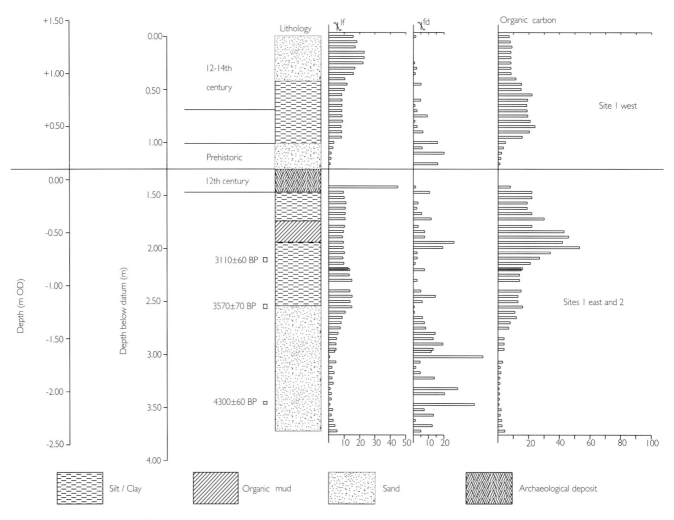

Fig 21 Lithological diagram from Palace Chambers South, Westminster

consisted not only of occupation debris, but also waterlain material – several shells of the freshwater molluscan genus *Bithynia* were noted in the sample tins. The sedimentological properties of these deposits reflect their inferred means of genesis, and it is notable that a peak in χ^{lf} occurs within these strata at *c* 50^{-8} m^3kg^{-1}. Organic content, however, declines to around 10%, suggesting that little biological material is included within the deposits.

The stratigraphy portrayed in Fig 21 as lying above the archaeological deposits relating to the river wall has no direct relationship to the stratigraphy previously discussed, but rather are strata investigated at Site 2. However, as noted in the introduction to this section the basal sand contained prehistoric pottery, struck flints and a Neolithic polished axe, suggesting a possible correlation with the sands at the base of the sequence previously discussed, despite a difference in altitude of almost 1.5m. The strata consist initially of well-sorted, light olive-brown (2.5Y5/3) sands between +0.15m OD and +0.35m OD, and of almost identical properties to those discussed above from the base of the main sequence (*ie* low χ^{lf} and organic carbon values, with wildly fluctuating χ^{fd}). As with the previous sands, these almost certainly formed within a channel environment and as a result of near bed-flow processes. Given the location of the sample site and the relative height at which

they occur it would seem most likely that accretion was in a tributary channel, rather than that of the Thames itself. Unconformably overlying the sands, and indicating a decline in depositional energy, are a series of very dark greyish-brown (10YR3/2) silt/clays, which extend upwards to an erosional contact at +1.00m OD. These are apparently structureless and contain moderate quantities of charcoal and small proportions of sand. They are iron stained throughout, which when considered alongside the frequent roots noted within the deposits would appear to be indicative of the operation of terrestrial processes. It would therefore seem likely that these deposits formed within a cut-off channel which was occasionally subject to flooding, during which time charcoal and sand were washed in from the nearby river, although during other periods water levels were relatively low. Organic carbon levels within the silt/clays average 25%, while χ^{lf} measurements are notably higher than those of the underlying sand. The upper part of the silt/clays (above +0.50m OD) contain 12th- to 14th-century ceramics, indicating that the unconformity with the underlying sands may represent a hiatus of as much as 2500 years.

Capping the sequence and with an unconformable boundary to the silt/clays below is a reverse bedded (*ie* coarsening upwards), very dark greyish-brown (10YR3/2) medium to fine sand which also contains 12th- to 14th-century ceramics. This is indicative of progressive increase in energy levels, and probably accreted as the previously abandoned channel became reoccupied by a tributary stream, or a new channel migrated across the sample site. The sands are of similar character to those noted elsewhere in the stratigraphy except that organic contents are noticeably higher (c 8%, compared to c 3% in the other sands), and χ^{lf} values substantially increased (c 22^{-8} m^{3}kg^{-1} compared to 4^{-8} m^{3}kg^{-1}). The latter property is almost certainly the result of the incorporation of ceramic microartefacts in the stratigraphy, and has been noted in Roman and later sand-rich alluvial deposits in the City of London (Wilkinson in prep), while the former may be indicative of the incorporation of finely divided plant matter eroded from contemporary channel sides. Thus the sedimentological data suggest slightly different depositional environments during the high-energy accumulation of sands in the channel during the two separate sand-accretion episodes, although both formed as a result of near bed-flow processes, and probably in a freshwater environment.

Pollen biostratigraphy

Pollen analysis was carried out on samples collected from Site 1 west and Site 2. Study during the assessment programme indicated that pollen was poorly preserved or absent in the basal arenaceous sediments and this proved to be the case in more recent analysis. However, organic muds and mineral silt/clays outcropping at between −0.79 and −0.09m OD, and which were not available in the earlier assessment, contained sufficient remains to construct a pollen sequence/diagram (Fig 22). These levels correspond to the Middle and Late Bronze Age, and possibly the Iron Age. Pollen in this part of the stratigraphy was generally well preserved, but was rather sparse, being in the order of 20,000–50,000 grains/ml.

Four local pollen assemblage zones are suggested for this sequence, although the upper and lowest zones are single levels only. Although tentative, they appear to show significant ecological differences relating to increasing wetness and a retrogressive hydrosere caused by a rising local water table. This was driven by positive RSL changes causing ponding back of the freshwater systems. The characteristics of these zones from the basal zone upwards are as follows:

WSS:1 −0.79m OD *Quercus-Tilia-Corylus avellana type-Alnus*

This level occurs at the interface of the organic and underlying sediments which do not contain pollen. Tree and shrub pollen are at their highest levels (60% and 27% respectively). *Tilia* (24%), *Quercus* (33%), *Alnus* (20%) and *Corylus avellana* type (26%) are dominant while herbs are at their lowest levels (12%) with only Poaceae being important. Cereal type (<5%) are also present. Wetland taxa comprise *Alnus* (20%) with Cyperaceae (22%) and *Alisma* (<5%), and spores of *Polypodium* are at their highest (10%).

WSS:2 −0.79 – −0.44m OD *Quercus-Corylus avellana type-Poaceae-Pteridium aquilinum*

This zone is characterised by reduced *Tilia* (to <5%) and a substantial increase in herbs. *Quercus* (c 30%) and *Corylus avellana* type (10–20%) remain at their previous levels. There are also sporadic occurrences of *Fagus* and *Fraxinus*. Herbs are dominated by Poaceae (expanding to 48%) with Lactucae (16%), *Plantago lanceolata* (8%), Chenopodiaceae (5%) and Cereal type (3%) of note. Marsh taxa remain dominated by *Alnus* (declining from 27%) with Cyperaceae (c 15%), sporadic *Salix*, *Rhamnus catharticus* (buckthorn), *Alisma plantago aquatica* (water plantain), *Iris*, *Typha latifolia* and *Typha angustifolia/Sparganium*. There is a very marked expansion of *Pteridium aquilinum* (60%) while *Polypodium* is much reduced from WSS:1.

WSS:3 −0.44 – −0.14m OD *Pinus-Quercus-Poaceae-Pediastrum*

Pinus expands to 16% along with peaks of large Poaceae, *Dryopteris* type spores and algal *Pediastrum*. *Tilia* declines to sporadic occurrences and absence while *Quercus* and *Corylus* remain similar to WSS:2 but with some expansion of *Quercus* (to 36%). Marsh/aquatic taxa are not as diverse as WSS:2. Cyperaceae are the most important but with *Potamogeton* (pondweed), and *Sagittaria sagittifolia* (arrow head) also present. There is a significant peak of algal *Pediastrum* and occasional Hystrichospheres/dinoflagellates.

WSS:4 −0.10 – −0.9m OD

This single level lies at the interface between mineral-rich silt/clays below and the overlying archaeological deposits. It differs from WSS:3 by a reduction in *Pinus* (to <5%) and *Pediastrum* (<5%) combined with a sharp increase in derived pre-Quaternary pollen and spores. Trees remain dominated by *Quercus* (17%) with sporadic *Picea*, *Betula* and *Fagus*. Herbs are dominated by Chenopodiaceae, Lactucae and Cereal type. Also noted are grains of *Plantago maritima* (sea plantain) type, large Poaceae and Hystrichospheres which may be halophytes. There are few aquatic and marsh taxa with only Cyperaceae and occasional *Potamogeton*.

Diatom biostratigraphy

Seven samples from the monoliths taken at Palace Chambers South from Site 1 west (*ie* the top part of Fig 20) were assessed for diatoms. Despite the obviously waterlain origin of these deposits, poor diatom preservation indicated that full diatom analysis of the sequence would not be possible (Cameron 1995). Diatoms were absent from the basal sands and a single valve of the brackish-water species *Nitzschia navicularis* was present at the base of the overlying silt/clays. The uppermost sample from this level, which as discussed above has been attributed to the medieval period, was dominated by the same estuarine species, along with the presence of other brackish,

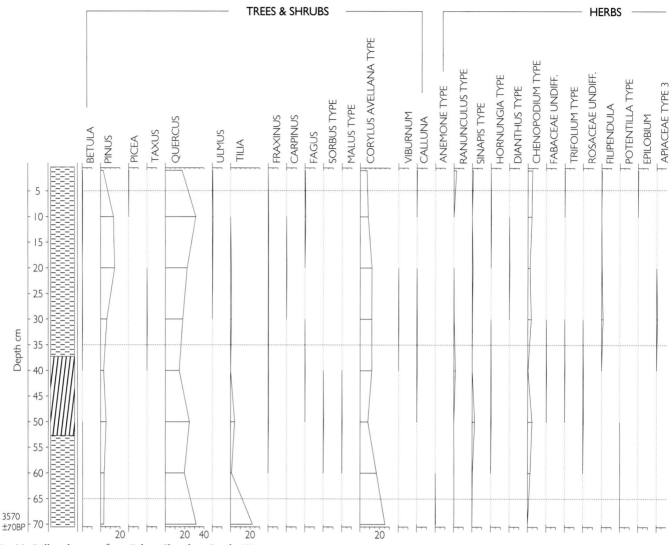

Fig 22 Pollen diagram from Palace Chambers South, Westminster

freshwater and marine diatoms. The low concentration and poor preservation of diatoms in the silt-rich deposit is consistent with the proposed origin of the sediments as a result of floods from a tidal channel or from the main course of the river. It was not possible to further identify the diatom fragments present in the upper, coarse sand.

Following the initial evaluation of material, samples were assessed for diatoms from the two basal monoliths from Site 1 east. As discussed above, the sand strata in this sample probably correspond with the strata found at the base of Site 1 west, but unfortunately, no diatoms were present.

Discussion

The data obtained from Palace Chambers South demonstrate changing depositional environments from a freshwater, sand-dominated meandering river to an estuarine system. The change seems to have occurred around 3200 cal. BP, and thus coincides with the Middle to later Bronze Age. The basal sands found in all the sequences investigated are remnants of the Early and mid Holocene meandering river, which from data obtained from Site 2 was still present c 4800 cal. BP, that is, in the later Neolithic.

Such strata probably formed as channel margin bars on a meander bend under a moderate flow regime. Flow in similar meandering rivers at the present day varies on a seasonal basis and thus some of the sand bars would be exposed during the later summer and early autumn at least. It would appear that the contemporary Neolithic and/or Bronze Age populations took advantage of this fact to utilise one such bar, leaving flint and ceramic artefacts, and excavating features such as pits and postholes. It is notable that all such archaeological remains were from sand strata on Site 1 west which are 1.5m higher than those on Site 2 and thus would have been exposed above floodplain surface for a longer period of time. Indeed it is possible that sands accreting on Site 2 were almost always submerged as there is little evidence for mechanical diagenetic processes, whereas the lamina structure of the sands at Site 1 west has been disrupted. Unfortunately the sands have proved to be unfossiliferous and therefore it cannot be determined whether sea-level rises had any impact on sediments forming on the site, or on the nature of the vegetation in which human activity was taking place.

At around 3800 cal. BP sediments accreting at Palace Chambers South began to change character, becoming increasingly dominated by silts and clays, while input of

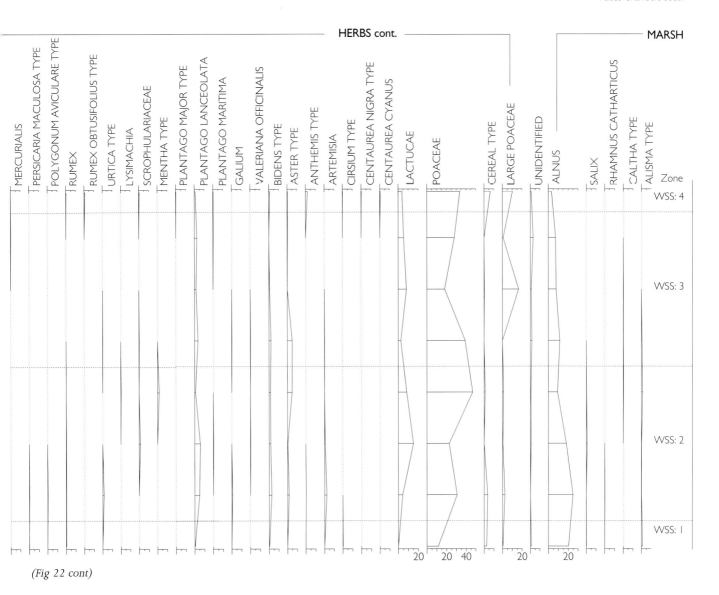

(Fig 22 cont)

organic material also rose. It is tempting to link this change to rises in sea level, and the influence of tidal waters, although it is also possible that the river had simply migrated away from the sample sites. Arguing for the latter hypothesis is the magnetic susceptibility data which suggest that the silts and clays which were forming at this point were exposed to subaerial processes, and thus there were substantial periods when the site was dry. Unfortunately there was no diatom preservation to aid interpretation in this regard. Although no direct evidence of human activity was noted, the presence of charcoal in the monoliths is almost certainly related to human action. Accretion of these overbank floodplain sediments continued until the later Bronze Age (4030–3450 cal. BP) at least, whereupon organic muds began to accumulate. Zone WSS:1 corresponds with the silt/clay sediments dating to around 3200 cal. BP, and which according to the palynological evidence may have undergone a period of pedogenesis. This is possibly evidenced by the strong representation of woodland pollen, dominated by *Tilia*. However, a substantial number of these grains appeared degraded and it is very possible that there has been differential preservation in their favour (Havinga 1964; Waller 1994a, 96) and indeed there is no magnetic susceptibility evidence for the

presence of a palaeosol. *Tilia* with *Quercus* and *Corylus* are typical of both Neolithic and Bronze Age woodland noted at other sites in London (see chapter 8). *Tilia* was clearly locally dominant on a range of soils, certainly including the better-drained soils of the interfluves which would have been located very close to the sample site, but also possibly on less rich soils. This is likely to have occurred in combination with *Quercus* and *Corylus* as constituents of communities growing on heavier valley side and bottom soils, also as part of the drier fen carr woodland. These conclusions are based on increasing evidence that, contrary to earlier views, *Tilia* only grew on good, well-drained soils while it may also have been an element of woodland on poorer soils (see chapter 8).

In lpaz (local pollen assemblage zone) WSS:2, which dates to just after 3200 cal. BP, values of lime are reduced as organic carbon content increases in the top of the silt/clays and into the organic muds. The latter are likely to have formed at the very margin of the floodplain, and thus represent a continued trend in the marginalisation of the site from the river. The decline in lime pollen is possibly an artefact of poorer (?soil) pollen-preserving conditions with over-representation of *Tilia* as a result of changing taphonomy in the underlying sediments.

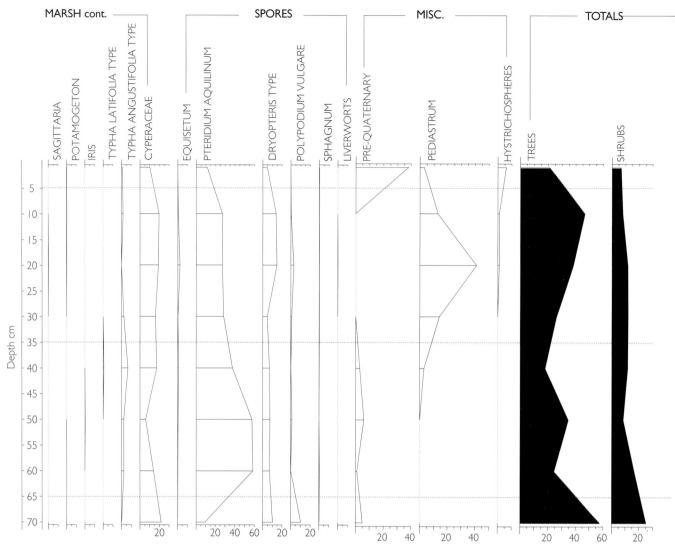

(Fig 22 cont)

Quercus and *Corylus avellana* remain the most important woodland elements, but with occasional elements of less well-represented secondary elements such as *Fagus* and *Fraxinus*. These may relate to the strong evidence for human activity with evidence of arable agriculture. Whether the floodplain was freshwater or tidally dominated during accretion of the mineral clay/silts and the organic muds cannot be determined in the absence of diatoms, while the palynological evidence is also inconclusive.

In lpaz WSS:3, which corresponds to the upper silt/clays which overlie the organic muds in which lpaz WSS:2 occurs, there are strong indications of increasing freshwater conditions suggested by *Pediastrum*, occasional *Potamogeton* (pondweed) and associated changes in taphonomy. WSS:3, however, may be separated from lpaz WSS:2 by an unconformity at the organic mud to silt/clay boundary, with a hiatus of perhaps 1200 years or more. It is notable for example that *Pinus*, which is previously found in very small numbers, is present in some quantity in WSS:3. Pine is noted to increase in pollen diagrams of the medieval period as a result of deliberate human planting (Greig 1992; Wilkinson *et al* 2000), perhaps explaining its occurrence, although it is also commonly over-represented in

lake and fluvial sediments due to its buoyancy (air sacs) (Faegri & Iversen 1975, 71). Apart from the changes in the local/autochthonous environment, terrestrial vegetation communities appear to have remained similar to the preceding zone. Sporadic cereals and synanthropic weeds attest to some human activity in this region during the Late Bronze and Iron Ages, presumably relating to arable agriculture, although this was apparently not as extensive/intensive as in other nearby areas such as Rainham and Barking (Scaife 1991).

Above the waterlain silt/clays that correspond with WSS:3 there is a further unconformity, before sediments relating to human activity began to accrete in the 12th century. WSS:4 relates to this boundary, and although consisting of just a single sample, demonstrates changes to the pollen assemblage which are attributed to both brackish-water/saline conditions and differential taphonomy consequent on mode of deposition. Palynologically the change is attested by the expansion of derived pre-Quaternary palynomorphs in the sediments and to a small number of contemporaneous halophytic taxa. The latter include *Plantago maritima*, and possibly Chenopodiaceae, *Aster* type and large (thin-walled, non-cereal) Poaceae and Hystrichospheres.

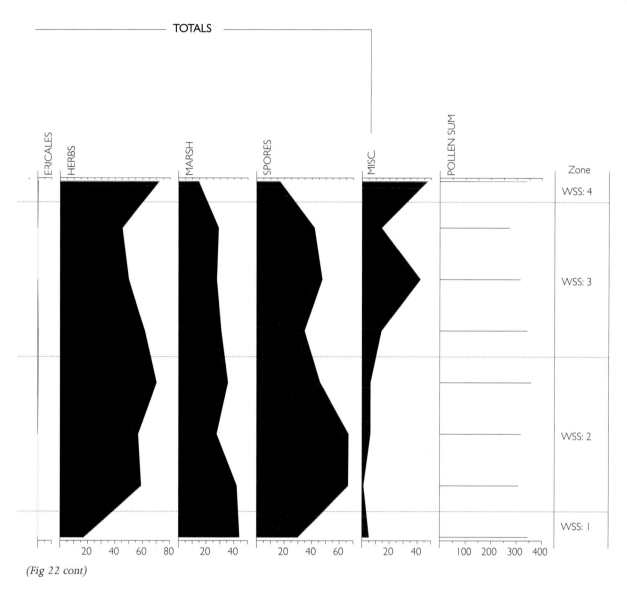

TOTALS

ERICALES HERBS MARSH SPORES MISC. POLLEN SUM Zone

WSS: 4

WSS: 3

WSS: 2

WSS: 1

20 40 60 80   20 40   20 40 60   20 40   100 200 300 400

(Fig 22 cont)

To summarise, following sand accretion in the Neolithic period and earlier, overbank silt/clays formed as a result of channel migration away from the site, while at the same time base levels on the floodplain rose (possibly as a result of positive trends in RSL). This initiated accumulation of organic mud at the site, which was now located at the floodplain edge. Accretion would thus seem to have mainly occurred in a freshwater environment, and only in the 12th century; there is new firm evidence of saline input in the form of polyhalobous/mesohalobous diatoms and halophytic pollen taxa. This level is also the first at which direct human impact on the site was made, while prior to this human action is attested from within the local environment by the presence of charcoal. Throughout the Bronze Age, as represented by the palynological data, the terrestrial vegetation was initially dominated by lime and, following its removal, by oak and hazel woodland with perhaps some secondary ash and beech, a characteristic pattern of late prehistoric woodland in the London area. Evidence of agriculture is present throughout with cereals and some weeds. However, this does not appear as extensive as in other sites examined and may not have been in close proximity to the sample site (being on the opposite side of the Tyburn) or may

have been of small/local extent on Thorney Island itself. Palynological data from the top of the sequence are more difficult to interpret in view of the complex taphonomy, but would appear to suggest the persistence of forested environments within the catchment and the deliberate human planting of pine. Nevertheless, frequency of both charcoal and cereal pollen suggests an increased human impact on the landscape in the medieval period than in later prehistory.

Westminster Underground Station

Introduction

In October and November 1995 archaeological investigations were carried out on the western side of St Stephen's House, at Westminster Station, prior to the construction of new parts of the underground station and a new parliamentary building. A previous evaluation had been made of the site in 1992, when 12 testpits were excavated. During the 1995 excavations an area

40m x 14m was investigated, initially by machine and then by hand. The topmost layers excavated related to 19th- and 20th-century activity and particularly basements of the demolished St Stephen's House. These overlay a complex series of ditches, foundation slots, pits, stakes and deliberately deposited layers relating to activities from the 14th to the 18th century, including a 16th-century barrel-lined well containing two complete ceramic watering cans. The earliest of these features was a series of pits containing middle and later 14th-century ceramics, suggesting that by this time the site was in a terrestrial setting. Possibly the land had been deliberately reclaimed when the area was granted by Edward III to the college of St Stephen's Chapel in the early 14th century. Many of the post-medieval features cut through much of the lower stratigraphy, even truncating pre-Late Bronze Age fluvial sands at the base of the investigated sequence. Elsewhere the later medieval and post-medieval archaeological stratigraphy sealed a series of channels, filled with poorly sorted silt/clays and sands, containing pottery from the 11th and 12th centuries. These channels are probably a mixture of both naturally developing creeks on the foreshore and deliberately constructed drainage channels. The channels were found to cut into organic muds, outcropping between +0.48m OD and −0.61m OD. These proved not to contain artefacts, but a sample taken for ^{14}C dating gave a result of 2800±70 BP (3156–2760 cal. BP) (Beta 88701). This later Bronze Age date suggests that there is a 2000-year hiatus between the accretion of the organic muds and the filling of palaeochannels that cut into them. Beneath the organic muds was a further complex of intercutting channels filled with silt/clays and sands, as well as larger spreads of fine-grained fluvial strata. The only artefacts from this part of the stratigraphy were flint flakes and a single core which cannot be attributed to any single period. At the base of the investigated sequence was a series of pale yellow bedded fluvial sands between +0.08m OD and −1.52m OD.

Four monolith samples were taken from three different sections during the evaluation in March 1992. However, two of the samples were from ephemeral features and are not considered here. The remaining samples were examined during the assessment, but it was decided not to carry out detailed analysis of the samples given the fact that only 1m of stratigraphy was represented. The following account is based on the morphological evidence obtained during the assessment, along with similar preliminary data obtained from initial pollen and diatom studies, which provided some useful points regarding the sedimentation history and depositional environments.

Lithostratigraphy

The base of the sampled sequence consisted of a dark greyish-brown (2.5Y4/2) well-sorted medium to coarse sand which was locally iron stained and present below −0.12m OD. Although structureless, this probably accumulated in a medium- or high-energy fluvial environment, and in common with other arenaceous deposits from Westminster is almost certainly a

channel fill. The iron staining noted in the sand indicates that there were occasional episodes when the sand was exposed to subaerial weathering. Unconformably overlying the sand was a very dark grey (10YR3/1) organic mud, rich in plant material, including large wood fragments and charcoal. The charcoal is indicative of human activity within the landscape. Whether this was actually on the sample site or within the wider environment cannot be determined given present data, although the deposit has been ^{14}C dated to 3110–2760 cal. BP, that is, the Late Bronze/Early Iron Age. As the organic mud almost certainly formed in a channel marginal position, or more plausibly in a cut-off channel, and given the erosional episode indicated at the interface, a hiatus between accumulation of the two deposits almost certainly exists. If this is the case the sand could be considerably older than the Late Bronze Age date obtained, and may, therefore, be correlated with similar deposits from St Stephen's East and Palace Chambers South, despite the fact that these lie at lower elevations. Deposits indicative of channel marginal accumulation conformably overlie the organic mud at +0.35m OD and are indicative of increasing river levels, which may have been tidally driven. These deposits consist of very dark greyish-brown (2.5Y3/2) silt/clays and contain small quantities of granular and pebble-sized sub-rounded flint clasts, but appear structureless as a result of diagenetic modification by rootlets. Given these properties these strata are likely to have accumulated as a result of overbank processes, which as suggested above may have been a product of tidal influence. Despite the apparent conformity between the organic muds and the overlying silt/clays it is likely that a period of hiatus exists, as the latter may date to the 11th or 12th century according to ceramic evidence, while the former is later Bronze Age. It is therefore possible that a 'blurring' of the interface between the strata has occurred as a result of bioturbation caused by roots growing in the silt/clays.

Pollen biostratigraphy

Pollen-assessment analysis carried out on the organic muds and overlying silt/clays produced well-preserved and abundant pollen. The pollen spectra consisted of a diverse range of taxa dominated by *Alnus* (to 45% of total pollen), but with substantial quantities of herb pollen and *Pteridium aquilinum* spores. Evidence of woodland is negligible excepting *Alnus* in local wetland habitats. Small percentages of *Tilia* in the organic muds suggest a post-lime decline age (see chapter 3). As the single ^{14}C date from the site suggests the organic muds were still accumulating at *c* 3000 cal. BP, the lime decline in this area must have occurred earlier. *Quercus* and *Corylus avellana* are consistent with this interpretation and indicate that these were the predominant woodland types which remained. This does not, however, preclude the growth of typically less well-represented trees such as *Fraxinus*. The herbs are dominated by Poaceae but with an admixture of taxa which include cereal pollen and weed taxa. Change from the organic mud, to silt/clays of predominantly mineral composition, shows an increased diversity of herbs which include *Armeria* 'A' line and Chenopodiaceae suggesting marine/tidal influences which imported salt marsh taxa from the east. The overall picture obtained here was one of openness: little local (dry-land) woodland with grassland/pasture and possibly cereal cultivation. However, pollen from the latter may also derive from secondary sources such as human and animal waste products which were readily disposed of in the Thames and its tributaries. The depositional environment represented on the site initially was apparently freshwater marsh with possible fringing alder. This was superseded by tidal/brackish-water conditions which transported pollen from further distances.

Diatom biostratigraphy

Five samples were initially assessed for diatoms from the Westminster Underground Station site. Diatoms were absent from the basal sands and from the lower organic muds. The absence of diatoms from the sand is consistent with the lithostratigraphic interpretation of a relatively high-energy fluvial environment, subject to drying; conditions which would be unlikely to favour the survival of diatoms. A poorly preserved assemblage of brackish-marine species (*Paralia sulcata*, *Cyclotella striata*, *Diploneis didyma*, *Nitzschia navicularis*) was present in the upper part of the organic mud and indicates that the diatoms originated in tidal waters. Given that other data (see above) indicate that the depositional environment was essentially terrestrial, the estuarine nature of the diatoms suggests that they represent material deposited by overbank flooding. Although subject to significant breakage and dissolution, a more diverse mixture of brackish, marine and freshwater species from the lower part of the overlying mineral silt/clays represents the prevalence of estuarine conditions and a more favourable preservational environment, perhaps as a result of infrequent drying or continuous submersion as the lithostratigraphic evidence also indicates. The assemblage present at the top of this deposit is very poorly preserved, but diatom fragments were thought likely to be those of brackish-water taxa.

Conclusions

As with the deposits at Parliament Square, the sequence sampled at Westminster Underground Station is almost certainly of a local derivation and caused by local processes. The basal sands and subsequent organic silt encountered probably accumulated within a single feature – possibly a channel – and were not found at the same altitude on St Stephen's East, a site that is only a few tens of metres to the north. Indeed it is quite possible that the sampled section at Westminster Underground Station is later than that at St Stephen's East, and represents a continuation of the same sedimentation pattern. The pollen data may be indicative of a similar pattern as all samples indicated relatively open conditions, typical of the Westminster sites following the lime decline. Diatom data suggest that the open

environment may be at least partially the result of RSL rise, as brackish-water diatoms appear in the organic muds. The subsequent deposits sealing the channel fills indicate that the area became terrestrial following channel abandonment by at least the early medieval period, but was marginal to the confluence of the Thames and the northern branch of the Tyburn and was intermittently flooded by tidal waters. The area appears to have been fully reclaimed by the mid 14th century, probably by the provision of river defences to the north and east.

St Stephen's East

Introduction

Excavations were carried out in October 1994 at the eastern side of Westminster Underground Station prior to its modification to accommodate both the Jubilee Line Extension and a new suite of offices for the Houses of Parliament, as discussed above (Westminster Underground Station). Two trenches measuring around 5m in length by 1.5m in width were dug by mechanical excavator and later by hand to examine a sequence of alluvial sands and associated archaeology. The first deposit encountered below modern deposits consisted of poorly sorted and unbedded sands, containing brick and tile fragments of Tudor (late 15th- to early 17th-century) date which has been interpreted as a deliberate deposition to raise ground surfaces above flood levels. That such a strategy had been required was demonstrated by the underlying deposits located between −0.50m OD and −1.08m OD which consisted of interbedded silt/clays and sands of undoubted fluvial origin, into which a number of stakes had been driven. These strata contained few artefacts, although ceramics of the 15th century and Tudor period were recovered from the uppermost sediments between −0.56m OD to −0.64m OD, while the lowest layer, a thinly bedded fine sand, contained a sherd of Kingston ware dating to between 1230 to 1400. This succession of fluvial deposits was found to sit on top of a series of hollows filled with organic material, which unfortunately contained no dating evidence. The hollows in turn were cut into further well-bedded fluvial silt/clays and sands, which extended from about −1.00m OD to −1.80m OD where coarse sands and gravels outcropped. No artefacts were found from either of these deposits and therefore a chronology for development of the basal metre of the succession is unknown.

Three monolith samples were taken from this sequence in Trench 1 spanning all the stratigraphy outlined above. Fig 20 displays the results of particle-size analysis and derived graphic statistics (Folk & Ward 1957), while the results of magnetic susceptibility and loss-on-ignition studies are presented in Fig 23. Figs 25, 26 and 27 show the results of molluscan, palynological and diatom study respectively.

Lithostratigraphy and sedimentology

(Figs 23 and 24)

Based on both lithostratigraphic description and sedimentary characteristics, the sampled part of the stratigraphy can be divided into three Facies Associations (Reading 1997), which almost exactly correspond with the archaeological layers described in the introduction.

Facies Association 1 – fining up sequence of sands into silt/clays

Strata comprising Facies Association 1 consist of a fining upwards sequence of initially dark greyish-brown (2.5Y4/2) fine sands which dominate until −1.49m OD, and then clays and to a lesser extent silts which are more important above (see Fig 20). At the very base of the sequence the sands include pebble to granular rounded and sub-rounded flint clasts. Despite the fact that these are supported by a matrix of medium sand, the gravels almost certainly accumulated during bed-flow, and therefore indicate that a relatively fast-flowing stream passed over the site during initial accretion. The sand particles within the deposit formed as a result of near-bed-flow processes (eg saltation), and although the matrix between the basal clasts may be broadly contemporary with gravel deposition and therefore occurred during a high-energy phase, the remaining part of the sequence indicates somewhat lower-energy accumulation. The particle-size distributions generated from samples taken in Facies Association 1 further confirm that deposition was as a result of a multiplicity of fluvial processes. The single distribution where graphic data could be generated shows that the lower sands are extremely poorly sorted and very finely skewed. Both properties are the result of fluctuations in energy levels, possibly on a seasonal basis, with the net result that clays and silts become incorporated within the sand matrix.

Organic carbon content is low throughout the sequence, averaging c 10%, although values do increase as particle size decreases and presumably as a result of localised plant growth (see Fig 23). Likewise χ^{lf} appears, in the absence of microartefacts (Wilkinson in prep), to be grain-size dependent and progressively increases upwards through the deposits as particle size decreases, from around 8^{-8} m^3kg^{-1} at the base to 15^{-8} m^3kg^{-1} at the top. A further change in property as silt/clay sizes begin to dominate above −1.49m OD is the first sign of bedding structures in the sediments. These consist of wavy, parallel laminations and are indicative of both extremely low energy levels and periodicity in deposition. The uppermost part of the silt/clays contain iron stains which, although a product of diagenesis, may indicate that these strata were exposed to subaerial erosion. Given that strata of Facies Association 2 are suggested (see below) to have accreted in a floodplain marginal or cut-off channel environment, this supposition would seem highly plausible.

The fining upwards properties seen through Facies Association 1 are a classic indication of progressive fall in energy levels (Boggs 1987, 115–17), a supposition further supported by the laminae structure and iron staining which is only found in the uppermost part of the sequence. The fall in energy levels is, in this case, likely to be a result of the migration of a channel away from the sample site. Gravels and sands at the base of the sequence are likely to have accumulated within the channel, while the silts and clays found further up will have been channel marginal, and deposited as fallout from suspension during individual flood events.

Facies Association 2 – laminated organic muds

The second Facies Association, between −1.23m OD and −1.09m OD, consists of a series of organic-dominated very dark grey to black (2.5Y3.5/1–2.5Y2.5/1) clay/silts and is separated from Facies Association 1 by an unconformity. The muds contain wavy, parallel lamination of the same sort as found at the top of Facies Association 1, although this is locally disrupted by rootlets. The particle-size properties of Facies Association 2 are not dissimilar from those in Facies Association 1 in terms of graphic indices (see Fig 20), but proportions of particle-size classes are quite different. The particle-size distribution of Facies Association 2 is extensively mixed with gravel (predominantly granular), sand and clay present in equal proportions, and with slightly less silt. The deposits also contain large quantities of organics (35–40%) when compared to other deposits in the sequence, and these data, when combined with the presence of roots, would seem to be indicative of in situ plant growth. The deposits also contain mollusc shell fragments, but these appear to be of the genus Lymnaea (most probably Lymnaea peregra), and therefore do not provide significant palaeoecological information beyond the fact that water was present (but see Molluscan biostratigraphy below). Charcoal fragments of around 2–4mm size are found in low concentrations towards the surface of the organic strata, but it would seem that these are redeposited as the magnetic susceptibility values in Facies Association 2 are even lower than in Facies Association 1, whereas extremely high readings would be expected if burning had taken place in situ.

Despite the fact that an unconformity occurs between Facies Associations 1 and 2, it nevertheless seems likely that Facies Association 2 represents a continuation of the same processes that were taking place during the accumulation of Facies Association 1 sediments, that is, channel migration away from the site. Therefore if any hiatus in deposition did occur, it is unlikely to have been long-lived. Sediments in Facies Association 2 almost certainly accumulated in an extreme channel marginal situation, for example in an abandoned channel or at the very periphery of the floodplain. All indications (ie laminations, grain size, high organic content) point to extremely low energy deposition, which would be typical of such locations. Indeed there is substantial evidence for the action of terrestrial processes in the form of rooting and a high organic content, while the extreme variation in particle size is also indicative of the beginnings of pedogenesis. The charcoal found suggests that humans were active in the environment during accumulation, although it would appear that this may not have been on the site itself.

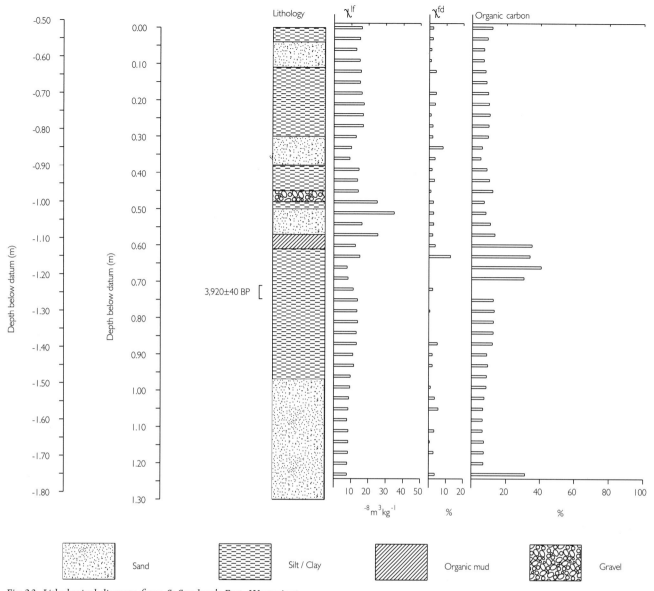

Fig 23 Lithological diagram from St Stephen's East, Westminster

Facies Association 3 – alternating thin-layered silt/clays and sand

Unconformably overlying Facies Association 2 at −1.09m OD is a sequence of sands and silt/clays that extend to at least −0.52m OD. The individual deposits comprising this part of the sequence are highly varied and bounding surfaces are always sharp, indicating many truncation episodes. The deposits consist of alternating bands of dark yellowish-brown (10YR4/4) coarse sands, mixed with granular, sub-rounded flint gravels and dark greyish-brown (2.5Y4/2) silt/clays (see Fig 22). Iron staining is frequent in the coarser deposits, while there is no recognisable bedding structure in any part of the facies. Particle-size analysis indicates widespread differences in proportions of sand, silt and clay between individual layers, while the graphic indices indicate that the distributions are even more poorly sorted than the sediments found below. As with Facies Association 1, this is almost certainly the result of 'overprinting' of different layers as a result of diagenesis and is indicative of a rapidly shifting fluvial environment. Organic carbon

values are relatively low throughout at between 10–15%, but χ^{lf} varies between 10–20^{-8} m³kg⁻¹. While it is likely that some of the χ^{lf} variation is grain-size driven – it being noticeable that silt/clays have higher χ^{lf} values than sands – there is one point in the sequence where χ^{lf} peaks at 40^{-8} m³kg⁻¹. That this high occurs in a sand deposit is significant, and is almost certainly the product of the incorporation of microartefacts in the sediments (Wilkinson in prep). Indeed Kingston ware ceramics were found at this altitude during the excavation. In the City of London the influx of microartefacts has been related to the initial development of Londinium in the Roman period (Wilkinson in prep) and it is quite conceivable that Facies Association 3 can be dated to the medieval period on the basis of magnetic data. Facies Association 3 is highly fossiliferous (in contrast to the facies below) and large quantities of mollusc shells occur throughout (see below), while charcoal is also present in profusion. As with Facies Association 2, χ^{lf} values are too low to suggest that any of the burning was *in situ*, and it would therefore seem that all charcoal was redeposited.

Facies Association 3 represents an entirely different mode of accretion to that of the preceding associations and therefore a significant change to the depositional environment. It is possible that there was some hiatus between the accumulation of the Facies Association 2 sediments and those comprising Facies Association 3. Indeed, a fine gravel lag found at the base of Facies Association 3 would seem to suggest that erosion of the top of Facies Association 2 took place. Given these assertions it is notable that Facies Association 3 exactly corresponds with the medieval and Tudor period fluvial layers described above, while the ^{14}C date from −1.23 to −1.27 gave a result of 3920±40 BP (4502−4239 cal. BP) (Beta 121716), suggesting the hiatus here is of the order of 3000 years. The sediments comprising Facies Association 3 are indicative of the remigration of a river channel across the site, and thereafter continuous changes in energy levels over a period of 200−500 years. This was perhaps associated with channel movement around the floodplain and/or the impact of the movement of the tidal head, or possibly even alterations to the flow of the Tyburn tributary. Whichever of these explains the change in sedimentation it would appear that in the newly created fluvial environment accretion was highly variable both temporally and spatially. Indeed, the deposits preserved at St Stephen's East can be assumed to be brief and highly localised 'snapshots' of wider fluvial developments. The coarser sediments found in Facies Association 3 formed within channels where flow energies were high, while the silt/clays formed on the margins of these channels or on inter-channel surfaces. Iron staining in the sands indicates that the sand bars on occasion dried out, allowing subaerial processes to operate, while gravel lag deposits in all the sediments are indicative of constant fluvial recutting. Charcoal throughout the sequence demonstrates the presence of people within the local environment, although there are no indications of *in situ* human activity. Nevertheless, it would seem that during Facies Association 3, pottery was deposited in the river channels, and can be observed in the effect of microartefacts on the magnetic record and as actual fragments from −0.65m OD upwards.

Molluscan biostratigraphy

Mollusc samples were taken from the organic muds (Facies Association 2) and the overlying alternating sands and silt/clays (Facies Association 3) (see Fig 23), which had been noted to be particularly shell-rich during excavation. Samples were 5cm in thickness and each consisted of around five litres of sediment. This was processed and sorted following the method of Evans (1972), although given the huge quantities of shell and the low variability only shells >1mm were recovered and identified (investigative methodology is covered in greater detail in the Appendix). During the sorting of the sample residues it was noted that considerable quantities of fish bone also existed. Although this seemed to be predominantly vertebral, several pharyngeal and stickleback teeth were also spotted. Similarly, ostracod valves were present in small numbers from samples 1−9. These groups of remains were not identified further, although both are indicative of aquatic environments.

Shell preservation throughout the sampled profile was good, with between 300−1000 quantifiable shell parts per sample being identified. This equates with between 250−800 shells per litre. In the three basal samples shell preservation was less good (ie 60−180 quantifiable shell parts per sample), but nevertheless enough shells were preserved to enable an interpretation to be made of local palaeoecology. A histogram (Fig 25) has been generated to show changes in molluscan frequency with time.

Aquatic palaeoenvironment

As has been demonstrated from the lithostratigraphic and sedimentological analysis above, accretion during the accumulation of both Facies Associations 2 and 3 was within a stream channel, albeit in a marginal location in the case of Facies Association 2 (mollusc sample 15). Thus the majority of the mollusc shells are likely to be allochthonous, having been transported to the sample site from different locations within

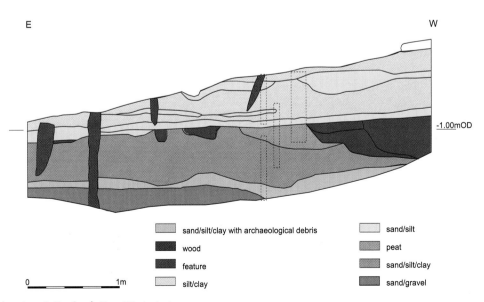

sand/silt/clay with archaeological debris	sand/silt
wood	peat
feature	sand/silt/clay
silt/clay	sand/gravel

Fig 24 Section drawing, St Stephen's East, Westminster

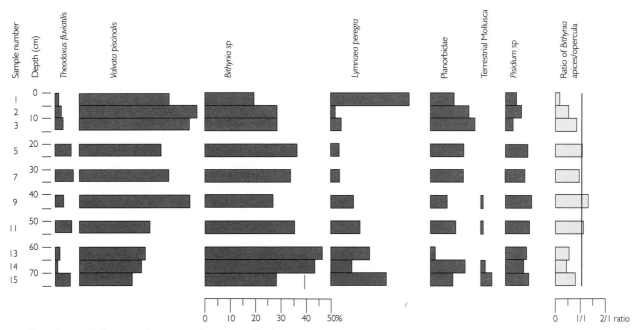

Fig 25 Mollusc (>1mm) frequency histogram from St Stephen's East, Westminster

the channel system. Therefore, the environment that can be reconstructed from the shell data is a composite one, reflecting riverine conditions within central and western London as a whole, rather than specific local environments directly relating to the site. Sample 15 is a possible exception, where a higher proportion of autochthonous shells should be expected. Nevertheless, all samples examined contained similar molluscan assemblages, dominated by *Valvata piscinalis* and *Bithynia* sp, with fewer numbers of *Lymnaea peregra*, *Planorbis planorbis* and *Theodoxus fluviatilis* (see Fig 25). It is notable that not one of the mollusc taxa recorded from the samples has tolerance of saline conditions and that the assemblages recovered are of completely different character to those found in the Thames at the present day, where the intertidal genus *Hydrobia* dominates (Wilkinson in prep).

At the broadest level it would appear that similar aquatic environments existed throughout the accretion of Facies Associations 2 and 3. The presence of *V. piscinalis* and *Bithynia* sp in the same samples and in such high proportions is indicative of a large waterbody. When these taxa are found alongside *T. fluviatilis*, which only lives in rapidly moving water within a river system (Boycott 1936, 141), a fully riverine environment is suggested. Indeed *T. fluviatilis* appears to be characteristic of larger rivers, rarely being found in small tributaries, and is common in the west London Thames at the present day. This may indicate that accretion was within the Thames rather than the Tyburn tributary, which during early medieval times emerged into the Thames close to the sample site. However, whether development of Facies Associations 2 and 3 was within the Thames channel or as a result of overbank flooding from that river is not immediately apparent from the molluscan data alone. The latter process appears to be more likely for Facies Association 2 (sample 15), as here proportions of *L. peregra* (a species of catholic preferences, but usually found in quieter waters than *T. fluviatilis*) are relatively high,

while terrestrial taxa are found in greater numbers than in later samples. The latter include *Discus rotundatus* (a shade-loving species) and *Trichia hispida*, which may have been living in drier areas on the extreme channel margin, although shells could also have been eroded from a nearby bank. The ratio of *Bithynia* apices to opercula is close to one for this sample suggesting that variable transport of different shell sizes and densities was minimal.

Above sample 15 there is a reduction in the proportion of *L. peregra* and terrestrial taxa and a corresponding increase in *V. piscinalis* and *Bithynia* sp, species of moving-water affinity, although it is interesting to note that the most significant indicator of moving water, *T. fluviatilis*, initially declines prior to increasing in frequency in sample 11. This decline is matched by a fall in the ratio of *Bithynia* apices to opercula of around 0.5, indicating a greater degree of shell sorting in samples 14–13, although by sample 11 ratios are close to 1 once more. These data suggest that shell derivation had changed in samples 13 and 14 from that in 15, and that allochthonous shells dominate the assemblages. Nevertheless all indications from samples 14–5 are that accretion was in a large, rapidly moving water body, and probably occurred within the river channel. There are some indications for the presence of aquatic vegetation at the margin of the channel from the presence of Planorbidae at frequencies of around 10%.

The assemblages in the uppermost three samples, which, significantly, were taken from levels above the monolith samples (see Fig 24), indicate a rapid decrease in influence of in-channel processes and suggest a return to an overbank flooding as a means of deposition. In these samples the proportion of *T. fluviatilis* falls indicating a reduction in the influence of high-energy fluvial conditions. The *Bithynia* apex to opercula ratio also falls, ultimately to the lowest ratio in the sequence, suggesting an increasing importance in shell sorting. Therefore, in this part of the sequence, it is likely that the assemblages

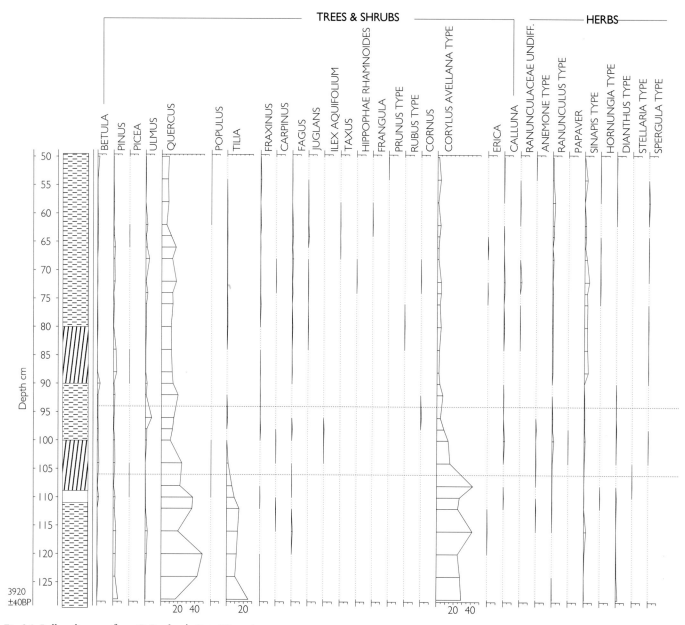

TREES & SHRUBS ——————————— ——— HERBS ———

Fig 26 Pollen diagram from St Stephen's East, Westminster

are derived from two sources: one from relatively still or slow-moving water (autochthonous), accumulating at the sample point or close by, and the other in sediment washed in as a result of flooding (allochthonous).

The molluscan data thus indicate a number of subtle changes in the aquatic environment during accretion, developments which largely match the sedimentary sequence. However, it is notable that processes operating either side of the suggested 3000-year hiatus between sample 15 and the remaining samples appear to have been very similar. Perhaps most significantly the molluscan data suggest that there is no indication from these assemblages for the presence of saline waters either in the late prehistoric period, or even, more surprisingly, in the medieval and Tudor period. This is a situation that is in marked contrast to the present day where movements of the river are controlled by the system of locks in west London.

Pollen biostratigraphy

Pollen was obtained from Facies Associations 2 and 3. Three local pollen assemblage zones (Fig 26) have been recognised and are delimited as follows:

SSE:1 –1.34 – –1.12m OD *Quercus-Tilia-Corylus avellana type-Alnus*

Trees and shrubs are dominant to 65% and 40% respectively while herb percentages are correspondingly low (25%). This basal zone is delimited by high percentages of *Quercus* (50%), *Tilia* (25%) and *Corylus avellana* type (to 40%). Herbs are at their lowest levels in this profile with only Poaceae having values greater than 10%. There are sporadic occurrences of *Plantago lanceolata*, Brassicaceae (*Sinapis* type), Caryophyllaceae, *Chenopodium* type and Asteraceae types. Cereal pollen/large

HERBS cont

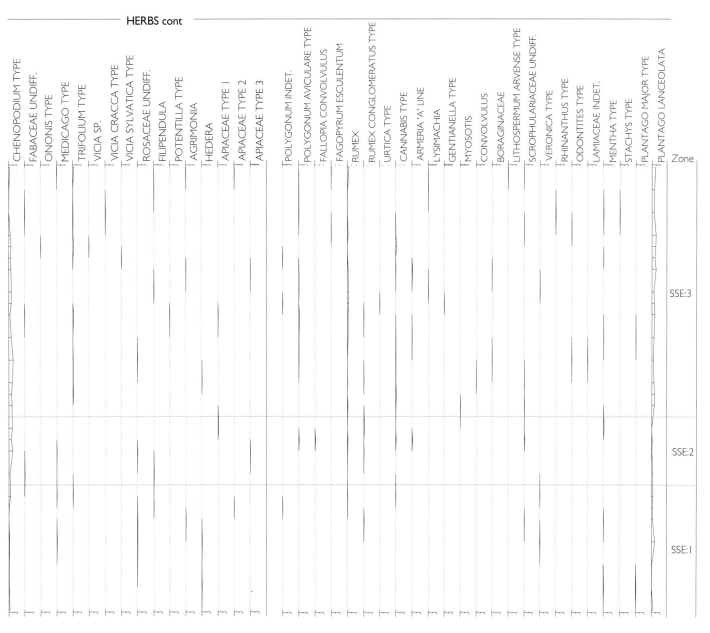

(Fig 26 cont)

Poaceae become increasingly important towards the top of the zone (from *c* −1.21m OD). Marsh types are dominated by *Alnus* (to 50%) with Cyperaceae (to 50%). The latter are initially more important (pasz 1) to −1.24m OD after which *Alnus* becomes dominant (pasz 2). Small percentages of *Salix* are present. Spores comprise *Pteridium aquilinum*, *Dryopteris* type and *Polypodium vulgare*; the latter is especially important (to 18%) in this zone.

SSE:2 −1.12 − −1.00m OD *Quercus-Corylus avellana* type-Poaceae-Cereal type

Stratigraphically, this zone marks the change from the organic muds of Facies Association 2 to minerogenic sediment of Facies Association 3. Palynologically the zone appears transitional. *Tilia*, previously present (SSE:1), becomes absent. *Quercus* and *Corylus avellana* type show progressive reduction (to 20% and 5% respectively). Conversely, there is a marked expansion of herb

taxa to dominance (80%). Poaceae and Cereal type/large Poaceae are dominant (50% and 20% respectively) while herbaceous diversity also increases, especially with Chenopodiaceae (6%) and Asteraceae types. There are sporadic occurrences of other weeds/ruderal types, and *Secale cereale* (rye) and *Centaurea cyanus* (cornflower) are also present. There are smaller percentages of marsh taxa, but *Alnus* and Cyperaceae remain relatively important. There is an expansion of *Typha angustifolia/Sparganium*, while *Polypodium vulgare*, which was significant in zone 1, now becomes absent. Pediastrum, derived pre-Quaternary palynomorphs and Hystrichospheres are incoming.

SSE:3 −1.00 − −0.56m OD Poaceae-Cereal type-*Plantago lanceolata*

Trees are consistent at 20–25% with *Quercus* dominating. Of note, however, are consistent but small values of *Picea*,

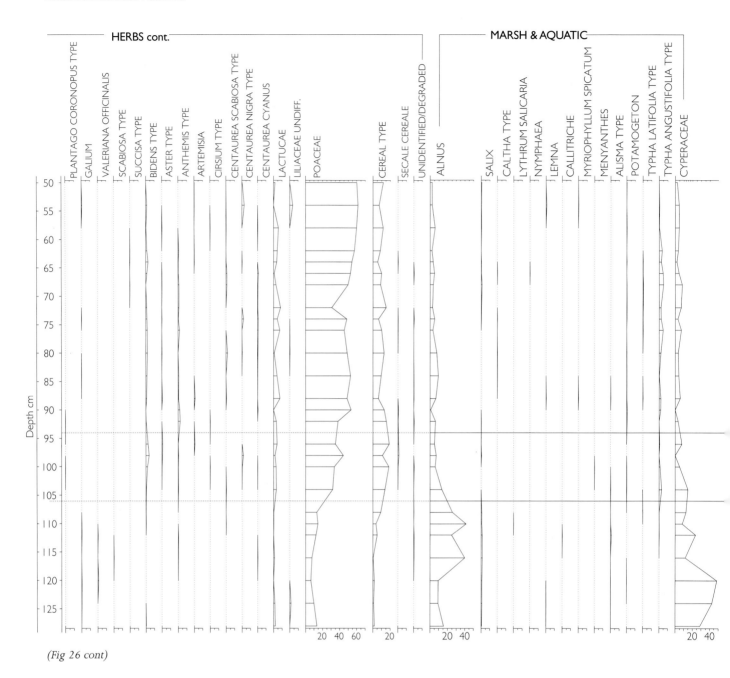

(Fig 26 cont)

Fraxinus, *Fagus*, *Juglans* and *Hippophae rhamnoides* (sea buckthorn). Herbs remain dominated by Poaceae (to 63%) with Cereal/large Poaceae (10–15%). There are further increases in *Sinapis* type (charlock), Chenopodiaceae, Polygonaceae spp, *Rumex* (dock), *Plantago lanceolata* and Asteraceae types. Of specific note are *Fagopyrum esculentum* (sweet chestnut), *Cannabis* type (hemp), *Secale cereale* and *Armeria* 'A' line. Spores of ferns, pre-Quaternary palynomorphs, Hystrichospheres and *Pediastrum* remain. A single intestinal parasite ovum of *Trichuris* cyst was noted.

Diatom biostratigraphy

Initially, 11 samples were assessed for diatoms from the St Stephen's East site. Diatoms were absent from most sediments of Facies Association 1 but were present in the overlying material and well preserved in both Facies Associations 2 and 3 (Fig 27).

In the units from which diatoms were absent, the lithostratigraphic evidence (see above) indicates that the environments in which these sand-rich deposits formed would have been unlikely to preserve diatoms. Two samples examined from the top of Facies Association 1 contained a low concentration of diatom valves which were dominated by freshwater species, but also included a small number of valves of the estuarine, planktonic species *Cyclotella striata*. These assemblages are consistent with lithostratigraphic interpretations discussed above for predominantly freshwater conditions, although the data make it clear that there were minor inputs of saline water. The sample at −1.16m OD contained mostly valve fragments of undifferentiated *Pinnularia* spp. The robust *Pinnularia* taxon or taxa present are likely to be terrestrial species. The diatom evidence for these strata is therefore also congruent with lithostratigraphical evidence for periodic exposure to air.

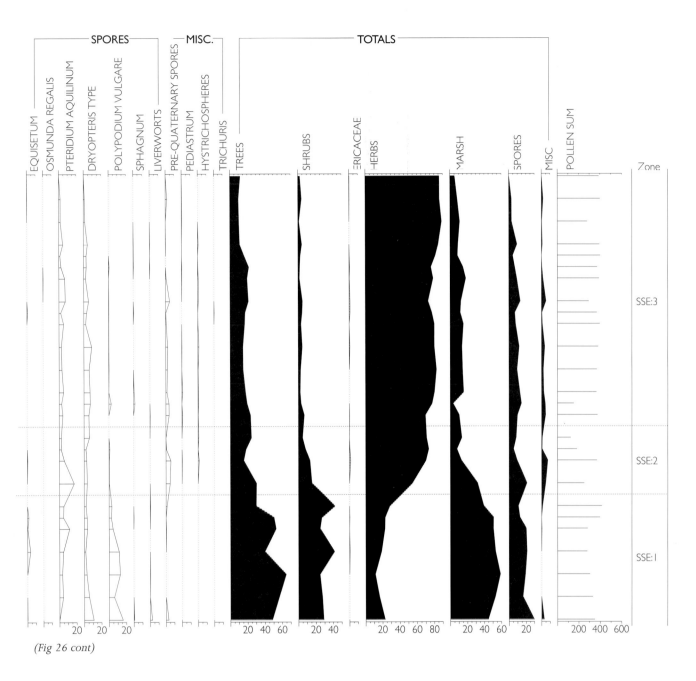

(Fig 26 cont)

Following the indications of semi-terrestrial/freshwater conditions at the very top of Facies Association 1, and after an initial maximum in salinity, diatom assemblages between −1.12m OD and the top of the sequence show a pattern of decreasing salinity and a maximum in the freshwater component at the surface. Polyhalobous taxa reach a maximum of almost 50% of the total diatoms in Facies Association 2 (at −1.12m OD) and decline to less than 2% in Facies Association 3 (at −0.82m OD). These outer estuary, planktonic diatoms are represented by taxa such as *Cymatosira belgica* and *Rhaphoneis* spp and indicate a strong tidal influence at this point. In parallel with the marine diatoms, mesohalobous species increase to a maximum of almost 35% at −0.70m OD from a minimum of less than 5% at −1.01m OD. The dominant brackish-water species is *Cyclotella striata* and it is also likely that the undifferentiated *Cyclotella* spp at −1.16m OD represent the dissolved and eroded central areas of this estuarine species.

The apparent total of mesohalobous taxa is therefore under-represented at this depth. Between −0.70m OD and the top of the sequence polyhalobous taxa are present only at low abundances (<5%) while mesohalobous diatoms decrease from 35% to less than 5% of the diatom assemblage. At the same time oligohalobous indifferent taxa increase from about 35% to almost 70% of the total diatoms.

More subtle changes in the diatom stratigraphy are also apparent within the major shift from partly marine to almost entirely freshwater-dominated assemblages. Immediately after the maximum in polyhalobous species and before the maximum in mesohalobous diatoms there is a peak in the abundance of halophilous to indifferent diatoms. This is almost entirely the result of a maximum percentage of the non-planktonic diatom *Rhoicosphaenia curvata* and follows the succession of maxima in polyhalobous and mesohalobous diatoms (assuming here that undifferentiated *Cyclotella* sp

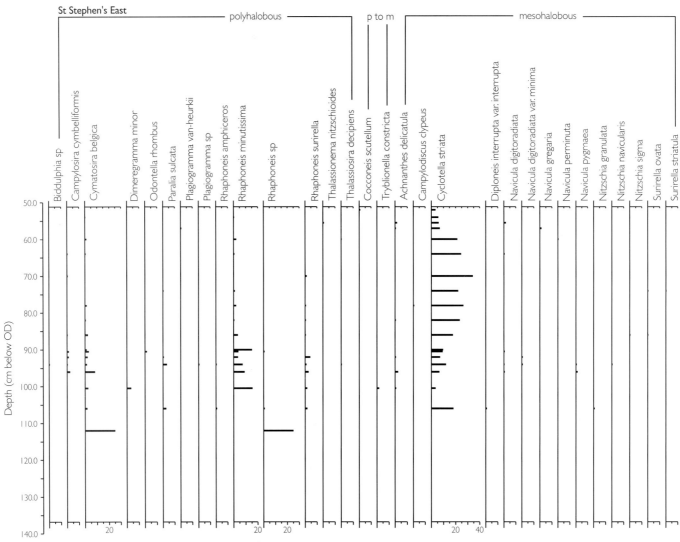

Fig 27 Diatom diagram from St Stephen's East, Westminster

= *Cyclotella striata*). The idea of a decreasing estuarine influence here is also supported by an initial peak in the percentage of oligohalobous indifferent diatoms at *c* −0.90m OD, before the percentages of mesohalobous taxa begin to increase. The curve of halophilous to indifferent taxa, represented by *Rhoicosphaenia curvata*, also precedes and follows the maximum in mesohalobous diatoms with minor maxima of *c* 12–15% at *c* −0.74 and −0.54m OD. Along with the cumulative abundance of *Cocconeis placentula* and its varieties, which although classified here as oligohalobous indifferent are sometimes considered to be halophilous/freshwater diatoms, *Rhoicosphaenia curvata* is likely to represent an epiphytic habitat in slightly brackish water. It is probable that these non-planktonic epiphytes were growing close to the site of deposition and may be considered autochthonous. Further, the growth of aquatic macrophytes and their epiphytic diatoms would have required relatively shallow water.

Discussion

The diatom sequence seen at St Stephen's East represents a complex pattern of change in the tidal and flooding regime at the site which corresponds closely with the lithostratigraphy. Initially, characterised by poor preservation and indications of

semi-terrestrial conditions (Facies Association 1), there is a phase of maximum marine influence where outer estuary diatoms are abundant (Facies Association 2). There follows in Facies Association 3 a period of increasing freshwater influence, although conditions remain tidal, where halophilous and oligohalobous indifferent taxa reach maxima. After their initial maximum, the percentages of polyhalobous taxa decline and remain low, but traces of marine diatoms reflect the tidal nature of the river and probably a degree of redeposition or reworking of sediment from elsewhere in the river and other levels in the sequence. The continuation of tidal conditions is confirmed by significant percentages of mesohalobous diatoms culminating in a maximum abundance at −0.70m OD. A second freshwater phase follows at −0.52m OD and at this level the absence of marine diatoms and very low percentage of (possibly reworked or redeposited fossil) brackish species suggest that the site was not tidal at this point at this time.

The complexity of the stratigraphy has undoubtedly influenced the pollen taphonomy; furthermore, the hiatus complicates interpretation of the profile. However, there are a number of significant vegetation changes evident. Zone SSE:1 illustrates the dominance of *Tilia*, *Quercus* and *Corylus avellana* woodland on the drier interfluves while the wetter floodplain

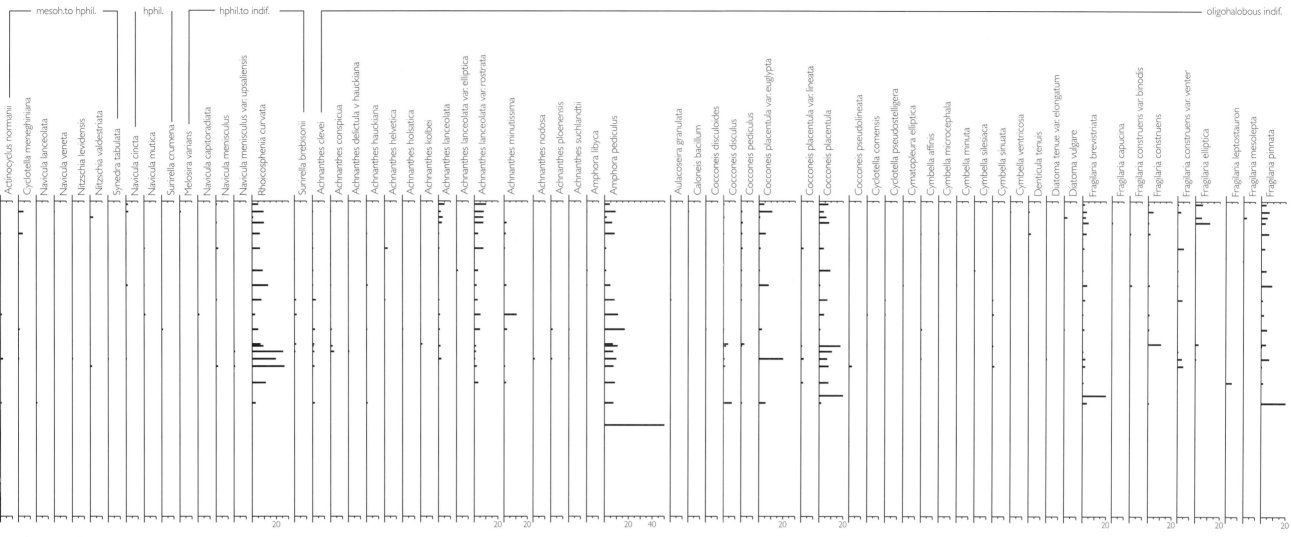

(Fig 27 cont)

supported *Alnus* and Cyperaceae fen. Expansion of *Alnus* in the top of the zone SSE:2 represents successional change to carr woodland and a peat/organic accumulation rather than riverine sediments, as the environment became drier. Higher values of *Polypodium vulgare* are associated with this woodland dominance (being an epiphyte). Furthermore, the consistent but small values of *Plantago lanceolata*, Cereal type and sporadic herbs imply localised, late prehistoric agriculture.

Zone SSE:2 appears to be a transitional phase where there is a clear reduction in woodland and a marked expansion of herbs. This is a progressive change which is also associated with a change in sedimentation. Thus, it is not clear whether this change from zone SSE:1 to SSE:2 marks a hiatus or whether there is evidence of forest reduction through human factors or base-level change factors. Given the progressive change noted, it seems plausible that the latter may be the case with the reduction of *Tilia* being the lime decline noted at other sites. After reduction of lime (during the Late Bronze Age), *Quercus* and *Corylus avellana* become the principle woodland elements with some secondary woodland of *Fraxinus*, *Fagus* and possibly *Ilex* and understorey shrubs.

In zone SSE:3 *Quercus* remains the most important tree but, given its relatively high pollen production, possibly represents

the background regional vegetation. There is also, however, a relatively diverse range of tree and shrub taxa which occur as small percentages or as sporadic, individual occurrences. These are significant, including exotic and markedly under-represented taxa. Of the former, *Juglans* and *Picea* are of particular note being Roman and post-Roman introductions respectively. *Tilia*, *Fraxinus* and *Fagus* are under-represented and grew within the pollen catchment (but see below). Contrasting with the domination of trees in the uppermost zone is the marked frequency and diversity of herbs dominated by Poaceae (both small/wild and large grains >45μm of Cereal type). There is a predominance of herbs/ruderals which are associated with waste ground and agriculture. The taphonomy of the pollen in these upper stratigraphic units is, however, complex, making interpretation of the pollen assemblages difficult. The data suggest that there were not only freshwater inputs of sediment (with aquatic macrophytes present and algal *Pediastrum*), but also indications of halophytes/salt marsh with *Chenopodium* type, *Armeria* 'A' line, large grasses, *Aster* type and Hystrichospheres/dinoflagellates – which all correspond with the diatom evidence for initial freshwater conditions succeeded by tidal waters influencing the area. These taxa and the reworked/derived pre-Quaternary palynomorphs are

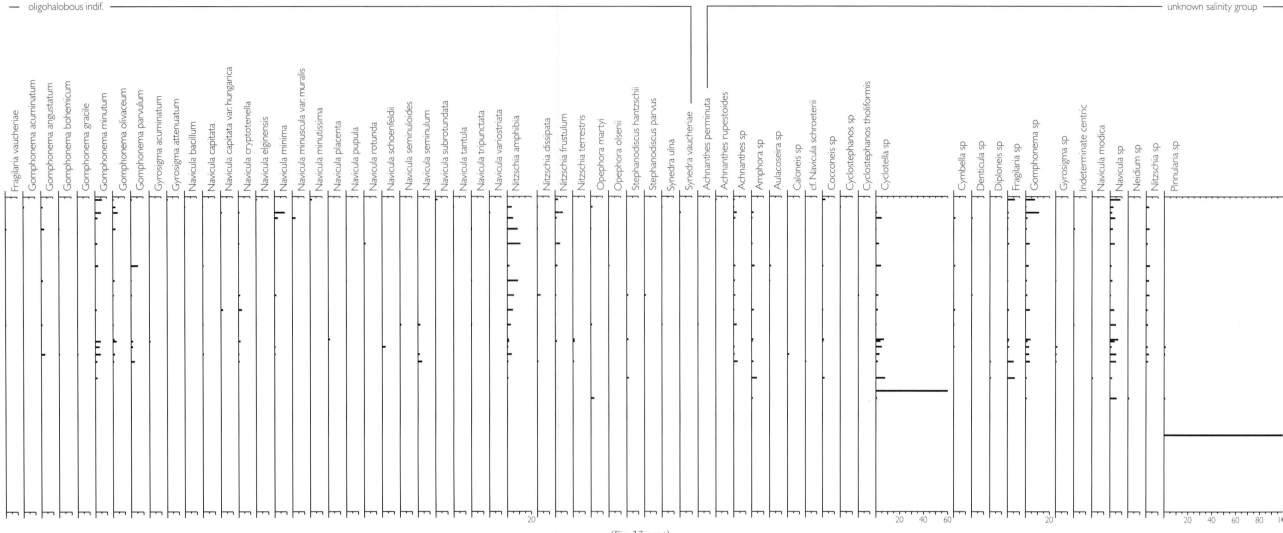

(Fig 27 cont)

further indications of the complexity of the pollen taphonomy with both airborne and fluvially transported microfossils. Thus tree and herb taxa may have been derived from further afield.

Conclusions

The Facies Associations ascribed to the sedimentary sequence from this site support a three-phase model of accretion. In conjunction with this, a major erosive event has been identified dating from the Bronze Age (or later) to the early medieval period. Initially, St Stephen's East appears to have been situated within a medium to high energy channel (probably the main channel of the Thames) which subsequently migrated away from this location, resulting in occasional exposure of the sediments accreting here. Unfortunately, no pollen evidence was recovered from the basal sediments, but diatoms were preserved from the end of this phase and confirm the picture of occasional exposure. The ^{14}C date obtained from this site is from the boundary of Facies Associations 1 and 2 and demonstrates that the first major change in sedimentation took place at *c* 4350 cal. BP, or in the Late Neolithic period. The second phase reflects

further channel migration away from the site; limited and probably slow accretion with the onset of vegetation colonising the site. It seems likely that at this point the site was in the environs of an abandoned channel or at the margins of the floodplain, leading to terrestrial phases and initial pedogenesis. There is limited evidence for contemporary human activity in the area, if not directly at the sampling location. The diatom evidence for the latter part of this phase indicates that marine influence has reached the site with the presence of outer estuary species such as *Cymatosira belgica* and provides extremely significant evidence for Early Bronze Age tidal movements. The local pollen information supports the picture of dry land locally and nearby, and the removal of forest cover in this period is evidence of the wider-scale transition to locally cleared areas, presumably for cultivation and livestock. The erosive event identified at this point is extremely frustrating and it is unfortunately not possible to date the onset of erosional processes. However, the suggestion that the site was now peripheral to a tidal river may indicate that the site was subject to tidal scouring. Sedimentation only recommences in the medieval period, leaving over three millennia unaccounted for. The picture is one of a rapidly shifting

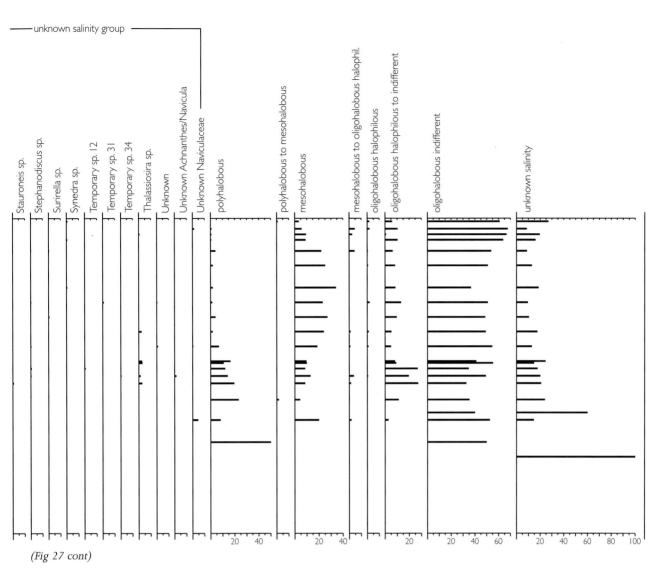

(Fig 27 cont)

environment located adjacent to, and sometimes in, the main body of the tidal river. Additionally, the site may have been occasionally influenced by the changing configuration of the Thames/Tyburn confluence. The diatom data indicate that although the sediment being deposited was derived from a tidal river, the marine influence at this point was not as strong as prior to the hiatus. Furthermore, in the late medieval/Tudor period (reflected at −0.52m in the sequence) the diatom evidence suggests conditions which are dominantly freshwater. This corresponds with the insertion of wooden stakes which may have been part of a revetment associated with water management. If so, it is possible that the change in diatom assemblages may reflect movement of fresh water from Thorney Island into the Thames, thus changing the balance in estuarine and freshwater species being incorporated into the sediments deposited at St Stephen's East. The pollen indicates that at this period cultivation of cereals was still taking place locally (although probably not on the Thorney Island itself now) and, in addition, species only introduced in the historic period could be found nearby. Finally, the site was reclaimed in the Tudor period by deliberate dumping to raise the ground above flood levels.

Conclusions: the sedimentation and environment of Westminster

(Fig 28)

At first sight the stratigraphy of Westminster would appear to be extremely complex, especially when combined with diatom data which appear to suggest a variety of relative river-level changes over a relatively short time span. However, the lower part of the lithostratigraphy, prior to human impact, can in the case of every site be readily correlated into a tripartite division of beds, each indicative of different depositional sub-environments (Table 5). This lithostratigraphy forms a new geological division: the Westminster member of the Maidenhead formation (Gibbard 1999), with type sites at Storey's Gate, Palace Chambers South and St Stephen's East.

The Westminster member represents deposition initially in a sand-dominated, meandering, freshwater river prior to 4350 cal. BP, which led to the formation of dune systems (Thorney sand bed) at the river margin. By 3800 cal. BP this depositional regime had changed and laminated silts and clays were being deposited as channel marginal, or even overbank

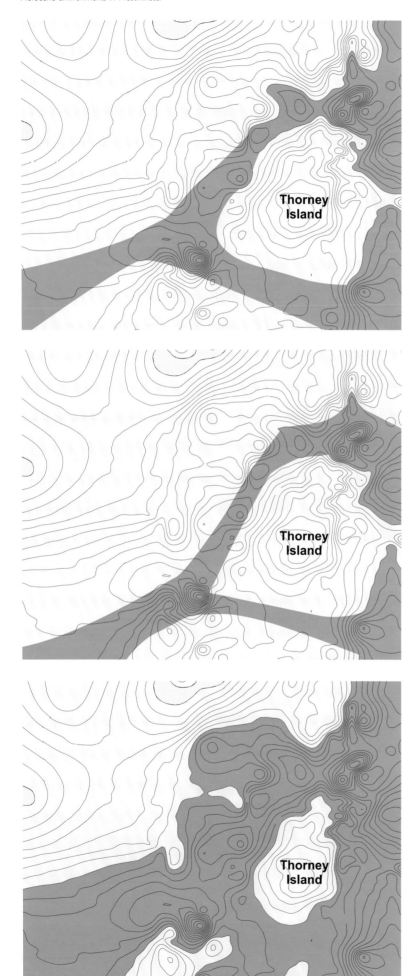

Fig 28 Reconstruction of dry-land topography and the Thames and the Tyburn at Westminster in the Mesolithic, Neolithic and Late Iron Age

Table 5 Beds of the Westminster member

Bed	Description	Type sites	Depositional sub-environment
Storey organic mud bed	Homogeneous and horizontally laminated organic muds	Storey's Gate, WSS	Channel margin marsh
Palace Chambers silt bed	Horizontally laminated, yellow-brown moderately to poorly sorted clays and silts	WSS, SSE	Channel margin flood deposits
Thorney sand bed	Planar cross-bedded medium and fine, moderately to well-sorted yellow sands	WSS, SSE	Meandering river, in-channel dunes

deposits (Palace Chambers silt bed), but still in a freshwater environment. A further development of this process occurred around 3500 cal. BP when a marsh became established across all the sites, leading to the formation of organic mud (Storey organic mud bed). The development of marsh in the Westminster area invariably coincides with a period of vegetation change, when the lime, oak and hazel woodland of the surrounding areas was being opened up by the Bronze Age populations. Lime can be noted in particular and declines in lime pollen occur in all diagrams from the Storey organic mud bed. The reduction in allochthonous arboreal pollen coincides with an increase in autochthonous marsh pollen, and in particular alder, which appears to have spread rapidly as the marsh developed. Cereal pollen also occurs in greater frequency following the lime decline providing further evidence of human impact on the landscape. A tentative identification of Bronze Age ard marks (tracks left by primitive ploughs) on the east side of Thorney Island (C Thomas, pers comm) may in fact represent the arable fields suggested by the pollen evidence. The marsh seems to have ceased forming around 2700 cal. BP, just as it was being subjected to contact with brackish, estuarine waters. The bed changes described appear to be broadly synchronous across the whole of the Westminster area investigated, and would appear to represent gradual falls in energy levels. Such reductions in energy could be associated with channel migration away from Westminster, although why this occurred is not immediately obvious.

Following accretion of the Storey organic mud bed, there is an unconformity at all the sites examined and a hiatus for 2000 years prior to renewed deposition. The hiatus is synchronous for all Westminster sites – that is, all accretion ceases at c 2700 cal. BP and begins again at c 1200 (800 cal. BP) – and it is this that suggests the operation of large-scale processes. It is almost certainly significant that the unconformity coincides with a period of increasing estuarine influence; perhaps the Westminster area was rapidly inundated by estuarine waters and became incorporated in a channel bed where little deposition took place. However, in all probability it is erosion that is the explanation, as in a tidal environment there are few areas where accretion does not occur. It is, therefore, likely that sedimentation at

Westminster continued after 2700 cal. BP albeit in a tidal environment, but subsequent events – for example movement of the Tyburn tributary across its lower floodplain – eroded the newly deposited sediments. Wave action may also have been a possible cause of erosion, particularly if during any point of the estuarine phase the Westminster sites were in an exposed position in relation to the east–west fetch. Support for the erosion thesis can be found in fine-grained stratigraphy of variable thickness overlying the Storey organic mud bed at Parliament Square and Palace Chambers South, which could not be dated, except as predating 1200. These deposits may have formed immediately following the deposition of the Storey organic mud bed and have been variably eroded, thereby explaining their absence at Storey's Gate and St Stephen's East. Pollen assemblages from both the latter sites further illustrate the hiatus in suddenly changing from floras dominated by oak and hazel woodland in the Storey organic mud bed, to one where cereals dominate, and where exotics such as spruce and walnut (both known to be historic introductions) are found.

The deposits overlying the Westminster member are dominated in the main by sediment derived from the river, although archaeological material dating from the 12th century onwards is ubiquitous. The latter occurs both as a general spread and within distinct features and structures. Diatom evidence indicates that the river was still tidal at Westminster in the 12th century, although evidence from St Stephen's East suggests that freshwater environments were beginning to dominate in this area at least. Possibly this was an effect caused by the Tyburn which drained areas to the north and has had its course altered on a number of occasions. An alternative is that increasing water management associated with the human population altered the balance of fresh to salt water at strategic riverside locations. That deposits of 12th-century date should be encountered in the uppermost stratigraphy on the Westminster sites is not surprising, since by this period Westminster was becoming increasingly heavily occupied, in part due to the presence of Westminster Abbey. The sediments examined from this period certainly contain widespread evidence of human activity in the form of artefactual inclusions, charcoal and high magnetic susceptibility readings, as well as pollen from imported species of tree.

5

Middle and Late Holocene environments in west Southwark

Keith Wilkinson, Robert Scaife, Nigel Cameron and Jane Sidell

Introduction

(Fig 29)

The Jubilee Line Extension cuts a swathe across the northern edge of Southwark from west to east where it crosses under the Thames to the Isle of Dogs. Several sites on the new route were located within the borough. Firstly, developments at Waterloo Station have been undertaken but did not produce any detailed sequences of palaeoenvironmental interest. A new underground station (Southwark Station) was constructed to the south of the Blackfriars Bridge approach. Several excavations were undertaken at this location, associated with the station construction. These were the Joan Street and Union Street sites. Neither of these proved to be archaeologically significant; however, they provided some of the most important organic sequences to be discovered along the route. Further east, the construction work at Borough High Street, associated with the development of London Bridge Station, has provided some of the most significant Roman archaeology so far excavated in Southwark. The results of this are being published in one of the monographs in the Jubilee Line series (Drummond-Murray *et al* in prep). The sites at Borough High Street were unfortunately not suitable for this project.

The archaeology of Southwark

The earliest signs of human activity in Southwark date to the Mesolithic period. Although the data are limited, the evidence does indicate that the area was populated on a seasonal or transient basis, typical for this period. Several sites can be dated to the Mesolithic; the first to be excavated was the B&Q site adjacent to the Old Kent Road where an impressive lithic assemblage of over 1500 struck flints was recovered (Sidell *et al* in prep a). Unfortunately, the adverse soil conditions led to poor bone preservation; only four fragments were observed. Several hearths were indicated by the remains and their distribution at this site presents the evidence for one of the earliest post-glacial camps in south London.

No Neolithic settlement evidence has yet been conclusively identified in Southwark, although several traces of activity have been recorded. A recent excavation at Hopton Street, very close to the current line of the Thames, uncovered a series of stakeholes and pits associated with Beaker pottery (Maloney & Gostick 1998). An excavation at Park Street, at the site of the former Courage Brewery, consisted of several firepits or hearths on the contemporary foreshore. A further site with possibly Neolithic material is Phoenix Wharf where a burnt mound (Bowsher 1991) and a series of ard marks were uncovered. These marks are made by the primitive plough used by early farmers which gouged rather than turned the soil. A series of sites has now been discovered with ard marks but these appear to represent the continuation of the tradition into the Bronze

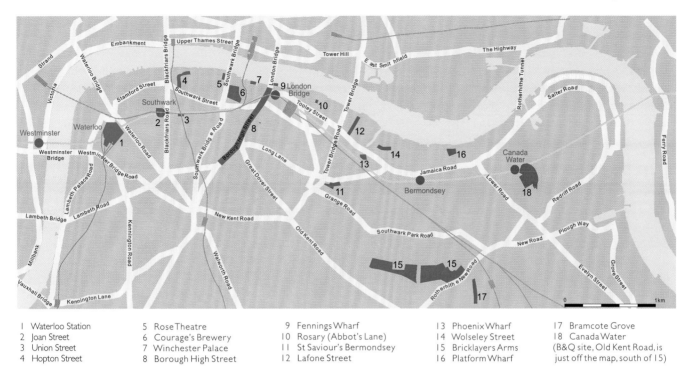

1	Waterloo Station	5	Rose Theatre	9	Fennings Wharf	13	Phoenix Wharf	17	Bramcote Grove
2	Joan Street	6	Courage's Brewery	10	Rosary (Abbot's Lane)	14	Wolseley Street	18	Canada Water
3	Union Street	7	Winchester Palace	11	St Saviour's Bermondsey	15	Bricklayers Arms		(B&Q site, Old Kent Road, is
4	Hopton Street	8	Borough High Street	12	Lafone Street	16	Platform Wharf		just off the map, south of 15)

Fig 29 Map of Southwark © Crown copyright. All rights reserved. Corporation of London LA 087254/00/12

Age and indeed there is some debate about the date of the site at Phoenix Wharf. The series of plough mark sites – including Lafone Street, Wolseley Street and Hopton Street – indicate that there was a considerable amount of Bronze Age agriculture taking place in Southwark. Although there is little direct evidence of settlement, some finds do suggest that people also lived in the vicinity. A timber platform was recovered from the Bricklayers Arms, Bermondsey at the interface of marshy and drier ground (Jones 1988). A further timber structure was found close by at Bramcote Green (Thomas & Rackham 1996), which has been identified as a trackway across marshland.

There has been limited evidence for settlement dating to the Bronze/Iron Age transition. At the Courage Brewery, traces of circular wooden huts (see Cowan in prep) were found in the form of postholes, while a rare (for London) burial mound has been uncovered adjacent to modern London Bridge at the site of Fennings Wharf (Sidell *et al* in prep a). Cremations have been uncovered from its ditch, including the remains of several children. Evidence for Iron Age occupation in Southwark is extremely scanty, but it appears to have consisted of small, isolated hamlets.

It was in the Roman period that Southwark first became occupied in a substantial manner. Initially the city of London on the Thames was settled following the Roman conquest, *c* AD 50. However, north Southwark lies directly across the Thames from the main Roman city of Londinium on the north bank, and south of the presumed location of the bridge. It may have been this location at the bridgehead and along the Roman road leading south to the Roman city at Canterbury (*Durovernum*) which led to the intensive settlement of Southwark. The major focus of the suburb is along the line of Watling Street (now marked by Borough High Street) and along the waterfront. The

south bank consisted of a series of sand islands or eyots with navigable inlets. However, this reduced the amount of land available for settlement, and signs of reclamation have been observed. Buildings have been found in the excavations along Borough High Street (particularly the Northern Line Ticket Hall site) and at London Bridge which precede the Boudican revolt of AD 60/61. This indicates that Southwark was settled either contemporaneously with or immediately after the foundation of Londinium itself. After the reconstruction of Roman London following the revolt, Southwark was rebuilt and extended. Borough High Street appears to have become a bustling commercial centre with a wide range of shops and businesses. Further away from Borough High Street, large stone buildings have been discovered which are possibly town houses of wealthy individuals or prestigious public buildings (Drummond-Murray *et al* in prep). As yet, the mechanism leading to the decline of Roman Southwark is not fully understood. It is likely that the suburb decayed along a similar pattern to that experienced by the main centre of London, which appears to have been gradually abandoned in the 5th century after military protection was withdrawn from the province (Esmonde Cleary 1989, 137).

The nature of human activity in the Saxon period is similar to that of the prehistoric periods in Southwark, that is, with very little evidence for occupation identified in the borough. What occupation there does appear to have been in Early Saxon London seems to have concentrated in small hamlets in locations such as Croydon and Hammersmith. Later Saxon settlement is concentrated in the Covent Garden area (Malcolm *et al* 1999): the trading emporium of *Lundenwic* mentioned by Bede in his *Historia ecclesiastica* (Colgrave & Mynors 1969, 142–3). It was only at the end of the Saxon period that

Southwark appears to have been densely settled. It is from this date that the name derives; the initial term *Suthringa geweorc(he)* is found in the Burghal Hidage, an early text which lists contemporary fortified settlements (Vince 1990, 86–7). The term *south work* came into being slightly later. The settlement was destroyed by William the Conqueror but was re-established and became a thriving and expanding community with its own Minster listed in Domesday Book. The settlement associated with the bridgehead gradually expanded to the east and west along the river frontage and came to include two royal residences, namely the Rosary of Edward II built in 1324–5 and a later residence in Rotherhithe (at Platform Wharf) constructed for Edward III in 1353–61 (Blatherwick & Bluer in prep). Other desirable residences and important establishments came to be built in Southwark which identified the area as more than a commercial centre, the poor relation of the City. These include the Abbey of St Saviour, Bermondsey, initially a Cluniac priory when constructed in the 11th century and subsequently a Benedictine abbey from the 14th century (Steele in prep). An additional example of these important buildings was the palace of the bishops of Winchester, located to the west of the Priory of St Mary Overie. Built in the 12th century, it became one of the largest buildings in London at over six acres (Seeley *et al* in prep).

The post-medieval period saw the decay of the large religious and public buildings with the dissolution of the monasteries and the passing of the royal and spiritual palaces into public hands. Southwark did not decay as a centre of settlement but rather changed its character. However, it was not entirely devoid of large public buildings, in fact some of the earliest additions in this period were the polygonal timber playhouses such as the Rose and Globe, justly famous through their association with the great playwrights of the period, William Shakespeare and Christopher Marlowe (Blatherwick 1998). The emphasis on commercial development seems to increase throughout this period, with a wide range of trades practised, such as lime burning, tanning, pottery manufacture, including delftware and porcelain, and the production of clay pipes.

Joan Street and Union Street are located close together in west Southwark at the site of the Southwark Station. The analysis of these sites is reported in this chapter. The site excavated at Canada Water, Rotherhithe, is reported on in the following chapter. Although there are similarities between the sites, their geographical disparity makes it appropriate for them to be discussed separately.

Joan Street

Introduction

The sites of Joan Street and Union Street lie only some 400m apart and are similar in many ways. The land-use history of the Joan Street site is relatively well understood for the later historic period, prior to which the area was termed 'Wideflet', or

willow stream, in recognition of its damp aspect. Indeed, even after the land had passed through the hands of the Priory of Bermondsey (1113–69), the Knights Templar (1169–1324), the Knights Hospitaller (1324–1536) and Henry VIII, certain areas, including the sample site, had not been developed because of the wet nature of the ground. In the 17th and 18th centuries the area was utilised for fulling and bleaching cloth because of the need in these processes for large quantities of water and it was only through the construction of Blackfriars Road in 1760 and provision of sewers in 1809 that construction of houses took place.

Two separate phases of investigation occurred at the Joan Street site where ventilation shafts were to be excavated. The first (Joan Street 1) took place over a period of a single week in September and October 1991 when a stepped trench with a footprint of 9m x 15m was excavated. Three separate steps were made, with cultural material (pottery, animal bone and tile) and walls dating to the 18th century being found in the lowest at about +1.60m OD. In the upper two steps, building foundations and a well associated with 19th-century material were found, while 19th-century cartographic evidence suggests that from 1872 at least the area lay in a yard behind a row of houses. At the base of the final step (+0.70m OD) a 2.50m^2 slot was machine excavated a further 3.50m downwards through mineral silt/clays and peat. Unfortunately, although the underlying gravel was reached it could not be investigated in detail due to flooding of the trench when the water table was breached. No archaeological material was found from anywhere within this lower stratigraphy, although monolith sampling was carried out of the peat in a single section prior to encasing it with shuttering. A total of five monolith samples were taken in this fashion through the peat stratigraphy, which has been dated to between 4850±80 BP (5737–5331 cal. BP) (Beta 119783) and 2340±60 BP (2706–2162 cal. BP) (Beta 119784).

A second smaller-scale investigation of the Joan Street (Joan Street 2) site took place in 1995 from a location 50m to the east of the earlier site during excavation of a ventilation shaft. During this stage of work no archaeological recording was carried out, although the exposed section was logged and two monolith samples taken from lower stratigraphy. The deposits revealed by the second investigation were essentially the same as the first, although because the depth of the deposits was not as great it was possible to investigate strata below the peats. However, due to safety constraints it was still not possible to sample down to the basal gravel. Therefore the monolith tins were taken from a sand which immediately overlay the gravel, various silt and clay deposits which overlay this and an organic mud, as well as the peat itself.

The stratigraphy of the Joan Street sites has been plotted alongside the mineral magnetic, loss-on-ignition and particle-size data in Fig 30. [14]C dating of the first sequence investigated has also allowed a curve to be constructed of the peat-accumulation rate, which in turn allows an approximate chronology to be determined for the peat stratigraphy. Such an approach may be seen as potentially hazardous as it does not allow for differential compaction or unconformities in the peat.

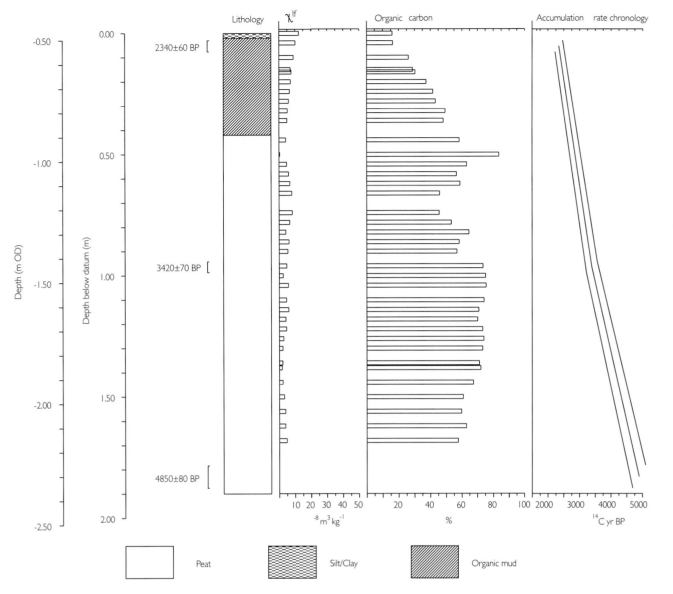

Fig 30a Lithological diagram from Joan Street, west Southwark

However, it is thought to be justified in the present locality as recent work on a series of London peats dating from the period c 5800 cal. BP to c 2600 cal. BP has demonstrated that accumulation at most sampled sites has been more or less continuous, while based on OD heights of peat surfaces variations in compaction between different peat sequences appear to be a minimal problem, especially when considered alongside the difficulties caused by the inherent errors of the ^{14}C dating (Thomas & Rackham 1996; Wilkinson *et al* 2000). The results of palynological and diatom studies are presented as histograms in Figs 31 and 32 respectively.

Lithostratigraphy and sedimentology

Underlying the Holocene stratigraphy on the Joan Street sites was a flint gravel, presumably relating to the Late Devensian Shepperton Gravel. However, this was only revealed following completion of both investigations at a depth of −2.8m OD

and could not be investigated due to the high water table. The earliest sampled deposits appear to unconformably overlie the gravel at Joan Street 2 at least and although undated are probably of the Early to Middle Holocene period. These comprise a fining upwards sequence at least 0.65m thick, of fine to medium sands, silts and silt/clays of an olive-grey (5Y5/2) colour. A further trend upwards through the sequence is the increase in organic content from levels of around 3% at −2.30m OD (Fig 30) to 22% at −1.70m OD. The latter increase is gradual within the coarser sediments at the base of the sequence, but rapid above −1.80m OD where sediments are finer. Changes in χ^{lf} values operate in the opposite direction with steadily decreasing values upwards, probably as a result of increasing organic content of low susceptibility diluting the higher susceptibility mineral particles. The evidence from the fining upwards sequence would seem to suggest that accumulation took place within a river channel that was gradually migrating away from the sample site. The consequent decrease in energy levels as the

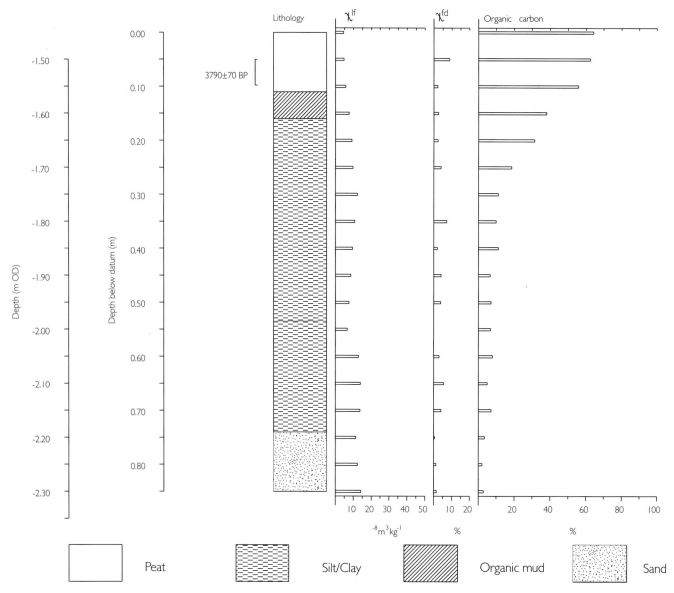

Fig 30b Lithological diagram from Joan Street, west Southwark

sample site became increasingly marginal to the main zone of river flow would have allowed plant growth during periods of low water, thereby explaining the increase in organic content.

Unconformably overlying the fining upwards sequence (at −1.61m OD) discussed above is a dark grey (2.5Y4/0) silt/clay. The apparent erosional contact between this and underlying deposits would at first sight appear to suggest that a hiatus may exist between the strata. However, this may not in fact be the case as the organic carbon record indicates a progressive increase in organic content through the top part of the underlying sequence and across the stratigraphic boundary, rather than the sudden 'jump' that may have been expected given the presumed hiatus. This pattern of gradually increasing organic carbon content continues through the overlying organic mud and into the peat capping this part of the sequence. Thus a plausible scenario is that the clay/silt and indeed the organic muds into which it grades simply reflect a continuation of the processes outlined above, with the sample site situated

on a floodplain at increasingly greater distance from the river. In this type of environment the area would only be subject to periodic flooding allowing increasing numbers of plants to colonise and hence explaining the higher organic contents. Sand lenses found within silt/clay are likely to reflect particularly intense flood events and therefore it is possible that minor unconformities as a result of these also exist in the sequence.

The organic sequence overlying the silt/clays has already in part been discussed and, as previously suggested, is probably indicative of increasing marginalisation from the river – perhaps caused by accumulation placing the sample site at increased elevation in relation to river levels – rather than to any movement of the latter. The organic strata consist of an organic mud outcropping at −1.61m OD (at Joan Street 2), conformably overlain by peat and organic muds, which at Joan Street 1 extends to −0.50m OD. The lower part of the sequence is, however, potentially problematic, for although the base of the organic sediments is encountered at −1.61m OD at Joan Street 2, it is found at −2.35m OD or lower at Joan Street 1, a difference of at least 0.74m. However, the chronology of the lower parts of the peat may provide an answer. At the base of the Joan Street 2 organic sequence a ^{14}C date of 3970±70 BP (4780–4185 cal. BP) (Beta 122928) was obtained from material between −1.50m OD and −1.55m OD, but at Joan Street 1, the base of the sampled peat produced a result of 4850±80 BP (5737–5331 cal. BP) (Beta 119783), which at two standard deviations is between 600 and 1300 years older. There are several possible explanations for this difference. Firstly, it is possible that peat initially formed in the lowest part of the floodplain, and as it accumulated upwards it spread to ever larger areas eventually covering the area of the Joan Street 2 site at around 4500 cal. BP. However, for this hypothesis to be accepted it would have to be assumed that the sediments below the organic sequence at Joan Street 2 accumulated prior to 5600 cal. BP, and that there is at least a 600-calendar-year hiatus between their deposition ending and the initiation of peat growth. As has been demonstrated above, the stratigraphic morphology does not seem to bear this out, while a further ^{14}C date from Joan Street 1 of 3420±70 BP (3839–3473 cal. BP) (Beta 119785) from material at a depth of between −1.41m OD and −1.46m OD (and thus similar to that from which the date from Joan Street 2 was obtained), is 350 to 1400 calendar years younger. Of course differential subsidence or compaction could explain the difference, but given the proximity of the two sites this does not seem likely. A more plausible alternative is that the varied chronology of peat growth initiation reflects facies differences within a floodplain. In other words, the peats at Joan Street 1 began forming while sands and mineral silt/clays were accumulating at Joan Street 2, but in areas further away from the river. A combination of river migration away from the site, sediment accretion and adjacent peat growth, eventually led to peat formation at the Joan Street 2 site, although it seems unlikely that this occurred on a level surface. If correct this interpretation would suggest that the river/stream channel responsible for the mineral accretion at Joan Street 2 was located in an easterly direction from this site.

Within the 1.5m thickness of peat at Joan Street 1 there are only minor fluctuations in morphology and generally the accumulation is of relatively unhumified wood peats containing moderate quantities of macroscopic remains. Sand is found throughout in variable quantities suggesting that although the peat formed in a largely terrestrial environment, inundation by flood water occurred on occasion. The trend in these inundation events can be tracked by variations in the organic carbon content where reductions in organics can be taken to be due to allochthonous mineral input. Organic contents are high throughout the lower part of the peat at levels of between 70–75%, but at −1.37m OD there is a sudden drop to levels of around 55–60%. This drop corresponds to a sharp boundary in the stratigraphic record and to the occurrence of a highly humified peat. The change, which can be dated to around

3600 cal. BP, may relate to an increase in flooding, but may also relate to a decrease in the rate of peat accumulation, perhaps relating to a change in hydrology or climate. However, it should be stated that the accumulation rate data, although crude, suggest that such a slowing of peat formation did not occur, but rather that it increased following 3600 cal. BP. The lower organic carbon levels then continue at a similar level with a single peak of 80% at around −1.0m OD into the overlying organic muds. The latter outcrop at −0.99m OD and mark a change to the accumulation pattern, almost certainly caused by increased flooding as a result of RSL rise. Organic carbon values drop steadily through the organic muds from levels of around 40% to 20%, while the deposits gradually develop a laminar structure indicating periodicity in deposition. These include occasional sand laminations indicating periodic high-energy deposition across the floodplain, while the overall trend is for increased frequency of mineral laminations upwards through the profile. A date of 2340±60 BP (2706–2162 cal. BP) (Beta 119784) from the top of the organic mud sequence indicates that inundation of the site by rising water levels occurred in the Early to Middle Iron Age, while the nature of this upper boundary suggests that there was no hiatus in deposition.

The deposits conformably capping the organic sequence consist of well-sorted dark greyish-brown (2.5Y4/2) silt/clays. Particle-size analysis on samples between −0.80m OD and −0.03m OD suggests that the sequence coarsens upwards from having equal proportions of clay and silt, to a domination by the latter. This property is probably related to increased energies as a result of greater turbidity in an increasingly tidal environment. The deposit is moderately rich in mollusc shell and includes the freshwater genus *Lymnaea*, but nevertheless almost certainly formed in brackish water.

Pollen biostratigraphy

Pollen was obtained from the detrital fen peat between −1.80m and −0.45m OD, and overlying silt/clay units between −0.45m and −0.20m OD. Five principal local pollen-assemblage zones have been delimited (Fig 31). These are characterised from the bottom of the profile at −1.80m upwards as follows:

JOA:1 −1.80 − −1.54m OD *Quercus-Tilia-Fraxinus-Alnus-Corylus avellana* type

Arboreal species are at their highest values (to 72%) dominated by *Quercus* (to 62%), *Alnus* (84% tdlp+marsh) with *Tilia* (9%) and *Fraxinus* (4%). *Corylus avellana* is the dominant shrub with sporadic numbers/occurrences of *Rhamnus catharticus*, *Malus* type (apple), *Sorbus* type (rowan), *Salix* and Viburnum. There are generally few herbs with Poaceae the most important (peak of 20%). Sporadic *Plantago lanceolata* and Cereal type are of note.

TREES & SHRUBS

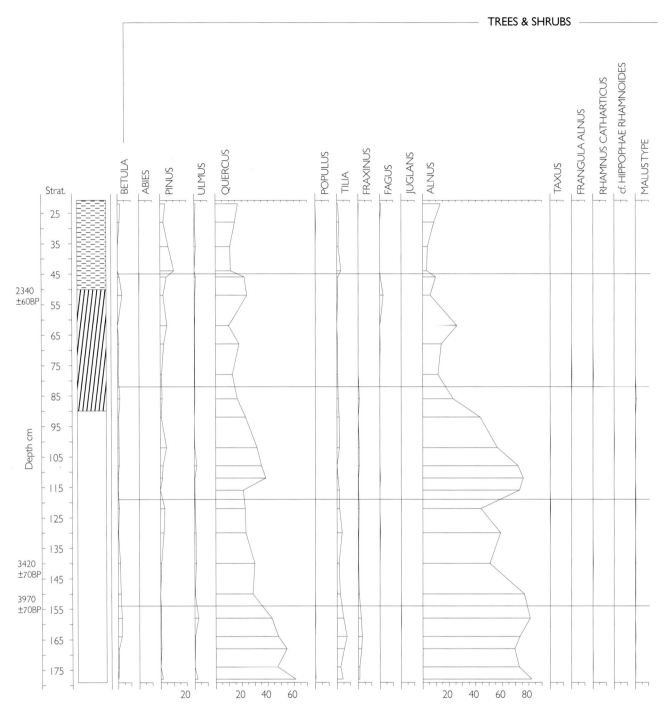

Fig 31 Pollen diagram from Joan Street, west Southwark

JOA:2 −1.54 − −1.19m OD *Quercus-Tilia-Alnus-Corylus avellana* type

There is an overall reduction in trees with declining *Quercus*, *Tilia* and *Alnus*. Conversely, there is substantial expansion of *Corylus avellana* type and lesser increases in *Pinus* and *Salix*. One of the characteristic features of this zone is the very marked expansion of herbs, especially Poaceae (expanding to 40%), *Plantago lanceolata* (to 7%), Lactucae (5%), *Chenopodium* type (5%) and *Rumex*. There are also increasing numbers of sporadic herb occurrences. Of note is a peak of Cereal type (pasz 1) corresponding with the expansion of *Plantago lanceolata* and Lactucae. Marsh types include increasing *Typha angustifolia* type and Cyperaceae. Spores become increasingly dominant/important with *Pteridium aquilinum* and some *Dryopteris* type (monolete spores).

JOA:3 −1.19 − −0.82m OD *Quercus-Alnus-Lactucae-Poaceae-Plantago lanceolata*

This zone is characterised by the strong expansion of Poaceae reaching high values (to 40% at the top of the zone) with *Plantago lanceolata* (10%), Lactucae (10%), plus a diverse range of other herbs. Trees are dominated by *Quercus* (45%) and *Alnus* (to 75% tdlp+marsh), both having peaks at the beginning of the zone but which decline consequently. *Tilia* remains consistent at low values (<3%) while *Fagus* is also present but *Fraxinus* dies out. Shrubs remain dominated by *Corylus avellana* type but it declines to its low values prior to further expansion. Local pollen-assemblage sub-zones can be delimited, dividing the lower part of the zone with dominance of *Alnus* (pasz 1) changing to Cyperaceae (to

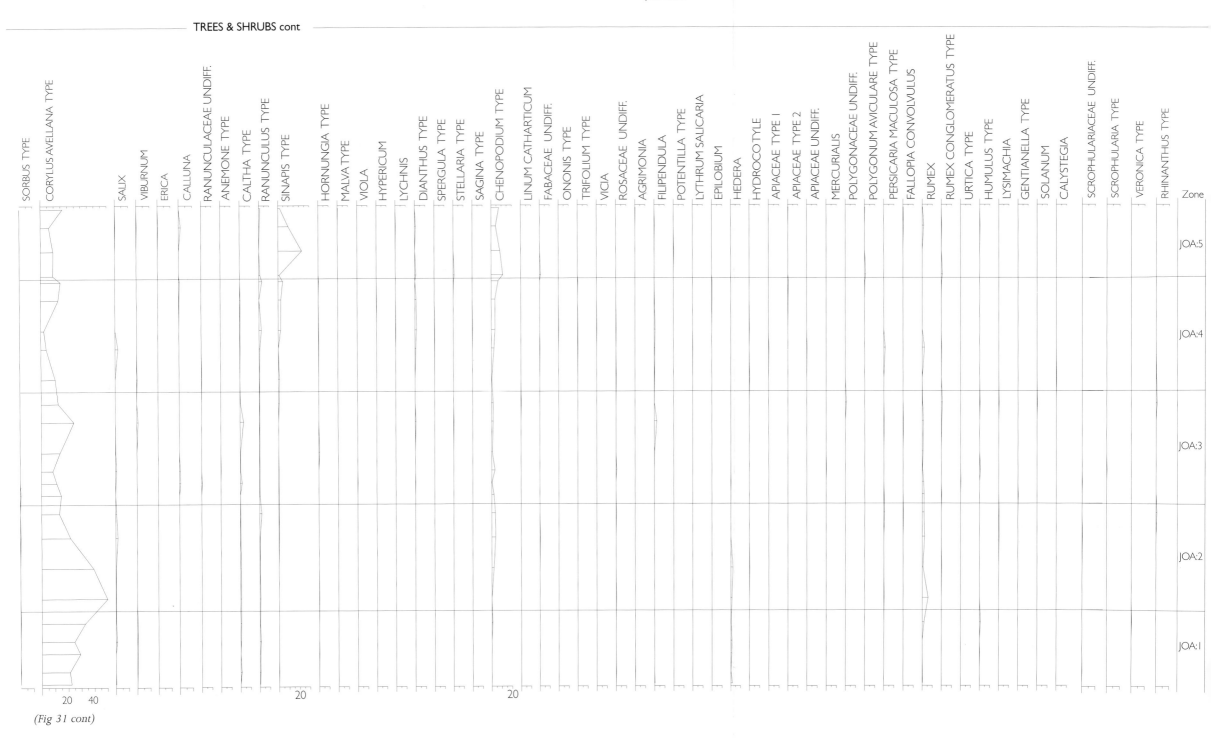

(Fig 31 cont)

50%) with *Typha angustifolia* (pasz 2). *Pteridium aquilinum*
(50%) and *Dryopteris* are the principal spore taxa with
constant but small values of *Polypodium* and *Sphagnum* (bog
moss). Cysts of the freshwater algae *Pediastrum* are present.

JOA:4 –0.82 – –0.45m OD Poaceae-Cyperaceae-Lactucae

Tree pollen declines including *Quercus* (30%) and *Corylus
avellana* type (<10%). Sporadic occurrences of *Betula*, *Ulmus*
and *Tilia* remain. There is a small peak of *Fagus*. Within the
herbs, Poaceae is dominant to 50% with peaks also of Cereal
type (10%) and other large (thin-walled) Poaceae (5%).
Chenopodium type starts to increase along with peaks of *Bidens*
type, *Aster* type *Anthemis* type (daisy family) and the highest

values of Lactucae. Marsh types are dominated by Cyperaceae
which attains its highest values (to 50%) with *Typha
angustifolia* type. Spores comprise *Pteridium aquilinum* and
Dryopteris type with small peaks of *Equisetum* (horsetails) and
Sphagnum.

JOA:5 –0.45 – –0.20m OD *Chenopodium* type-Lactucae-Poaceae-Cereal type

This zone corresponds broadly with the upper waterlain unit
which has been described as comminuted. Herbs are dominant
with Poaceae (to 30%), Lactucae (10%), *Chenopodium* type
(15%), Cereal type (15%) and *Sinapis* type (peak of 25%). The
most important trees are *Quercus* and *Pinus* but are subordinate

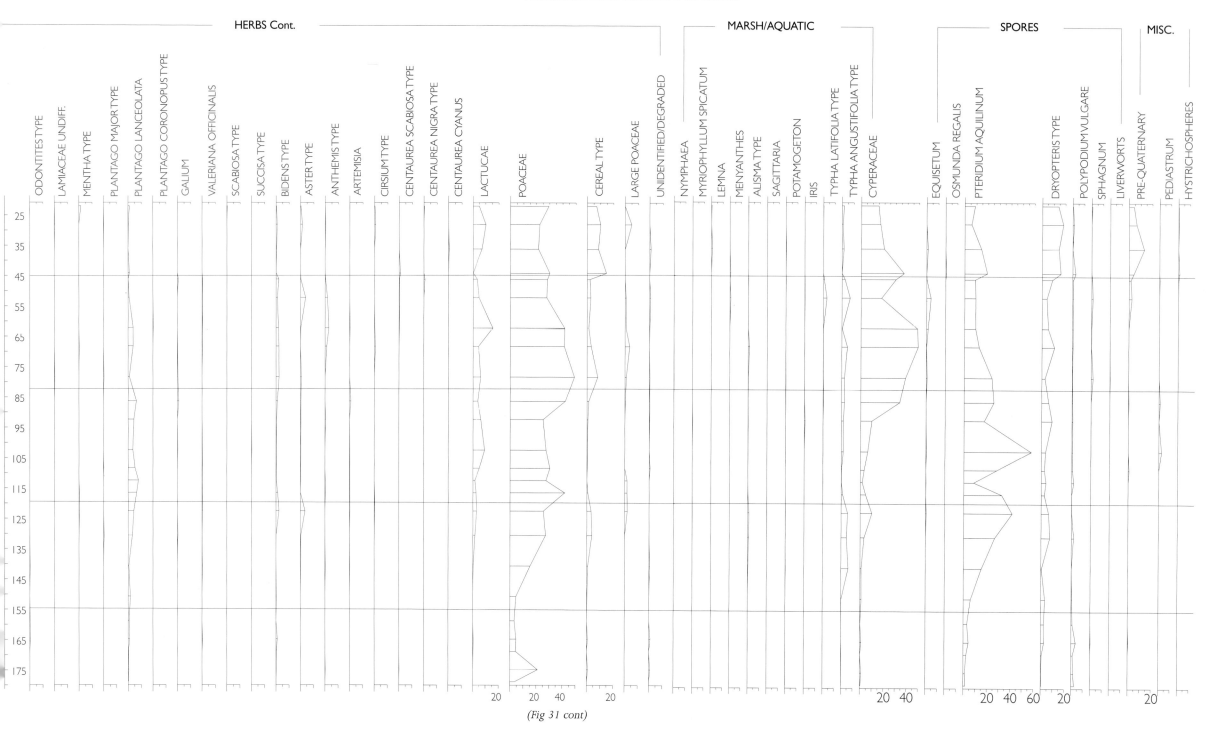

(Fig 31 cont)

to herbs. *Pinus* attains its highest values. Marsh taxa include Cyperaceae. There is an increase in Dryopteris type, *Pteridium aquilinum* and derived pre-Quaternary palynomorphs.

Diatom biostratigraphy

Sixteen samples were initially assessed from the peats, organic muds and silt/clays of the Joan Street 1 sequence. As would be anticipated, diatom preservation in the peat was generally poor; however, exceptionally a freshwater-halophilous diatom assemblage was found at the base of the peat. The overlying organic silt and waterlain clay/silt was found to contain a mixture of fresh, brackish and marine taxa. Further material was assessed for diatoms from two monolith samples collected

during the second phase of fieldwork at Joan Street 2 (Wilkinson 1996a). However, despite the varying lithostratigraphy of this material, including sand, silt, peat, terrestrial and archaeological units (Wilkinson 1996a), diatoms were absent from all the samples assessed (Fig 32).

The diatomaceous sample from the base of the peat, below −2.1m OD, is dominated by non-planktonic, freshwater diatoms with a smaller, non-planktonic halophilous element (*Anomoeoneis sphaerophora* and *Navicula cincta*). Planktonic mesohalobous and polyhalobous species, typical of estuarine conditions, are absent. However, the presence of halophilous species suggests that the environment was slightly brackish and was subject to some influence of saline water. A poorly preserved diatom assemblage from the middle part of the peat

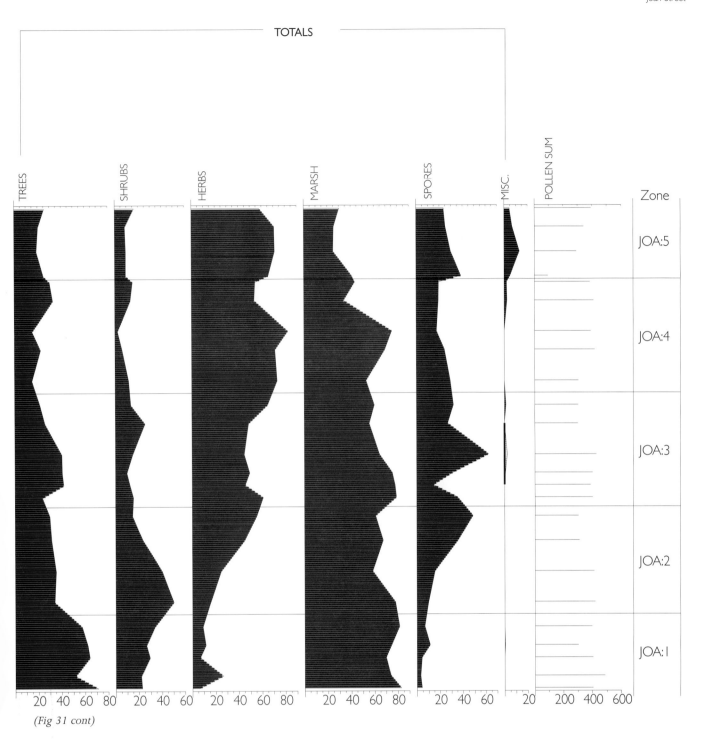

TOTALS

TREES SHRUBS HERBS MARSH SPORES MISC. POLLEN SUM Zone

JOA:5

JOA:4

JOA:3

JOA:2

JOA:1

20 40 60 80   20 40 60   20 40 60 80   20 40 60 80   20 40 60   20   200 400 600

(Fig 31 cont)

contains indeterminate species, identifiable only to generic level. However, these are most probably freshwater taxa.

The upper part of the organic mud contains freshwater diatom assemblages with only traces of polyhalobous, mesohalobous and halophilous taxa. Diatom assemblages in the base of the overlying waterlain silt/clays shift from oligohalobous indifferent dominated diatom assemblages to an assemblage dominated (>35%) by polyhalobous species with no transitional assemblage of brackish-water species. A high proportion of the diatoms (60%) at this level are poorly preserved and could not be assigned to any halobian group. It is likely that differential preservation has resulted in the over-representation of robust taxa such as *Paralia sulcata*. However, the switch to dominance of this coastal species gives clear

evidence for an increase in salinity perhaps as a result of flooding from the river rather than continuous immersion of the site by tidal waters.

In the uppermost silt/clays, the percentages of polyhalobous species decline to between *c* 5–10% and marine taxa are absent at the surface. At the base of this stratum, freshwater taxa comprise almost 80% of the assemblage and include both non-planktonic *Fragilaria* spp and planktonic *Cyclotella* spp. Mesohalobous taxa, best represented by *Cyclotella striata*, then increase to almost 40% while freshwater species decline to 20% of the assemblage. At the surface of the sequence the non-planktonic brackish-water species *Nitzschia granulata* becomes dominant, but again this is likely to partly reflect the effects of differential preservation and survival of a robust species.

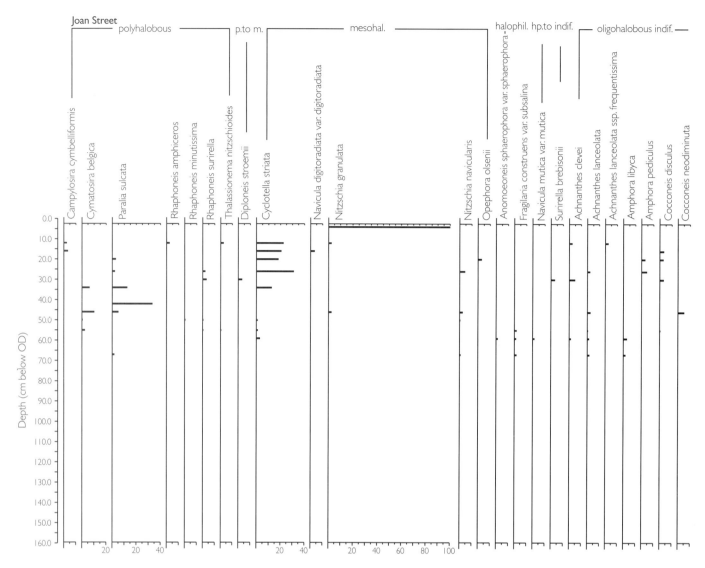

Fig 32 Diatom diagram from Joan Street, west Southwark

Nitzschia granulata is a species associated with epipelic habitats, for example the mud surface of a tidal foreshore. Despite the species-preferential survival, its presence clearly indicates the prevalence of brackish to marine conditions. The diatom assemblages of the upper silts indicate that, although the habitat and preservation conditions were changing, the sedimentary environment was a tidal one with some indication for decreasing salinities towards the surface.

Discussion

It was very fortunate that a second phase of groundworks at Joan Street was undertaken, allowing a watching brief to be carried out and allowing the collection of the Joan Street 2 samples. Although it was not possible to collect gravel, this is now known to occur at *c* −2.9m OD on the Joan Street site. The initial sedimentation reflects sediments derived from channel flooding, in all likelihood the channel migrating away from the sample site. This is thought to be a north or north-eastward migration, based on analysis of the Southwark sites and also topographic data. The minerogenic sediments are

replaced at Joan Street 2 by organic muds at −1.61m OD, dating to *c* 4500 cal. BP. However, at Joan Street 1, the organic muds are found at lower altitude (−2.35m OD) and date to *c* 5800 cal. BP. When a 95% confidence range is calculated for these dates, the age difference is between 600 and 1300 years. Although the sites are only 50m apart, this is a significant difference and it is difficult to suggest explanations other than organic sedimentation took place asynchronously in the lower parts of the floodplain in which Joan Street 1 is located. The organic muds rapidly developed into well-preserved peats. Unfortunately, no diatom evidence was recovered from the lowest deposits. Pollen evidence is available, however. The base of the peat at −2.25 to −2.35m OD illustrates that organic accumulation was initiated shortly after the primary elm decline. The date of 4850±80 BP (5737–5331 cal. BP) (Beta 119783) is comparable with a number of other sites examined in central and east London. A date of 2340±60 BP (2706–2162 cal. BP) (Beta 119784) for the upper part of the organic silts at −0.50 to −0.55m OD gives a date for organic accumulation prior to the Iron Age intertidal deposits.

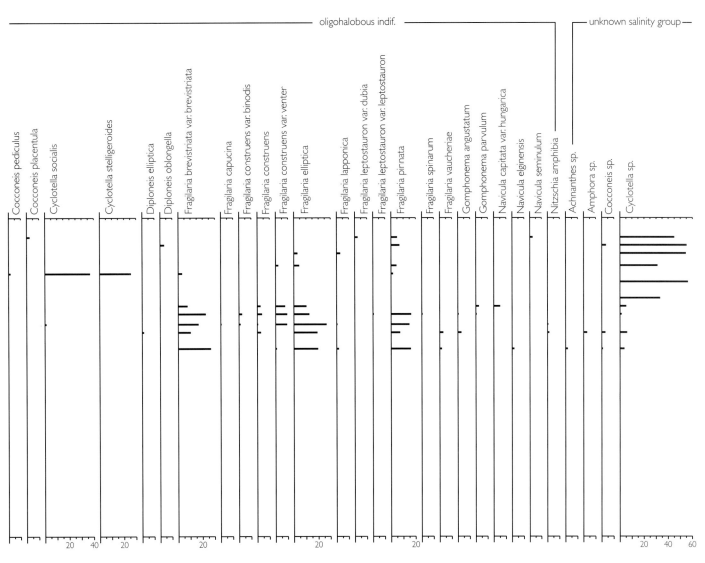

(Fig 32 cont)

Pollen zone JOA:1 clearly shows the dominance of tree and shrub pollen. High values of *Alnus* clearly indicate the dominance of alder carr locally to the site and is also accompanied by other fen carr taxa such as *Rhamnus catharticus*, *Salix*, *Caltha* type and *Humulus* type (cannabis and hop, but here thought to be hop). There are some indications of standing water with *Potamogeton* and *Alisma plantago-aquatica*. The drier soils of the terrestrial zone were dominated by *Quercus*, *Corylus avellana*, *Tilia* and *Fraxinus*. It can be noted here (but see chapter 8) that *Tilia* and *Fraxinus* are poorly represented in pollen assemblages and, as such, it is likely that they were of substantial importance in the environment. Whether these woodland elements formed a mixed deciduous community or areas of separate importance is not clear. It is most likely that *Quercus* and *Corylus* may have formed a dominant woodland community on, or adjacent to, the floodplain on heavier gleyed soils. *Tilia* was, however, perhaps dominant on well-drained soils. There are now substantial data illustrating such importance of lime in the Middle Holocene and later prehistoric environment.

As mentioned above, the small quantity of *Ulmus* pollen indicates a post-elm-decline date for the base of this column. While woodland was dominant in proximity to the sample site, there are some typical indications of prehistoric impact. Firstly, it can be postulated that the *Fraxinus* is secondary woodland consequent upon the elm decline and Neolithic woodland disturbance. Secondly, cereal pollen and *Plantago lanceolata* occur sporadically throughout this zone and, given that the pollen catchment under heavily wooded conditions was small/very local, this may indicate agricultural activity in the local area.

From −1.75m OD to −0.70m OD (c 4500 cal. BP) there is the start of a marked expansion of herbs with Poaceae, Cereal type, *Plantago lanceolata* and other ruderals (Asteraceae types), *Rumex*, Polygonaceae and *Chenopodium* types, providing clear evidence for extension of human activity and agriculture in proximity to the site. This is also manifested by the apparent clearance of woodland – *Quercus*, *Tilia*, *Fraxinus* all decline, while *Corylus* expands to its highest values. This is attributed to opening of the woodland canopy promoting growth of understorey hazel. This opening of the canopy is also indicated by the input of other pollen types such as *Pinus* and *Fagus*,

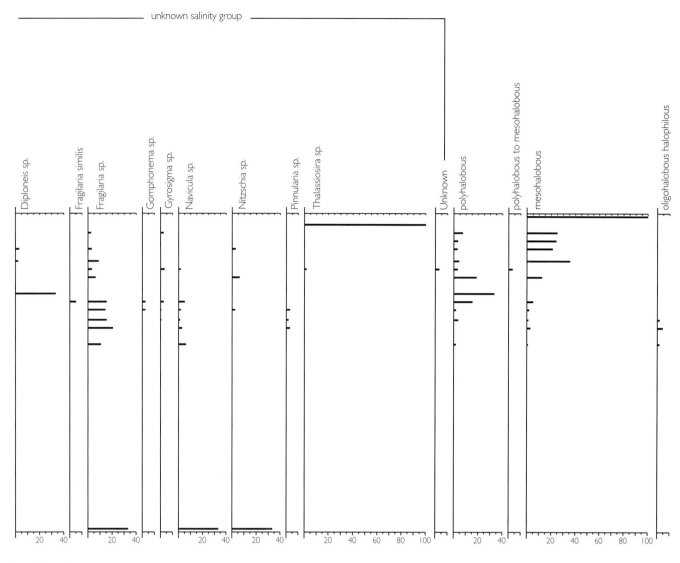

(Fig 32 cont)

whose representation is increased as the pollen catchment of the site became extended. *Pteridium aquilinum* demonstrates the extension of waste ground, although the sporing may also be a function of increased light to the ground flora.

Human activity also appears to have had autogenic effects on the mire ecology after c 3600 cal. BP. Decline in alder (carr) is mirrored by an expansion of *Typha angustifolia/Sparganium* type, Cyperaceae, *Alisma* type and other local fen taxa indicating localised waterlogging of the floodplain. This may be attributed to woodland clearance, reduction in evapotranspiration, higher groundwater table and also increased overland flow (Moore & Willmot 1976; Scaife 1980). In zone JOA:3 there was stabilisation which saw the regeneration of *Quercus* and re-establishment of alder with reduction of the wetter fen elements (this has been designated pasz 2). This was, however, short-lived and there appears to be an expansion of wetter fen elements (especially Cyperaceae) in JOA:4 at the expense of the alder carr seen in zone JOA:3. As with the earliest phase, this was associated with expansion of herbs including strong indications of cereal cultivation and agricultural land use (*Plantago lanceolata*, cereal pollen and many weed types). This situation

lasted until the Late Bronze Age/Iron Age as demonstrated by the ^{14}C date of 2340±60 BC (Beta 119784). While this increased wetness of the mire community may be due to human activity as described, it is also possible that regionally rising base levels caused by positive RSL change was responsible.

The change to pollen floras in JOA:5 occurs at a stratigraphic break/change associated with fewer organic deposits, with some lamination, indicating periodic sedimentation. Pollen changes associated with this indicate marine and/or brackish-water influences; *Chenopodium* type are diagnostic. *Sinapis* type, while including numerous taxa, may have derived from halophytic Brassicaceae. Also present are occasional hystrichospheres and derived pre-Quaternary palynomorphs. There are also increased numbers of cereal pollen, characterised by thick exine, large pores, annuli and coarse columellae, and also other large Poaceae with thinner walls and smaller pores. The latter possibly come from halophytic grasses. This uppermost pollen and lithostratigraphic zone is attributed to the proposed Iron Age marine transgression/influences suggested by Devoy (1979) which strongly affected the taphonomy of pollen transported from within the estuary.

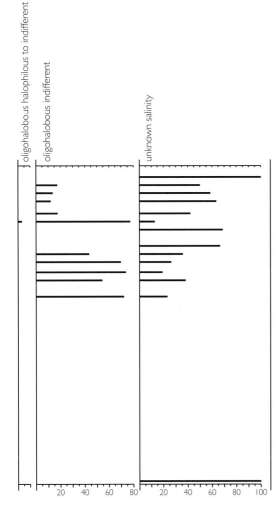

oligohalobous halophilous to indifferent

oligohalobous indifferent

unknown salinity

20   40   60   80   20   40   60   80   100

(Fig 32 cont)

Conclusions

The base of the sequence from the two Joan Street sites has shown that significant changes in sedimentary pattern can take place over quite short distances. The basal sediments show a change from freshwater fluvial to a long-lived period of semi-terrestrial organic deposition, spanning over two thousand years. Oak, lime, ash and hazel woodland was dominant on soils above the floodplain, while the floodplain supported a dominant alder carr community. There is evidence for increased human activity/pressure with woodland clearance during the later Neolithic and Early Bronze Age and subsequent agricultural activity. A second lime decline at *c* 3200 cal. BP (Bronze Age) occurred with further evidence of increased human activity and expansion of agriculture. This habitat saw a possible change from alder carr to wetter sedge fen. This may in part have been due to autogenic human effects or from base-level changes caused by RSL change. Certainly, after *c* 2300 cal. BP there is clear evidence for change to marine/brackish-water conditions of sedimentation which appears to have taken place initially as periodic flooding rather than complete inundation of the site.

Towards the top of the sampled sequences, there is a suggestion that the marine influence is decreasing, possibly suggesting a migration of the tidal head downstream, a trend well known from the Roman period (Sidell submitted).

Union Street

Introduction

Excavations were carried out within the footprint of a 5m diameter ring shaft at 206 Union Street in October 1991 by the DGLA. During the course of the two-week field project a depth of 8m of sediments was examined in a stepped trench and subsequently – following the excavation of *c* 4.5m (*ie* at +1.37m OD) of material – in a 3m² shaft. Artefacts dating to the post-medieval period were found from the ground surface (+1.90m OD) to +0.60m OD. Part of the stratigraphy comprised a series of ploughsoils representative of the site's documented arable use from the Tudor period until the mid 18th century. The palaeosols were capped by rubble and levelling material relating to the construction of buildings fronting Union Street and William Street which date from the middle 1700s. The palaeosols in turn seal deliberately deposited household waste dating to the 1550s and later, which in turn overlies a sequence of fine-grained alluvial deposits and peats which extends from +0.75m OD to at least −2.60m OD. This part of the sequence dates from around 4630±110 BP (5594–4974 cal. BP) (Beta 119783) at the base of exposed peat, to the 16th–17th centuries (450–250 cal. BP) at the top of the uppermost silt/clays. Unfortunately it was not possible to reach the gravel at the base of the Holocene sequence due to the high water table.

Sampling was concentrated on the fine-grained silt/clays and underlying peat. Seven monolith samples were taken from +0.78m OD to −2.60m OD and sedimentary tests carried out on subsamples at 5cm intervals. Fig 33 illustrates the results of χ^{lf}, χ^{fd} and loss-on-ignition tests, and in common with Fig 30 (Joan Street) provides data regarding peat-accumulation rates. In the case of Fig 33 (Union Street) the latter data have been extended upwards to the top of the silt/clay strata based on data from artefacts within these fine-grained deposits. The accuracy of such a projection is uncertain as the length of any hiatus represented by the contact between the mineral deposits and the underlying organic muds can only be estimated, although the diatom evidence suggests more or less continuous accretion. Palynological (see Fig 34) and diatom analysis (see Fig 35) was undertaken (respectively) on subsamples primarily concentrating on the organic and inorganic sequences.

Lithostratigraphy and sedimentology

The base of the sampled sequence (−2.60m OD to −0.88m OD) consists of a moderately humified wood peat with interleaving horizontally bedded fine layers of organic mud. The peat horizons date from at least 4630±110 BP (5594–4974 cal. BP), and possibly significantly earlier, that is, the base was not located. They are generally medium to thickly bedded, have little structure and contain variable quantities of wood and other plant macro fragments. Particularly well-preserved organic remains occur concentrated as a continuous bed between −1.98m OD and −1.88m OD and as discontinuous fine layers between −1.73m OD and −1.01m OD. Organic carbon contents are likewise variable with values of around 60% at levels below −1.80m OD and between 60–80% above −1.70m OD, while above −1.20m OD there is a declining trend in organic content to levels of around 30%. Rooting associated with the layers of well-preserved organic macrofossils indicates that many of the remains are not detrital, but are instead *in situ* accumulations of local vegetation. Thus, the data may indicate that during the episodes represented by high organic preservation the peat was forming as marsh above the contemporary river level, probably at the channel margins. In contrast the fine layers of organic mud (occurring at −1.79m OD to −1.77m OD, −1.75m OD to −1.73m OD and −1.01m OD to −0.98m OD) are almost certainly representative of flood events when river levels rose and inundated the marsh. These deposits do not only consist of silts and clays, but also contain a moderate quantity of fine sands which may indicate the floods were of moderately high energy, although the events may have been short-lived. The two earlier inundations are likely to date from *c* 4700–4450 cal. BP, if continuous deposition is assumed between the basal ^{14}C date of 4630±110 BP (5594–4974 cal. BP) and that of 3930±80 BP (4570–4099 cal. BP) (Beta

119788), at −1.60m OD to −1.55m OD. The last flood event in the peat dates to *c* 3450–3350 cal. BP based on the same assumption, but using the depositional rate between Beta 119788 and the date of 2290±90 BP (2707–2069 cal. BP) (Beta 119786) recorded at −0.60m OD to −0.55m OD.

Water levels appear to have gradually risen from the Late Bronze Age (−0.88m OD), and accumulation until at least 1800 cal. BP (pottery recovered adjacent to a feature cut from within the organic muds has been identified as 1st- and 2nd-century AD Verulamium ware) changed from predominantly peat to organic mud. Nevertheless, the Union Street site almost certainly remained a back swamp at the margin of the floodplain, but flood frequency is likely to have increased, while the formation of semi-permanent pools will have also been a characteristic not previously seen. Indeed the decline in organic content from −1.20m OD at 80% to around 30%, immediately below the organic muds, also suggests that flooding of the peat surface had gradually increased from *c* 3200 cal. BP. Organic material within the muds probably accumulated as a result of both *in situ* plant growth and decay, and also from locally transported plant material incorporated in flood waters. Sand-sized particles within the sediments from this period attest to occasional higher-energy flood events, but there is no evidence from the sequence for scouring, and deposition seems to have been more or less continuous. However, the sand content of the organic muds (and indeed the underlying peats) does not seem to have led to variations in χ^{lf} values which remain uniformly low throughout the lower part of the sequence.

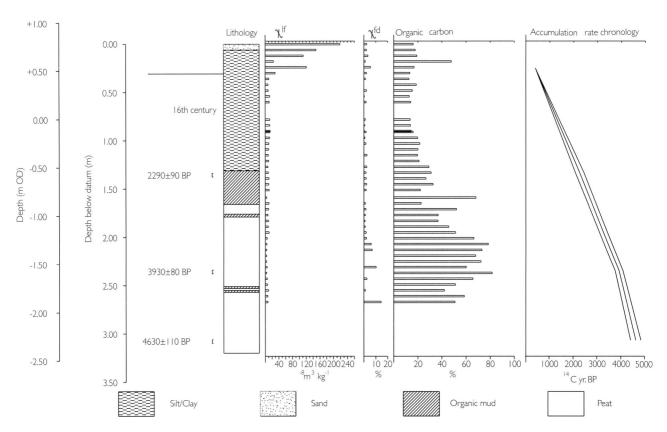

Fig 33 Lithological diagram from Union Street, west Southwark

At the top of the organic mud sequence (−0.53m OD) is an unconformity. Lack of dating evidence from the overlying sediments means that the length of any hiatus cannot be judged, but diatom assemblages either side of the contact are similar, suggesting continuity of deposition mechanism. These sediments comprise thickly bedded sequences of dark grey silts and clays, locally rich in mollusc shell. Particle-size analysis demonstrates constant fluctuations in the relative proportions of silt and clay, although it is possible that the deposits are coarsening upwards in a similar manner to that observed at Joan Street. Notably sand contents are locally high, suggesting that higher-energy depositional events (possibly as a result of storms) occurred, particularly in the medieval period. The deposits have slightly higher χ^{lf} values than the underlying organic stratigraphy as a result of a higher mineral content, although there is little significant variation in either these or organic carbon content until the upper 0.20m of the layer. The sediment morphology and the nature of the molluscan assemblages suggest that deposition occurred as a result of flooding from the adjacent river. By this time, Union Street must have been located well within the floodplain, and have been subject to inundation on a frequent basis. Initially, flooding seems to have occurred in relatively low-energy conditions, although in addition to the particle-size data discussed above, there is a general morphological trend for increasingly poorly sorted deposits with decreasing depth − particularly above 0.0m OD − suggesting that energy levels increased with time. Above +0.40m OD there is evidence for human input into the sediments in the form of domestic rubbish such as oyster shell, charcoal and ceramic fragments. Many of the latter are fluvially reworked Roman types among a ceramic assemblage that is otherwise dominated by 16th-century and later wares. The later ceramics were almost certainly thrown on to the accreting floodplain from adjacent habitation, while the former were transported over longer distances by the river. Indeed, there is little doubt that by the medieval period at the latest, ceramics (particularly of Roman fabrics) were a significant component of the Thames's clastic content (Wilkinson in prep) and were thus regularly deposited by flood events. The inclusion of both directly deposited artefacts and river-transported 'microartefacts' (Stein & Teltser 1989) is also clearly seen in the sedimentological records where there are sharp peaks and troughs in both the organic carbon and χ^{lf} curve. Rapidly oscillating records of this nature are typical of channel margin archaeological sediments and represent alternate depositions of deliberately deposited material and flood-transported, fine-grained sediments. χ^{lf} values of greater than 160^{-8} m³kg⁻¹ are also characteristic of human activity, and are in this case almost certainly a product of microartefact incorporation.

The clay/silt sequence at Union Street is unconformably capped at +0.72m OD by a poorly sorted sand, rich in coarse clastic components and including large quantities of cultural material such as bone, oyster shell and pottery. The latter

date to the period 1550–1650 and include the Tudor period Brown ware fabric as well as green-glazed wares. Magnetic susceptibility data provide further evidence for human involvement in the formation of this layer with values exceeding 200^{-8} m³kg⁻¹, probably as a result of both burning activities and the incorporation of ceramic fragments. Therefore this stratum is likely to be a deliberately deposited levelling horizon placed on the floodplain to remove the site from any risk of flooding. Although no sampling was undertaken on horizons at greater elevations than +0.78m OD, field description suggests that these mainly relate to a succession of ploughsoils and indeed, as has already been stated, documentary records suggest that the area comprised open fields until the middle 1700s. Therefore some 0.5m of soil seem to have formed between the first use of the area as farmland − probably in the early 17th century − and the construction of houses in the mid 18th century.

Pollen biostratigraphy

The peats and overlying organic sediments examined span the period from approximately 5600–4980 cal. BP at −2.27m OD to 2695–2065 cal. BP at −0.60m OD. A total of five local pollen assemblage zones have been recognised (Fig 34).

UNION:1 −2.30 − −2.0m OD *Ulmus-Quercus-Tilia*

Arboreal pollen is dominant (to 82%). This zone is characterised by maximum values of *Ulmus* (5%) and *Tilia* (to 40%) along with relatively high values of *Quercus* (45%) and *Corylus avellana* type (increases throughout to 35%). Also present is *Pinus* (to 5%). Herbaceous diversity is low but there are minor peaks of Poaceae (to 10%) with *Plantago lanceolata* and Lactucae. Small numbers of Cereal type pollen are recorded. Marsh taxa are dominated by *Alnus* (45%) with small numbers of Cyperaceae, *Typha/Sparganium*, *Typha latifolia* and *Alisma* type. Spore values of *Pteridium* and *Dryopteris* type are higher than in the subsequent zone (18% and 13% respectively). *Polypodium vulgare* is also important.

UNION:2 −2.0 − −1.46m OD *Quercus-Tilia-Corylus avellana* type

This zone is defined by reductions of *Ulmus*, *Pinus* and *Tilia* and herbs (Poaceae) noted in zone 1. Conversely, *Corylus avellana* type expands to its highest values (50%). *Quercus* (50%) and *Tilia* remain important. The latter declines to <10% in the lower half of the zone but subsequently peaks to 30% (−1.85 to −1.60m OD). This is designated as a pollen-assemblage sub-zone (1) and subsequently declines to 15–12%. There is a constant but sporadic record of *Pinus* and *Ulmus*. Herbs are at their lowest diversity and percentage values. There is, however, a constant record of Poaceae. Cereal pollen shows a small peak at the top of the zone with Poaceae (to 10%) and has been designated as a pasz (2) (−1.00 to −1.4m OD). Mire taxa remain dominated by *Alnus* (fluctuating 25–65%).

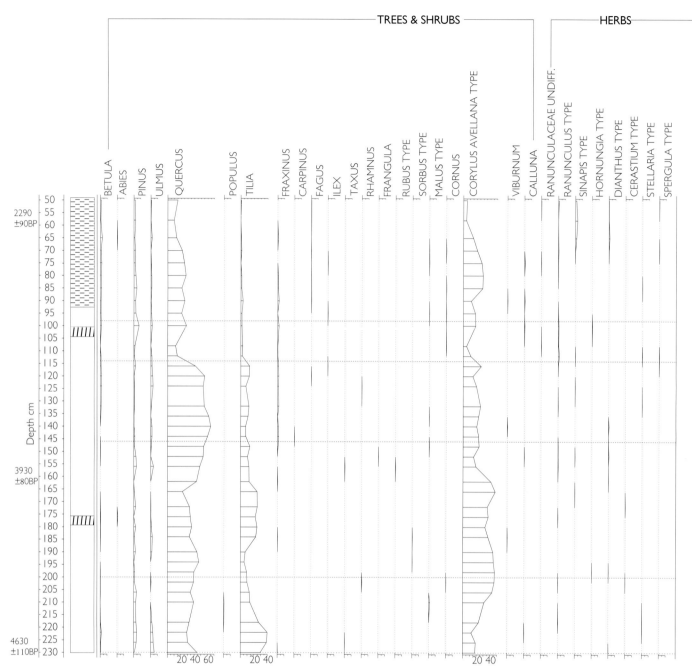

Fig 34 Pollen diagram from Union Street, west Southwark

UNION:3 −1.46 − −1.14m OD *Quercus-Tilia-Fraxinus*

Quercus attains its highest values (to 66%) along with *Tilia* (15%) and *Corylus avellana* type (25%). *Fraxinus* expands and becomes constant (5%). There are relatively few herbs. A peak of *Hedera* (ivy) occurs at −1.25 to −1.20m OD. Marsh taxa remain dominated by *Alnus* which attains its highest values at the top of the zone (87%). Cyperaceae is the only continuous marsh taxon.

UNION:4 −1.14 − −0.98m OD **Poaceae-Cyperaceae-Pteridium aquilinum**

There are significant declines in tree pollen taxa with *Quercus* and *Tilia* declining sharply at −1.13m OD to 10% and 5% respectively. There is also some reduction in *Corylus avellana* type (to 10%). Conversely, there is some expansion of *Pinus*. The zone is, however, characterised by the sharp overall

expansion of herbs, including especially *Chenopodium* type, *Plantago lanceolata* (10%), Lactucae (10%), Poaceae (60%) and Cereal type (15%). In the marsh category, *Alnus* declines to 15% while there is a strong expansion of Cyperaceae and *Typha/Sparganium* with some increase in diversity. There are declines in *Polypodium vulgare* and *Dryopteris* type but a marked peak of *Pteridium aquilinum* (to 77%).

UNION:5 −0.98 − −0.50m OD *Chenopodium-Poaceae-Cyperaceae*

This zone corresponds with lithostratigraphic changes. Herbs are more diverse and dominant (to 85%). There is, however, some recovery of trees and shrubs with *Quercus* and *Corylus avellana* type reaching peaks of 30% and 25% respectively. *Chenopodium* continues from the base of zone 4 and expands to 9% at −0.55m OD.

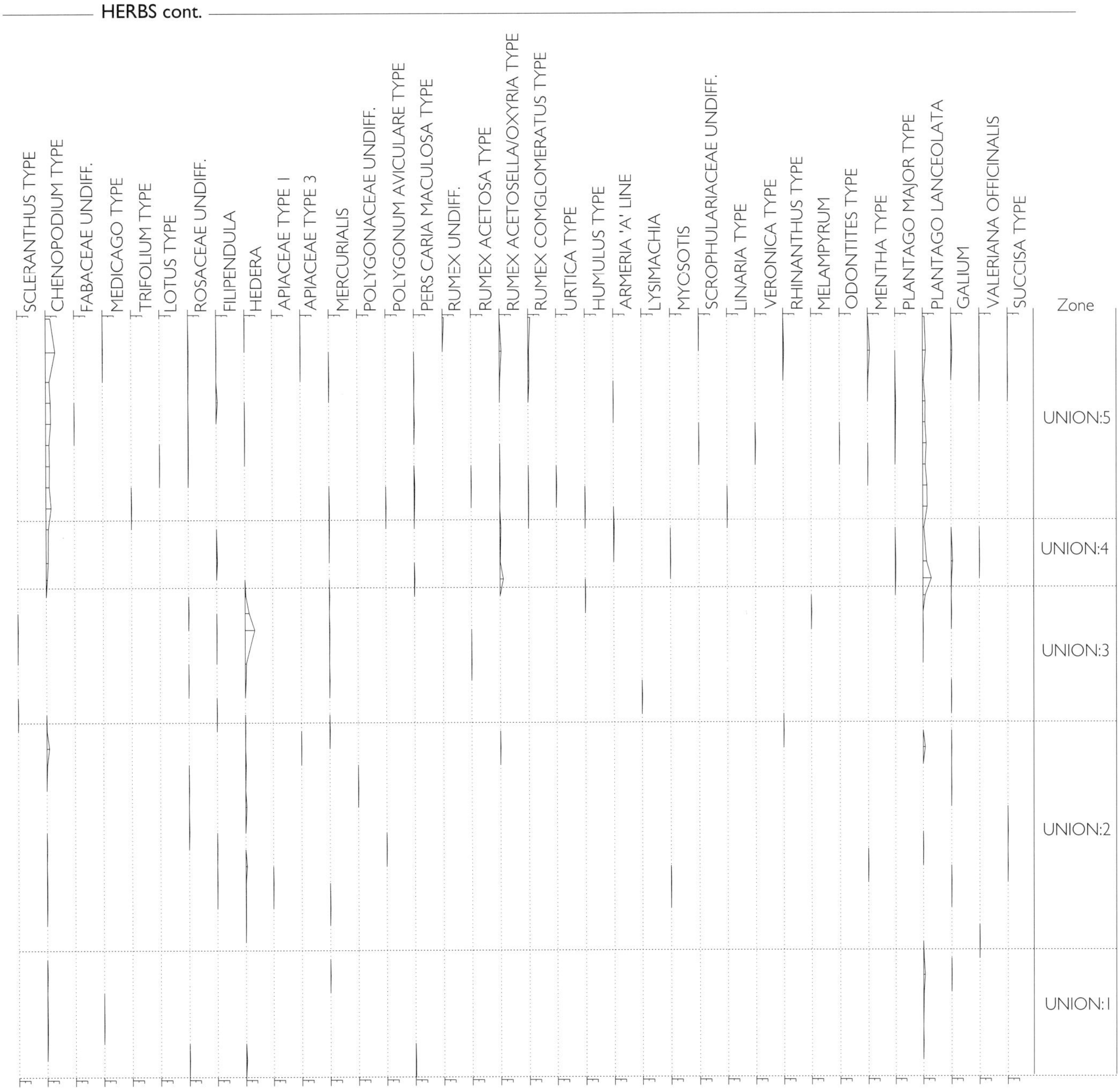

—— HERBS cont. ——

SCLERANTHUS TYPE · CHENOPODIUM TYPE · FABACEAE UNDIFF. · MEDICAGO TYPE · TRIFOLIUM TYPE · LOTUS TYPE · ROSACEAE UNDIFF. · FILIPENDULA · HEDERA · APIACEAE TYPE 1 · APIACEAE TYPE 3 · MERCURIALIS · POLYGONACEAE UNDIFF. · POLYGONUM AVICULARE TYPE · PERS CARIA MACULOSA TYPE · RUMEX UNDIFF. · RUMEX ACETOSA TYPE · RUMEX ACETOSELLA/OXYRIA TYPE · RUMEX COMGLOMERATUS TYPE · URTICA TYPE · HUMULUS TYPE · ARMERIA 'A' LINE · LYSIMACHIA · MYCSOTIS · SCROPHULARIACEAE UNDIFF. · LINARIA TYPE · VERONICA TYPE · RHINANTHUS TYPE · MELAMPYRUM · ODONTITES TYPE · MENTHA TYPE · PLANTAGO MAJOR TYPE · PLANTAGO LANCEOLATA · GALIUM · VALERIANA OFFICINALIS · SUCCISA TYPE

Zone

UNION:5
UNION:4
UNION:3
UNION:2
UNION:1

(Fig 34 cont)

In addition to the overall herb diversity, *Plantago lanceolata*, Lactucae, Poaceae (60%) and Cereal type (15%) are the principal taxa. A single grain of *Secale cereale* is present. Marsh taxa remain dominated by Cyperaceae (23%) while *Alnus* continues to decline (to 5%). There are also aquatic macrophytes present, including *Nymphaea* (water lily), *Nuphar* (water lily), *Potamogeton* cf *Lemna*. The high *Pteridium* values of zone 4 are much reduced (10–15%) with *Dryopteris* and *Equisetum*. Of note is the increase in derived, pre-Quaternary palynomorphs.

Diatom biostratigraphy

Eighteen samples were initially scanned from Union Street. As in the Joan Street sequence, diatoms were found to be poorly preserved in the peats, here covering the deposits occurring between −2.3m OD and −0.6m OD. However,

fragmentary or dissolved diatom remains were found in some of the peat levels and well-preserved diatom assemblages were present in sections of the overlying organic muds and silt/clays (Fig 35). In the basal part of the peat, below −1.12m OD, the assessment found remains of heavily silicified diatom taxa, particularly freshwater or terrestrial taxa such as *Pinnularia* spp. Polyhalobous species were also present in the peat and this indicated that there was contact with the estuary. Diatom analysis focused on the section of the sequence between −1.12m and −0.38m OD.

The samples examined from between −1.12m OD and −1.02m OD are dominated either by freshwater diatoms and taxa of unknown salinity preference or only by the latter group. Polyhalobous, mesohalobous and halophilous taxa are absent and it is therefore probable, from the type and generic composition of the taxa of the unknown salinity

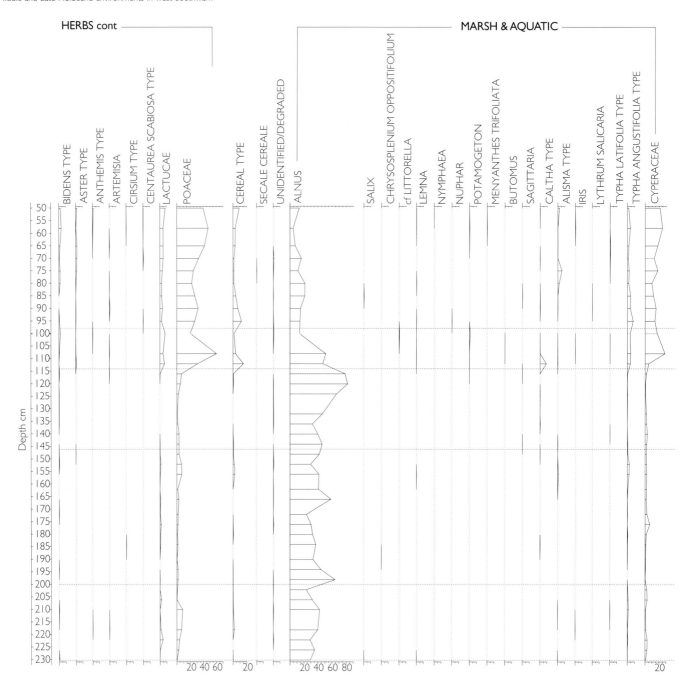

(Fig 34 cont)

group (*eg Amphora* sp and *Gomphonema* sp), that all the diatoms represent freshwater or semi-terrestrial freshwater habitats. The remainder of the sequence from just below −1.0m OD (top of the peat) to the top shows a number of diatom-assemblage changes resulting from salinity and habitat changes.

Throughout this part of the sequence, oligohalobous indifferent diatoms are the dominant group, varying between *c* 30–70% abundance. Marine and brackish species are present at significant frequencies from approximately −1.0m OD and therefore tidal conditions can be inferred for the whole of the later period of accumulation. However, the percentage of polyhalobous taxa declines from around 15% at −1.02m OD to less than 2% at the top. The input of these planktonic, outer estuary taxa – for example *Paralia sulcata, Cymatosira belgica,*

Rhaphoneis spp and *Thalassionema nitzschiodes* – represents a background input of allochthonous taxa and confirms the tidal nature of the environment. The cumulative percentage of mesohalobous taxa, dominated by the brackish-water species *Cyclotella striata* (Fig 36), mirrors the total of marine diatoms with maxima at depths of approximately −1.00m OD, − 0.72m OD and −0.45m OD. The minima of freshwater diatoms coincide with the maxima of marine and brackish diatom abundance, and maxima of oligohalobous indifferent taxa occur in the intervening periods. In addition, therefore, to the overall decline in the input of outer estuary taxa, which perhaps suggests a longer-term downstream migration of the tidal head, there may have been intervening periods of marine transgression reflected by the enhanced transport of marine and brackish plankton to the site. The idea that the uppermost

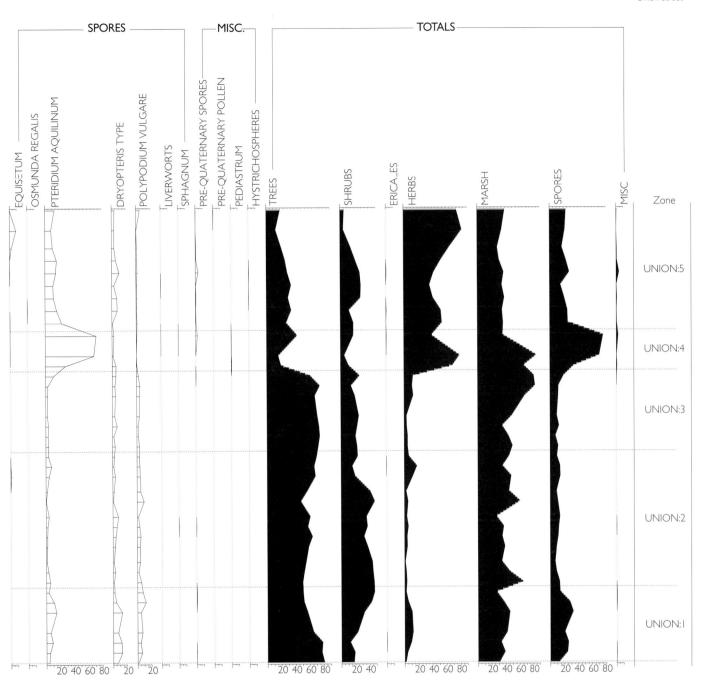

(Fig 34 cont)

Discussion

sediments represent the least saline phase in the sequence is supported by the presence at low abundances of a number of oligohalobous indifferent to halophobous and halophobous *Eunotia* spp. Elsewhere, diatoms such as *Cocconeis disculus* which has maxima of almost 20% both at the base and towards the top of the profile indicate that freshwater to slightly brackish conditions and a shallow water depth allowed the growth of a significant macrophyte flora which would have provided a habitat for this species.

Discussion

Unfortunately as the sediments underlying the peats could not be excavated for safety reasons, it is not possible to discuss this sequence in as much detail as the sequences from Joan Street

and Canada Water which are comparable in many ways. Peat formation had begun by the Neolithic at a depth of at least −2.3m OD. This appears to have occurred as thickly bedded horizontal stratigraphy rather than in a cut-off channel. Formation continues almost uninterrupted until −0.88m OD, *c* 2300 cal. BP (Early Iron Age), when the organic content at the floodplain margin sediment decreased. Several brief flood events have been identified within the organic sequence at *c* 4700–4450 cal. BP and subsequently *c* 3450–3350 cal. BP, but otherwise this sequence does not appear to have been overtly influenced by the river. This is consistent with the sampling site being located slightly above high water in a semi-terrestrial situation. Thus, organic deposition outstripped the rate of rising river levels and, with the exception of several discrete flood events depositing fine sand/clay/silt units,

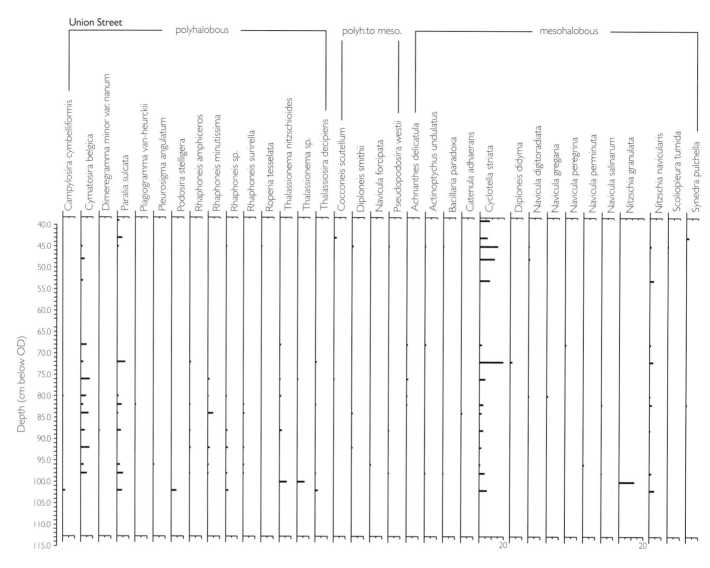

Fig 35 Diatom diagram from Union Street, west Southwark

remained relatively dry. Very limited diatom remains were recovered from the peats. However, although the majority of identifiable fragments were of freshwater taxa, the presence of several polyhalobous species indicates that tidal processes could have operated at a relatively early date, although it is more likely that these are derived from the flooding events previously discussed and so are atypical of general accretion.

The pollen sequence covers the Middle Neolithic to Iron Age, that is, from immediately after the primary elm decline at *c* 6300–5750 cal. BP to *c* 3200 cal. BP. Embodied in this profile is evidence of the principal late prehistoric woodland/shrub communities and their progressive demise in response to forest clearance, agriculture, secondary woodland development and RSL/base-level changes. Representation of the basic woodland prior to extensive clearance is seen in zone 1. Percentages of lime are at their highest and given the marked under-representation of this taxon in pollen spectra (Andersen 1970; 1973), it is likely that lime woodland was dominant in the local area. Oak and hazel were possibly also important constituents of this

community or in separate discrete areas, perhaps of heavier soils along the floodplain margins or on drier areas of fen carr. Sharply declining elm in the basal zone is interesting and enigmatic since it is not clear whether this is the primary elm decline or a secondary elm decline after a period of Middle Neolithic regeneration (Scaife 1987). Given the date of 4630±110 BP (5594–4974 cal. BP), the latter seems more likely as a regional date of *c* 6300–5750 cal. BP is usual for the primary elm decline. The on-site habitat during the early phase of peat deposition was alder carr which, with the dominance of woodland noted, suggests that the pollen catchment was restricted. In spite of this, however, small numbers of cereal pollen grains and *Plantago lanceolata* are indicative of local activity in the later Neolithic.

Thereafter, the pattern of woodland change is complex, with notable periods of lime reduction and regeneration at different time periods. This is dealt with in more detail in Part 3. Briefly, however, it appears that there was a decline in areas of lime from *c* 5200 cal. BP which may have caused expansion of hazel woodland scrub. A phase of regeneration occurs

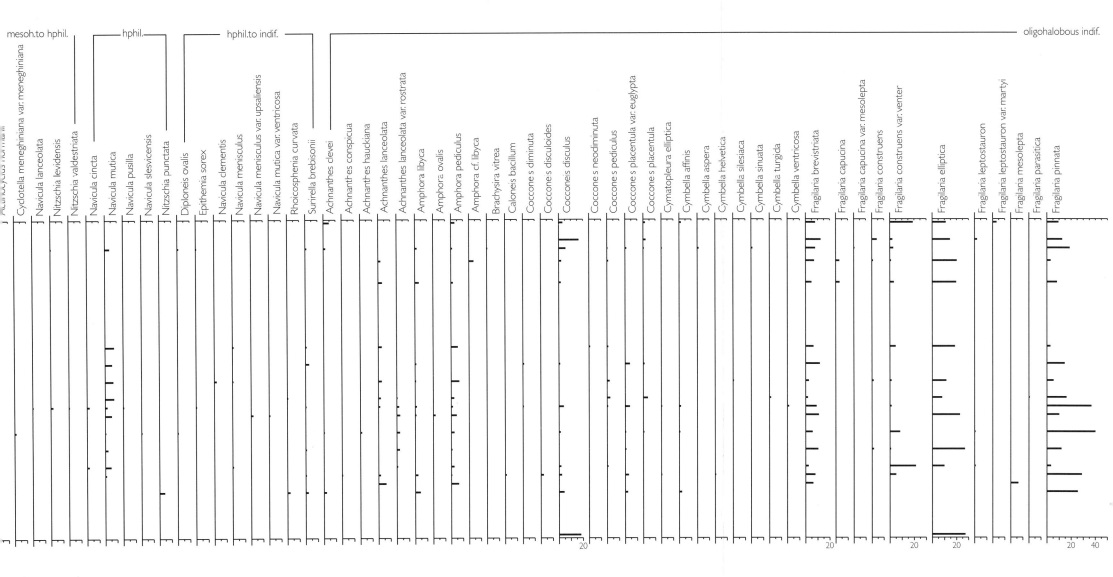

(Fig 35 cont)

between −2.3 and −2.05m OD (pasz at an estimated date of *c* 4750–4350 cal. BP). There are further reductions after *c* 4250 cal. BP which are associated with an increase in secondary *Fraxinus* woodland. A final reduction of *Tilia* occurs at −1.55m OD with values down to <5% for the remainder of the profile. This marks the final decline in lime and, although not specifically dated here, is likely to relate to 4200 cal. BP, based on accumulation rates in Fig 33, a date commensurate with the lime decline at other London and regional sites.

Subsequent to this event, woodland communities comprised of *Quercus*, *Corylus avellana* and *Fraxinus* are the most important. This was maintained until the top of the pollen profile dated at *c* 2350 cal. BP (*ie* Middle to Late Iron Age). Change in sedimentation from peat to organic muds is also reflected in pollen taphonomic changes, for example by extension of the pollen catchment through the inclusion of fluvially transported pollen and spores. These include *Pinus* and possibly *Fagus* and *Ilex*, although for the latter, any opening of the woodland/forest canopy would also allow ingress of pollen from further afield. Such opening of the canopy (on site) is reflected by a sharp

reduction of alder (carr) in pasz 4 and increase of the fen marsh taxa including Cyperaceae *Typha/Sparganium* and *Alisma*.

Changes in woodland character noted above may also be attributed to both anthropogenic effects and RSL rise. Clearly, for the bulk of the peat sequence, the changes noted are attributed to human deforestation and are mirrored by the continuous but low frequency of cereal pollen and associated weed taxa (*eg Plantago*), wild grasses and *Pteridium aquilinum*. It is notable that there are peaks of these associated with the different phases of lime decline. However, changes in the peat, from *c* −1.55m OD and manifested by the falling organic carbon contents, show a response to local increase of base level at *c* 4200 cal. BP causing the habitat to become wetter. This is illustrated by the progressive reduction of *Alnus* and perhaps caused by the alder carr constantly being drier further away from the sample site as conditions became wetter with aquatic herb/fen vegetation community developing in this part of the floodplain. From pasz 4 alder carr gave way to open grass, sedge, reed fen with reed mace and burr reed, a change which coincides with the first countable diatom assemblages

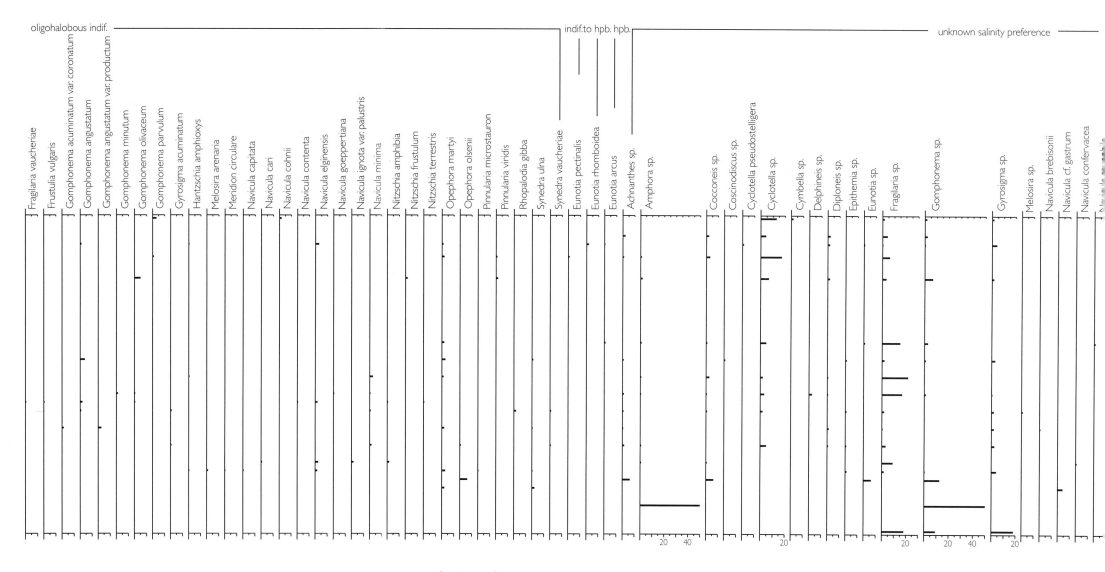

(Fig 35 cont)

which indicate accretion in freshwater environments. Zone Union:4 may be a transitional, more freshwater phase with fluvially transported bracken spores (Peck 1973) characteristic of fluvially derived sediment and the presence of freshwater algal *Pediastrum* which are only found in this zone. Aquatic macrophytes are also noted (*Lemna, Potamogeton, Littorella*). Indeed there is some evidence for changes (positive tendency) in RSL on a regional scale. From zone Union:4, *Chenopodium* type increase which, along with *Armeria* and Hystrichospheres, are indicative of estuarine conditions. However, as the diatom floras are dominated by oligohalobous indifferent taxa until −1.02m OD, it is likely that, locally, the river remained dominantly freshwater. Above −1.02m OD diatom evidence is supported by the pollen data; marine and brackish species initially peak and then decrease in proportion and this trend is continuous to the top of the sequence. This swing takes place following a storm event at *c* 3450–3350 cal. BP. Thereafter, the site was dominated by a combination of estuarine and freshwater processes, although the gradual reduction in polyhalobous species indicates lessening tidal influence at Union Street from the Late Bronze Age until the late medieval period.

In the estuarine clay/silts which cap the organic sequence, there is grain-size evidence of increasing energies, perhaps suggestive of periodic storms. It is not until the 16th century that any sign of human activity is seen in the stratigraphy, where deliberately dumped deposits containing domestic waste were used, presumably to reclaim and raise up the land, probably as flood defences. The area appears to have stabilised and developed a soil that appears to have been farmed until the 18th century when the area was finally built upon.

Conclusions: the sedimentation and environment of west Southwark

The sampled sequence at Union Street appears to have been initially dominated by semi-terrestrial processes. It is very unfortunate that it was not possible to sample the units underlying the peat and thereby establish the date of organic

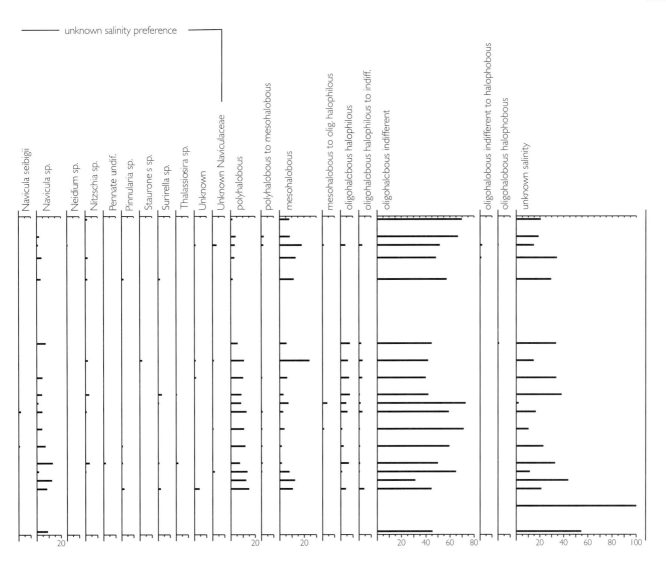

(Fig 35 cont)

formation, and also to establish the depositional conditions prior to peat formation. This would have led to a more valid comparison with the site at Joan Street.

The peat formation reflected in this sequence accumulated over a period of approximately 2000 years, extended to c 2300 years with the accretion of the subsequent organic mud. It is suggested that the organic mud marks the transition from semi-terrestrial alder carr conditions to inundation by the Thames. It has been possible to date this transitional period to approximately 300 years in length, while organic accumulation of the local vegetation stands fought it out with silting incurred through Thames-side flooding. According to extrapolated accumulation rates, the swing to tidal inundation began in the later Bronze Age (c 4200 cal. BP) which corresponds roughly with the information derived from the analysis of the Westminster sediments, although the suggestion there is that tidal influence was present slightly earlier. As Westminster is located slightly upstream from Union Street, it seems likely that tidal influence was felt first at Union Street and therefore vagaries in dating may be causing the apparent anomaly. Looking at this point in a wider context, however, the date corresponds extremely well

with the three-stage model proposing estuary expansion at c 4200 cal. BP in the Thames, Severn and Southampton Water (Long *et al* submitted). This would suggest that the changes occurring in the Thames at this point, evidenced from Southwark and Westminster, were part of wider, regional trends. The early historic period is likely to have been one of eroding, as well as accreting, sediments. Although Roman pottery was recovered from this site in waterlain deposits, it is probable that this is in fact part of foreshore and river deposits of the medieval period, deposited by continued flooding prior to reclamation in the late medieval period.

The patterns of environmental change shown from the examination of Union Street and Joan Street are similar. Although sediments underlying the organic muds were not available from Union Street, both sequences show a transition from water-dominated to semi-terrestrial conditions. In terms of date, this is slightly confused at Joan Street, but has taken place by c 5300 cal. BP, while peat formation began at Union Street by at least 5100 cal. BP, but is present at a slightly lower altitude at Union Street. This again is likely to reflect asynchronous 'filling' of the floodplain as the Thames migrated northwards. The vegetation changes shown in the peat

Fig 36 Electron micrograph of Cyclotella striata

sequences are generally consistent, with the very interesting exception that there is no direct evidence for cereal cultivation from Union Street, while there is from Joan Street. This not only suggests that activity is concentrated in the western part

of the area (perhaps, significantly, closer to Westminster where there is also evidence for farming), but also demonstrates the local distinctions which may be achieved through pollen analysis. Both sites appear to have gone through a period when the area was subject to flooding, although the very specific events recorded at Union Street were not observed so distinctly at Joan Street. Inundation of the sites appears to have begun before *c* 3450 cal. BP (approximately −1.0m OD), with total inundation taking place at Joan Street *c* 2450 cal. BP (approximately −0.8m OD), and at Union Street taking place at *c* 3200 cal. BP at an altitude of *c* −0.9m OD. These figures indicate that the timing is asynchronous, while the altitude is reasonably consistent. However, differential compaction may have affected the relative variation in height between the two sites. The difference in the dates when the two sites were finally inundated rather than periodically flooded is interesting, and it is possible that, while Union Street is likely to have been flooded first by tidal waters (being further downstream), the timing of the event at Joan Street may not have been so much later, owing to the error factor and ranges ascribed to ^{14}C dates.

6

Holocene environments in Rotherhithe and Canning Town

Keith Wilkinson, Robert Scaife and Jane Sidell

Introduction

Initially, a series of archaeological interventions was proposed along the stretch of the JLE running from Rotherhithe across the Isle of Dogs and into Canning Town. However, a number of these had to be abandoned owing to difficulties such as excessive contamination which rendered access and particularly sampling unfeasible. Several of these sites were in known areas of important stratigraphy. Durands Wharf on the eastern edge of the Rotherhithe peninsula is located adjacent to a site at Bryan Road (Sidell *et al* 1995) where an important Neolithic and later sequence had been examined. The conclusions derived from this study relate to the study of peat formation and the developing vegetation of this period, and it had been hoped that Durands Wharf would provide more detailed information on these issues. A further case was that of North Greenwich, the new underground station to serve the Millennium Dome (Fig 37). This area was notoriously contaminated as a result of the industrial processes taking place on the peninsula in the past, such as the gasworks. The sedimentary sequences on the site consist of substantial stacks of intercalated peats and waterlain silt/clays (J Bowsher, pers comm and E J Sidell, personal observation). However, it was not safe to sample these sequences. Therefore the site at Canada Water has been taken as the focal point for the eastern stretch of the route, along with data collected from investigations at Canning Town and Culling Road.

The archaeology of Rotherhithe and Canning Town

(Fig 38)

The areas of Rotherhithe and Canning Town do not contain extensive evidence for settlement and activity in the archaeological record. The area was never occupied to the same extent as the central areas of London such as Southwark and the City of London. Isolated prehistoric activity has been recorded through the recovery of stray finds (see Beck 1907). Many of these have been identified through antiquarian sources, for example the discovery of prehistoric bones during the construction of Canada Dock. Several struck flints were recovered from Rupack Street and prehistoric pottery is recorded from Cherry Gardens in Rotherhithe. The evidence from Canning Town is even more scanty with rare Bronze Age artefacts identified, including urns, possibly from a cemetery, but with little other evidence for prehistoric activity (Environmental Resources Ltd 1990).

There is evidence of Roman activity from Rotherhithe, although there is no evidence for any substantial Roman settlement. A structure, possibly an embankment or revetment, was revealed during the construction of the Grand Surrey Canal in 1809. A group of artefacts was discovered at the

Fig 37 North Greenwich Station and the Millennium Dome

interface of peats and river silts at Bryan Road (Sidell *et al* 1995), while a coin hoard was found at Plough Way. The focus of activity in Rotherhithe seems to have been concentrated at the waterside. The date of the first river wall is not conclusively known. Saxon use of the area is inferred through place-name rather than archaeological evidence. The name Rotherhithe is derived from *Aethelreds Hithe*, or Mariners Haven. Another Saxon name, *Redriff*, is thought to have applied to the same area, meaning harbour to offload cattle. Documentary evidence survives mentioning several areas around Canning Town and Stratford, named as *Hame* in 1086. *Hame* obviously develops and expands, for by the next century, the western sector is known as *Westhamme*, the precursor of modern West Ham (Environmental Resources Ltd 1990).

Rotherhithe became more significant in the early medieval period. It seems to have been used for settlement; documents referring to the construction of Edward III's moated manor house at Platform Wharf in 1353 show that a series of old houses were present on the site. Evidence from the post-medieval period suggests that the area was developed as a commercial centre. The construction of the first of the great docks in Rotherhithe was in 1700–3, the Howland Great Wet Dock, but by the end of the century another 10 had been built. This expansion continued and led to significant settlement and the development of service industries to cater for the increased occupation of the area (Cowan 1986).

The Canning Town area is documented as containing marshlands as late as the 18th century, for instance the Laywick and Hendon Hope marshes, but several printing industries developed, including calico and silk-screen printing (Drummond-Murray *et al* 1998). The construction of the Queen Victoria Dock led to the commercial development and increased domestic occupation of Canning Town.

Culling Road

Introduction

The land-use history, even in the recent past, of the Culling Road site is not clear. However, it appears that the site remained 'dry' throughout the later Holocene as a result of the deeply stratified sand and gravel sequences that were deposited during the Devensian cold stage and the Early Holocene. These appear to have formed an effective island within an area of marshland and river, so that in the late 19th century the site was part of the 'seven islands'. In the 14th century the site lay immediately to the south of walled gardens belonging to Edward III's manor of Southwark Park and was probably in use for market gardening from at least this period until the end of the 19th century. At that point terraced houses were built across the site and survived until relatively recently.

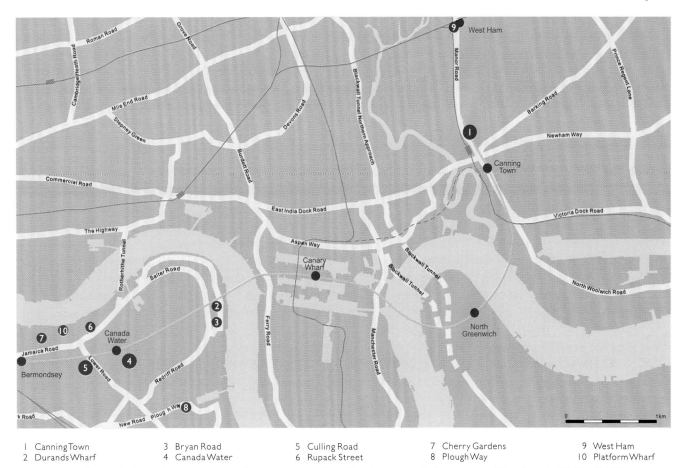

| 1 Canning Town | 3 Bryan Road | 5 Culling Road | 7 Cherry Gardens | 9 West Ham |
| 2 Durands Wharf | 4 Canada Water | 6 Rupack Street | 8 Plough Way | 10 Platform Wharf |

Fig 38 Map of Rotherhithe and Canning Town © Crown copyright. All rights reserved. Corporation of London LA 087254/00/12

Investigations at Culling Road took place prior to the construction of a 30m deep ventilation shaft between 22–30 December 1993, followed by a second phase of archaeological investigation between 27 January – 9 February 1994. A 14m x 9m trench was excavated during the first investigation along with a 2m x 2m testpit, whereas during the second, two trenches 2m wide by 12m and 15m long were examined. Cut features dating on the basis of ceramic inclusions to the late 18th and early 19th centuries were found immediately below the surface and extending down to the sands below. At about +1.2m OD, 0.8m below ground level, were the remnants of a poorly sorted sand horizon, cut through by the post-medieval features described above. Within this deposit were found many charcoal fragments and fire-cracked flints, while in an extension trench two flint blades dating to the Neolithic or Mesolithic and two sherds of Peterborough ware pottery of Late Neolithic date (2500–2000 BC or *c* 4500–4000 cal. BP) were collected. While reworking cannot be discounted these data would seem to suggest that the sand-rich colluvium dates to the later Neolithic period. Cutting from above the Neolithic artefacts was a steep-sided channel found cut to a depth of 0.90m into the underlying sands which contained a single sherd of Roman Grey ware pottery in its fill. This feature took up most of the area of the second-phase excavation trenches, which did not therefore recover any further Neolithic material.

Underlying the archaeological stratigraphy was a 3.5m sequence of initially horizontally bedded and then finely laminated sands comprising the bulk of the eyot, which in turn overlay gravels, presumably of the Shepperton terrace. These sands were revealed in trench section (but were not bottomed) and also in a single borehole, sunk during geotechnical investigations prior to the excavation. Unfortunately there is no dating evidence for the sand sequence except that it predates the Neolithic archaeological layer above. Therefore, the sand sequence cannot easily be correlated with similar sequences elsewhere in London where a chronology has been obtained. Despite these problems four monolith tins were taken from the sand sequence and the palaeochannel and subsequently examined in the laboratory with the primary objective of determining whether any terrestrial surfaces existed within the sequence. As well as detailed description, mass specific magnetic susceptibility measurements and X-radiographs were made of the sequence.

Lithostratigraphy and sedimentology

The gravel found below the sands relating to Culling Eyot was not sampled, although it was noted to outcrop at *c* −2m OD from borehole records. The base of the sampled sequence (+0.53 to −0.12m OD) consisted of a pale yellow 2.5Y7/4 medium sand, darkening (to light brownish-grey 2.5Y6/2) and fining upwards to a silt/fine sand, laminated irregularly throughout with ferruginous medium to coarse sands. Throughout this part of the sequence there are a series of minor discontinuities, which are likely to be the result of short-lived erosional processes operating within the stream channel.

This part of the sequence is likely to have formed in a moderately fast-flowing river with gradual reductions in energy levels upwards. This could have occurred through increasing water depths as a result of a rise in river levels, or more plausibly in this case through increased marginalisation as a result of channel migration away from the sample site. The iron-stained laminae are the product of diagenesis, and most likely caused by subaerial weathering of exposed surfaces. If correct this would suggest that although during this period flow energies were relatively high, stream flow was nevertheless discontinuous – a finding that is perhaps indicative of seasonality, or at least periodicity of water flow.

A further discontinuity separates the fining upwards sequence at 0m OD from a series of horizontally bedded medium and fine sands. These have been diagenetically modified by rooting, and include not only former root holes present as darker mottles within the sediments, but also the actual roots themselves. However, the sands are likely to have originally formed in the same type of moderately rapidly running river as the base of the fining upward sequence discussed above, and are therefore suggestive of a remigration of the river channel towards the sample site. The roots appear to originate from further up in the sequence and there are no indications for the type of subaerial weathering noted in the lowest stratigraphy. In contrast, deposits unconformably overlying the horizontally bedded sands appear to be the source of the roots and are largely terrigenous.

Immediately above the sands (+0.53m OD) and separated from them by a major unconformity is a silt/clay deposit, highly disrupted by rooting, which has resulted in the presence of sand casts derived from material further up sequence. This silt/clay is the first deposit to have formed within a palaeochannel cut into the sands and is almost certainly a low-energy fluvial unit deposited from suspension. However, it has been modified by pedogenesis in the layer above, which indicates that the channel was relatively dry by the time it had filled with sediment (perhaps in the Roman period). The latter consists of a poorly sorted silt-dominated horizon which seems to be the source of all rooting. The poorly sorted nature of the deposit suggests that it is in part reworked as a result of colluvial erosion, while sufficient pedogenetic properties exist to suggest that the erosional material later underwent soil formation and was buried by later archaeological activity. For colluviation to have occurred and a soil to have formed conditions must have been relatively dry and it is therefore likely that these processes occurred a long time after the formation of the eyot. Therefore, archaeological use of the site in both the Neolithic and Roman periods took place on a terrestrial ground surface.

Magnetic susceptibility measurements indicate that no long-lived phases of weathering occurred within the sand sequence, and indeed values were low throughout, even in strata thought to represent palaeosols. These properties are similarly indicative of the absence of direct human activity during aggradation, although the relatively coarse grain size of the deposits (predominantly fine and medium sands), may in part also be responsible for the low readings (Thompson & Oldfield 1986).

Discussion

The largest problem when further discussing the Culling Road stratigraphy is the absence of dating evidence from the pre-archaeological stratigraphy. This is especially unfortunate in view of the apparent changes that seem to have occurred in fluvial process, from in-channel sedimentation of sands, interspersed with terrestrial weathering and channel migration, to colluviation and pedogenesis. A few suggestions as to chronology can be made on the basis of sediment morphology, stratigraphic position and limits placed by the artefacts, which indicate that the sands date to the Neolithic period or earlier. Such complexity of process as found in the sand stratigraphy is typical of dune development within a large river (eyots are commonly formed from fluvial dune systems) (Collinson 1986), but in the Thames is more characteristic of areas of central (eg Westminster – Thorney Island) and western (eg Chiswick Eyot) London than areas to the east. For example Early Holocene (ie pre-7000 cal. BP) dune sequences recently examined at Silvertown (Wilkinson et al 2000) and Erith (E J Sidell et al unpublished data) appear to be structurally simple, consisting solely of horizontally bedded sands with no size trend properties, whereas, as has already been demonstrated for Westminster, sequences here are more complicated. One of the reasons given for the complexity of dune systems in central and western London has been the almost continuous development of such features from the Early Holocene to the Bronze Age and the impact on this process of rising sea level during the Middle and later Holocene. Such a scenario cannot be put forward for Culling Road, located in the east, which must have been affected by rising RSL significantly earlier. Therefore, the Culling Road dune system must reflect changes in behaviour of the freshwater river for this locality in the Early Holocene not seen at other sites, but which are thought to be characteristic of sandy bedform meandering rivers (see Miall 1996).

Canada Water

Introduction

Excavations were carried out during a five-week period from May to July 1991 by the DGLA prior to the construction of Canada Water Station (see Fig 38). The location now lies to the immediate west of Surrey Commercial Docks, and until recently the station site had been partially occupied by Canada Docks which were built some 11 years after Surrey Commercial Docks in 1875. Prior to 1875 the site would seem to have been occupied in part by a late 18th- or early 19th-century building of unknown function, although cartographic sources suggest that prior to this the whole area had consisted of intertidal creeks and channel marginal marshland. A series of boreholes sunk prior to the excavation indicate that a sequence of some

7.5m Holocene deposits overlay Pleistocene river gravels. A considerable proportion of the upper part of this stratigraphy consists of estuarine muds which must relate to pre-19th-century intertidal environments, and are thus evidence of their longevity. Also found within the borehole stratigraphy was a thin peat – which subsequently became the main focus of the sampling programme – some 5.8m below ground surface.

The initial excavation trench had a footprint of 30m x 15m and as it was excavated downwards from a surface of around 5m OD, was stepped in by 1.5m after each 1.2m depth. The stratigraphy revealed by this process consisted of around 1.2m thickness of modern rubble and service ducts relating to the previous dock structures, overlying 3m or more of deliberately deposited silt/clays and sands. The latter contained 19th-century bricks and are almost certainly levelling horizons associated with measures taken in 1875 to raise the ground surface for construction of Canada Dock. Below the deliberately deposited material was a 0.25m thick organic horizon of domestic rubbish, containing 18th-century ceramics. This is likely to be a midden formed as a result of the disposal of refuse from adjacent properties when the area was still occupied by marsh. In contrast, the deposits found in two separate testpits excavated below this layer, that is, from +0.10m downwards, formed entirely as the result of tidal and channel marginal processes. The stratigraphy consisted of up to 1m of mineral silt/clays overlying organic muds and peat dating from around 4000 cal. BP, which in turn sealed further fine-grained silt and sand deposits. The peat contained several large pieces of wood, including oak, while a red deer antler was also found on the peat surface. A single archaeological feature was found in the lower stratigraphy in the form of a ditch cutting downwards from the surface of the silt/clay above the peat. The fill consisted of further clay and contained a wooden tile, a bronze pin and an undiagnostic sherd of prehistoric pottery. Nevertheless, as Horwood's map of 1799 clearly shows a ditch in a similar position, and as the ditch was cut from the top of the clay (which on comparative grounds is unlikely to have ceased forming before the post-medieval period), this would seem to be a relatively late feature. As stated above, the peat and associated deposits were targeted for monolith sampling in order to reconstruct the pre-18th-century environment. This was carried out by accessing sections from within one of the testpits and sampling it through a gap left in the shuttering.

Lithostratigraphy

(Fig 39)

Although it was not possible to sample the gravel at the base of the sequence, the overlying sand was collected in the basal monolith, but the vertical extent of the sand could not be determined beyond −1.95m OD. This proved to be a well-sorted, horizontally bedded, olive-grey (5Y4/2) fine to medium sand, containing occasional plant macro remains. These deposits are most likely to have formed in a relatively rapidly moving stream, while the plant remains were probably derived from erosion of the banks, or could have been washed

in during periods of lower-energy flow. The sands fine upwards and darken, so that by −1.60m OD they are dominated by silt and are of a very dark grey (5Y4/1) colour while plant remains continue to occur in moderate quantities. The fining upward trend represents a decrease in energy, which in this case could be either as a result of an increase in water depth, or migration of the river away from the sample site. In the first scenario, sedimentation would have continued within the stream channel as lateral accretion; in the second, as fallout from suspension following overbank flooding events (vertical accretion). Unfortunately, no sedimentary structures have been retained by the silts, which makes further interpretation difficult. However, charcoal and rooting were noted in the field descriptions, which would appear to suggest the operation of terrestrial processes and thus favouring the overbank model of accretion.

Unconformably overlying the silt/sand sequence at −1.30m OD is a series of peats and organic muds. Although the presence of an unconformity would appear to suggest erosion of the surface of the underlying silt/clays, this may have been minimal. Indeed, accretion of an organic mud above the overbank silts is most likely to simply reflect a continuation of the processes previously operating, with the sample site becoming increasingly marginalised from the river channel. The organic muds almost certainly formed at the interface between riverine and terrestrial environments, allowing plant growth, but were nevertheless occasionally inundated by flood water. It is notable that between −1.30m OD and −1.20m OD there is evidence for occasional erosive inundation of the organic muds by relatively high-energy flood waters in the form of coarse sand and granular clast laminae. Above −1.20m OD the organic mud is overlain by a highly humified peat, which is likely to have formed by a further continuation of the marginalisation process. The peat would have formed just above the floodplain and would have been inundated by flood water only on an irregular basis, and would thus have been a highly suitable location for plant growth. Dating of the initiation of peat growth is provided by a single ^{14}C date of 3650±100 BP (4245–3692 cal. BP) (Beta 122968), at −1.19m OD to −1.21m OD, suggesting that the peat was forming in the Late Neolithic and/or Early Bronze Age. The evidence can in turn be used to date a single struck flint found at −1.19m OD, which also confirms the terrestrial nature of the peat surface and indicates that the sample site was utilised by the contemporary population, presumably as hunting territory. Nevertheless peat growth appears to have been relatively short-lived as at −0.93m the peat is conformably overlain by a very dark grey (2.5Y3/1) organic mud, indicating the sample site had resumed a location lower down on the floodplain. The reason for this change in accretion pattern cannot be discerned from the sediments alone, but RSL rise, and the consequent increase in both the width of the floodplain and frequency of flood events, is perhaps the most likely. During this time the sample site is likely to have been once more at an interface between riverine/estuarine and terrestrial environments, although unlike the previous organic mud there is no evidence for high-energy flood events in the form of laminae of coarse particles, and it would appear that flooding was of both greater frequency and lower magnitude.

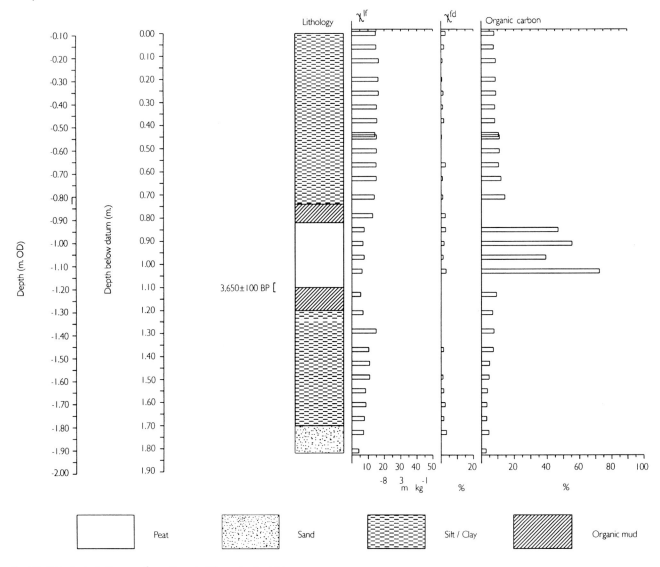

Fig 39 Lithological diagram from Canada Water, Rotherhithe

At −0.85m OD the organic sequence is unconformably overlain by a homogeneous, very dark greyish-brown (2.5Y3/2) silt/clay, marking a return to mineral deposition, almost certainly as a result of sea- and river-level rise. Despite this inferred genesis, freshwater mollusc shells were noted in the deposit, although these were mostly of the ubiquitous *Lymnaea peregra*, which has some tolerance to salinity. This part of the sequence cannot be dated precisely, although accretion had undoubtedly finished by the 18th century when midden deposits covered the site.

Pollen biostratigraphy

Pollen was sparse and poorly preserved in the oxidised peats at the base of the sequence. Consequently the pollen sum (tdlp) counted was low, in the order of 100–220 grains per level, although the pollen counts (*ie* including marsh) were substantially higher. Three pollen assemblages (Fig 40) have been recognised and are characterised as follows from the base of the sequence upwards:

CW:1 −1.27m – −1.17m OD *Quercus-Tilia-Corylus avellana type-Alnus*

Trees and shrubs are dominant (66% and 45% respectively) but decrease progressively throughout this zone. *Tilia* is dominant to 37% in the basal level along with *Quercus* (25%) and *Corylus avellana* type (to 48%). In the wetland category *Alnus* also attains highest values (40% tdlp+marsh). Non-arboreal pollen is at its lowest, increasing upwards through the zone. Poaceae is the main herb taxon increasing to 15%. There are sporadic occurrences of *Plantago lanceolata*, spores of *Pteridium aquilinum*, *Dryopteris* type and *Polypodium vulgare*. The latter is significant in this zone (to 25%).

CW:2 −1.17m – −0.99m OD *Quercus-Corylus avellana type-Poaceae-Alnus*

This zone is delimited by a sharp decline in *Tilia* and the start of a sharp rise in herb totals and diversity. *Quercus* remains important to 30% with *Corylus avellana* type decreasing progressively to 20% and *Tilia* (<5%). There is also an expansion of marsh types including *Typha angustifolia/Sparganium* type and Cyperaceae. *Alnus* type remains important while *Polypodium vulgare* declines sharply.

CW:3 –0.99m – –0.16m OD *Quercus-Corylus avellana* type-Poaceae

In this zone the sampling interval is broad due to the poor pollen preservation in these upper sediments. Consequently only a single broad zone has been recognised. Overall, *Quercus* remains the most important tree with constant *Corylus avellana* type. *Alnus* remains present at relatively low levels. Poaceae, Cereal type Poaceae, *Secale cereale*, Lactucae, *Chenopodium* type, *Sinapis* type and *Plantago lanceolata* are the most important herbs. Within the marsh category, Cyperaceae are important in the lower part of the zone (to 60%) but are diminished upwards. There is evidence of aquatics and marginal aquatics (*Potamogeton, Typha latifolia, Typha/Sparganium* type). Spores comprise *Dryopteris* type and *Pteridium aquilinum* with sporadic *Polypodium* and sporadic *Osmunda regalis, Sphagnum* and Liverworts. Pre-Quaternary palynomorphs, Hystrichospheres and algal *Pediastrum* are present.

Diatom biostratigraphy

Twelve samples were examined for their diatom content during the assessment stage of the project, although due to poor valve preservation no detailed analysis was undertaken. Given the low valve numbers the validity of any inferences of salinity made from the assemblage type is open to debate. Despite the examination of several samples from sediments underlying the peat only a single identifiable valve of the freshwater benthic species *Achnanthes minutissima* was found at −1.45m OD. Therefore the sands found at this elevation are, as suggested above, likely to be of freshwater derivation, although the poor valve preservation would appear to be more indicative of a shallow alluvial, that is, floodplain environment, rather than a deep-water channel fill. Further valves of *Achnanthes minutissima* were found together with another oligohalobous indifferent genus, *Aulacoseira*, at the surface of the peat (−0.85m OD) indicating freshwater flooding of the peat surface. However, a single valve fragment of *Nitzschia navicularis*, a mesohalobous species, was found at the same level, indicating some tidal influence. In the organic muds overlying the peat at −0.80m OD a diverse oligohalobous indifferent assemblage was recovered – including *Aulacoseira* sp, *Fragilaria* cf *brevistriata* (Fig 41), *Fragilaria* cf *construens* var. *binodis, Tabellaria flocculosa, Nitzschia* cf *recta* and *Achnanthes microcephala* – suggesting that deposition during this phase was still at the margins of a freshwater river. Valve preservation in the overlying inorganic silt/clays was very poor, with identifiable valves being limited to strata above −0.30m OD. Nevertheless it was notable that in this area of the stratigraphy all identified species (*Cyclotella striata, Diploneis didyma* and *Nitzschia navicularis*) are mesohalobous, indicating brackish-water conditions characteristic of an estuary.

Discussion

The area in which the site of Canada Water Station is located was not intensively occupied until the late post-medieval/modern period. Cartographic evidence suggests that until the late 18th/early 19th centuries, the area was one of tidal creeks and marshland. The evidence collected from the analysis of the samples from this site suggests that there has been little human impact upon this area, and since the later prehistoric period at least, the pattern of meandering channels and marshes is a consistent one.

The lowest units (−1.95m OD) suggest that the sampling site was either in or peripheral to a channel which was slowly accreting sands from flooding events. A gradual decrease in energy of flow was observed, suggesting the channel was migrating away from the sampling site, and that the deposits were derived from overbank flooding. Unfortunately, no microfossils were recovered from these deposits which could have been used to obtain further information about the depositional conditions, with the exception of one freshwater diatom valve, *Achnanthes minutissima*, suggesting a fluvial derivation, and therefore that the site at this point was above mean sea level. The sands were succeeded by an organic mud (−1.3m OD) which indicates that the site was located at the interface between terrestrial and aquatic conditions, with very low-energy fluvial input and limited vegetation growth. The presence of fine sand laminae within the organic mud indicates periods of high-energy flooding which may have eroded the accreting organic muds, and suggests this was a period of relatively unstable sediment accumulation. The organic muds are sealed by a highly humified peat horizon (−1.2m OD), suggesting a gradual transition to a semi-terrestrial environment with a very limited input of minerogenic sediment from flood waters, which according to the extremely limited diatom evidence appear to be freshwater and suggest that the strata in question were still deposited above mean sea level and that the Thames was not yet tidal to this point. One brackish species fragment (*Nitzschia navicularis*) was recovered from this stratum, perhaps suggesting the beginnings of tidal migration towards the site. A worked flint flake at −1.19m OD supports the suggestion of a semi- or seasonally terrestrial surface located at or above the highest river levels. The ^{14}C measurement of 3650±100 BP (4245–3692 cal. BP) at −1.21 to −1.19m OD provides a date for the decline in dominance of the lime woodland (see below and discussion in Part 3) and also demonstrates that the organic/peat accumulation was initiated during the Neolithic period. This was, however, certainly post-elm decline as percentages of *Ulmus* are low. The paucity of herbs and dominance of woodland is similar to, and comparable with, evidence from other London sites. The local woodland community in this zone consisted of *Quercus, Corylus* and *Tilia* on drier soils while *Alnus* formed the dominant community on the floodplain and its margins. Such high values of *Tilia*, especially at the base of zone 1 (to 36%), firmly illustrates that this usually under-represented taxon must have been the dominant woodland component in

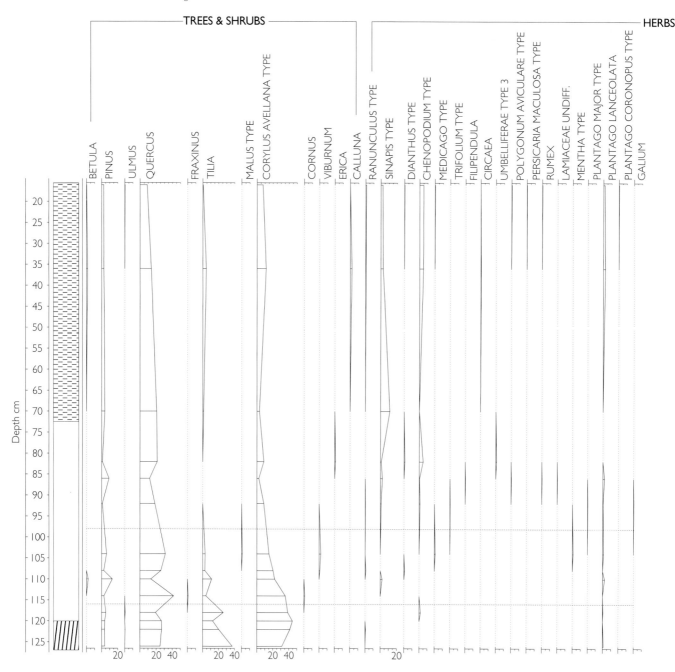

Fig 40 Pollen diagram from Canada Water, Rotherhithe

close proximity to the floodplain/sample site. Values of *Polypodium vulgare* are high and with this fern commonly being an epiphyte on mature trees, is a further indication of the local dominance of woodland. Such dominance of woodland in the drier and wetter habitats is also reflected in the paucity of non-arboreal pollen present. There is no cereal pollen present although sporadic records of *Plantago lanceolata* may be indicative of clearance and human activity at some distance.

Reasons for this peat initiation are not clear but may be associated with base-level changes caused by positive marine tendency. It is from the subsequent zone that substantial changes in the dominance of this woodland caused by or associated with evidence of human activity (cereal pollen and herbs) are seen along with a local environment which was becoming progressively wetter, that is, change from alder

domination to sedge/reed swamp. The thin peat layer appears to have been relatively short-lived. It is sealed by a further organic mud at −0.93m OD which indicates higher levels of flood water penetrating to this height, probably as a result of relative river levels increasing and inundating the floodplain. The sediments are homogeneous with no sand laminae as observed below and indicate a more stable and gentle environment. The pollen indicates that in zone CW:2, *Tilia* continues to decline along with *Corylus*. This progressive woodland clearance is also clearly associated with the expansion of herbs and agriculture. This may have been pastoral, but there is also significant evidence for cereal cultivation from the top of zone CW:2. However, this may not be as straightforward as it appears. Associated with the reduction in *Tilia* is a sharp decline of alder and marked expansion of wetter fen elements including largely

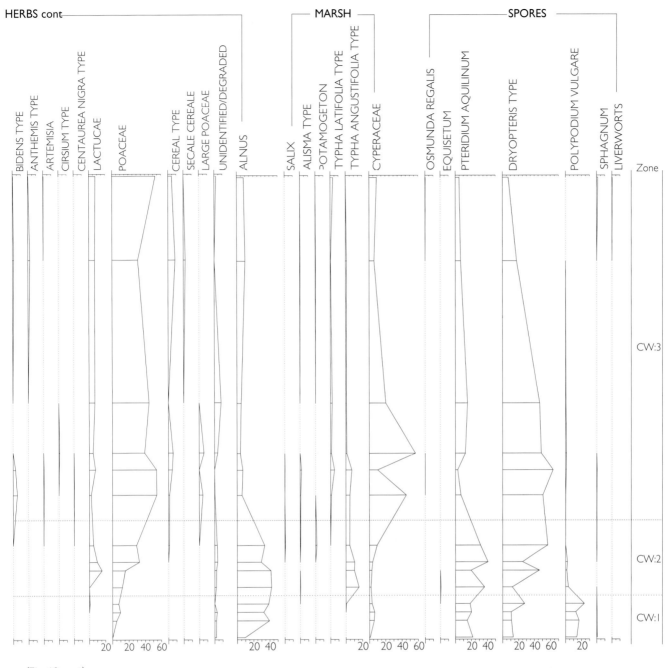

(Fig 40 cont)

Cyperaceae and *Typha angustifolia/Sparganium* but also a range of other wet fen taxa and algal *Pediastrum* in the overlying sediments. An alternative possibility, therefore, is that the pollen catchment may have become enlarged as a result of the reduction of on-site alder carr woodland. This would have allowed ingress of pollen from further afield, both airborne and fluvial. Furthermore, the inundation (paludification) of the floodplain will have pushed the growth areas of the terrestrial trees (such as *Tilia*) away from the sample site and thus reducing the representation of certain taxa especially where insect pollinated such as *Tilia* (Waller 1994b). It is clear, however, that both of these events occurred together during the Early to Middle Bronze Age. The progressive waterlogging is probably associated with processes similar to or the same as that causing Thames Stage III (Devoy 1979), leading to waterlogging of carr woodland

and then sedge fen which was inundated by estuarine sediments presumably during the Late Bronze Age–Iron Age. Such change to brackish/tidal conditions may be illustrated by the increases of *Chenopodium* type and Hystrichospheres/dinoflagellates although a strong freshwater element persists – possibly carried downstream from beyond the tidal margins. *Secale cereale* is consistent with an Iron Age/Romano-British date for the upper sediments sampled in this profile (zone CW:3).

The final phase of sedimentation, from −0.85m OD, suggests that the site was finally submerged beneath estuarine silt/clays which continued to be deposited until reclamation began in the late 18th century. Again, only very fragmentary diatom remains were recovered but confirm the picture of inundation under estuarine conditions, reflected by classic indicator species such as *Cyclotella striata* and *Nitzschia*

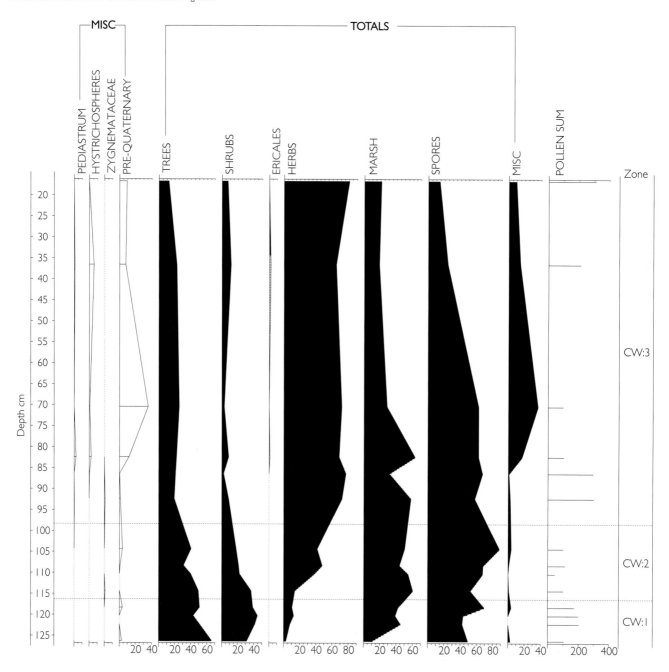

(Fig 40 cont)

navicularis. Although some archaeological evidence was recovered in the form of several artefacts, it is apparent that this area appears to have been of fairly limited significance to the human population throughout much of the Holocene.

Conclusions

The sequence of sedimentation at Canada Water has followed a relatively simple pattern, with fluvially lain sands, presumably of Early Holocene date, overlying Pleistocene terrace gravel. The energy of deposition decreased during the Middle Holocene as the river migrated northwards. As the site was marginalised, organic muds and peats formed, which allowed vegetation to develop at the sampling site, providing evidence of woodland dominated by lime, oak and hazel and, subsequently, an

Early–Middle Bronze Age date for the *Tilia* decline prior to 3950 cal. BP. This is comparable with all other late prehistoric *Tilia* decline sites investigated in this region and appears to be associated with prehistoric woodland clearance for arable and pastoral agriculture. However, the circumstances at this site are complicated by the fact that base levels were rising causing pollen taphonomic and stratigraphical changes.

The site appears to have been subject to estuarine inundation from the Late Bronze/Early Iron Age until post-medieval reclamation took place. There is extremely limited evidence for any human occupation or impact upon the area, with the exception of the changes brought about by the woodland clearance. This is hardly surprising given the apparent nature of the area: mudflats, marshland and wholly submerged in parts. It cannot have been particularly hospitable at any time. However, the presence of some artefacts suggests that the area was at least traversed occasionally if not actually settled during the Neolithic or Bronze Age. The evidence from the pollen suggests that there was human activity some distance from the site. Potentially the area contained resources important to the late prehistoric communities, and it may be that in the future, further, albeit ephemeral (*ie* timber trackways similar to that found in Bermondsey: see Thomas & Rackham 1996), archaeological discoveries may be made in this area.

Canning Town (Station and Limmo sites)

Introduction

The Canning Town archaeological site consisted of a 500m long strip of land, 13–30m wide, running north-north-west to south-south-east, some 400m north of the point where the River Lea joins the Thames, and directly south of the A13 (see Fig 38). The site was investigated in two phases: the first and most northerly, due to the construction of Canning Town Station, and the second in a more southerly location as a result of the emergence of the Jubilee Line from its tunnel on to the surface. Excavations within the Station footprint in November 1991 revealed stratigraphy similar to that from the Limmo site, and as no detailed geoarchaeological analytical work was carried out on the Station site, only the Limmo site is considered further here. Both investigations were undertaken by the Oxford Archaeological Unit (OAU), with the geoarchaeological component of the study on the Limmo site being conducted by the former Geoarchaeological Service Facility (GSF) of University College London (UCL). Prior to the fieldwork the Limmo site had consisted of railway track and associated installations relating to

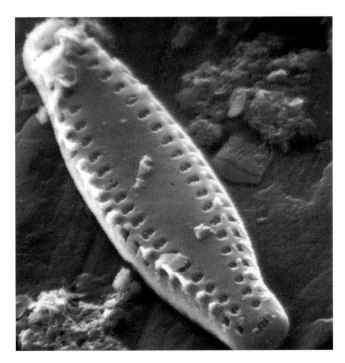

Fig 41 Electron micrograph of Fragilaria brevistriata

British Rail's North London Line, although parts of the site also lay within a former area of yards belonging to J C Mare and Co (the yards were originally part of an iron foundry owned by Thames Iron Works, Shipbuilding and Engineering Co and were developed in 1916). The North London Line was formerly the North Woolwich Railway and had been opened in 1846 to provide communication with the then burgeoning docklands. Prior to 1845, maps show the site to have been intertidal marshland.

Investigations at the Limmo site were carried out over a two-week period in November and December 1993. There was a twofold division to the investigative strategy. Firstly, two trenches were excavated in locations determined by where the adjacent railway would not be undermined. These were machine excavated from the ground surface to the top of the first peat layer encountered (2.3m below surface), and then subsequently hand dug to a depth of 3.2m in Trench 1 and 3.8m in Trench 2. In neither trench were artefacts predating the 19th century found. The second part of the investigation strategy consisted of a borehole survey carried out using a cable percussive drilling rig, equipped with a U4/100 sampler. A total of six boreholes were drilled along the length of the site from the ground surface to the top of the underlying Pleistocene gravels. Description of the stratigraphy was made on site where U4 samples were not taken followed by more detailed recording of the extruded cores in the laboratory.

Lithostratigraphy

The stratigraphy of the site as exposed in the boreholes and the archaeological trenches is displayed in Fig 42. A total of seven lithostratigraphic units were recognised sitting on an undulating basal gravel outcropping between −0.40 and −3.08m OD, but averaging −2.5m OD. There is a general tendency for the gravel to slope downwards to the north, a trend that continues to the Station site where it was encountered at −1.73m OD. This poorly sorted flint sand and gravel represents the eroded surface of the Shepperton Gravel (*sensu* Gibbard 1994), a Late Devensian stratum forming in either the Lea or the Thames. The undulating surface is likely to have had a considerable impact on later sedimentation, which occurred preferentially in topographic lows. A well-bedded, shell-rich coarse sand occurs above the gravels in a single borehole (BH6) and appears to have been rooted. This suggests episodes when terrestrial processes were operating during, or immediately following, its accretion. Such sand deposits are frequently found in similar stratigraphic sequences from areas adjacent to the east London Thames (*eg* Masthouse Terrace, Isle of Dogs (K N Wilkinson unpublished data), Silvertown (Wilkinson *et al* 2000) and Erith (E J Sidell *et al* unpublished data)), and are thought by Wilkinson *et al* (2000) to be remnants of an Early Holocene fluvial dune system, forming in a sand-dominated meandering river.

Unconformably overlying the gravels in BH1 is a 0.40m sequence of wood peat/organic mud capped by further organic muds. Plant macrofossils were visible throughout, while the organic muds contain evidence of bedding indicating, firstly,

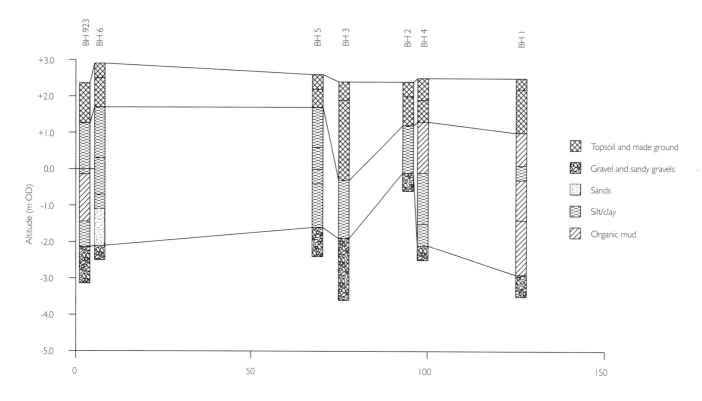

Fig 42 Representation of the stratigraphy recorded at the Canning Town Limmo (modified from Bates et al 1994)

channel margin development of marsh, followed by increased inundation, presumably as a result of rising sea level. This association was similarly encountered in the two archaeological trenches where large pieces of wood were found. This opportunity of examining large areas of the peat/organic mud demonstrated that it had been heavily eroded by subsequent fluvial activity, suggesting that it was formerly present in both a greater thickness and over a larger spatial area. It is perhaps notable that despite a relatively large area being exposed in a trench on the Station site, no peat was encountered – suggesting that these organic deposits may thin northwards. The base of the silt/clays that conformably overlie the peat/organic mud, and unconformably cap the sand and gravel sequences, contain relatively high proportions of organic material at their base, which may be eroded remnants of the peats. This deposit is most likely to have formed as a result of tidal flooding of channel margin areas and is indicative of the inundation of the peat surface as a result of rising sea level. The fact that the deposit fines upwards is suggestive of decreasing energy levels and is probably caused by sedimentation in the increasing water depths consistent with RSL rise. However, it is apparent that bedding structures and lamination frequency decrease upwards, indicating either that deposition became more continuous with time, or that post-depositional disturbance has preferentially disrupted the upper strata. If the rising sea-level scenario is accepted, the former is perhaps more likely. The silt/clays outcrop at between +0.25m OD and −0.50m OD, and are conformably overlain in the south of the site (BH1 and BH4) by an organic mud and in the north of the site by a palaeosol. The former contains low frequencies of

macrofossils, but the fact that *Phragmites* was noted suggests that the organic mud formed in brackish conditions. If correct this would suggest a negative tendency in RSL, possibly as a result of sediment stacking. The palaeosol is a further indication of a continuation of the same process as it would seem to have formed in a predominantly terrestrial environment (as indicated by the presence of land snails), although iron stains are indicative of occasional flooding. Capping the whole sequence is a series of deliberate human depositions made to heighten ground level in order to construct the railway and the yards. Most of this material seems to have been of redeposited riverine clay and silt of broadly similar properties to the bedded silt/clays detailed above.

Discussion

Strata at Canning Town are highly variable, with deposits in adjacent boreholes (eg BH923 and BH6) often proving difficult to correlate. Nevertheless the sequences have much in common with a number of sites investigated in east London in recent years, and are also broadly similar to that already discussed for Canada Water (4.5km west-south-west of Canning Town). The main difference from such sites as Masthouse Terrace, Isle of Dogs (K N Wilkinson unpublished data; 3km south-west of Canning Town), Silvertown (Wilkinson *et al* 2000; 1km east) and Bramcote Green (Thomas & Rackham 1996; 3km south) is the lack of thick peat strata. Indeed the archaeological excavations at Canning Town have demonstrated that peats once existed above the basal gravels, but they have subsequently been eroded and survive only in highly localised pockets.

Such erosion is likely to be a result of the location of the Canning Town site at the confluence of the Thames and Lea, where turbidity currents are likely to have been particularly active and eroded the peat surface. Only in those areas protected from such scour (BH1 may be such an example) could peat strata have survived. Indeed similar processes may have been operating even before the formation of the peats as the underlying gravel is highly undulatory suggesting the migration of stream channels across the area. Dating the sequences is of course problematic in the absence of a ^{14}C chronology, although if data from adjacent sites are applied this would suggest that the organic strata are of Middle and Late Holocene date. Therefore if the basal gravels date to the Late Devensian, channel incision and migration must have occurred in the Late Glacial or Early Holocene, while a 1m sequence of bedded sands outcropping above the gravel in BH6 probably relates to the Early Holocene sand-dominated meandering river. Erosion of the peat surface must have taken place in the Middle or later Holocene.

Conclusions: the sedimentation and environment of Rotherhithe and Canning Town

The sites examined from the JLE in Rotherhithe and Canning Town are separated by 5km (almost the same east–west difference as from Storey's Gate to Joan Street) and by sediment accretion in different depositional sub-environments, possibly at different times. Therefore it is difficult to correlate the sequences, and indeed arguable if such an activity is worthwhile at all. Sequences at Culling Road in particular are quite different to those at the other two sites, and indeed from those in Southwark or east London. The Culling Road deposits probably relate to accretion of dunes on a meander bend of the Early Holocene (based on the ceramic chronology) river, then unaffected by tidal processes. The result of such accumulation appears to have been to raise the site above the floodplain, so that it was not inundated by Middle Holocene sea-level rises, hence explaining its use by both Neolithic and Romano-British populations during the formation of largely terrestrial sediments. Deposits that may relate to the Early Holocene meandering river have also been found at Canada Water and Canning Town, but these bedded-sand sequences are thinner than at Culling Road, and appear to have suffered erosion prior to being covered by intertidal sediments. Indeed sequences at both Canada Water and Canning Town are largely the products of estuarine processes, with peats forming at the floodplain margins and clay/silts on intertidal mudflats. Unfortunately in the absence of an absolute chronology for Canning Town it cannot be determined if phases of peat formation on this site and Canada Water were synchronous. It is notable that peat forming at the latter site occurred over both silt/clay and sand strata, whereas at Canning Town it developed on the surface of the gravel, perhaps suggesting an earlier date for accretion at that site. A further argument for earlier peat development east of Canada Water are ^{14}C dates from lower bounding surfaces of peat strata at such sites as Silvertown, where results of around 6300 cal. BP have been obtained, rather than 4300–3650 cal. BP as at Canada Water. Strata overlying the peats at both Canada Water and Canning Town relate to similar development of mudflats and creeks which are well attested in the historic literature, while diatom evidence from Canada Water suggests that salinity gradually increased with time. Industrial activity that terminated accretion of mudflats also occurred more or less at the same time in the 19th century at both sites, after which their history has been inextricably linked to the fortunes of London's docklands.

Part 3:
Correlation, discussion and conclusions

7

Late Glacial and Holocene development of the London Thames

Keith Wilkinson and Jane Sidell

Introduction

(Fig 43)

The preceding chapters have outlined the results of both lithostratigraphic and biostratigraphic investigations. These conclusively demonstrate that the major factors affecting patterns of accretion, stasis and erosion on all the sites investigated were changes in fluvial and intertidal depositional environments (*sensu* Reineck & Singh 1980). Ultimately, alterations to both depositional environment and sub-environment and the associated facies changes, occurred primarily as a result of RSL change, which is in turn a product of post-glacial climate amelioration causing eustatic sea-level rise and isostatic downwarp (Clark *et al* 1978). Therefore humans had a relatively limited impact on sedimentation along the JLE until at least the medieval period, by which time many of the sites investigated had been protected from flooding by river defences (see chapter 9). Given the importance of fluvial and intertidal depositional environments to the sedimentary stratigraphy of the JLE sites, the evolution of the Thames from a braided, gravel- and sand-dominated river of the Devensian to an estuary accumulating predominantly fine-grained and organic sediment, is of vital importance for interpretation. Indeed, the stratigraphy of the JLE sites provides a wealth of information on these depositional environments which until now has only been available from widely disparate sites, simply

Fig 43 Aerial view of the JLE eastern section

Table 6 Facies of the Jubilee Line Extension

JLE facies	Depositional environment/ sub-environment	Miall (1996, 79) facies codes
a. Structureless gravels and sands	Braided river, channel bars	Gcm
b. Cross-bedded well-sorted medium to fine sands	Fresh water, in-channel dunes	Sp, Sh
c. Cross-bedded poorly sorted sands	Fresh water, in-channel ripples	Sr, Sm
d. Parallel laminated silt/clays (fw)	Fresh water, overbank and channel margin	Fl
e. Parallel laminated silt/clays (e)	Estuarine, flood deposits	Fl
f. Massive silt/clays (fw)	Fresh water, overbank and channel margin undergoing diagenesis	Fm
g. Massive silt/clays (e)	Estuarine flood deposits undergoing diagenesis	Fm
h. Organic muds (fw)	Floodplain margin and cut-off channel	Fsm
i. Organic muds (e)	Floodplain margin with estuarine flood input	Fsm
j. Peats	Terrestrial, floodplain margin	C

Key

C	Organic mud and peat	Gcm	Clast supported, massive gravel
e	estuarine	Sh	Horizontally laminated sand
Fl	Finely laminated clay/silt	Sm	Massive sand
Fm	Massive clay/silt	Sp	Planar, cross-bedded sand
Fsm	Massive organic mud	Sr	Ripple, cross-laminated sand
fw	fresh water		

because engineering works on such a scale have not previously been undertaken in London with a comparable scale of archaeological mitigation. Therefore, data obtained from the project provide a firm foundation for examining the mechanisms and chronology of the evolution of the London Thames during the Late Devensian and subsequent Holocene period. In this chapter the project data are examined alongside those from other sites recently investigated in the Thames in order to provide a detailed account of river change.

Lithostratigraphic sequences: depositional environments, chronology and diagenesis

Despite the fact that the lithostratigraphy of 10 sites was examined during the project and that in excess of 150 sedimentary beds were described, these can be attributed to just 10 facies based on lithological characteristics and associated diatom assemblages (Table 6). In the main these have behaved according to Walther's (1894, 535–1055) *Law of facies*, where facies occurring in a conformable vertical sequence formed in laterally adjacent depositional environments and sub-environments. Thus, conformable Neolithic to Iron Age sequences comprising mineral silt/clays and peats indicate that

intertidal mudflats were found adjacent to brackish/freshwater peats during the Middle and later Holocene, while sand strata bedded with silts and clays indicate lateral association of freshwater stream channels and floodplains. However, unconformities do occur in most of the sequences when Walther's Law is not applicable, and it is unfortunate that these hiatuses often coincide with periods when it is known that the Thames was undergoing change.

When the facies found at the JLE sites are plotted against an absolute timescale of calibrated years BP (Fig 44) the operation of Walther's Law can clearly be seen, particularly for Westminster, where there is a time-transgressive facies change on an east to west axis. Thus, this progression from initially cross-bedded sands accreting in a freshwater meandering river, through horizontally laminated silt/clays accumulating as freshwater overbank flood deposits, to organic muds forming firstly at the margin of a freshwater then a brackish-water channel, occurs first at St Stephen's East and lastly at Storey's Gate. Plotting lithostratigraphy against time also emphasises the unconformity at the top of the Storey organic mud bed and the succeeding hiatus of approximately 2000 years.

Away from Westminster the picture is less clear, although in part this is undoubtedly a result of the smaller number of sites studied further to the east. However, peat development at both Joan Street and Union Street is broadly synchronous at around 5200 cal. BP, although it is noticeably later at Canada Water (4200 cal. BP). Reasons for the late development at Canada Water are not obvious, especially in view of the fact that the latter is not on a topographic high. Perhaps the site was particularly exposed to wave erosion during RSL rise prior to 4200 cal. BP, or conversely the site may have been separated from the river channel by a high levee system, isolating it from accretionary mechanisms. The Culling Road site is the obvious exception from the eastern part of the transect in having no organic sediments and consisting solely of bedded sands dating from before the Neolithic period, overlain by floodplain silt/clays of Roman and later date. These properties, and the lack of organic sediments, are primarily the result of rapid sand accretion during an Early Holocene fluvial phase which raised ground level to an elevation above that at which it would be affected by later sea-level rises. It is noteworthy in this respect that although the Culling Road and Westminster sequences are often as thick as those from Southwark, the latter represent almost continuous deposition from the Neolithic to the 16th century, whereas the former are characterised by a staccato style of sedimentation, where rapid accretion was followed by prolonged periods of stasis or erosion. Indeed the latter mechanism seems to be a feature of many freshwater fluvial systems (Miall 1996).

Plotting the lithostratigraphic and diatom-derived sea-level trend data of each site against elevation provides a more complex picture than that based entirely of chronology, especially so for the Westminster member (see Fig 44). For example, sand strata, which would appear to date from c 12,000 cal. BP to 6400 cal. BP, outcrop on different sites

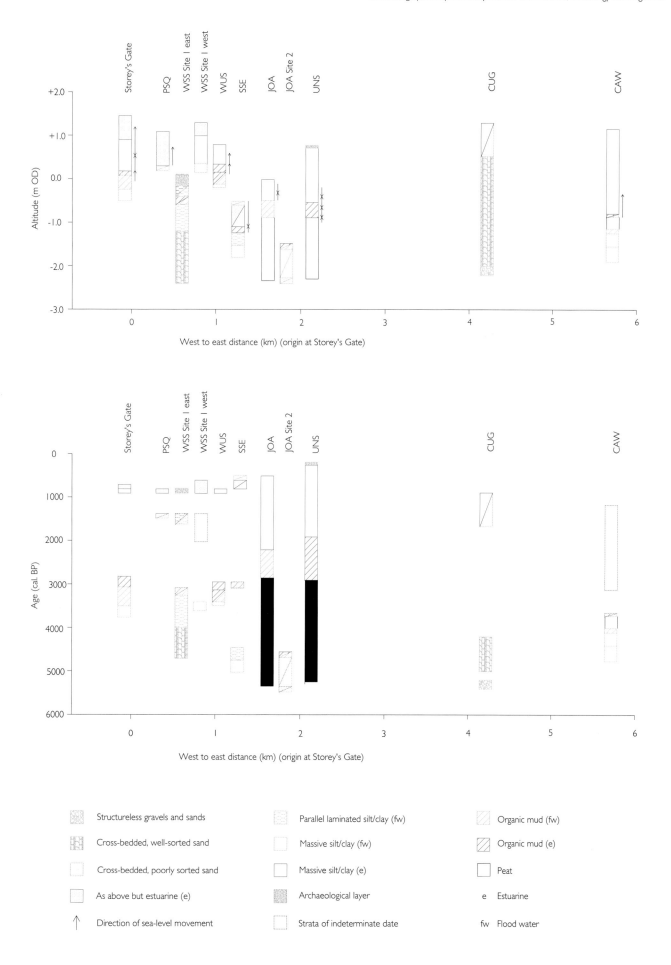

Fig 44 Facies of the JLE sites plotted against altitude and chronology

between +0.2m OD and −2.4m OD, with upper surfaces varying between −1.5m OD and +0.2m OD. Although these differences could be explained solely by fluctuations in deposition resulting from upstream variation in tidal range over this c 5600-year period, it is perhaps more likely that an unconformity exists above the sands in this area, probably caused by channel development after 6400 cal. BP. Indeed the thickest sequences of silts and clays occur where the upper surface of the sands is lowest, namely Palace Chambers South and St Stephen's East, and are therefore likely to be vertically accreting flood deposits preferentially accumulating in low-lying areas, such as abandoned channels. Given the location of these sites near the confluence of the Tyburn and Thames (see Fig 28), it could be changes in course of the former that have carved out the channels beneath Westminster Underground Station.

A similar observation can be made of the Storey organic mud bed, which, as has already been seen in chapter 4, occurs almost ubiquitously across the Westminster sites, and appears to have formed more or less synchronously as a general spread across the area in channel marginal marsh between 3200 cal. BP and 2900 cal. BP. However, despite the apparent synchronicity in deposition, outcrop heights vary between +0.3m OD and −1.0m OD. Given the widespread distribution of this stratum, some of the undulation must be a result of differential compaction under later sediments, it being notable that the thickest sequences are at Storey's Gate and Westminster Underground Station where overlying deposits are the thinnest. Nevertheless, this is not the complete explanation as the maximum thickness of the bed is only 0.4m – that is, less than the height variation – while the underlying sands and clay/silts often retain structures, such as laminated and cross-bedding, that would be lost, or at least disrupted, by compression. Therefore it would seem that the marsh in which the Storey organic mud bed accreted originally formed at a range of elevations bordering the Thames and the Tyburn tributary.

Peat units further to the east at the Joan Street and Union Street sites occur at very similar elevations. However, it is notable that the Joan Street 2 site – where the basal peat occurs at a higher elevation than the other two sites – demonstrates that when initially forming the peat filled hollows in the underlying deposits. It is notable that the top of the peat strata at both Joan Street and Union Street plots at lower elevations to the Storey organic mud bed of Westminster, despite being of comparable age. Similarly strata from Westminster containing diatom evidence for increasing estuarine influence outcrops at higher elevations than comparable strata of the same age in Southwark. If it is accepted that sea-level rise within a river basin affects channel locations at the same elevations simultaneously, the only explanation for these observations is the operation of diagenetic processes. In this case it would appear that the Southwark peats have been preferentially affected by post-depositional compaction as a result of sediment loading, when compared to organic deposits in Westminster. Indeed Allen (1999) has recently argued that peat strata are more readily compressed than any other deposit type, due in

part to high moisture contents and pore space. In organic deposits of similar properties the potential for compaction is therefore related to deposit thickness, which in the case of the Southwark examples is 1.5m, when compared to 0.4m in Westminster, allowing much greater compaction to occur in Southwark compared to Westminster.

Despite the effects of diagenesis, the presence of unconformities and the apparently contradictory nature of much of the stratigraphic data highlighted above, it is nevertheless possible to suggest on the basis of the JLE and other recently examined strata, a model of river change from the Late Glacial period through until the 16th century.

The braided river of the Late Devensian

The exposures examined as part of JLE contribute relatively little to the knowledge of Pleistocene environments of the Thames. Strata attributable to the Shepperton Gravel were found in trenches at Joan Street (−2.8m OD), Union Street (−2.5m OD), Culling Road (−2.0m OD), Canada Water (−2.0m OD) and Canning Town (between −0.40m OD and −3.08m OD), but no associated fine-grained deposits were noted. At all these sites (except possibly Canning Town) the gravels are separated from the overlying strata by unconformities, marking periods of erosion (also indicated by the undulating nature of the gravel surface) and therefore hiatus. It is of particular note that gravels were not found in any of the Westminster sites, where bedded sands extended down to at least −2.0m OD. Despite this lack of evidence from the JLE sites, previous investigations in London outlined in chapter 3 demonstrate that the Shepperton Gravel had accumulated in a braided river during the last glacial maximum and that it had ceased forming before the Late Glacial period (ie prior to 15,500 cal. BP). This is in marked contrast to evidence of the Thames west of London (Gibbard & Hall 1982; Gibbard 1985; Gibbard 1988), the Kennet Valley (Collins et al 1996) and the lower Thames Valley (Briggs et al 1985; Parker & Chambers 1997) for continued aggradation until after 13,500 cal. BP. These data may be representative of an east to west trend in the cessation of braided river-gravel accretion, as it is also notable that no evidence of such accumulation dating from after 15,500 cal. BP has been found to the east of London (although it must be stated that the Shepperton Gravel is deeply buried beneath post-glacial deposits in these locations, so exposures are extremely rare). In London the Windermere interstadial (c 15,500–13,000 cal. BP) is not represented by any deposits other than the lowermost marls at Bramcote Green, which are characterised by a birch pollen flora (Thomas & Rackham 1996). In contrast, several organic channel fills at sites such as Silvertown (Wilkinson et al 2000) and Masthouse Terrace (K N Wilkinson unpublished data), containing herb-dominated floras, are known from the subsequent Loch Lomond stadial (c 13,000–11,500 cal. BP).

Collins et al (1996) suggest the cessation of gravel sedimentation in the Late Glacial to be a result of river competence exceeding sediment supply, while Rose (1995) hypothesises that the latter was in part due to the relative density of vegetation during the Windermere interstadial. If these assertions are correct such conditions must have persisted in the London area into the following Loch Lomond stadial, despite the changing vegetation evidenced from pollen data. Thus during the Windermere interstadial it would appear that the London Thames was simply utilising its existing braid plain, without depositing any further gravels, and indeed perhaps even cutting into the existing gravel surface. However, during the Loch Lomond stadial, the evidence of organic channel fills suggesting abandonment would appear to indicate that fewer and fewer channels were being utilised, perhaps as a result of a lower flow. Such transition phases where the number of channels utilised by a river are progressively reduced have been noted for several rivers on the European mainland, namely the Maas (Bohncke et al 1987; Vandenberghe et al 1987; Tebbens et al 1999) and Warta (Starkel 1994), albeit from earlier periods in the Late Glacial.

A meandering river of the Early and Middle Holocene

As has been demonstrated in the previous section and in chapter 3, the Late Glacial period saw a reduction in the number of channels utilised by the Thames in the London area, almost certainly as a result of loss of flow competence due to reduction of spring ice melt. It is probable, based on the, admittedly limited, altitudinal data, that during the Early Holocene the Thames adopted a single channel form, with the primary calibre of sediment being sand. Exactly when this change occurred is not at present clear as sequences comprising sand facies are not easily dated, while such facies always unconformably overlie the Late Devensian Shepperton Gravel, suggesting a period of hiatus. Organic muds at Masthouse Terrace and Silvertown (Wilkinson et al 2000) which are stratigraphically older than the sands have been dated to around 12,000 cal. BP, indicating that accretion began after this. However, evidence from organic deposits beneath horizontally bedded sands at Richmond suggests that here at least sand accretion was only initiated in the Early Holocene. A molluscan fauna associated with these dates indicates that these formed within or at the margins from a channel transporting moderate-energy fresh water, probably as part of a dune system (R Cowie & K N Wilkinson unpublished data). A Mesolithic flint scatter has also been found from within similar sand deposits in the Erith marshes (Sidell et al 1997), indicating that accretion in a similar depositional environment was occurring in this area of east London during the Early Holocene. Taking the evidence from the Maas, along with the limited data from the Thames, it is safest to assume that accretion in a sandy bed river began sometime at the end of the Late Glacial or in the very Early Holocene, primarily as a response to variations in sediment supply consequent on climate change.

Evidence of in-channel dune systems have been found at all the sites along the JLE in Westminster (the lower Westminster member), and at Culling Road in Rotherhithe, forming part of the topographic features of Thorney Island and Bermondsey Eyot respectively. It is likewise possible that sands underlying mid Holocene organic deposits at Canada Water and Joan Street 2 may relate to this phase of river development. The sand strata from Palace Chambers South and Culling Road in particular are thickly bedded, with good evidence for planar cross-bedding, indicating formation as part of two-dimensional dunes (Miall 1996, 109–12). Such structures typically accumulate within channels of moderate and large meandering rivers, where flow velocities are between 0.5m/s and 0.7m/s (assuming the average grain sizes generated for Palace Chambers South are typical) (Ashley 1990). At the other sites in Westminster sand strata appear homogeneous and poorly sorted, suggesting either that several depositional episodes of variable energy have been overprinted, or that bioturbation or reworking has occurred. Nevertheless all sand facies are likely to have formed in a similar depositional environment, which would have consisted of a relatively shallow (ie there is no evidence for three-dimensional dunes indicative of deep water and high flow velocities) meandering river, probably of relatively low sinuosity. The fact that such thick sequences of sand have survived in locations 3.5km apart, with little evidence of comparable deposits in between, indicates that the Westminster area and Culling Road are either exceptional accretion zones or have been protected from later tidal scour. In the case of Westminster this was probably as a result of the confluence at this location with a tributary (the modern Tyburn) leading to the formation of channel junction bars (Kellerhalls & Church 1989), while Culling Road is likely to have been situated on the inner bend of a meander where point bars could form. Reconstruction of the 'Mesolithic' topography (Fig 45) would appear to confirm the former presence of this meander and also suggests that in the Early Holocene the Westminster site locations may have been on the inner bend (south bank side) of a now lost meander. If this is indeed the case, the Early Holocene Thames channel would have passed on a south-west to north-east course beneath the Victoria and Pimlico area. The topographic data also suggest that the west to east section of the Thames currently passing between Charing Cross and West India Docks ran 0.5km to the south, along an axis through Waterloo, Borough, Bermondsey and Rotherhithe. The same source also presents tantalising evidence for a north to south channel, presumably draining the south London area passing through Camberwell and Elephant and Castle, to a confluence with the Thames at Borough. It is notable that Mesolithic finds cluster along the eastern side of this route.

There is little evidence for change in depositional environment/sub-environment for the majority of the time represented by the sand accretion with the meandering river system. For example, in the 2m of bedded sands that occur at both Palace Chambers South and Culling Road there is little variation in either lithology or structure, beyond occasional gravel stringers. It would also seem likely that such sequences

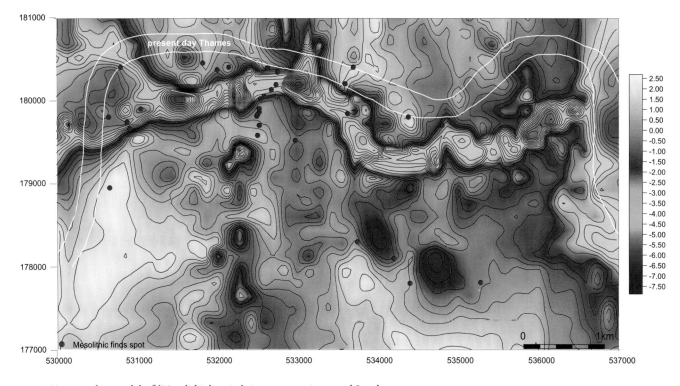

Fig 45 Topographic model of 'Mesolithic' period river systems in central London

would have been found at the other Westminster sites if excavation had not ceased as soon as the top of the sands was encountered. Significantly there is no evidence for overbank flooding contemporary with sand accretion, as vertical accretion deposits are not found. This would appear to suggest that the river was well constrained within its channel, possibly as a result of a similar flow competence throughout the year, combined with a high levee. Therefore during the Early Holocene the river and the adjacent 'dry' land are likely to have remained as separate entities in central London with little interaction taking place between the two. However, from about 4000 cal. BP there is evidence for vertical accretion of silts and clays at all Westminster sites except Storey's Gate. These data suggest the main area of flow had migrated southwards towards the present course of the Thames, and that, as at present, Westminster formed the northern margin of the river channel, on which low-energy vertical accretion deposits could form. All diatom floras recovered from these deposits are indicative of freshwater environments, and so this change in accretion is not directly related to RSL rise. Indeed the timing of the change correlates with Long *et al*'s (submitted) phase of estuary contraction throughout southern Britain, when the influence of tidal waters would have declined. A possible alternative to channel migration in the formation of the mineral clay/silts overlying the Thorney sand bed across Westminster is the input of sediment derived from agriculture elsewhere within the Thames catchment (Brown 1992; 1997). Evidence of such erosion in the upper Thames Valley indicates that silt/clay-dominated vertical accretion deposits began to form about 2000 cal. BP as a result of Iron Age agricultural intensification (Robinson 1992), and thus if this hypothesis were correct it would suggest similar events occurring earlier in the London

area. Whichever the true cause it is almost certainly the case that evidence for similar changes had occurred sometime before in areas to the east of Westminster, but unfortunately no evidence remains as to when. Alternatively it might exist, but buried deeply beneath later peat and intertidal deposits.

While it is still unclear when accretion of in-channel sand facies started, there is a certain amount of information indicating when it ceased, both from sites along the JLE (see Fig 44) and from others recently investigated in London. Despite the fact that there are problems with this chronology (*ie* most ^{14}C dates are on organic muds or peats unconformably overlying the sand strata) it is possible to suggest that sands continued to form later in the west than in the east (Fig 46), that is, in-channel sands had ceased to form by at least 6400 cal. BP in the Erith marshes, but continued to accrete as late as 3500 cal. BP at Storey's Gate. The associated facies changes, from in-channel sands, through overbank silt/clays to peats in

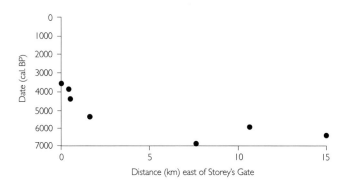

Fig 46 Minimum age by which in-channel sand strata have ceased accreting, plotted on a west–east axis

central London is therefore most likely to be the result of Middle Holocene sea-level rise and estuary development, which pushed freshwater facies progressively westwards. Fig 46 also demonstrates that date of peat formation, which is related to position relative to RSL, is progressively younger the further west a site occurs. By 3500 cal. BP the whole of the Thames reach in central London was dominated by tidal processes, and these, with limited fluctuations, have persisted to the present day.

Transition to a tidal river

The gradual change of the central London Thames from an essentially freshwater system before 6400 cal. BP to an estuarine one after 3500 cal. BP is undoubtedly the result of an incremental positive trend in RSL, caused by a combination of eustatic sea-level rise and isostatic downwarp (Devoy 1979; Fairbridge 1983; Shennan 1987). Unfortunately the lack of sites examined along the eastern part of the JLE means that the rate at which tidal waters passed into the river system cannot be tracked. There is some evidence to suggest that Early and Middle Holocene estuary expansion was not unidirectional (Long *et al* submitted). This phase of estuary contraction took place at about 5300 cal. BP, almost certainly caused by a reduction in the rate of RSL rise, accompanied by an increase in peat formation, which outstripped river-level rise. Such stratigraphy was encountered along the JLE at Joan Street, Union Street and Canada Water, where peat formation lasted for over 2000 years (until *c* 3000 cal. BP), but has also been found at numerous sites from the Isle of Dogs eastwards (Sidell submitted). Prior to this phase of estuary expansion there is no evidence, biological or lithological, for the ingress of tidal waters into central London in contrast to the situation at Tilbury and sites to the east (Devoy 1979). Estuary contraction does not appear to have been accompanied by a migration of freshwater facies eastwards, as no such deposits characteristic of freshwater fluvial processes have been found within any peat stratigraphy recently investigated. Indeed, estuary contraction would appear to have been just that, a reduction in channel width, best exemplified by the data collected by Devoy (1979) at Crossness, where a decrease in channel width from 4.7km to 0.67km is recorded from *c* 6000 cal. BP (Long *et al* submitted). Nevertheless, as has already been noted, freshwater sand facies continued to accrete during the contraction phase on the Westminster sites.

Chronologically the next evidence for the impact of tidal waters on the JLE sites is from Westminster, just before 3000 cal. BP, where diatom evidence from within the Storey organic mud bed suggests transition from fresh- to brackish-water deposition. This change seems to have occurred slightly before that of the Southwark sites despite the relevant Westminster strata occurring at higher elevations and Westminster being located further upstream. However, an apparently short-lived event was recorded at Union Street which reflected tidal conditions, occurring at *c* 3200 cal. BP, but which did not

continue (although after 3000 cal. BP tidal conditions did prevail), and possibly represents an atypical flood deposit. These data confirm the thesis proposed above that it was just channel width which had been reduced during the contraction phase (*ie* there was no actual drop in river levels), and that brackish waters were able to penetrate upstream. Indeed, the channel constriction may actually have encouraged continual penetration of tidal waters (A J Long, pers comm).

The evidence for the impact of estuarine waters on the Southwark sites at around 3000 cal. BP is unclear. At Union Street the change from peat formation to organic mud accretion which coincides with a *c* 3000 cal. BP ^{14}C date is accompanied by a shift from a fresh- to brackish-water diatom assemblage, but at Joan Street freshwater floras persist in the organic mud (see Fig 44). It is possible that the Joan Street area may have been protected from inundation by estuarine waters, perhaps by barrier islands or spits, or may have been supplied directly by a freshwater stream draining northwards. The difference may have also been associated with a movement of the Thames channel northwards from its location in the Early to Middle Holocene to a position similar to that of the present day.

Therefore, a trend in expansion of estuarine conditions upstream that had begun on the Isle of Dogs at *c* 4200 cal. BP (Wilkinson 1995b), and earlier to the east (*ie* 4800–4400 cal. BP; Q1333; Devoy 1979) at Crossness, had reached Southwark and Westminster by 3000 cal. BP. Although this advance is not likely to have been linear, an average rate of 5.4m upstream movement of the tidal head every year can be suggested from the existing data. Data from non-JLE sources suggest that estuary expansion was not only upstream, but lateral as well, as tidal waters penetrated into the east London marshes (Rackham 1994; Meddens 1996) and areas of southern Southwark and Rotherhithe (Tyers 1988; Sidell *et al* 1995) for the first time, depositing mineral-rich silt/clays.

The data from this project have allowed five sea-level index points to be constructed. These are dated points in the sequence which are from the interface between minerogenic and organic deposits, and exhibit marine influence in the microfossil record. An assumption has been made that the deposits in question – organic muds – formed at approximately mean high water of spring tides (MHWST), and in order to plot these new data on the curve previously shown in chapter 3 (see Fig 9), the altitudes have been converted to reflect mean sea level (MSL). The index points are all from intercalated sequences; none are from 'basal' peats and therefore cannot be viewed as of the highest quality (Shennan 1994). Nevertheless, the new plot (Fig 47) indicates that they are consistent with index points already generated for the Thames estuary. They fall within the upper end of the dates generated by Devoy (1979), Long (1995) and Wilkinson *et al* (2000) and are more closely comparable with those from the inner rather than mid estuary. On the whole they fall slightly lower, altitudinally, than those from Silvertown which is further downstream and so this appears slightly anomalous, but may be a factor of individual errors (*ie* results of compaction and ^{14}C error) associated with each point.

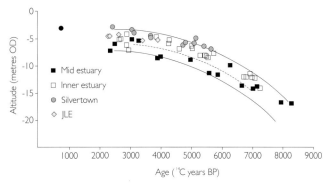

Fig 47 Current age–altitude curve for relative sea-level fluctuations (MSL) in the Thames estuary based on published data with five additional points from JLE sites

The tidal river of the Late Holocene

By c 3000 cal. BP (ie Late Bronze Age) the Thames was consistently tidal to at least as far upstream as Thorney Island. Initially, the tidal reach seems to have extended as far upstream as Westminster, as outer estuary diatoms occur in some frequency in floras otherwise dominated by inner estuary types. Following initial evidence for tidal conditions, the Westminster and Southwark sites show a declining trend in marine influence in the microfossil record, and it would appear that after an initial 'surge', the location of the tidal head gradually shifted downstream from the Late Bronze Age onwards (a trend that is noted in several other British estuaries: A J Long, pers comm). Unfortunately, at this period, there is a significant hiatus in the sedimentary sequence across the Westminster sites, dating from c 2900 cal. BP in some locations until c 1000 cal. BP. The reason for this is still unclear, but is almost certainly linked to tidal scour of the margins of Thorney Island which was, by this point, situated on the outside of a meander bend, the zone of highest erosion (Miall 1996). Additionally, the confluence of the Tyburn and Thames may also have played a part in generating turbidity currents which eroded existing deposits. A further possibility is that under the tidal regime, sediments gently accreted on these sites, but were later removed during a substantial storm event. One such event has been identified from the mid 11th century which appears to have flooded the higher ground of Thorney Island, to a depth of at least 1m (see Thomas et al in prep). However, the sequences in west Southwark do not exhibit a similar hiatus, and if an erosional event of such magnitude had occurred in the medieval period, it seems likely that it would also have been experienced in west Southwark. Therefore, local processes associated with the location of Thorney Island on a meander and tributary confluence are probably the explanation for the hiatus.

The record from west Southwark confirms the Westminster microfossil data: that the pattern of the tidal river was one of steadily decreasing marine influence in central London from the Late Bronze Age onwards. However, this does not appear to have been continuous as the Union Street sequence suggests that there were a number of fluctuations, reflected by a more strongly marine diatom flora, which could represent periodic upstream migrations of the tidal head. After the initial change to tidal conditions on this site at c −1.0m OD, a gradually declining marine presence was observed, with returns to marine input at −0.72m and −0.45m OD, at c 2800 cal. BP and c 1950 cal. BP respectively.

Previously recorded data for the history of the tidal Thames (see chapter 3) have suggested that there was a significant downstream migration of the tidal head in the Roman period (AD 43–410, or 1907–1540 cal. BP) (Milne et al 1983; Brigham 1990), which had a serious effect on the waterfront quays and jetties. This appears to have been reversed in the later Roman/Early Saxon period (1650–1300 cal. BP). Indeed, it is possible that both the Roman city of Londinium and Saxon *Lundenwic* were located at the approximate location of the tidal head, for which there is historical precedent (see Wheeler 1928). Recent evidence gathered from sequences of the Saxo-Norman period (Wilkinson in prep; Sidell submitted) indicates that there was a renewed downstream migration of the tidal head until at least 1181 (769 cal. BP), coinciding with the construction of the first London bridge built in stone. There is then evidence for river-level rise in the City from the 12th century. Data gathered during the JLE archaeological project at Westminster support this date for a rise in relative river levels, as river defences on Thorney Island were constructed in the 12th century (Thomas et al in prep). Data for the historic period are limited from the sites examined in this project; however, renewed accretion is seen at Westminster from c 1200, characterised by mixed diatom floras indicating both brackish and freshwater environments. These are probably a result of varied water input from the Thames (intertidal and freshwater) and Tyburn (freshwater). Evidence from the Southwark sites also confirms a weakly tidal river here, although there is no dating evidence for the mineral silt/clays that formed above the late prehistoric peats until the 16th century. In the early historic period limited river defences were in place, but were almost certainly not influencing the tidal range of the Thames to any significant degree. However, much of the marshy and intertidal areas of the central London area were reclaimed from the early medieval period onwards, coinciding with the expansion of Westminster and the City, which would have begun to constrain the course of the Thames and may have artificially extended the tidal head upstream. By the 14th century, evidence from City sites (Milne & Milne 1982) suggests that the tidal influence was much stronger than it had been throughout the historic period and this trend has continued with river levels rising to the present day.

8

Holocene vegetation development in London

Robert Scaife

Introduction: the natural vegetation

During the Jubilee Line project, none of the peat or minerogenic sequences produced material of Early or Middle Holocene age. This is in spite of the number of such sites attributable to Flandrian Chronozones I and II (the pre-Boreal, Boreal and Atlantic) which are now known in the London region. The earliest deposits examined here date back to the Early Neolithic and appear to immediately postdate the primary elm decline, that is, between *c* 6300–5800 cal. BP from Joan Street and Union Street. With the exception of elm, which had become substantially less important due to the effects of disease, the preceding woodland remained largely the same, and thus these sites provide data on the environment of these areas prior to subsequent human activity. From this period onwards, however, we can see the progressive late prehistoric modification of the 'natural' woodland at these sites which had been established during the Middle Holocene (the Atlantic period; Flandrian Chronozone II).

Traditionally, the vegetation of the Middle Holocene, Atlantic period was viewed as being dominated by a climax forest of mixed oak (*Quercetum mixtum*) with *Tilia*, *Ilex* and *Fraxinus*, and thermophiles including *Lonicera* (honeysuckle), *Hedera* and *Viscum album* L. The sites of Union Street and Joan Street demonstrate that this was not the case since pollen percentages of lime attain high values at Union Street to 40% of total pollen (lpaz UNION:1) whereas in the nearby site of Joan Street values are only 9% (lpaz JOA:1). This demonstrates that there was in fact much local variation, with the former site showing clear dominance of lime woodland whereas *Quercus* was locally more important at the latter. In spite of such local variations, all sites examined which span the late prehistoric period illustrate the great importance of lime woodland until its removal locally by Neolithic and Bronze Age land clearance (see below). These and other sites in the London region – *ie* Hampstead Heath (Girling & Greig 1977; 1985; Greig 1989) and Runnymede Bridge (Scaife in prep) – clearly show that a polyclimax view is more appropriate, that is, with differing woodland communities dominant on varying soil types which were themselves developed on different bedrock types and under different groundwater conditions. In earlier work, lime growth was considered to be a characteristic only of the well-drained soils of the interfluves and here, on the localised islands which occur on the Thames floodplain. Some recent studies are now, however, indicating that far from being restricted to such 'good' soils, lime may have also been a constituent of poorer sandy soils (Waller 1994a, 96) and even very 'damp' woodland on peaty substrates (Tomalin *et al* in press). The latter may well be the case at some JLE sites (*eg* Union Street) where peat was formed under damp (but dry in a mire ecological sense) woodland with other typical fen carr woodland elements (oak, ash, birch, hazel, yew and understorey shrubs). Heavier soils developed on alluvial deposits and London Clay are likely to have supported more typical oak, elm and hazel with the possibility of an element of lime as noted.

The wetter clay valley bottoms and floodplain habitats supported alder carr woodland which, although not evidenced here, became locally dominant at the start of and during the Early Atlantic period in response to post-glacial rising sea levels. This is seen in Devoy's (1979) work in the lower Thames. This woodland community remained in many areas until further, Late Bronze Age, positive eustatic change caused local changes to grass/sedge fen. The sites of Joan Street, Union Street, Canada Water and St Stephen's East all demonstrate typical floodplain alder carr with a range of associated trees, understorey shrubs and herbs during the Neolithic and Early to Middle Bronze Age. Typically, at Union Street and Joan Street, *Frangula alnus* (alder buckthorn), *Rhamnus catharticus*, *Salix* and *Viburnum* (wayfaring tree) are evidence of the richness of the fen carr woodland. Of note is the presence of *Taxus* at Joan Street and Union Street. Now regarded as a tree of the chalk downlands and churchyards, in the past it appears that yew was an important constituent also of dry alder carr woodland. Initially noted in the fen peats of East Anglia (Godwin 1975a), macrofossils and tree boles have now also been found in the fen peats of London and from its pollen in the JLE sites. It seems that there is no modern analogue for this community. This type of alder carr is, however, a clear representation of the environment which became established during the Late Mesolithic, Atlantic period which because of its inhospitable nature was not influenced to any great extent by human activity. A Neolithic wooden trackway found in peats at Silvertown (Wessex Archaeology 1994b) which traverses such an environment is perhaps the only evidence for human penetration of this environment.

While the Atlantic period is associated with the Late Mesolithic, there has been no real evidence here for woodland modification/disturbance in this region. This is not surprising given the likely ephemeral encampments of the small numbers of the hunting and foraging human communities. Small numbers of herb pollen taxa including *Plantago* spp at other London sites (eg Runnymede) are enigmatic. While these may be attributable to human activity, woodland disturbance caused by tree throw or animal/herbivore activity may also have caused soil disturbance. It is against a background of stable woodland that the first indisputable effects of human activity on the local landscape can be seen and is first evidenced at sites along the Jubilee Line.

Influences of the Neolithic

Union Street and Joan Street have the best representation of the Neolithic vegetation and, of the sites examined in this project, the former is the only one which has some evidence for elm in its lowest levels. This indicates that the often described 'Primary Elm Decline' had occurred. Elm was undoubtedly an important constituent of the preceding Middle Holocene vegetation and here in the basal pollen levels the last vestiges of this woodland

type are seen. In sites examined along the Jubilee Line, organic deposits started to accumulate early during the 4th millennium – immediately at, or after, the elm decline – with peat inception occurring because of rising sea levels and increase in groundwater tables which initiated the anaerobic conditions suited to peat accumulation. However, there is evidence for the elm decline in London from non-floodplain sites. Of importance is Hampstead Heath (Girling & Greig 1977; 1985; Greig 1989; 1992) from which the late Dr Girling (1988) established that disease carried by the elm bark beetle *Scolytus scolytus* was the principal cause for the widespread and broadly synchronous demise of elm at *c* 6300–5800 cal. BP. This was apparently aided by Neolithic opening of the forest canopy which allowed or even promoted the spread of this insect/disease vector. This hypothesis coupled with the more recent spread of Dutch Elm Disease from the late 1960s and 1970s in Britain effectively disproved the earlier views of the elm decline causation as due to climatic change, use of leaves for fodder or forest clearance (see Smith 1970; 1981; Scaife 1988a, for general discussions). However, this event although not directly anthropogenically controlled is, nevertheless, strongly associated in many instances with the first indication of human (Neolithic) agricultural activity (Godwin 1944; Smith 1970; Scaife 1988a). At the JLE sites (especially Union Street and Joan Street), this significant event unfortunately occurred just prior to the start of peat accumulation at these sites. The immediate effects of this event and adoption of Neolithic subsistence are clearly seen in the pollen record with changes in woodland structure caused by the disappearance of elm and secondary woodland regeneration of areas occupied or disturbed by Neolithic activities.

The first agriculture is evidenced at the Union Street and Joan Street sites, where the basal peats associated with declining elm contain such sporadic occurrences of cereal pollen and also show minor peaks in grasses and herbs (*Plantago lanceolata*, Asteraceae types and *Pteridium aquilinum*). At Union Street this early agricultural phase has been dated to 4630 BP±110 (Beta 119787) and is, therefore, of Early to Middle Neolithic Age and possibly shows typical localised clearances of woodland for cultivation. Union Street and Joan Street show similar peaks of herbs and cereals which may be associated with such typical and relatively short-term clearance of woodland for agriculture. Here, however, this clearance was not perhaps in close proximity to the sample site since quantities of herbs are fewer than at other terrestrial sites noted above.

Although the two sites are geographically close, there are some differences in the woodland characteristics which show that the pollen catchment of these sites was small. It seems that the woodland was a mosaic of different types within this small region. There is some evidence for expansion of secondary woodland types, notably lime at Union Street and ash at Joan Street. The latter is typical of secondary woodland regeneration replacing earlier areas of elm and, here at Joan Street, it became more important along with some birch and an expansion of hazel. At Union Street (lpaz UNION:2), there are comparable peaks of hazel and lime, undoubtedly caused by opening of the woodland canopy. It should be noted that ash and lime are very much under-represented in pollen assemblages and any presence in pollen spectra is usually regarded as being ecologically significant. In the pollen diagrams these differences are complex. Local pollen assemblage zone JOA:2 appears to correlate with zone UNION:2. However, zone JOA:2 is more enigmatic since there may be a hiatus between zones JOA:1 and JOA:2 given that there is a gap of 550 ^{14}C years spanning only 10–15cm across the zone boundaries. However, the peat at these levels is highly humified, having accumulated under mature, damp but not wet alder carr woodland. Accumulation rates may thus have been very slow.

The data presented here, along with Greig's earlier work at Hampstead Heath, mark the first pollen evidence for human environmental disturbance and agriculture in the London region. The 'blip' (grasses and herbs) in zone UNION:1 is typical of the pollen evidence of Neolithic activity and may be of the *Landnam* type (literally land clearance) originally described by Iversen (1941; 1949) for Denmark and in Ireland at Ballynagilly (Pilcher & Smith 1979) as transient clearances of the slash and burn type. Originally postulated as being of short duration – in the order of 30 years – by Iversen, he later suggested a period of some hundreds of years' duration, for occupation and agriculture occurred prior to regeneration of secondary woodland. This is a more realistic time span and has been demonstrated in Britain using close-spaced pollen sampling at Tregaron Bog (Turner 1964); Hockham Mere (Sims 1973), and Gatcombe Withy Bed, Isle of Wight (Scaife 1980; 1987; 1988a).

The Bronze Age woodland

All of the sites studied have yielded information on the character and development of the woodland structure and environment of the Bronze Age. It is this period which saw the first major environmental changes caused by human activity substantially reducing woodland in the London region. As important as the earlier decline in elm was the clearance or reduction of lime and the diminution of remaining oak and hazel. Also, during the latter part of the Bronze Age period, dense valley-bottom, alder-dominated carr which had remained for some millennia was subject to major changes as a result of RSL change. Rising base levels set in motion a retrogressive hydrosere, resulting in a progressive change to reed swamp, poor fen communities and freshwater aquatic conditions. There is also, towards the end of this period, the first evidence towards brackish-water conditions with pollen of halophytes introduced fluvially from downstream salt marsh communities.

Lime woodland

Perhaps the most characteristic phenomenon of the late prehistoric woodland in many areas of south and east England is the importance of lime woodland. Its decline at various times during the late prehistoric period (especially during the Middle–Late Bronze Age) is equally significant and is well evidenced in London from the JLE sites. Lime became an important or even dominant constituent of the Middle Holocene (Atlantic; Flandrian Chronozone II) after its arrival in the Late Boreal (Godwin 1940; 1956; 1975a; 1975b) or Early Atlantic period immediately prior to flooding of the Straits of Dover by rising sea level. Its subsequent importance during the Atlantic is now well established for southern and eastern England (Birks *et al* 1975; Birks 1989; Moore 1977; Scaife 1980; 1987; Greig 1981; 1982b). While identification of *Tilia* pollen to species level is possible (Andrew 1971), this is not always easy and is not usually undertaken. Some records of *Tilia platyphyllos* (broad-leaved lime) are known from southern England (Dimbleby 1965) at Addington, Kent, Amberley Wild Brooks, Sussex (Thorley 1971) and in the Isle of Wight (Scaife 1980). These are, however, very occasional occurrences. Where lime pollen is consistently found in quantity it appears that this is usually *Tilia cordata* L (small-leaved lime). Later introductions of lime from Europe facilitated hybridisation, and the resultant *Tilia europaea* is frequently found today growing in parks, gardens and along roadsides.

The importance of lime in the late prehistoric vegetation of London has now been established at a substantial number of sites; few of these, however, are published. Exceptions to this are Hampstead Heath (Greig 1989; 1992), Runnymede Bridge (Greig 1991; 1992) and Bryan Road, Rotherhithe (Sidell *et al* 1995). Extensive redevelopment in the City and London suburbs has produced further extensive evidence of its importance. Of note are sites at Beckton (Scaife 1997), Ferndale Street (Scaife 1995), Silvertown, east London (Wilkinson *et al* 2000) and Rainham (Scaife 1991).

The lime decline

Rapidly declining percentages of lime pollen in pollen spectra from southern England were initially attributed to climatic change by Godwin (1940; 1956). This was based on few early analyses and insufficient detailed data from a region where it was considered that there were few satisfactory pollen-preserving sites (Turner 1970; Pilcher & Smith 1979; Scaife 1980). Furthermore, without radiometric dating, it was assumed that the lime decline was synchronous and represented climatic worsening from the sub-Boreal to sub-Atlantic period. Turner (1962) first highlighted the possibility that prehistoric clearance for agriculture may have been a major factor by identifying the expansion of agricultural weeds which occurred along with, or shortly after, declining lime pollen percentages. This has subsequently been widely illustrated from sites in southern England (Haskins 1978; Scaife 1980; Waton 1982; Waller 1993). The development of ^{14}C dating has demonstrated that the decline was not synchronous but took place from the Neolithic period onwards. The majority of dated events do, however, fall within the Middle to Late Bronze Age, that is, as originally postulated for the period of climatic deterioration. However, dates as late as the Saxon period (in Epping Forest) have been determined (Baker *et al* 1978). Other explanations for the lime decline have also been forthcoming, of which taphonomic causation may be foremost. Waller (1994a, b) has demonstrated that owing to poor pollen-dispersal characteristics (Andersen 1970; 1973), expanding wetland (paludification) may have driven lime-dominated woodland/communities farther away from the mire/sample site, thus causing reduction in pollen percentages at that site. It is conceivable that both human and pollen taphonomic factors may have played a role in the lime decline seen at a number of sites from the Jubilee Line and others recently examined in London.

Two principal phases of lime reduction and/or removal have been recognised. Firstly, in the Neolithic, all sites except Parliament Square exhibit a lime decline. Very substantial pollen percentages were found at those sites which date back to the Neolithic. Union Street perhaps illustrates the changing woodland most clearly and has provided ^{14}C dating for some of these changes. Here, high percentages of lime pollen (40%) in zone UNION:1 are dated to 5594–4974 cal. BP (Beta 119787). This illustrates the importance of lime in the local (Neolithic) landscape after the elm decline at *c* 6300–5800 cal. BP. However, from the middle of pollen zone UNION:1, percentage pollen values of >40% decline to *c* 10% and are then followed by an expansion to 30% in zone UNION:2. This is associated with expansion of hazel woodland; however, unlike the later, Middle to Late Bronze Age decline discussed below, there is no apparent expansion of cereal pollen or herbs associated with the decline. Whether or not this early lime decline was clearance for agriculture is uncertain since there are no other apparent reasons for its diminution such as paludification. It is possible that extensive woodland (including on-site alder) may have restricted ingress of airborne pollen to the site (Tauber 1967). Furthermore, lime may have been used as leaf fodder or bast fibres at this time. Subsequently (before *c* 4300 cal BP), there is evidence of lime regeneration to relatively high percentage values which may reflect woodland expansion.

Joan Street also shows a Neolithic decline at the boundary of zones JOA:1 and JOA:2 which also corresponds broadly with the period of regeneration at Union Street, that is, at 3970±70 BP). The decline here is, however, from lower percentages (*c* 10%) than seen at Union Street. The difference in pollen percentages and dates of these phases is interesting given the close spatial proximity of the two sites and further illustrates that lime pollen is very poorly represented in pollen spectra (Andersen 1970; 1973). Keatinge (1982) has demonstrated the rapid decline away from the boles of the trees. It is possible that regeneration in one area may indicate changing areas of land use during the Late Neolithic at a local level; alternatively, purely taphonomic factors such as changes in vegetation screening may account for this variation. Overall, it is felt that the sites of Joan Street and Union Street provide valuable information on local woodland modification or clearance and agricultural activity during the Middle to Late

Neolithic. There is a marked expansion of hazel pollen to high values at Joan Street again possibly caused by removal of lime and/or opening of the wood canopy enabling spread of hazel scrub or possibly coppice. It is also interesting to note that there is some increase of pine and beech pollen which may be evidence of an expanding pollen catchment caused through this woodland removal allowing greater ingress of pollen.

It was during the Bronze Age that all sites show a significant diminution of lime woodland. Of these, Canada Water shows an Early–Middle Bronze Age decline at 4245–3692 cal. BP (Beta 122968). This is associated with a sharp expansion of typical arable weeds and cereals. The latter increase alongside Chenopodiaceae, *Plantago lanceolata*, *Rumex*, Poaceae and *Pteridium aquilinum*. The latter become increasingly important, reaching maxima during the Middle–Late Bronze Age. This is interpreted as an increase in land pressure during the Late Neolithic/Early Bronze Age with local woodland clearance. However, there is also a significant increase in marsh/fen taxa (*Typha/Sparganium* and Cyperaceae) which might be a result of increased wetness that may have also caused the demise of local lime woodland. Such removal of woodland may itself have caused localised waterlogging through reduced evapotranspiration and increased surface run-off giving conditions suited to growth fen development.

A second lime decline higher in the profile at Union Street is thought to be of Middle/Late Bronze Age date. At Joan Street it occurs after 3839–3473 cal. BP; possibly at *c* 3200 cal. BP. This is characteristically associated with significant increases of cereal pollen (especially at Union Street) and taxa such as *Plantago lanceolata* and other weeds of agriculture. At Storey's Gate, samples from the basal organic mud levels have high percentages (26%) which decline to 5–10%. This decline is again of Middle to Late Bronze Age date with a second later reduction from *c* 2800 cal. BP. The latter, final decline in the Storey's Gate profile may, however, be caused by taphonomic changes brought about by change from organic to predominantly mineral stratigraphy.

At St Stephen's East, Westminster, the decline is very strongly associated with cereal pollen and expansion of herbs. This event has not been specifically/radiometrically dated but is attributed to the Bronze Age. The site is complicated by the fact that there is a distinct change in the stratigraphy between pollen zones SSE:1 and SSE:2. Thus, taphonomy may be significant since, at the lime decline, there is also an increase in Chenopodiaceae and taxa which may indicate tidal- and brackish-water influences. Paludification/waterlogging, therefore, may have been responsible for this decrease in lime pollen. The expansion of cereal pollen and herbs from these levels may also be fluvially derived, being transported from farther afield. The phenomenon is complex and while largely attributed to human activity, may also be linked to regional base-level changes and changes in pollen taphonomy.

All of the pollen diagrams presented here have yielded data on the character and development of woodland structure and environment during the Bronze Age when major changes to the region's woodland occurred. Second only to the decline in elm at 6300–5800 cal. BP was a reduction of lime from the environment and diminution of oak and hazel. During the latter part of the Bronze Age period dense valley-bottom, alder-dominated (carr) wood, which had remained little changed for some millennia, was also subject to change in many areas. This was caused by RSL change and local/regional autogenic changes causing retrogressive hydroseres with the transition to grass/sedge/reed fen. There is also the first evidence of brackish-water conditions with halophytes introduced fluvially from farther afield (downstream). These changes are particularly prominent at Palace Chambers South where peat developed on an earlier land surface (Neolithic/Bronze Age transition) which in turn developed on fluvial sediments. Initially, alder, grass and sedge communities became increasingly inundated by freshwater conditions and subsequently by saline-/brackish-water conditions in the Late Bronze Age.

The Iron Age

The removal of lime woodland during the Middle to Late Bronze Age was the most significant event in the pollen spectra examined from the JLE sites. Nevertheless, there is pollen evidence for the local and regional woodland and land use during the Iron Age and historic periods.

At Joan Street, after 2706–2162 cal. BP and at Union Street after c 2700 cal. BP, the upper sequences date to the Iron Age and Roman period. These sites (with Canada Water) demonstrate that *Quercus* and *Corylus avellana* remained the most widespread woodland elements. Pollen values of *Quercus* typically range between 10–20%. These taxa have a generally good pollen dispersion (being anemophilous) and the data are likely to represent the regional background vegetation. It is not clear, however, whether this was of remaining woodland or scattered trees and small copses. Woodland continued to be pressurised causing further reduction in its percentages/representation. At Canada Water, for example, values decline from 20% in the Iron Age and this continued diminution is mirrored by increases in agricultural crops including *Triticum/Hordeum* and *Secale cereale* at this site and Union Street. These are useful records of oats being grown during the Iron Age which in the past were considered to be a Roman introduction. Apart from the remaining oak and hazel woodland, all of the sites referable to the Iron Age and later periods display a diversity of trees and shrubs, albeit in low values. Joan Street and Union Street contain sporadic occurrences of *Tilia, Fraxinus, Fagus, Abies, Ilex, Pinus* and fen shrubs. Interpretation of the extent of their importance is difficult and further complicated by taphonomic problems

Roman and post-Roman periods

Sites which are dated to the Roman and post-Roman periods include the upper sections of Union Street, Joan Street and Storey's Gate, Westminster Underground Station and Parliament Square. Sediments associated with these periods are predominantly minerogenic rather than the organic peat associated with the later prehistoric period. Deposition of these silts was widespread under varying freshwater and brackish-water conditions causing the change from alder carr (*eg* at St Stephen's East, Joan Street, Canada Water and Union Street) to wetter freshwater reed-swamp (grass-sedge fen). This was, therefore, a retrogressive hydrosere. Pollen preservation in these units was found to be very variable with some sites such as London Bridge, examined during earlier assessment, proving to be of little value. However, at the sites noted above, it was possible to make a general reconstruction of the vegetation of the historic period. Interpretation of pollen spectra in these sediments is, however, more complex with both aerial and fluvial transport of pollen, human factors (domestic waste) and the possible reworking of earlier material in this fluviatile and estuarine environment. The growing importance of London from the Roman period also resulted in the introduction of exotic plant taxa (food and drink)(Willcox 1977) which add a further dimension to an understanding of the pollen spectra and character of the vegetation. Of particular interest from the study of the JLE sites are the, albeit sporadic, records of taxa that are less well represented which also include possible exotic introductions into London. Some of the more interesting of these are discussed below.

Fagus (F. sylvatica L): (beech)

Fagus has been found in Bronze Age contexts at Joan Street and Palace Chambers South as well as in medieval levels at Storey's Gate, Union Street (especially in UNION:5), St Stephen's East, Palace Chambers South and Parliament Square. Although beech produces copious quantities of pollen this tree is generally poorly represented in pollen assemblages because the grains are heavy and rarely spread far away from the tree canopy. Its presence in even the small quantities at these sites may thus attest to its local growth. It should also be considered that pollen fluvially transported from further away may also have contributed to these Iron Age and later records.

Tilia (lindens/lime)

While this tree was clearly abundant during the Atlantic and the sub-Boreal, there is a consistent presence in Iron Age, Roman and post-Roman contexts at Joan Street, Canada Water and Thorney Island. This suggests local growth of lindens since the tree is insect pollinated and poorly represented in pollen spectra. Its presence here and at other London sites such as the Tower of London (R G Scaife unpublished data) and Falcon House may also be evidence of the introduction of exotic/non-native types (*ie* not the small-leaved lime *Tilia cordata*). There is some indication of this from the differing pollen morphology in these cases. As lime blossom was an important constituent of herbal tea and also of mead, it is possible that trees were planted within the urban area in gardens in this region. Introduced limes were certainly planted for ornamental reasons, as has been clearly shown at Hampton Court where pollen and plant macrofossils of *Tilia* cf x *europaea* L were recovered from the moat fills.

Juglans regia L (walnut)

Walnut pollen was found consistently in the upper levels at Storey's Gate and especially at St Stephen's East where it is an important continuous record of this introduced tree in the historic period. Although there are now occasional records in pre-Roman sediments (Long *et al* 1999) and at Joan Street, it is generally regarded as a Roman introduction into western Europe as a whole (Godwin 1975a). Most occurrences are from Roman and post-Roman sequences such as an early Roman record from the Temple of Mithras (Scaife 1982b). Overall, this suggests that once introduced into London by the Romans, it continued to grow or be grown locally presumably for its nuts (*Juglans regia* L) which have been found in a number of London sites. Its pollen has been found from sites of all later periods, including post-medieval, Tudor sediments at Broad Sanctuary, Westminster (Mills 1982), Saxon at Cromwell Green (Greig 1992) and in the uppermost recent levels of Hampstead Heath (Greig 1992). Earlier occurrences (*ie* pre-Roman) – such as at Joan Street, in Poole Harbour (Long *et al* 1999) and in Northern Ireland (D Weir, pers comm) – may be attributed to long-distance airborne or fluvial/ocean currents, perhaps from North America where other important species of *Juglans* occur.

Picea (spruce) and *Abies* (fir)

Abies and *Picea* pollen have been recorded from JLE sites which have sediments of Roman and post-Roman age. *Abies* has a fairly consistent record throughout the upper sediments at Storey's Gate and at Parliament Square with sporadic occurrences at Union Street and Joan Street. *Picea* has been found at sites which include Palace Chambers South, St Stephen's East and in Bronze Age levels at Storey's Gate. These records of spruce and fir are enigmatic and possibly important since these trees are clearly also not native to Britain during the Holocene. Pollen records are, however, now relatively frequent for analyses which span the historic period. There is a possibility that these pollen taxa may have been reworked and derived from earlier Pleistocene sediments such as terrace sequences where they occur in varying degrees of abundance in the different preceding interglacial stages. The preservation of the grains was, however, largely comparable with the contemporary Holocene pollen while the pre-Quaternary palynomorphs, which were also present, were typically stained much darker, had different reticulation of the saccae and were

easily differentiable. The derivation of the spruce and fir pollen recorded at these JLE sites is enigmatic and, as with *Juglans*, may be from the planting of exotic trees in parks and gardens or alternatively derived from fluvial/marine transport. With regard to the latter, *Picea* has been noted in marine sediments on the south coast by Jennings and Smyth (1982) at Lottbridge Drove, East Sussex and in Poole Harbour, Dorset (Long *et al* 1999) indicating possible long-distance marine transport, a possibility indicated by the studies of Dyakowska (1947) and Stanley (1969) for marine-borne pollen. It is plausible that spruce and fir were introduced into gardens by the Romans and there are now various sites in London exhibiting small numbers of these taxa. Locally, these conifers have been recorded from the sediment fills of the Tower of London moat (R G Scaife unpublished data). For the post-medieval period occurrences are commonplace in pollen spectra through introduction into parks and gardens.

Miscellaneous taxa

A range of other tree and shrub taxa are present which may derive from regional sources or occasional local growth in proximity to the JLE sites examined. These taxa include *Carpinus betulus* L, recovered at St Stephen's, at Palace Chambers South and Union Street, *Populus* at Joan Street and St Stephen's East, and more common taxa (birch and pine) which are likely to be from airborne transport representing growth within the region. *Ilex aquifolium*, *Fraxinus* and *Fagus sylvatica* L (see above) are taxa which are generally substantially under-represented in pollen spectra and, if not fluvially transported from elsewhere in the catchment, probably indicate local growth.

After the Late Bronze Age and Iron Age, shrubs decline sharply, as well as trees, leaving predominantly *Corylus avellana* as the principal background shrub. However, as with trees, there occurs an increased diversity of shrub types. These again pose the problem of whether the taxa are from local growth or are regional representations. *Rhamnus catharticus* (alder buckthorn) at St Stephen's East and Joan Street are likely to have been growing in the damp alder fen carr woodland. Other taxa are less easily attributable to ecological community types. These include notably *Viburnum lantana*, *Cornus* cf *sanguinea* (dogwood) and *Prunus/Malus* type. *Hippophae rhamnoides* L recorded at St Stephen's East is associated with some other halophytic elements which include *Armeria* at Westminster Underground, *Plantago maritima* (at Palace Chambers South) and possibly Chenopodiaceae, *Aster* type and hystrichospheres/dinoflagellates. These along with diatoms have clearly been transported from estuarine/salt marsh areas downstream in the Thames estuary.

Roman and post-Roman evidence of cultivation

Cereal pollen recovered from Jubilee Line sites comprise barley type, rye/wheat type and oats. The latter is especially characteristic of the Roman and post-Roman periods but here has been found at Union Street and Canada Water in what are thought to be Iron Age contexts. As outlined above, the marked expansion of cereal cultivation at and after the Bronze Age 'lime decline' suggests increased population, food demand and land pressure during the later Bronze Age and hence clearance of lime on suitable agricultural soils. This was perhaps associated with the socio-economic changes and land apportionment mooted by Bowen (1975) for the chalklands of southern England. There is no apparent expansion of agriculture resulting from changes that took place with the onset of the Iron Age or Romano-British periods. The overall increase in the numbers and diversity of herbs relates to, and may be associated with, the preceding Late Bronze Age deforestation and increased agriculture. There are few other cultivated plants in the JLE sequences. This is unsurprising since most of the sites consist of floodplain marsh and as such were doubtless removed from the main areas of cultivation; that is, with the exception of ard-mark sites on the dunes in Southwark.

9

The interaction of environmental change and human habitation

Jane Sidell and Keith Wilkinson

Introduction

This final chapter is concerned with using the data gathered during this project in a wider context. As was stated in the introduction to this book, the project was conceived as one whereby data relating to the topography and vegetation along the line of the JLE could be generated and could act as context for 'mainstream' archaeological interpretation. It is hoped that this will be an ongoing and interactive approach which will, over the next few years, lead to the revision and hopefully refinement of models suggested in this volume and other archaeological publications relating to the JLE and London. The chapter focuses on how the changes that have been identified in the palaeoecological record are likely to have affected the societies occupying the central London area. A review of the techniques and research objectives combined with some suggestions for developing this type of research in London concludes the volume.

Prehistoric site location, taphonomy and representation

Until now this account has concentrated on providing a developmental history of the London Thames for the Late Devensian glacial and Holocene periods, based on data obtained from the JLE investigations. In this section the intention is to go beyond such a narrative to look at processes of landscape modification resulting from the sorts of river and estuary development outlined in the preceding chapters, and examine how these are likely to have affected prehistoric archaeological site survival in central London. That the archaeology of the historic period is not covered is mainly due to the fact that comparatively little of the stratigraphy investigated during this project is later than the Iron Age and that the main impact of Holocene RSL change and river development occurred during the later prehistoric periods. It is also true to say that taphonomic processes operating on historic period sites adjacent to the Thames have been rather better studied, simply because sequences of Roman, Saxon and medieval date are readily available throughout much of central London (Milne *et al* 1983; Brigham 1990; Steedman *et al* 1992; Milne *et al* 1997).

Palaeolithic

As has been noted above, despite the presence of such well-known Pleistocene fossil-bearing strata as those found at Trafalgar Square (Franks *et al* 1958; Franks 1960; Preece 1999), relatively few *in situ* Palaeolithic artefacts have been recovered from central London. Findspots of Palaeolithic stone tools are largely confined to reworked examples found in gravel strata relating to braided river environments developing during cold stages of the Pleistocene. Such reworked artefacts have been located at either end of the JLE from around St James's Square and Stratford, but not from the area in between according to the Greater London Sites and Monuments Record (GLSMR). *In situ* Palaeolithic remains are few in central London, mainly as a result of the dominance of gravel-dominated, braided river facies for much of the Pleistocene. The dynamic nature of such depositional environments would have caused almost certain destruction to any sites located on, or close to, the surface of the floodplain, even if the Palaeolithic population chose to utilise areas adjacent to the river. Such reworked material is of relatively limited archaeological significance, except perhaps for stylistic studies, as when removed from primary context it is arguable to what extent artefacts can be indicative of human activity and interaction.

Survival of Palaeolithic artefacts *in situ* is more likely to occur in channel marginal conditions during episodes when the Thames adopted a meandering bedform, or in periods when braid plains were being abandoned. Such occurrences are associated with interglacial, and occasionally interstadial, episodes of the Pleistocene. Thus Late Upper Palaeolithic sites, relating to the Windermere interstadial, are known from the floodplain deposits in the Colne (Lewis 1991; Lewis *et al* 1992) and Lea (Reid 1916; Sidell *et al* in prep b) tributaries. Lower and Middle Palaeolithic sites that are almost certainly *in situ* most famously include Swanscombe (Conway & Waechter 1977; Conway *et al* 1996), but Middle Palaeolithic artefacts have also been found lying on the top of Taplow Terrace deposits at West Drayton (Wymer 1988). In central London, however, such sites are all but unknown, although fine-grained Late Glacial deposits occur as localised channel fills in the Shepperton Gravel (for example at Bramcote Green, Masthouse Terrace and Silvertown). Ipswichian organic and other floodplain deposits are of course also known for the Trafalgar Square, Green Park, Strand and Whitehall area (Preece 1999), but as already discussed the Ipswichian appears to be the one interglacial of the Middle and later Pleistocene when humans were not present in the British Isles (Sutcliffe 1995). Nevertheless, possible Palaeolithic flakes were found, apparently *in situ*, in deposits adjacent to Trafalgar Square during construction of the Admiralty Offices (Abbott 1898). However, the association of these artefacts with the dwarf birch *Betula nana*, would suggest they are of Devensian Late Glacial and hence Late Upper Palaeolithic date, while on typological grounds Lacaille (1961) assigns them to the Mesolithic. No Palaeolithic finds have been made from other Late Glacial deposits as yet (although this may be a result of the limited exposure available), but it is highly likely that artefacts will be recovered in the future, especially as recent studies of the final Upper Palaeolithic suggest site locations are associated with rivers (Barton 1997). Fills of abandoned channels can rarely, unfortunately, be detected from the modern ground surface in London where the thickness of post-glacial sequences and modern building obscure the features. It is notable for example that the Late Glacial sequences of Bramcote Green, Masthouse Terrace and Silvertown were chance discoveries during archaeological evaluations carried out to investigate other strata.

Mesolithic

As has been discussed in previous chapters, the Mesolithic period was a time of rapid climatic and vegetation change in London. For most of the Mesolithic period the area encompassed by the JLE was characterised by the meandering, sand-dominated river that had developed either at the end of the Devensian Late Glacial or in the Early Holocene. Despite the ameliorating climate and rapidly developing deciduous woodland, the Thames appears to have been well constrained within its channel. Within the channel areas various bar features developed, particularly in meanders (*eg* Culling Road) and at confluences (Westminster). These are likely to have prograded downstream over time accompanied by localised erosion as a result of chute channel development and channel migration. Thus the picture is of stability on the floodplain and continuous change within the channel itself. However, the evidence presented in chapter 7 suggests that the Early Holocene meandering river ran along a slightly different course from the present-day Thames, passing through Pimlico, Victoria, Westminster, Waterloo, Borough, Bermondsey and Rotherhithe, rejoining the present-day channel near Canada Water. If these data are correct it would suggest that no *in situ* Mesolithic sites should be expected along this route, as people are unlikely to have exploited river channels for anything other than occasional fishing expeditions. However, areas adjacent to the river channel would be ideal for exploitation given the inherent ecotonal environment of a river margin. Nevertheless, it is unlikely that *in situ* Mesolithic sites will survive in locations between this Early Holocene river course and the present one, as processes associated with river migration are likely to have reworked any archaeological material. The only archaeological material to be found *in situ* in these areas will postdate the episodes of channel migration, which cannot be precisely dated on the basis of present data. However, the potential for Mesolithic sites to the south of this Early Holocene route is high, and should be considered when planning investigations in Southwark and Lambeth.

In common with Palaeolithic populations, the Mesolithic hunter-gatherers do not appear to have occupied permanent settlements, and thus their activities are less visible in the archaeological record than those from later periods. Sites in the London area mainly take the form of flint scatters (*eg* Three Ways Wharf, Uxbridge (Lewis *et al* 1992), the Erith Spine Road (Sidell *et al* 1997) and the B&Q site, Old Kent Road Sidell *et al* in prep a), although seasonal settlements have been found elsewhere in the Thames Valley, notably at Thatcham on the River Kennet in Berkshire (Wymer 1962). However, by far the majority of Mesolithic sites in central London consist of isolated findspots of flint blades and scrapers, antler picks, and perforated and tranchet axes. These cluster particularly in Westminster, with other finds from Waterloo and Stratford, but are largely absent elsewhere, probably for the sorts of reasons discussed above. There can be little doubt that the numerous Mesolithic finds in Westminster, which from descriptions appear to be primarily of Late Mesolithic date, have eroded out of the Thorney sand bed, and are likely to have been originally deposited during hunting/foraging expeditions on the surface of emergent channel bars during periods of low river flow. *In situ* evidence of such activity has recently been found in Erith (Sidell *et al* 1997), where finds included microliths, a tranchet axe, an awl, scrapers, blades and many flakes (Taylor 1996). The lack of finds of Early Mesolithic date in Westminster would appear to suggest either that the population of this period did not exploit the area, or more plausibly that such sites are deeply buried within channel marginal bars and have not been uncovered by either erosion or excavation. East of Westminster there is a rapid drop in the frequency of Mesolithic findspots, which given the reconstructed route of the Thames channel would have been readily available for exploitation. However, the topography of these areas of Southwark, Bermondsey and Rotherhithe has been severely affected by sedimentation as a result of RSL rise in the Middle Holocene, which has filled the areas between sand bars developed in the earlier Holocene with both peats and estuarine silt/clays. Thus Mesolithic sites are likely to be deeply buried, and are all but undetectable. It is notable that the few Mesolithic finds that have been made are associated with the eyots, which have not been buried by such a thickness of later sediment. The same sorts of processes are likely to have obscured sites on the Isle of Dogs and Canning Town, but to an even greater degree because of the absence of Early Holocene sand islands. Notably no Mesolithic findspots are known from these areas.

Neolithic

There are even fewer Neolithic findspots in central London than from the Mesolithic period. According to the GLSMR, flint axes have been found adjacent to Westminster Bridge, at London Bridge Station and at Stratford, while a polished axe has been found at Downing Street. Elsewhere a Neolithic site consisting of *c* 200 flint pieces and located within organic muds topping Chiswick Eyot has recently been found by the Thames Foreshore Survey and is currently being prepared for publication (F Haughy, pers comm). Scatters of Neolithic artefacts were also found during the course of the JLE investigations at Palace Chambers South, Westminster and Culling Road, Rotherhithe. The one factor that all these sites have in common is that they are situated on localised topographic highs above the channel of the Thames. The key question to ask is whether such a distribution truly represents Neolithic land utilisation, or whether it is an artefact of later sedimentation obscuring Neolithic sites in low-lying situations. Evidence from recent projects in central London and from the JLE investigations suggests the latter is almost certainly the case. For example, excavations at Silvertown demonstrate that a Neolithic trackway extended from a sand island out into a marsh (although where it terminated is not known), suggesting that the latter was used by the contemporary population (Wessex Archaeology 1994b; Meddens 1996). If this was the case further sites should be expected from within the peat

deposits that characterise much of Southwark eastwards, and which are known from both the JLE and other recent investigations to date from at least *c* 5400 cal. BP (*ie* the Middle Neolithic). It is true that no Neolithic material was found during excavations at Joan Street, Union Street or Canada Water, but as trench sizes were small these represent an infinitesimally small sample of the total area occupied by the peat. A further problem with the distribution of Neolithic findspots is that in the Westminster area the sand strata which are classified by most authors (*eg* Meddens 1996; Merriman 1992) as comprising the 'topographic highs' so favoured for discard of artefacts, were still forming. Therefore Early and Middle Neolithic material can be expected from within the sands, and only the very latest Neolithic artefacts will be found on the surface of such strata. Indeed it is likely that many of the casual finds made in the Westminster area prior to the JLE investigations have eroded, or been pulled, from the sand strata during construction in the last two centuries. If the change in the course of the Thames from its Early Holocene route through Victoria, Westminster, Waterloo and Bermondsey to its present form occurred in the Mesolithic period (there is no precise chronology for this migration), Neolithic sites will have been little affected by the scouring processes of such a migration, and can thus be expected in almost any location in central London. Thus the Neolithic archaeology of central London is undoubtedly hugely under-represented in the artefactual records, and sites are almost certainly located beneath the sands of the Westminster member and the peat and intertidal sediments of the south bank. Such artefacts only occur close to the present-day surface where pre-Neolithic fluvial sands were not covered by subsequent estuarine sediments as at Culling Road. Perhaps significantly large quantities of Neolithic artefacts have been dredged from the Thames, but are not included on the GLSMR (F Haughy, pers comm).

Bronze Age

The discussion of the previous section is also of relevance to the situation regarding central London's Bronze Age archaeology. Although there are just occasional findspots along the western part of the JLE (*eg* a socketed axe recorded adjacent to Westminster Bridge and various ceramic finds from Palace Chambers South), and a ring-ditch from near London Bridge, there is a wide range of data emerging from areas to the east suggesting widespread Bronze Age activity (Meddens 1996). As has already been discussed, this evidence is primarily in the form of trackways that criss-cross the peats in areas to the east of the Isle of Dogs (Meddens & Sidell 1995; Meddens 1996). Little evidence for such features has been found so far from south of the Thames beyond the trackway at Bramcote Green (Thomas & Rackham 1996) and Erith (Sidell *et al* 1997), although this might be a result of the larger number of investigations in north-eastern areas. Trackways have not been found in Southwark or Rotherhithe, but given the number of 'islands' that are known to occur within the peat and intertidal sediments in this area (Tyers 1988), such structures are likely, linking the 'topographic highs'. Thus Bronze Age sites in Southwark and areas to the east almost certainly exist, but are obscured by the great depths of peat and intertidal sediments that outcrop in these areas. In Westminster the situation is somewhat different. The Bronze Age saw a change in sedimentation from firstly sands to vertically accreting mineral silts and clays and then organic muds. Utilisation of such a depositional environment for settlement and agriculture would have been limited, but ard marks have been noted, as mentioned above. The majority of evidence of archaeological features and artefacts of Bronze Age date, however, is found cut into sand deposits at elevations above the floodplain that then existed, as at Site 2, Palace Chambers South.

Iron Age

There are fewer Iron Age finds and sites in central London than from almost any other archaeological period (a coin hoard from St James's Park is the only listing from the JLE route in the GLSMR), and this is mirrored by the discoveries, or rather their absence, during the JLE investigations. Indeed the majority of Iron Age finds made have been of items dredged from the river (eg the famous 'Battersea Shield') or found redeposited on the foreshore. There are several reasons for such a state of affairs. Firstly, in Southwark and areas to the east there is widespread evidence for RSL rise causing widespread inundation of lower-lying areas by the end of the Bronze Age, with the previous alder carr environments of the Bronze Age being replaced by intertidal mudflats. Evidence from Joan Street and Union Street suggests that this process was completed by c 2300 cal. BP (the Middle Iron Age), while for some time previously the area would have been occupied by salt marsh. Neither salt marsh nor mudflats would have been particularly favourable areas for occupation, or indeed any activity beyond hunting waterfowl, and therefore it is unlikely that the Iron Age population utilised much of the Southwark, Rotherhithe, Bermondsey or Isle of Dogs areas, except on an extremely infrequent basis. The situation may have been different in Westminster, but unfortunately almost all deposits dating between the Bronze Age and the 12th century have been removed by channel scouring (which cannot be precisely dated). Therefore evidence for Iron Age activity in this area will always be limited and restricted to reworked finds.

The influence of the changing river on human occupation

The River Thames has been a dominant feature in the central London region for much of the period of human occupation. Even now, when it is heavily managed, constrained within a narrow course and overshadowed by the network of streets and buildings surrounding it, it is still a focal point of the city.

Therefore, in an undeveloped landscape and with the ability to follow an unconstrained course, the Thames must have been an extremely impressive feature; at times the evidence suggests that the floodplain was nearly 5km wide (Devoy 1979). However, the data collected during this project have suggested that the Thames has undergone a series of changes throughout the Holocene, which are likely to have affected the human population to a greater or lesser degree, dependent on time period and geographical location. This, potentially, would have affected the choice of activity/settlement locations for the contemporary societies and also their archaeological preservation and recovery at the present day.

Braided channel/meandering channel transition

The change from a braided system to a meandering single channel river would have significantly altered the appearance of the floodplain. This appears to have taken place at some point in the Late Upper Palaeolithic or Mesolithic. However, during these periods, there is limited evidence for human activity in the central London region; this is likely to be a factor of the cultural patterns of a transhumant society, which leaves very little solid archaeological evidence. On the whole, evidence for Palaeolithic activity tends to be restricted to isolated flint scatters, which may indicate that sites were only visited once, or perhaps a handful of times, if traditions of using specific areas continued over years or seasons. It can be assumed that the people generating the remains were highly mobile; the question is: how was the river traversed? Or indeed was the river traversed? This would certainly have been easier with a braided river, where distinct, relatively shallow channels were separated by solid ground, at least during the later summer and autumn. The transition to a single channel is likely to have made traversing the river altogether more difficult, by concentrating the flow and increasing the depth in that location. Additionally, although the Thames in central London was not directly affected by the increasing sea levels following glacial retreat at the Devensian/Holocene transition, the gradient of the freshwater river is likely to have been affected, thereby potentially increasing the relative altitude of the river. However, it is impossible to actually establish whether it would have been necessary or desirable for the communities to cross the river at all. It is unlikely that there would have been any distinction in resource availability on a north–south axis, and therefore the Thames potentially acted as a boundary not simply because it became difficult to cross, but also because there was little reason to cross it.

Although a region split by a meandering river could potentially have some deleterious effects upon the population using the marginal areas, this still does not seem to have been a period of major settlement. The Mesolithic communities continued a mobile tradition, with only isolated flint scatters – such as that recovered from Three Ways Wharf, Uxbridge (Lewis et al 1992) – testifying to their presence. Therefore, a slowly migrating river is likely to have only the most minor of effects, for instance causing previously dry land adjacent to the river to become slowly submerged. Nevertheless, there would also have been potential benefits of new areas of foreshore becoming available. The Late Mesolithic site at Spine Road, Erith (Sidell *et al* 1997) is an example of a marginal site located on the south bank, illustrating that the foreshore was used at this period. In fact, waterside locations are a prominent theme for Mesolithic findspots including central London. The topographic plot of Mesolithic Southwark (see Fig 45) identifies a series of findspots along a linear course, probably a relict channel which has not previously been observed. Three Ways Wharf itself is marginal to the River Colne, and a number of ephemeral sites have been identified on the margins of the River Lea. It is unlikely, though, that the speed of the changing river course would be such that a migrant society could not adapt itself and its needs.

The situation in the Neolithic contrasts significantly with that of the Mesolithic, although the terms Neolithic and Mesolithic are perhaps becoming slightly redundant with the considerable overlap that is now recognised in the cultural aspects which make up the last migrant societies and the earliest farming society. Having said this, there is evidence from the central London area for settled communities which would presumably have adapted to change in a very different way. In the Neolithic, buildings, animals and fields would have represented major investments of labour and resources; abandoning these owing to changing river conditions would have been much more of a blow to these more settled people than the preceding society.

Meandering channel/tidal river transition

Changes from the meandering river of the Mesolithic/Neolithic to intertidal conditions by the Bronze Age will almost certainly have had a substantial effect upon the people living close to the Thames. There are substantially more archaeological sites from this period, not least from the wetlands to the east of London, where a series of Middle Bronze Age timber trackways have been recovered from the upper strata of peat sequences associated with this change in environment. Stratigraphic and palaeoecological analysis have suggested that these were constructed to offset increasing wetness in the marshlands which was presumably related to RSL rise (Meddens & Sidell 1995; Meddens 1996; Thomas & Rackham 1996). More dramatic evidence comes from riverside sites in Southwark and Westminster where the soils through which rip ards have cut are submerged under waterlain silts, for example at Phoenix Wharf (Sidell *et al* in prep a) and Hopton Street. The data collected from the JLE project have suggested that the tidal inundation was a relatively rapid event with a strong tidal surge taking place in the Middle–Late Bronze Age. Again, it seems unlikely that societies were unable to react to the change in floodplain configuration that this would have entailed. It is possible, though, that within generations, those fields which were farmed on the Southwark islands and possibly also on Thorney Island were no longer available, making a retreat to higher and drier ground necessary. Without information on

how land was held within the contemporary societies, it is impossible to identify how this abandonment of land would have affected smaller units (*ie* families within the wider community). Nevertheless, it is fascinating to speculate on both this issue and where the fields were relocated – that is, off the floodplain entirely and on to the gravel terraces to the south and north?

The tidal river in the Bronze Age may not have caused serious problems to contemporary communities after the initial reconfiguration of the floodplain, because the data from this project suggest that the tidal head gradually progressed downstream in the Bronze and Iron Ages. Information collected from other sources suggests that this downstream migration progressed into the late Roman period. This indicates that the dry ground at the margins of the floodplain at the period of initial tidal progression upstream is likely to have remained dry from the Bronze Age to the end of the Roman period. The hiatus identified at Thorney Island, however, is undated, yet attributed to the tidal river and would have almost certainly had a significant effect upon the inhabitants of Thorney Island, by redefining its shape. In the absence of dating evidence, though, knowing that this would have made life difficult for the inhabitants is of little use; it is to be hoped that this problem can be addressed through future analysis.

The Jubilee Line Extension and future palaeoenvironmental studies of the London Thames

In the early 1990s palaeoenvironmental and geoarchaeological studies were just beginning to be viewed as important components of the rescue archaeology of London. As a result of this realisation the Jubilee Line Palaeoenvironmental Project was conceived and was subsequently supported by London Underground. However, as a result of various delays the project is being published at the end of the 1990s when multidisciplinary studies in archaeology are the norm, and when research techniques have moved on apace from procedures of the early 1990s. Therefore it is important to view the results of this project in the historical context of archaeology of the early 1990s, a period when compulsory developer funding of projects was in its infancy, and when relatively little was known of London's prehistory. Nevertheless the project has been largely successful in tackling the objectives outlined in chapter 1. Lithostratigraphic data were collected and suggestions have been made as to causes and processes leading to the formation of the sediment accumulating on the study sites. It was possible, particularly in Westminster, to correlate episodes of sedimentation and additionally to propose a new lithostratigraphic unit – the Westminster member – purely on the basis of data from the JLE project. Although the use of topographic modelling has been limited, the maps of Mesolithic

Southwark/Lambeth (including the borders to the City and Westminster) and Westminster have been informative at a basic level, and in fact identified a clustering of Mesolithic findspots along a previously unidentified south bank tributary in Southwark. The question of tidal influence is one which has dominated the investigation of these sites, and the information regarding tidal conditions in the Bronze Age is a significant breakthrough in interpreting the later prehistoric archaeology of central London.

These data should assist archaeologists in developing interpretations of individual areas, such as the history of Thorney Island, and also in addressing broader questions of the pattern of prehistoric settlement on the Thames floodplain. Although the project has been undertaken in an archaeological context, the data are more widely applicable. The stratigraphic and river-level data will be of importance to geologists and physical geographers alike, while information on vegetation changes will provide a firm base for future palaeoecological study of the London area.

Future research priorities

Techniques and methodological review

In considering future priorities in relation to palaeoenvironmental research, both techniques and specific themes can be addressed. As discussed in the introduction to this book, the project was derived from a programme of rescue archaeology, and although not governed by PPG16, it was subject to the usual constraints on time and funding. As a result of this, only a limited range of techniques was utilised. These included dating using the ^{14}C method, biological characterisation using pollen and diatom analysis, and facies modelling through sample description and sedimentological analysis; sound and valid techniques enabling generalised models to be proposed for the research issues under investigation. However, it is certain that a more wide-ranging use of available, if uncommon, techniques would have refined the data sets. The most obvious area is in obtaining chronological information in situations where organic material suitable for ^{14}C measurement is either absent, or judged to be unreliable (for example in the mineral-dominated strata in Westminster and at Culling Road). Although luminescence methods, that is, optically stimulated luminescence (OSL), are beginning to be used increasingly in archaeology to date alluvial and intertidal stratigraphy, such techniques were not readily available in the early 1990s. Therefore, samples were not taken from the first sites investigated such as Joan Street and Union Street. The exception is Canada Water where a thermoluminescence (TL) date was collected from the basal sands as part of a student project (although in this case the error margins are too wide to make the result useful). Recent success in using a combination of optically (OSL) and infra-red (IRSL) stimulated techniques to date later Holocene intertidal deposits in London (Frechen & Wilkinson in prep), suggests that there is little excuse for poor chronological control in fine-grained alluvial/intertidal deposits in future projects.

A second area where use of additional techniques could have enhanced the results of the project is palaeoecology. Diatom and pollen analysis are commonly considered the most appropriate techniques for the investigation of Holocene estuarine development; however, examination of further biological groups could have provided high-resolution data. Plant macrofossils may have enhanced the information relating to ultra-local vegetation, while the use of foraminiferal analysis – organisms which are less readily transported from outer estuary sources than diatoms – could possibly have refined some of the conclusions reached regarding tidal conditions. With regard to the lithological analysis, although a fairly limited range of techniques was used, one significant area where improvements can be made is in allowing the analyst access to sections in the field to describe sediment morphology and structure. The primary field records are of greater importance than the records generated by the samples collected from them. That this did not happen during the JLE project was due to the organisation that pertained in London in the early 1990s, where environmental archaeologists had rigidly defined roles (eg field sampling officers and specialists), with 'specialists' being largely laboratory-based. This situation was changed relatively soon after the samples for the JLE were taken to one which allows specialists much greater freedom to visit sites and sample them.

Topographic modelling was carried out on a basic level to reconstruct palaeotopography using data from boreholes and archaeological sites. These techniques are currently being further developed in archaeology in conjunction with Geographic Information System (GIS) software, both as an aid to research and as a predictive tool for identifying locations of potential archaeological significance. Numerous difficulties are associated with such activities; most notably, limitations of available and affordable software, but also the nature of the geotechnical data itself. Nevertheless, as more and more sites are excavated, and further synthetic projects are carried out, there will be increased need for detailed palaeotopographic data. This type of modelling is a simple and rapid means of establishing a broader context for both individual sites and groups of such sites. Although the quality of geotechnical data available from commercial companies may continue to vary in quality, archaeological trench data should improve, with better descriptions, greater geoarchaeological input and more accurate surveying. Improvements in modelling software are currently being developed and tested by archaeologists, all of which should lead to improved resolution of topographic data.

This project has benefited and been relatively successful in addressing its objectives by utilising techniques allied to the three principle components of geoarchaeology: bio-, litho- and chronostratigraphy (Butzer 1982). It must be stated, however, that in future projects (where funding allows), designs should allow for the employment of a greater range of techniques to address their research questions, most notably additional biostratigraphic methods such as foraminiferal analysis and chronometric dating techniques, as well as the development of high-resolution palaeotopographic models.

Research questions

Although this project has provided significant new data on several issues – for instance the development of the tidal river, the definition of sedimentation models in Westminster and the occurrence of the lime decline – it has also highlighted areas where data were not available. Consequently, it has been possible to identify issues which urgently require primary data collection and research to take forward palaeoecological reconstruction in central London. One such has been highlighted through the palynological studies. Although evidence for agriculture has been suggested from a number of the sequences from the pollen record, these data cannot be regarded as conclusive proof of localised agricultural communities. Further data are required to test the evidence, particularly for Bronze Age farming on Thorney Island. This can only be achieved through excavation, for instance with conclusive identification of plough marks or field systems. However, now that the possibility has been identified, it is a research theme that can be pursued through evaluations and excavations carried out as part of the PPG16 planning process.

One of the most obvious gaps revealed by this project relates to the development of the river between the Iron Age and the Saxon period. At Westminster, where arguably the best data concerning the Early and Middle Holocene river have been found, this period is not represented in the stratigraphy due to major scouring in the earlier medieval period. Although such data were available from Southwark in the form of mineral silt/clays forming on mudflats, Westminster is perhaps a more crucial location, as human settlement is known to have been located in the area for much of the period of hiatus. The location of the tidal head, representing the extent that brackish water reached up the river, has a critical bearing on the past land use and settlement distribution, and this is particularly true of the later prehistoric and the early historic periods. It is obvious from the data collected during this study that there was significant migration of the tidal head throughout the last three thousand years. Nevertheless, practically no data are available from the Iron Age in complete contrast to the Bronze Age

where the tidal status of the river is relatively clearly understood. Similarly the Thames in the Roman period has been studied from the City, and is comparatively well understood. The history of the tidal river is therefore an area of some debate and thus a research topic of prime significance.

In addition to the gaps in current knowledge of the tidal river, the pre-Bronze Age Thames in central and western London is also poorly understood, this project having only gleaned very limited data for this period. It was only possible to obtain one date on the freshwater sands, of *c* 5000 cal. BP, from Palace Chambers South, and this was from relatively close to the interface of the sands and overlying silts. The sand islands, eyots or dunes are an interesting phenomenon; unfortunately, there is a tendency among archaeologists to stop excavating once sand has been reached, it being perceived as the geological 'natural' and of no interest. Although these fluvial sands are generally non-artefact bearing, this is not always the case – for example the site at Erith (Sidell *et al* 1997) where a substantial Late Mesolithic flint scatter was located within such deposits. Unfortunately, this tendency affected some of the early sampling exercises on the project, in that complete sequences (*ie* penetrating to Pleistocene terrace gravels) were not always recovered. Additionally, this project was reliant upon the records of field archaeologists for the earlier sites; again, strata perceived as of no archaeological importance are necessarily treated in a more summary fashion. This in itself is understandable, and it is perhaps the role of geoarchaeologists or palaeoecologists to emphasise the significance of these strata and promote rigorous sampling and recording. Several major sand islands are present in the central London region, and doubtless more are present along other stretches of the lower Thames that have been buried by later prehistoric intertidal deposits. However, very little is known about their morphology, date and depositional history. This project has supplied some preliminary data on Thorney Island, and rather less on Bermondsey Eyot. However, only when more detailed chronological and sedimentological work is undertaken on these and the central Southwark islands, can the Early Holocene history of the freshwater river become clearer.

10

Appendix Analytical methodologies

Introduction

This appendix outlines the detailed methodology of data collection and the analytical procedures. All sites were sampled in essentially similar manners. Trenches were opened, for archaeological investigation, or for construction work where an archaeological watching brief was maintained. Where a site was considered suitable for sampling, sections were cleaned and recorded (either by drawing or photography) and the most appropriate location selected. This was generally the most representative location of the overall stratigraphy and all contaminated or anomalous areas were avoided. Monolith tins were used to collect undisturbed samples of the sediment stack. These were constructed of stainless steel, 500mm x 50mm x 50mm and in some, but not all, cases, were lined with plastic drainpipe to enable removal of the core from the tin. All samples were overlapped in order to ensure complete recovery. Tins were marked with the site code (*eg* WSS94 at Palace Chambers South, Westminster), the number of the tin within the sequence, the top and bottom and the overlap with the adjacent tin(s). These samples were then marked on the section drawing and were levelled to OD. They were then carefully cut out, wrapped in plastic and sealed for safe transport. When not prepared immediately, they were placed in cold storage.

Bulk samples were taken adjacent to the series of monolith tins. These were collected for a variety of techniques, such as particle-size analysis and ^{14}C assay. The methodology for collecting these was slightly varied from site to site, but generally followed a consistent pattern, which was as follows. The section was cleaned and recorded and samples were cut from the section face and placed into sample buckets or bags. All potentially contaminated and anomalous areas were avoided. The samples were generally collected in a consecutive sequence, controlled by volume. This was generally 300mm x 300mm x 100mm (Fig 48). Samples were double labelled and stored cool until required.

The monolith samples were used to provide additional subsamples. Following sedimentary description (see below, Lithostratigraphy), 1cm thick subsamples were cut using clean scalpels and knives for pollen and diatom analysis. These were submitted to the analysts for individual preparation (see below).

Sedimentology

Lithostratigraphy

The sediments retained within the monolith tin were cleaned with a scalpel and described using standard criteria on to pro forma record sheets (held in the Museum of London Archive). Features detailed were colour (Munsell value), grain size, nature and quantity of inclusions, sorting, bedding characteristics and

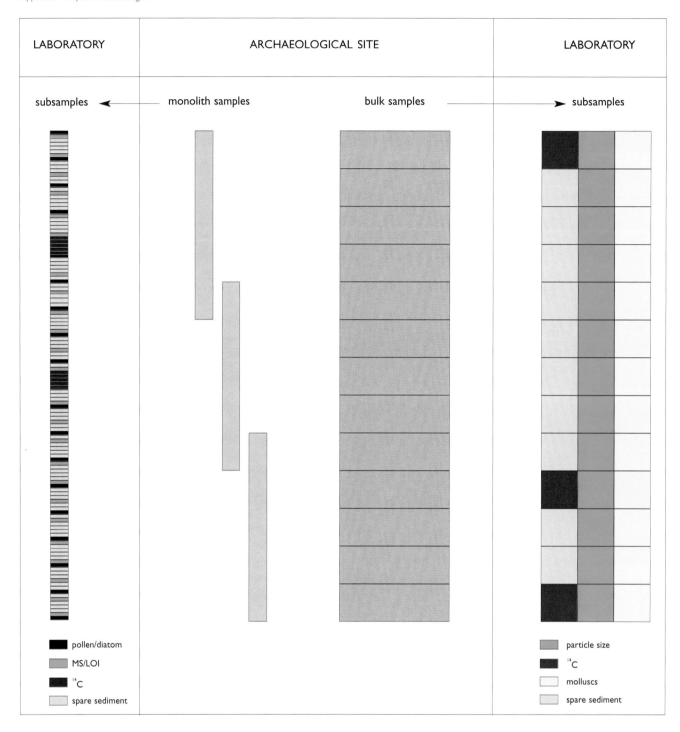

LABORATORY	ARCHAEOLOGICAL SITE		LABORATORY
subsamples ◄	monolith samples	bulk samples	► subsamples

pollen/diatom
MS/LOI
¹⁴C
spare sediment

particle size
¹⁴C
molluscs
spare sediment

Fig 48 Sample production chart

the nature of boundaries between individual sedimentary units. During this procedure a unique identification number was given to each sedimentary unit.

1cm thick subsamples were taken as a continuous sequence through the monolith for palynological and diatom assessment, and for later detailed sedimentological, palynological and diatom analysis. If the monolith tin contained a plastic insert this was removed for magnetic susceptibility measurement of the contained sediments. Sediments in the insert were thoroughly cleaned to produce a surface flush with the top of the insert. The insert was then passed through a loop sensor attached to a Bartington MS2 magnetic susceptibility meter taking volume-

specific readings at 2cm intervals. The data produced a rapid means of assessing human effect on sedimentation, besides giving information on the presence of palaeosols/iron pans etc, and depositional rates (Thompson & Oldfield 1986). Based on these results it was decided to undertake analysis of subsamples for the selected sites using mass susceptibility techniques (see below).

Magnetic susceptibility (MS)

The subsamples obtained from the selected cores were initially air dried at temperatures of <40°C. They were then manually ground in a mortar and pestle, sieved through a 2mm mesh and placed into weighed, numbered 10cl plastic pots. The analytical procedure then followed that of Gale and Hoare (1991, 204–20) for both low-frequency (χ^{lf}) and high-frequency measurement (χ^{hf}). On completion the data were transferred to Microsoft Excel to calculate mass specific susceptibility (χ^{lf}) and percentage frequency differences (χ^{fd}). The data were then loaded into Tilia and Tilia*Graph (Grimm 1991) alongside the loss-on-ignition for histogram plotting.

Loss-on-ignition (LOI)

The subsamples which had been used for the magnetic susceptibility measurements were subsequently used for loss-on-ignition measurements. This was done in order to determine organic carbon content as a proportion of total sediment mass. Loss-on-ignition procedure followed that recommended by Gale and Hoare (1991, 262–4). The samples contained within the plastic pots used for magnetic susceptibility were transferred to weighed, numbered porcelain crucibles and fired in a Carbolite muffle furnace at 550°C for four hours. The weight loss expressed as a proportion of the original sediment mass provides an approximation of organic carbon content.

Particle-size analysis

Particle-size analysis of 20 samples from three sites (Joan Street, Union Street, St Stephen's East) was undertaken by Jerry Lee of the Department of Geography, Royal Holloway, University of London.

Table 7 Particle-size samples examined during the project

Site	Code	OD height
JOA	PSA1	-0.03 ▸ -0.08m OD
JOA	PSA2	-0.23 ▸ -0.25m OD
JOA	PSA3	-0.48 ▸ -0.51m OD
JOA	PSA4	-0.75 ▸ -0.80m OD
JOA	PSA5	-0.95 ▸ -1.0m OD
UNS	PSA1	+0.37 ▸ +0.42m OD
UNS	PSA2	+0.17 ▸ +0.22m OD
UNS	PSA3	-0.08 ▸ -0.13m OD
UNS	PSA4	-0.40 ▸ -0.45m OD
WSS	PSA1	-1.34 ▸ -1.39m OD
WSS	PSA2	-1.39 ▸ -1.44m OD
WSS	PSA3	-1.49 ▸ -1.54m OD
WSS	PSA4	-1.64 ▸ -1.69m OD
WSS	PSA5	-1.69 ▸ -1.74m OD
WSS	PSA6	-1.95 ▸ -2.00m OD
WSS	PSA7	-2.00 ▸ -2.05m OD
SSE	PSA1	-0.54 ▸ -0.59m OD
SSE	PSA2	-0.69 ▸ -0.74m OD
SSE	PSA3	-0.84 ▸ -0.90m OD
SSE	PSA4	-0.90 ▸ -0.95m OD
SSE	PSA5	-1.10 ▸ -1.15m OD
SSE	PSA6	-1.15 ▸ -1.20m OD
SSE	PSA7	-1.25 ▸ -1.30m OD
SSE	PSA8	-1.29 ▸ -1.31m OD
SSE	PSA9	-1.44 ▸ -1.49m OD
SSE	PSA10	-1.54 ▸ -1.59m OD
SSE	PSA11	-1.69 ▸ -1.74m OD

A further seven samples from Palace Chambers South were analysed by Jane Sidell at the sedimentology laboratories, Department of Archaeology, King Alfred College, Winchester. The preparation procedure once again followed the methodology outlined by Gale and Hoare (1991, 80–96), with 15% hydrogen peroxide used to remove the organic content and sodium hexametaphosphate ('calgon') acting as a deflocuating agent. Sand- and gravel-size fractions were divided into size classes by dry sieving at 0.5phi (ϕ) intervals, while silt and clay fractions were separated into 0.5ϕ intervals by use of a Sedigraph 5100 particle-size analyser fitted with an 18-sample auto-sampler. Particle-size analysis was carried out on the samples shown in Table 7.

Biostratigraphy

Pollen

The monolith tins were subsampled for pollen in the laboratories of the (former) Centre for Environmental Change and Quaternary Research (CECQR), Cheltenham and Gloucester College of Higher Education. The sampling was undertaken by Keith Wilkinson and John Naylor in conjunction with the sedimentological description and volume magnetic susceptibility measurements described above. Pollen extraction was carried out in the Quaternary Environmental Change Research Centre (QECRC) of the Department of Geography, University of Southampton. During the assessment subsamples were examined at an approximate 8–16cm interval from all the sites, whereas during the analytical phase subsamples were only examined from Union Street, Joan Street, St Stephen's East, Storey's Gate, Palace Chambers South and Canada Water.

Owing to the diverse range of sediment types examined, ranging from coarse sands to fine silt/clay and organic peat, sample sizes analysed ranged from 5–7ml in the former to standard 1ml for peat. Extraction procedures followed those outlined by Moore and Webb (1978) and Moore *et al* (1991). Thus samples were deflocculated using 8% KOH (potassium hydroxide) and coarse debris removed through sieving at 150μm. Fine inorganics were removed by micromesh sieving at 10μm and the remaining silica was digested with 40% hydrofluoric acid. Finally Erdtman's acetolysis was carried out to remove cellulose. The concentrated pollen and spores were stained with safranin and mounted in glycerol jelly. Pollen grains were then identified and counted using an Olympus biological research microscope with phase contrast facility at magnifications of x400 and x1000.

Pollen diagrams have been constructed using Tilia and Tilia*Graph. The diagrams are based on a minimum count of 100 grains for the sites where full analysis was not carried out and where preservation allowed, and using a count of 300 grains where full analysis was undertaken. Pollen is calculated as a percentage of total dry-land pollen (tdlp), while the common practice of excluding *Alnus* from the sum has not been carried out as this taxon is generally present in fluctuating and/or low values. Spores and mire taxa are calculated as a percentage of the pollen sum plus spores and the pollen sum plus marsh taxa respectively. Throughout the text taxonomy follows that of Stace (1991) and Moore and Webb (1978).

Diatoms

The monolith tins were subsampled for diatoms in the laboratories of the CECQR. The sampling was undertaken by Keith Wilkinson and John Naylor in conjunction with the sedimentological work and pollen subsampling described above. Preparation of diatom slides was undertaken by Simon Dobinson in the laboratories of the Environmental Change Research Centre (ECRC), University College London. Preparation followed standard procedures (Battarbee 1986). Cleaned solutions from each subsample were evaporated on two coverslips at differing concentrations and were mounted in Naphrax. Slides were examined using a Leitz or Zeiss research microscope with phase contrast illumination at a magnification of x1000 or x1200. Where necessary, diatom identifications were confirmed using the collection of diatom floras and publications lodged at the ECRC and in the authors' collection.

Diatom species have been assigned to halobian groups according to the system of Hustedt (1957). The principal source of data on species ecology used was the survey of Denys (1992). The diatoms in the halobian groups have optimal growth in water with salinity equivalent to the ranges proposed by Hustedt (1953; 1957) (see Table 2).

Mollusca

Mollusc assessment and analysis were only carried out on samples from a single site, that of St Stephen's East, where mollusc remains formed an intrinsic part of the stratigraphy. Samples of approximately 5l volume were taken by officers of the Environmental Archaeology Section, MoLAS in October 1994, during archaeological investigation of the site. The samples were weighed and then soaked for 24 hours in a solution of water with 30% hydrogen peroxide. The sample sediment was then washed through a 500μm mesh and the material retained on the sieve air dried.

Due to the highly fossiliferous nature of the sampled deposits and therefore to ease assessment a quarter of each sample was separated by use of a riffle box, and only this was examined. These subsamples were passed through a series of mesh sizes to aid sorting, although because of time constraints fractions less than 1mm were not analysed. The procedure for assessing each sample residue was as follows:

1) All molluscan apices, bivalve valves including a hinge fragment, Limacid plates and *Bithynia* opercula were picked from the residue either by eye (>2mm) or using a low-power binocular microscope (>1mm).
2) All the shell parts picked out were identified to genus

(eg *Bithynia* sp and *Pisidium* sp), species (eg *Theodoxus fluviatilis*, *Valvata piscinalis*, *Lymnaea peregra* etc), or family (eg Limacidae) level. This was achieved in many cases with the aid of a modern comparative reference collection.

3) The identified shell parts for each sample were quantified, and in the case of samples where both >2mm and >1mm residues had been examined, were totalled. Throughout the text species these nomenclature is after Kerney (1976) for freshwater and Kerney and Cameron (1979) for terrestrial Mollusca.

4) Following quantification a percentage histogram was plotted for samples where both >2mm and >1mm residues had been examined using Tilia and Tilia*Graph software (see Fig 25). This diagram also includes the ratio of *Bithynia* apices to opercula as an index of 'assemblage transport', *ie* an *in situ* accumulation should have equal numbers of both; over-representation of either is indicative of transport.

Dating

¹⁴C (radiocarbon)

^{14}C dating has been most heavily relied upon for the Palaeoenvironmental project which, by its nature, has focused more upon sites which produced important sedimentary sequences, but tended to lack substantial archaeological features. Therefore, it was not possible to date them using established archaeological methods such as artefact typology (Renfrew & Bahn 1996, 116–18). It was necessary to collect subsamples containing organic material (these were generally split from the monolith samples) which could be used for ^{14}C assay. (See Lowe & Walker 1997, 240–7 for detailed discussion of the ^{14}C methodology.)

A combination of conventional radiometric, extended counting and accelerator mass spectrometry (AMS) techniques have been used. All samples specifically obtained by this project were measured by Beta Analytic Inc, Miami and full references are given in the text and in Table 8.

Luminescence-dating

One sample was submitted for luminescence-dating in 1993. This was as part of a student project undertaken at the Department of Archaeology, University of Durham. The sample was taken from the basal minerogenic sediments at Canada Water and was processed using the fine-grained particles, between 2 and 10 microns in size. The technique used was the infra-red stimulated luminescence (IRSL) method. Unfortunately, the resolution was low, with a result of 6200±2200 years before 1993 obtained (Dur93IRSL172-1Sed, 1σ).

Table 8 ¹⁴C dates obtained from the sites (calibration using curve of Stuiver et al 1998)

Lab no.	Code	OD height	¹⁴C age (BP)	2σ (95%) calibration	
Beta 119783	JOA1	-2.25→-2.35m OD	4850±80	3787-3381 cal. BC	5737-5331 cal. BP
Beta 119784	JOA2	-0.50→-0.55m OD	2340±60	756-212 cal. BC	2706-2162 cal. BP
Beta 119785	JOA3	-1.41→-1.46m OD	3420±70	1889-1523 cal. BC	3839-3473 cal. BP
Beta 122928	JOA4	-1.50→-1.55m OD	3970±70	2830-2235 cal. BC	4780-4185 cal. BP
Beta 119786	UNS1	-0.55→-0.60m OD	2290±90*	757-119 cal. BC	2707-2069 cal. BP
Beta 119787	UNS2	-2.27→-2.32m OD	4630±110*	3644-3024 cal. BC	5594-4974 cal. BP
Beta 119788	UNS3	-1.55→-1.60m OD	3930±80*	2620-2149 cal. BC	4570-4099 cal. BP
Beta 119789	WSS1	-0.73→-0.78m OD	3110±60	1517-1135 cal. BC	3467-3085 cal. BP
Beta 119790	WSS2	-1.17→-1.22m OD	3570±70	2135-1694 cal. BC	4085-3644 cal. BP
Beta 122929	WSS3	-2.09→-2.12m OD	4300±60**	3082-2709 cal. BC	5032-4659 cal. BP
Beta 127617	SG1	-0.20→-0.24m OD	3300±70	1741-1428 cal. BC	3691-3378 cal. BP
Beta 127739	SG2	+0.08→+0.07m OD	2640±40**	890-788 cal. BC	2839-2737 cal. BP
Beta 127616	SSE1	-1.23→-1.27m OD	3920±40**	2553-2290 cal. BC	4502-4239 cal. BP
Beta 122968	CAW1	-1.17→-1.21m OD	3650±100	2295-1742 cal. BC	4245-3692 cal. BP

*   Extended counting

** AMS dating

Topographic modelling

Geotechnical data were obtained from the library of the British Geological Survey, and also from the JLEP. In addition, point data were derived from trench sections arising through archaeological excavation. These data were entered on to Microsoft Excel as three-dimensional national grid coordinates separating major lithological units by OD heights.

Data were then selected from specific geographical areas and dropped into Golden Software's Surfer program to model images and surfaces of gravel and peat. These were then manipulated to add the course and the estimated approximate altitude of the Thames at the relevant period.

The raw data generated by this project for the techniques outlined above may be found in the Museum of London Archive.

French and German summaries

Résumé

Ce livre est basé sur l'étude paléoenvironnementale du projet de la Jubilee Line. Cette étude a été entreprise afin de fournir un cadre d'ordre géoarchéologique à l'ensemble du projet archéologique de la Jubilee Line et a donné lieu à un nombre recherches importantes à Westminster, Southwark et Stratford. Les objectifs de cette étude ont été de caractériser les séquences sédimentaires découvertes le long de la nouvelle extension de la ligne et de retracer les changements survenus et le développement de la plaine de la Tamise au niveau de la région du centre de Londres. Ceci peut fournir le cadre biophysique nécessaire à l'interprétation des sociétés humaines vivant dans cette partie de Londres pendant le Holocène.

L'étude a été concentrée sur quatre secteurs principaux: l'île de Thorney, Southwark Ouest, Rotherhithe et Canning Town. Pour chacun de ces secteurs, des modèles de sédimentation, de changement du régime du fleuve et du développement de la végétation ont été élaborés. Les descriptions individuelles de ces modèles sont présentées en détail ainsi que les nombreux schémas des données qui les accompagnent. A partir de celles-ci, on a pu observer des tendances d'ordre local et également tirer des conclusions pour l'ensemble de la région étudiée s'étendant sur 12km dans une des régions d'Angleterre les plus riches en archéologie.

Un modèle en trois étapes montrant le développement de la Tamise pendant le Holocène a été proposé: d'abord la rivière post-glaciale sinuant dans une large plaine inondable puis ensuite dans un seul lit en méandres. La phase finale est représentée par la progression en amont de la tête des marées qui fait que la région étudiée fait dorénavant partie de la zone de l'estuaire de la Tamise. Ce dernier épisode prit place pendant l'Age de Bronze et aurait bien sûr influencé les occupants de la plaine alluviale; des preuves de plus en plus nombreuses de cet effet sont peu à peu mises en évidence.

Zusammenfassung

Dieses Buch beschreibt die Ergebnisse palaeo-umweltlicher Untersuchungenwährend des Ausbaus der Jubilee-Untergrundbahn. Das Ziel war, dengeo-archäologischen Zusammenhang für die gesamte Ausgrabung zu erstellen.Es wurden deshalb größere Untersuchungen in Westminster, Southwark und Stratford durchgeführt, um die bei dem Ausbau freigelegten Sedimentsequenzen zu beschreiben und die Veränderunund Entwicklungen der Themseniederung im Zentral-Londoner Bereichfestzustellen. Das Ergebnis konnte dann als biophysischer Rahmen für die Interpretation menschlicher Tätigkeit in der Londoner Umgebung während des Holozäns verwendet werden.

Die Studien konzentrierten sich auf vier Gegenden: Thorney Island, West Southwark, Rotherhithe und Canning Town. In allen wurden die Sedimente, die Veränderungen des Flussverlaufes und der Vegetationsentwicklung untersucht. Die einzelnen individuellen Berichte werden durch ausführliche Diagramme ergänzt. Das Ergebnis der Untersuchungen lokaler Entwicklungen in den einzelnen Gegenden erlaubten Schlussfolgerungen für das gesamte Studiengebiet, der 12 km langen Strecke in einer der archäologisch reichsten Gebiete Englands.

In einem Modell wird die Entwicklung der Themse während des Holozäns in drei Stadien dargestellt. In der ersten, nacheiszeitlichen Phase floss der Fluss in vielen Läufen durch eine weite Niederung. Dem folgte ein meandernder Verlauf in einem einzigen Flussbett. Die letzte Phase ist gekennzeichnet durch einen flussaufwärts zunehmenden Einfluss der Gezeiten. Dieses fand in der späten Bronzezeit statt und beeinflusste entsprechend die Bewohner der Niederung, worüber wir nach und nach mehr erfahren.

BIBLIOGRAPHY

The Research Archive

This is a list of the unpublished reports which relate to the individual excavations carried out for the Jubilee Line Extension Project.

Bates, M R, Pine, C A & Williamson, V D, 1994 *A report on the stratigraphy at the Canning Town site, Jubilee Line Extension Project*, Geoarchaeological Service Facility Report, Institute of Archaeology, University College London

Bluer, R, 1993 *Ventilation shaft, Jubilee Line Extension, Culling Road, Rotherhithe SE16, London Borough of Southwark: an archaeological evaluation*, MoLAS

Bluer, R, 1994 *Ventilation shaft, Jubilee Line Extension, Culling Road, Rotherhithe SE16, London Borough of Southwark: an archaeological assessment*, MoLAS

Bowsher, J M C, 1991 *Jubilee Line Extension: report on the archaeological evaluation at Joan Street, SE1*, MoLAS

Cameron, N G, 1995 *A diatom assessment of borehole sediments from the Jubilee Line Extension*, ECRC, University College London, Archive Report 25

Cowie, R, 1992 *Archaeological evaluation of 1 Bridge Street and St Stephen's House, Westminster, SW1*, MoLAS

Cowie, R, 1996a *New Palace Yard, the Palace of Westminster, City of Westminster: an archaeological post-excavation assessment*, MoLAS

Cowie, R, 1996b *Westminster Station site 4 (formerly St Stephen's House East), SW1, City of Westminster: an archaeological post-excavation assessment*, MoLAS

Cowie, R, 1996c *Westminster Station site 5 (formerly St Stephen's House West), SW1, City of Westminster: an archaeological post-excavation assessment*, MoLAS

Environmental Resources Ltd, 1990 *Jubilee Line Extension archaeological impact assessment: report of survey*, Environmental Resources Ltd Assessment Report

Mason, S, 1991 *Jubilee Line Extension: report on the archaeological evaluation at Canada Water, Rotherhithe*, MoL

Mason, S & Steele, A, 1991 *206 Union Street, Southwark: archaeological evaluation*, MoLAS

Oxford Archaeological Unit, 1991 *Canning Town Station: archaeological field evaluation*, OAU

Oxford Archaeological Unit, 1994 *Canning Town Limmo site: archaeological field evaluation 1993*, OAU

Scaife, R G, 1995 *A palynological assessment of the borehole sediments from the Jubilee Line Extension*, Palaeopol

Sidell, E J, 1995 *Jubilee Line Extension: the palaeoenvironmental research project: project design*, MoLAS Archive Report

Sidell, E J, 1997 *The Jubilee line extension palaeoenvironmental research project: updated project design*, MoLAS Archive Report

Thomas, C, 1995 *A post-excavation assessment of the archaeological excavations at Westminster in Canning Green*, MoLAS

Thomas, C, 1997 *A post-excavation assessment of the archaeological excavations at Westminster in areas 1, 2 and 6 south of Westminster Station*, MoLAS

Wessex Archaeology, 1994c *Storey's Gate, Westminster, London: archaeological on-site trial work*, Wessex Archaeology

Wilkinson, K N, 1994 *An examination of sediment from a sand eyot at Culling Road, Rotherhithe*, Cotswold Archaeological Trust

Wilkinson, K N, 1995a *Assessment of the molluscan remains from St Stephen's East, Westminster*, Cotswold Archaeological Trust

Wilkinson, K N, 1995c *A molluscan assessment of St Stephen's East, Westminster*, Cotswold Archaeological Trust

Wilkinson, K N, 1996a *An assessment of monolith samples taken from Joan Street in 1995*, Cotswold Archaeological Trust

Wilkinson, K N, 1996b *Sedimentary assessment of the monolith samples from Redcross Way (REW92)*, Cotswold Archaeological Trust

Wilkinson, K N, 1996c *The sedimentary stratigraphy of Palace Chambers South*, Westminster, Cotswold Archaeological Trust

Wilkinson, K N & Naylor, J, 1995 *A sedimentological assessment of deposits from the Jubilee Line Extension*, Cotswold Archaeological Trust

Published works and other reports

Place of publication given for titles published outside the United Kingdom.

Abbott, W J L, 1898 'The section exposed in the foundations of the new Admiralty Offices', *Proceedings of the Geologists Association* 12, 346–56

Akeroyd, A V, 1972 'Archaeological and historical evidence for subsidence in southern Britain', *Philosophical Transactions of the Royal Society of London* A272, 151–69

Allen, J R L, 1999 'Geological impacts on coastal wetland landscapes: some general effects of sediment autocompaction in the Holocene of northwest Europe', *The Holocene* 9, 1–12

Andersen, S T, 1970 'The relative pollen productivity and pollen representation of North European trees, and correction factors for tree pollen spectra', *Danmarks Geologiske Undersøgelse*, Series I 196, 99

Andersen, S T, 1973 'The differential pollen productivity of trees and its significance for the interpretation of a pollen diagram from a forested region', in *Quaternary plant ecology* (ed H J B Birks & R G West), 109–15

Andrew, R, 1971 'Exine pattern in the pollen of British species of Tilia', *New Phytologist* 70, 683–6

Andrews, D & Merriman, N, 1986 'A prehistoric timber structure at Richmond Terrace, Whitehall', *Trans London Middlesex Archaeol Soc* 37, 17–21

Ashley, G M, 1990 'Classification of large-scale subaqueous bedforms: a new look at an old problem', *J Sedimentary Petrology* 60, 160–72

Aston, M, Martin, M & Jackson, A, 1998 'Soil analysis as part of a broader approach in the search for low status sites at Shapwick, Somerset', in *The Shapwick Project: an archaeological, historical and topographical study: the eighth report* (ed M A Aston, T A Hall & C M Gerrard), University of Bristol Department for Continuing Education, 51–68

Ayre, J, Wroe-Brown, R & Malt, R, 1996 'Aethelred's hythe to Queenhithe: the origin of a London dock', *Medieval Life* 5, 14–25

Baker, C A, Moxey, P A & Oxford, M, 1978 'Woodland continuity and change in Epping forest', *Field Studies* 4, 645–69

Barber, B, Chew, S & White, B, in prep *Excavations at the Abbey of St Mary, Stratford Langthorne, Essex*, MoLAS

Barham, A J, 1995 'Methodological approaches to archaeological context recording: X-radiography as an example of a supportive recording, assessment and interpretative technique', in *Archaeological sediments and soils: analysis, interpretation, and management* (ed A J Barham & R I Macphail), Institute of Archaeology, University College London, 145–82

Barton, R N E, 1997 *Stone Age Britain*, English Heritage

Battarbee, R W, 1986 'Diatom analysis', in *Handbook of Holocene palaeoecology and palaeohydrology* (ed B E Berglund), 527–70

Battarbee, R W, 1988 'The use of diatom analysis in archaeology: a review', *J Arch Science* 15, 621–44

Beck, E J, 1907 *A history of Rotherhithe*

Belcher, J H & Swale, E M, 1986 'Notes on some small *Thallasiosira* species (Bacillariophyceae) from the plankton of the lower Thames and other British estuaries (identified by transmission electron microscopy)', *British Phycological J* 21, 139–45

Bell, M G & Walker, M J C, 1993 *Late Quaternary environmental change: human and physical perspectives*

Bennion, H, 1994 'A diatom-phosphorus transfer function for shallow, eutrophic ponds in southeast England', *Hydrobiologia* 275, 391–410

Birks, H J B, 1989 'Holocene isochrone maps and patterns of tree spreading in the British Isles', *J Biogeography* 16, 503–40

Birks, H J B, Deacon, J & Peglar, S, 1975 'Pollen maps for the British Isles 5000 years ago', *Proceedings of the Royal Society* B189, 87–105

Blatherwick, S, 1998 'London's pre-Restoration purpose-built theatres of the sixteenth and seventeenth centuries', English Heritage, unpub

Blatherwick, S & Bluer, R, in prep *Medieval mansions of Southwark: The Rosary, Rotherhithe and Fastolf Place*, MoLAS Monograph

Boggs, S, 1987 *Principles of sedimentology and stratigraphy*, New Jersey

Bohncke, S, Vandenberghe, J, Coope, G R & Reiling, R, 1987 'Geomorphology and palaeoecology of the Mark Valley (southern Netherlands): palaeoecology, palaeohydrology and climate during the Weichselian Late Glacial', *Boreas* 16, 69–85

Bowen, H C, 1975 'Pattern and interpretation: a view of the Wessex landscape', in *Recent work in rural archaeology* (ed P J Fowler)

Bowsher, J, 1991 'A "burnt mound" at Phoenix Wharf, south-east London: a preliminary report', in *Burnt mounds and hot stone technology: papers from the second international burnt mound conference, Sandwell* (ed M A Hodder & L H Barfield), 11–20

Boycott, A E, 1936 'The habitats of freshwater Mollusca in Britain', *J Animal Ecology* 5, 116–86

Boyd, P D A, 1981a 'The micropalaeontology and palaeoecology of medieval sediments from the Fleet and Thames in London', in *Microfossils from recent and fossil shelf seas* (ed J W Neale & M D Brazier), 274–92

Boyd, P D A, 1981b *Report on the qualitative analysis of diatoms from sediments associated with the Roman waterfront at New Fresh Wharf, 1978*, DUA/MoL

Brickley, M, Miles, A & Stainer, H, 1999 *The Cross Bones Burial Ground, Redcross Way, Southwark, London*, MoLAS Monograph 3

Bridgland, D R, 1988 'The Pleistocene fluvial stratigraphy and palaeogeography of Essex', *Proceedings of the Geologists Association* 99, 291–314

Bridgland, D R, 1994 *Quaternary of the Thames*

Bridgland, D R, 1995 'The Quaternary sequence of the eastern Thames basin: problems of correlation', in *D R Bridgland et al*, 35–52

Bridgland, D R, Allen, P & Haggart, B A, 1995 *The Quaternary of the lower reaches of the Thames: field guide*, Quaternary Research Association

Briggs, D J, Coope, G R & Gilbertson, D D, 1985 *The chronology and environmental framework of early man in the upper Thames Valley*, BAR British ser 137

Brigham, T, 1990 'The late Roman waterfront in London', *Britannia* 21, 99–185

Brigham, T, Watson, B & Tyers, I, 1996 'Current archaeological work at Regis House in the City of London', *London Archaeol* 8

Brown, A G, 1992 'Slope erosion and colluviation at the floodplain edge', in *Past and present soil erosion: archaeological and geographical perspectives* (ed M G Bell & J Boardman), Oxbow Monograph 22, 77–87

Brown, A G, 1997 *Alluvial geoarchaeology: floodplain archaeology and environmental change*

Butzer, K D, 1982 *Archaeology as human ecology*

Canti, M, 1995 'A mixed approach to geoarchaeological analysis', in *Archaeological sediments and soils: analysis, interpretation and management* (ed A J Barham & R I Macphail), Institute of Archaeology, University College London, 183–90

Chambers, F M, Mighall, T M & Keen, D H, 1996 'Early Holocene pollen and molluscan records from Enfield Lock, Middlesex, UK', *Proceedings of the Geologists Association* 107, 1–14

Chen, F, Wu, R, Pompei, D & Oldfield, F, 1995 'Magnetic property and particle size variations in the late Pleistocene and Holocene parts of the Dadongling loess section near Xining, China', in *Wind blown sediments in the Quaternary record* (ed E Derbyshire), 27–49

Clark, A, 1996 *Seeing beneath the soil: prospecting methods in archaeology*

Clark, J A, Freell, W E & Peltier, W R, 1978 'Global changes in post-glacial sea level: a numerical calculation', *Quaternary Research* 9, 265–87

Colgrave, B & Mynors, R A B, 1969 *Bede's ecclesiastical history of the English people*

Collcutt, S N, 1987 'Archaeostratigraphy: a geoarchaeologist's viewpoint', *Stratigraphica Archaeol* 2, 11–18

Collins, P E F, Fenwick, I M, Keith-Lucas, D M & Worsley, P, 1996 'Late Devensian river and floodplain dynamics and related environmental change in northwest Europe, with particular reference to a site at Woolhampton, Berkshire, England', *J Quaternary Science* 11, 257–375

Collinson, J D, 1996 'Alluvial sediments', in H G Reading, 20–62

Colvin, H M, Allen-Brown, R & Taylor, A J, 1963 *The history of the King's works, I*

Conway, B, McNabb, J & Ashton, N, 1996 *Excavations at Barnfield pit, Swanscombe 1968–72*, British Museum

Conway, B W & Waechter, J D A, 1977 'Lower Thames and Medway Valleys – Barnfield Pit, Swanscombe', in *South-east England and the Thames Valley: guide book for excursion A5, INQUA Congress, Birmingham* (ed E R Shephard-Thorn & J J Wymer)

Coope, G R, 1959 'A late Pleistocene insect fauna from Chelford, Cheshire', *Proceedings of the Royal Society* B151, 70–89

Coope, G R & Angus, R B, 1975 'An ecological study of a temperate interlude in the middle of the last glaciation, based on fossil Coleoptera from Isleworth, Middlesex', *J Animal Ecology* 44, 365–91

Coope, G R, Gibbard, P L, Hall, A R, Preece, R C, Robinson, J E & Sutcliffe, A J, in press 'Climatic and environmental reconstructions based on fossil assemblages from the Middle Devensian (Weichselian) deposits of the River Thames at Kensington, Central London', *Quaternary Science Reviews*

Cowan, C, 1986 'LDDC Surrey Docks area: archaeological survey', MoL and London Docklands Development Council, unpub

Cowan, C, in prep *The development of north-west Roman Southwark: excavations at Courages Brewery 1974–90*, MoLAS

Davis, A, Scaife, R G & Sidell, E J, 1995 *Assessment of the environmental samples from the Elizabeth Fry School, Newham, London*, MoLAS Archive Report

Denys, L, 1992 *A check list of the diatoms in the Holocene deposits of the western Belgian coastal plain with a survey of their apparent ecological requirements, I: Introduction, ecological code and complete list*, Brussels, Service Géologique de Belgique

Devoy, R J N, 1977 'Flandrian sea-level changes in the Thames estuary and the implications for land subsidence in England and Wales', *Nature* 270, 712–15

Devoy, R J N, 1979 'Flandrian sea-level changes and vegetational history of the lower Thames estuary', *Philosophical Transactions of the Royal Society of London* B285, 355–410

Devoy, R J N, 1980 'Post-glacial environmental change and man in the Thames estuary: a synopsis', in *Archaeology and coastal change* (ed F H Thompson), Society of Antiquaries, 134–48

Devoy, R J N, 1982 'Analysis of the geological evidence for Holocene sea-level movements in southeast England', *Proceedings of the Geologists Association* 93, 65–90

Dimbleby, G W, 1965 'Pollen analysis at a Mesolithic site at Addington, Kent', *Grana Palynologica* 4, 140–8

Drummond-Murray, J, Thomas, C J & Sidell, E J, 1998 *The big dig: archaeology and the Jubilee Line Extension*, MoLAS

Drummond-Murray, J, Thompson, P with Cowan, C, in prep *Roman Southwark: the origins of the settlement: archaeological excavations (1991–1998) for the London Underground Limited Jubilee Line Extension Project*, MoLAS Monograph

Dyakowska, J, 1947 'The pollen rain on the sea and coasts of Greenland', *Bull Internat Academy Polonaise* B, 25–33

Ellison, R A & Zalasiewicz, J A, 1996 'Palaeogene and Neogene', in *British regional geology: London and the Thames Valley* (ed M G Sumbler), British Geological Survey, 92–109

English Heritage, 1991 *Management of archaeological projects* (MAP2)

Esmonde Cleary, S, 1989 *The ending of Roman Britain*

Evans, J G, 1972 *Land snails in archaeology*

Faegri, K & Iversen, J, 1975 *Textbook of pollen analysis*

Fairbridge, R W, 1983 'Isostacy and eustacy', in *Shorelines and isostacy* (ed D E Smith & A G Dawson), 3–28

Farrand, W R, 1984 'Stratigraphic classification: living within the law', *Quarterly Review of Archaeol* 5, 1–5

Folk, R L & Ward, W C, 1957 'Brazos river bar: a study in the significance of grain size parameters', *J Sedimentary Petrology* 27, 3–26

Franks, J W, 1960 'Interglacial deposits at Trafalgar Square, London', *New Phytologist* 59, 145–52

Franks, J W, Sutcliffe, A J, Kerney, M P & Coope, G R, 1958 'Haunt of the elephant and rhinoceros: the Trafalgar Square of 100,000 years ago – new discoveries', *Illustrated London News* 14 June, 1011–13

Frechen, M & Wilkinson, K N, in prep 'Luminescence dating of the Kennet Wharf bed', in K N Wilkinson

Gale, A J & Hoare, P G, 1991 *Quaternary sediments: petrographic methods for the study of unlithified rocks*

Gibbard, P L, 1985 *Pleistocene history of the middle Thames Valley*

Gibbard, P L, 1988 'The history of the great northwest European rivers during the past three million years', *Philosophical Transactions of the Royal Society of London* B318, 559–602

Gibbard, P L, 1994 *Pleistocene history of the lower Thames Valley*

Gibbard, P L, 1995 'Palaeogeographical evolution of the lower Thames', in D R Bridgland, P Allen & B A Haggart, 5–34

Gibbard, P L, 1999 'The Thames Valley, its tributary, valleys and their former courses', in *A revised chronology of Quaternary deposits in the British Isles* (ed D Q Bowen), 45–58

Gibbard, P L, Coope, G R, Hall, A R, Preece, R C & Robinson, J E, 1982 'Middle Devensian deposits beneath the "Upper Floodplain" terrace of the River Thames at Kempton Park, Sunbury, England', *Proceedings of the Geologists Association* 93, 275–89

Gibbard, P L & Hall, A R, 1982 'Late Devensian river deposits in the lower Colne Valley, west London, England', *Proceedings of the Geologists Association* 93, 291–9

Gibbard, P L, Wintle, A G & Catt, J A, 1987 'The age and origin of clayey silt brickearth, west London, England', *J Quaternary Science* 2, 3–9

Girling, M A, 1988 'The bark beetle *Scolytus scolytus* (Fabricius) and the possible role of elm disease in the early Neolithic', in *Archaeology and the flora of the British Isles* (ed M Jones), Oxford University Committee for Archaeology, 34–8

Girling, M A & Greig, J R A, 1977 'Palaeoecological investigations of a site at Hampstead Heath, London', *Nature* 268, 45–7

Girling, M A & Greig, J R A, 1985 'A first fossil record for *Scolytus scolytus* (F.) (elm bark beetle): its occurrence in elm decline deposits from London and the implication for the Neolithic elm decline', *J Arch Science* 12, 347–51

Godwin, H, 1940 'Pollen analysis and forest history of England and Wales', *New Phytologist* 39, 370–400

Godwin, H, 1944 'Age and origins of the "Breckland" heaths of East Anglia', *Nature* 154, 6–10

Godwin, H, 1956 *The history of the British flora: a factual basis for phytogeography*

Godwin, H, 1975a *The history of the British flora*, 2nd ed

Godwin, H, 1975b 'History of the natural forests of Britain: establishment, dominance and destruction', *Philosophical Transactions of the Royal Society of London* B271, 47–67

Graham, A H, 1978 'The geology of north Southwark and its topographical development in the post-Pleistocene period', in *Southwark excavations 1972–1974* (ed SLAEC Committee), London and Middlesex Archaeological Society & Surrey Archaeological Society

Greensmith, J T & Tucker, E, 1976 'Major Flandrian transgressive cycles, sedimentation and palaeogeography in the coastal zone of Essex, England', *Geologie en Mijnbouw* 55, 131–46

Greig, J, 1981 'The investigation of a medieval barrel-latrine from Worcester', *J Arch Science* 8, 265–82

Greig, J R A, 1982a 'The interpretation of pollen spectra from urban archaeological deposits', in *Environmental archaeology in the urban context* (ed A R Hall & H Kenward), CBA Research Report 43, 47–65

Greig, J R A, 1982b 'Past and present lime woods of Europe', in *Archaeological aspects of woodland ecology* (ed M G Bell & S Limbrey), BAR International ser 146, 23–55

Greig, J R A, 1989 'From lime forest to heathland – five thousand years of change at West Heath Spa, Hampstead, as shown by the plant remains', in *Excavations at the Mesolithic site on West Heath, Hampstead 1976–1981* (ed D Collins & J D Lorimer), BAR British ser 217, 89–99

Greig, J R A, 1991 'The botanical remains', in *Excavation and salvage at Runnymede Bridge 1978: the Late Bronze Age waterfront site* (ed S Needham)

Greig, J R A, 1992 'The deforestation of London', *Review of Palaeobotany and Palynology* 73, 71–86

Grimm, E, 1991 *Tilia / Tilia*Graph 1.12*, Springfield, Illinois State Museum

Haggart, B A, 1995 'A re-examination of some data relating to Holocene sea-level changes in the Thames estuary', in D R Bridgland *et al*, 329–38

Harris, E C, 1979a *Principles of archaeological stratigraphy*

Harris, E C, 1979b 'The stratigraphic sequence: a question of time', *World Archaeol* 11, 109–21

Harris, E C, 1989 *Principles of archaeological stratigraphy*, 2nd ed

Haskins, L E, 1978 'The vegetational history of south-east Dorset', University of Southampton, unpub

Havinga, A J, 1964 'Investigation into the differential corrosion susceptibility of pollen and spores', *Pollen et Spores* 6, 621–35

Hollin, J, 1977 'Thames interglacial sites, Ipswichian sea levels and Antarctic ice surges', *Boreas* 6, 33–52

Holyoak, D T, 1983 'A Late Pleistocene interglacial flora and molluscan fauna from Thatcham, Berkshire, with notes on Mollusca from interglacial deposits at Aveley', *Geological Magazine* 120, 623–9

Huntley, B & Birks, J J B, 1983 *An atlas of past and present pollen maps for Europe 0–13,000 years ago*

Hustedt, F, 1953 'Die Systematik der Diatomeen in ihren Beziehungen zur Geologie und Ökologie nebst einer Revision des Halobien-systems', *Sveriges Botaniska Tidskrift* 47, 509–19

Hustedt, F, 1957 'Die Diatomeenflora des Fluss-system der Weser im Gebiet der Hansestadt Bremen', *Abhandlungen naturwissenschaftlicher Verein zu Bremen* 34, 181–440

Iversen, J, 1941 'Landnam i Danarks Stenalder', *Danmarks Geologiske Undersøgelse, Series II* 66, 1–67

Iversen, J, 1949 'The influence of prehistoric man on vegetation', *Danmarks Geologiske Undersøgelse, Series IV* 80, 87–119

Jelgersma, S, 1961 'Holocene sea-level changes in the Netherlands', *Meded Geol Sticht* C 6, 1–100

Jennings, S & Smyth, C, 1982 'A preliminary interpretation of coastal deposits from East Sussex', *Quaternary Newsletter* 37, 12–19

Jones, H, 1988 *Excavations at Bricklayers Arms (BLA87)*, MoL/DGLA

Juggins, S, 1988 'A diatom/salinity transfer function for the Thames estuary and its application to waterfront archaeology', University College London, unpub

Juggins, S, 1992 *Diatoms in the Thames estuary, England: ecology, palaeoecology and salinity transfer function*, Berlin

Keatinge, T, 1982 'Influence of stemflow on the representation of pollen of Tilia in soils', *Grana Palynologica* 21, 171–4

Kellerhalls, R & Church, M, 1989 'The morphology of large rivers: characterisation and management', *Proceedings of the International Large Rivers Symposium* (ed D P Dodge), Canadian Special Publication of Fisheries and Aquatic Sciences 106, 31–48

Kerney, M P, 1971 'Interglacial deposits in Barnfield Pit, Swanscombe and their molluscan faunas', *J Geological Soc London* 127, 69–93

Kerney, M P, 1976 'Fresh water Mollusca of the British Isles', *J Conchology* 29, 26–8

Kerney, M P & Cameron, R A D, 1979 *A field guide to the land snails of Britain and north-west Europe*

Kerney, M P, Gibbard, P L, Hall, A R & Robinson, J E, 1982 'Middle Devensian river deposits beneath the "Upper Floodplain" terrace of the river Thames at Isleworth, West London', *Proceedings of the Geologists Association* 93, 385–93

King, W B R & Oakley, K P, 1936 'The Pleistocene succession in the lower parts of the Thames Valley', *Proceedings of the Prehistoric Society* 2, 52–76

Kukla, G, Heller, F, Liu, X M, Xu, T C, Liu, T S & Am, Z S, 1988 'Pleistocene climates dated by magnetic susceptibility', *Geology* 16, 811–14

Lacaille, A D, 1961 'Mesolithic facies in Middlesex and London', *Trans London Middlesex Archaeol Soc* 20, 101–49

Lewis, J S C, 1991 'Excavation of a Late Glacial and Early Flandrian site at Three Ways Wharf, Uxbridge: interim report', in *Late glacial settlement in north-west Europe* (ed R N E Barton, A J Roberts & D A Rowe), CBA Research Report 77

Lewis, J S C, Wiltshire, P E J & Macphail, R I, 1992 'A Late Devensian / Early Flandrian site at Three Ways Wharf, Uxbridge: environmental implications', in *Alluvial archaeology in Britain* (ed S P Needham & M G Macklin), Oxbow Monograph 27, 235–47

Long, A J, 1995 'Sea-level and crustal movements in the Thames estuary, Essex and East Kent', in D R Bridgland *et al*, 99–105

Long, A J, Scaife, R G & Edwards, R J, 1999 'Pine pollen in intertidal sediments from Poole Harbour, UK: implications for Late Holocene sediment accretion rates and sea-level rise', *Quaternary Internat* 55, 3–16

Long, A J, Scaife, R G & Edwards, R J, submitted 'Stratigraphic architecture, relative sea-level and models of estuary development in southern England: new data from Southampton Water', in *Coastal and estuary environments: sedimentology, geomorphology and geoarchaeology*, Geological Society Special Publication

Long, A J & Tooley, M J, 1995 'Holocene sea-level and crustal movements in Hampshire and Southeast England, United Kingdom', *J Coastal Research: Special Issue 17: Holocene Cycles: Climate, sea-levels and sedimentation*, 299–310

Lowe, J J & Walker, M J C, 1997 *Reconstructing Quaternary environments*

Maddy, D, Lewis, S G, Scaife, R G, Bowen, D Q, Coope, G R, Green, C P, Hardaker, T, Keen, D H, Rees-Jones, J, Parfitt, S & Scott, K, 1998 'The Upper Pleistocene deposits at Cassington, near Oxford, England', *J Quaternary Science* 13, 205–31

Malcolm, G, Bowsher, D & Cowie, R, 1999 *Excavations at the Royal Opera House, London, 1989–97*, MoLAS

Maloney, C & De Moulins, D, 1990 *The upper Walbrook in the Roman period*, CBA Research Report 69

Maloney, C & Gostick, T J, 1998 'London fieldwork and publication round-up 1997', *London Archaeol* 8 supplement 3

Meddens, F & Beasley, M, 1990 'Wetland use in Rainham, Essex', *London Archaeol* 6

Meddens, F & Sidell, E J, 1995 'Bronze Age trackways in east London', *Current Archaeol* 12, 412–16

Meddens, F M, 1996 'Sites from the Thames estuary wetlands, England, and their Bronze Age use', *Antiquity* 70, 325–34

Merriman, N, 1992 'Predicting the unexpected: prehistoric sites recently discovered under alluvium in central London', in *Alluvial archaeology in Britain* (ed S P Needham & M G Macklin), Oxbow Monograph 27, 261–7

Miall, A D, 1996 *The geology of fluvial deposits: sedimentary facies, basin analysis and petroleum geology*, Berlin

Middleton, G V, 1976 'Hydraulic interpretation of sand size distributions', *Geology* 84, 405–26

Mills, P, 1980 'Excavations at Cromwell Green in the Palace of Westminster', *Trans London Middlesex Archaeol Soc* 31, 18–28

Mills, P, 1982 'Excavations at Broad Sanctuary, Westminster', *Trans London Middlesex Archaeol Soc* 33, 345–65

Milne, G, 1985 *The port of Roman London*

Milne, G, Bates, M & Webber, M, 1997 'Problems, potential and partial solutions: an archaeological study of the tidal Thames, England', *World Archaeol* 29, 130–46

Milne, G, Battarbee, R W, Straker, V & Yule, B, 1983 'The London Thames in the mid-first century', *Trans London Middlesex Archaeol Soc* 34, 19–30

Milne, G & Milne, C, 1982 *Excavations at Trig Lane 1978*, London Middlesex Archaeol Soc Special Paper 5

Mitchell, G F, Penny, L F, Shotton, F W & West, R G, 1973 *A correlation of Quaternary deposits in the British Isles*, Geological Soc of London Special Report 4

Moore, P D, 1977 'Ancient distribution of lime trees in Britain', *Nature* 268, 13–14

Moore, P D & Webb, J A, 1978 *An illustrated guide to pollen analysis*

Moore, P D, Webb, J A & Collinson, M D, 1991 *Pollen analysis*

Moore, P D & Willmot, A, 1976 'Prehistoric forest clearance and the development of peatlands in the uplands and lowlands of Britain', *Sixth international peat conference, Poznan, Poland*, Poznan, Poland, 1–15

Needham, S P, 1992 'Holocene alluviation and interstratified settlement evidence in the Thames Valley at Runnymede Bridge', in *Alluvial archaeology in Britain* (ed S P Needham & M G Macklin), Oxbow Monograph 27, 249–60

Oldfield, F, Rummery, T A, Thompson, R & Walling, D E, 1979 'Identification of suspended sediment sources by means of magnetic susceptibility measurement: some preliminary results', *Water Resources Research* 15, 211–18

Parker, A G & Chambers, F M, 1997 'Late Quaternary palaeoecology of the Severn, Wye and Thames', in *The Quaternary of the South Midlands and Welsh Marches: field guide* (ed S G Lewis & D Maddy), Quaternary Research Association, 31–48

Peck, R M, 1973 'Pollen budget studies in a small Yorkshire catchment', in *Quaternary plant ecology* (ed H J B Birks & R G West), 43–60

Pilcher, J R & Smith, A G, 1979 'Palaeoecological investigations at Ballynagilly, a Neolithic and Bronze Age settlement in County Tyrone, Northern Ireland', *Philosophical Transactions of the Royal Society of London* B 286, 345–69

Poole, H, 1870 'Some account of the discovery of the Roman coffin in the north green at Westminster Abbey', *Arch J* 27, 119–28

Preece, R C, 1999 'Mollusca from the last interglacial fluvial deposits of the River Thames at Trafalgar Square', *J Quaternary Science* 14, 77–89

Rackham, D J, 1994 'Prehistory in the lower Thames floodplain', *London Archaeol* 7, 191–6

Rapp, G J & Hill, C H, 1998 *Geoarchaeology: the Earth-Science approach to archaeological interpretation*, New Haven, Connecticut

Reading, H G (ed), 1996 *Sedimentary environments and facies*

Reid, C, 1916 'The plants of the late glacial deposits of the Lea Valley', *Quarterly J Geological Soc London* 71, 155

Reineck, K E & Singh, I B, 1980 *Depositional sedimentary environments*, New York

Rendell, H, Worsley, P, Green, F & Parks, D, 1991 'Thermoluminescence dating of the Chelford interstadial', *Earth and Planetary Science Letters* 103, 182–9

Renfrew, C & Bahn, P, 1996 *Archaeology: theory, method and practice*

Robinson, M A, 1992 'Environment, archaeology and alluvium on the river gravels of the South Midlands', in *Alluvial archaeology in Britain* (ed S P Needham & M G Macklin), Oxbow Monograph 27, 197–208

Roper, F C S, 1854 'Some observations on the Diatomaceae of the Thames', *Microscopy J* 2, 67–80

Rose, J, 1995 'Late Glacial and Early Holocene river activity in lowland Britain', *Palaeoclimate Research* 14, 51–74

Rose, J, Allen, P & Hey, R W, 1976 'Middle Pleistocene stratigraphy in southern East Anglia', *Nature* 263, 492–4

Ross, R, 1976 'Diatom analysis: in excavations of the palace defences and abbey precinct wall at Abingdon Street, Westminster, 1963', *J British Archaeol Assoc* 129, 59–76

Round, F E, Crawford, R M & Mann, D G, 1990 *The diatoms: biology and morphology of the genera*

Scaife, R G, 1980 'Late Devensian and Flandrian palaeoecological studies in the Isle of Wight', PhD thesis, King's College London, unpub

Scaife, R G, 1982a 'Late Devensian and Early Flandrian vegetation changes in southern England', in *Archaeological aspects of woodland ecology* (ed M G Bell & S Limbrey), BAR International ser 146, 57–74

Scaife, R G, 1982b 'Pollen analysis of Roman peats underlying the Temple of Mithras, London', Ancient Monuments Laboratory Report 3502

Scaife, R G, 1983 'Stratigraphy and preliminary palynological results for Peninsula House, City of London', Ancient Monuments Laboratory Report 4001

Scaife, R G, 1987 'The Late Devensian and Flandrian vegetation of the Isle of Wight', in *Wessex and the Isle of Wight: field guide* (ed K E Barber), Quaternary Research Association, 156–80

Scaife, R G, 1988a 'The elm decline in the pollen record of south-east England and its relationship to early agriculture', in *Archaeology and the flora of the British Isles* (ed M Jones), Oxford University Committee for Archaeology, 21–33

Scaife, R G, 1988b 'Pollen analysis of the Mar Dyke sediments', in *Archaeology and environment in south Essex* (ed T J Wilkinson), Essex County Council, 109–14

Scaife, R G, 1991 *Rainham Marshes: pollen analysis*, Palaeopol

Scaife, R G, 1997 *Assessment of the pollen from Beckton*, Palaeopol

Scaife, R G, in prep 'Runnymede Bridge: palynology and palaeoenvironment', in *Runnymede Bridge research excavations 1* (ed S Needham)

Scaife, R G, Rackham, D J & Perry, J, in prep 'Palaeoenvironmental analysis of peat and the sedimentary sequence at Point Pleasant, Wandsworth, London'

Seeley, D C, Carlin, M & Phillpotts, C, in prep *The palace in Southwark of the medieval bishops of Winchester: excavations at Winchester Palace, London, 1983–90: part 2*, MoLAS

Sengupta, S, 1975 'Size sorting during suspension transportation – lognormality and other characteristics', *Sedimentology* 22, 257–73

Sengupta, S, 1979 'Grain-size distribution of suspended load in relation to bed materials and flow velocity', *Sedimentology* 26, 63–82

Shennan, I, 1987 'Global analysis and the correlation of sea-level data', in *Sea surface studies* (ed R J N Devoy), 198–230

Shennan, I, 1994 'Models of coastal sequences', in M Waller 1994a

Shepherd, J D, 1998 *The Temple of Mithras, London: excavations by W F Grimes and A Williams at the Walbrook*, English Heritage Archaeol Report 12

Sidell, E J, 1998 *Relative sea-level change and archaeology in the inner Thames estuary during the Holocene*, University of Durham Graduate Discussion Paper, unpub

Sidell, E J, submitted 'Archaeology and sea-level change: improved resolution through the combined use of geographical and archaeological methodologies', in *Proceedings of the 1997 Archaeological Sciences Conference, Durham* (ed A R Millard), BAR International ser

Sidell, E J, Cotton, J, Rayner, L & Wheeler, L, in prep a *The topography and prehistory of north Southwark and Lambeth*, MoLAS

Sidell, E J, Scaife, R G & Bowsher, D, in prep b 'Early Holocene environmental change and archaeology in the Lea Valley, London'

Sidell, E J, Scaife, R G, Tucker, S & Wilkinson, K N, 1995 'Palaeoenvironmental investigations at Bryan Road, Rotherhithe', *London Archaeol* 7, 279–85

Sidell, E J, Scaife, R G, Wilkinson, K N, Giorgi, J A, Goodburn, D, Gray-Rees, L & Tyers, I, 1997 *Spine Road Development, Erith, Bexley (RPS Clouston Site 2649): a palaeoenvironmental assessment*, MoLAS ENV01/97

Sims, R E, 1973 'The anthropogenic factor in East Anglian vegetational history: an approach using APF techniques', in *Studies in the vegetational history of the British Isles* (ed H J B Birks & R G West), 223–36

Smith, A G, 1970 'The influence of Mesolithic and Neolithic man on British vegetation: a discussion', in *Studies in the vegetational history of the British Isles* (ed D Walker & R G West), 81–96

Smith, A G, 1981 'The Neolithic', in *The environment in British prehistory* (ed I G Simmons & M J Tooley), 125–209

Spence, C, 1990 *Archaeological site manual*, 2nd ed, MoL

Spurrell, F C J, 1889 'On the estuary of the Thames and its alluvium', *Proceedings of the Geological Society* 11, 210–30

Stace, C, 1991 *New flora of the British Isles*

Stanley, E A, 1969 'Marine palynology', *Oceanography and Marine Biology Annual Review* 7, 277–92

Starkel, L, 1994 'Reflection of the glacial-interglacial cycle in the evolution of the Vistula river basin, Poland', *Terra Nova* 6, 486–94

Steedman, K, Dyson, A & Schofield, J, 1992 *Aspects of Saxo-Norman London III: the bridgehead and Billingsgate to 1200*, London Middlesex Archaeol Soc Special Paper 14

Steele, A, in prep *Excavations at the Cluniac Priory of St Saviour, Bermondsey, London*, MoLAS

Stein, J K, 1987 'Deposits for archaeologists', *Advances in Archaeological Method and Theory* 11, 337–95

Stein, J K & Teltser, P A, 1989 'Size distributions in artefact classes: combining macro- and micro-fractions', *Geoarchaeology* 1, 1–30

Stuiver, M, Reimer, P J, Bard, E, Beck, J W, Burr, G S, Hughen, K A, Kromer, B, McCormac, F G, van der Plicht, J & Spurk, M, 1998 'Calibration curve', *Radiocarbon* 40, 1041–83

Sutcliffe, A J, 1995 'Insularity of the British Isles 250,000–30,000 years ago: the mammalian, including human, evidence', in *Island Britain: a Quaternary perspective* (ed R C Preece), The Geological Society, 127–40

Tauber, H, 1967 'Investigation of the mode of pollen transfer in forested areas', *Review of Palaeobotany and Palynology* 3, 277–87

Taylor, H, 1996 'Time and tide: a study of a site at Erith in the Thames estuary', BA dissertation, University of Sheffield, unpub

Tebbens, L A, Veldkamp, A, Westerhoff, W & Kroonenberg, S B, 1999 'Fluvial incision and channel downcutting as a response to Late Glacial and Early Holocene climate change: the lower reach of the River Meuse (Maas), The Netherlands', *J Quaternary Science* 14, 59–76

Thomas, C, Cowie, R & Sidell, E J, in prep *Excavations at Thorney Island, Westminster: archaeological excavations (1991–98) for the London Underground Limited Jubilee Line Extension Project*, MoLAS

Thomas, C & Rackham, D J, 1996 'Bramcote Green, Bermondsey: a Bronze Age trackway and palaeoenvironmental sequence', *Proceedings of the Prehistoric Society* 61, 221–53

Thompson, R & Oldfield, F, 1986 *Environmental magnetism*

Thorley, A, 1971 'Vegetational history of the Vale of Brooks', *Institute of British Geographers Conference* 5, 47–50

Tomalin, D J, Loader, R & Scaife, R G, in press *Coastal archaeology in a dynamic environment: a Solent case study*, English Heritage

Tooley, M J, 1976 'Flandrian sea-level changes in west Lancashire and their implication for the "Hillhouse Coastline"', *Geological J* 11, 137–52

Tucker, M E, 1982 *Sedimentary rocks in the field*

Turner, J, 1962 'The Tilia decline: an anthropogenic interpretation', *New Phytologist* 61, 328–41

Turner, J, 1964 'The anthropogenic factor in vegetational history: I Tregaron and Whixhall Mosses', *New Phytologist* 63, 73–90

Turner, J, 1970 'Post-Neolithic disturbance of British vegetation', in *Studies in the vegetational history of the British Isles* (ed D Walker & R G West), 97–116

Tyers, I, 1988 'The prehistoric peat layers (Tilbury IV)', in *Excavations in Southwark 1973–76, Lambeth 1973–79* (ed P Hinton), London Middlesex Archaeol Soc/Surrey Archaeol Soc, joint pub 3, 5–12

Vandenberghe, J, Bohncke, S, Lammers, W & Zilverberg, L, 1987 'Geomorphology and palaeoecology of the Mark Valley (southern Netherlands): geomorphological valley development during the Weichselian and Holocene', *Boreas* 16, 55–67

Vince, A, 1990 *Saxon London: an archaeological investigation*

Vonder Haar, S P & Johnson, W H, 1973 'Mean magnetic susceptibility: a useful parameter for stratigraphic studies of glacial till', *J Sedimentary Petrology* 43, 1148–51

Waller, M, 1993 'Flandrian vegetational history of south-eastern England: pollen data from Pannel Bridge, East Sussex', *New Phytologist* 124, 345–69

Waller, M (ed), 1994a *The Fenland Project, Number 9: Flandrian environmental change in Fenland*, East Anglian Archaeology

Waller, M, 1994b 'Paludification and pollen representation: the influence of wetland size on Tilia representation in pollen diagrams', *The Holocene* 4, 430–4

Walther, J, 1894 *Einleitung in die Geologie als historische Wissenschaft*, Jena

Waton, P V, 1982 'Man's impact on the chalklands: some new pollen evidence', in *Archaeological aspects of woodland ecology* (ed M G Bell & S Limbrey), BAR International ser 146, 75–91

Watson, B & Brigham, T, in prep *Medieval London Bridge*, MoLAS

Wessex Archaeology, 1994a *Fieldwork recording manual: Wessex Archaeology guideline 1 (revised version)*, Wessex Archaeology

Wessex Archaeology, 1994b *Fort Street (West), Silvertown, London, E16: archaeological excavation assessment report*, Wessex Archaeol Report 37917/a

Westlake, H, 1923 *Westminster Abbey*

Westman, A, 1994 *Archaeological site manual*, 3rd ed, MoL

Wheeler, R E M, 1928 *An inventory of the historical monuments in London, vol III: Roman London*

Wilkinson, K N, 1995b *A borehole survey and geoarchaeological assessment of deposits at Masthouse Terrace, Isle of Dogs*, Cotswold Archaeol Trust Report 95309

Wilkinson, K N (ed), in prep *Urban waterfront geoarchaeology: stratigraphic investigation of the City of London's Roman and Saxon bank side sites*, MoLAS Monograph

Wilkinson, K N, Scaife, R G & Sidell, E J, 2000 'Environmental and sea-level changes in London from 10,500 BP to the present: a case study from Silvertown', *Proceedings of the Geologists Association* 111

Wilkinson, K N, Scaife, R G & Sidell, E J, in prep 'Mesolithic environment and people in London: new evidence from Wandsworth', *J Environmental Archaeol*

Wilkinson, T J & Murphy, P, 1986 'Archaeological survey of an intertidal zone: the submerged landscape of the Essex coast, England', *J Field Archaeol* 13, 177–94

Willcox, G H, 1977 'Exotic plants and animals from Roman waterlogged sites in London', *J Arch Science* 4, 269–82

Willis, J, 1997 *Extending the Jubilee Line: the planning story*, London Transport

Wymer, J J, 1962 'Excavations at the Maglemosian sites at Thatcham, Berkshire, England', *Proceedings of the Prehistoric Society* 28, 329–61

Wymer, J J, 1988 'Palaeolithic archaeology and the British Quaternary sequence', *Quaternary Science Reviews* 7, 79–97

INDEX

Compiled by Susanne Atkin

Page numbers in **bold** refer to illustrations and tables.
Not all pollen names have been indexed.

Abbey Precinct see Westminster
Abies see fir
Addington (Kent), lime 113
Admiralty Offices, Palaeolithic flakes 119
Aethelreds Hithe 90
agriculture 12, 108
  Neolithic 1, 112
  Bronze Age 19, 21, 65, 113, 114, 117, 121, 122, 124
  Iron Age 108, 117
  Roman/Romano-British 116–17
  medieval, Storey's Gate 35, 36
  Canada Water 96, 98, 114, 115
  Joan Street 75, 76, 77, 112, 114
  Palace Chambers South 46, 47
  St Stephen's East, late prehistoric 59, 60
  Thorney Island 21
  Union Street 84, 86, 112, 114
  Westminster 1, 63, 108
alder (*Alnus*) 19, 28, 29, 30, 36, 37, 43, 48, 49, 55, 59, 63, 69, 70, 75, 76, 80, 81, 85, 94, 95, 96, 128
alder (*Alnus*) carr 59, 75, 76, 77, 84, 85, 87, 97, 112, 113, 114, 115, 116, 121
algae (algal cysts; pollen; diatoms) 37, 43, 59, 71, 86, 95, 97
Alnus see alder
Amberley Wild Brooks (Sussex), lime 113
AMS (accelerator mass spectrometry), Palace Chambers South 39
antler picks, Mesolithic 119
antlers, deer 3, 93
ard marks, Bronze Age 21, 63, 64–5, 117, 121, 122
Armeria (sea lavender and thrift) 29, 49, 56, 59, 86, 116
ash (*Fraxinus*) 9, 29, 43, 46, 47, 48, 56, 59, 69, 70, 75, 77, 80, 85, 111, 112, 115, 116
Aster type 28, 46, 59, 71, 116
Atlantic period 12, 111–12, 113, 115
Aveley 13, 14
axes
  Mesolithic 119, 120
  Neolithic 38, 42, 120
  Bronze Age 120

B&Q site, Old Kent Road, Mesolithic 64, 119
bar features 107, 119; see also channel bars
Beckton 19
  Bronze Age trackways 19
  lime 113
Beckton Alp 19
bed structures 7, 8
beech (*Fagus*) 9, 114, 115, 116
  Joan Street 70, 71, 75
  Palace Chambers South 43, 46, 47
  St Stephen's East 56, 59
  Storey's Gate 29, 34, 37
  Union Street 85
birch (*Betula*) 9, 14, 18, 19, 29, 43, 71, 106, 111, 112, 116
Bermondsey 120
  Bronze Age 65
  Iron Age 121
  medieval 66
Bermondsey Eyot 107, 124
Betula see birch
biostratigraphy 4, 5, 7, 8-9, 16, 127–8;

see also diatoms; molluscs; pollen
Birdcage Walk 25
Black Park Gravel 13, **13**
Boreal and sub-Boreal 12, 18, 19, 111, 113, 115
boreholes 10
Borough High Street 65
Boyn Hill Gravel 13, **13**
bracken see *Pteridium aquilinum*
brackish-water environment 9, **10**, 17, 104, 109, 110, 113, 114, 115, 124
  Canada Water 95, 97
  Canning Town 100
  Joan Street 69, 72, 73–4, 76, 77
  Palace Chambers South 43, 46
  Parliament Square 37
  St Stephen's East 57, 58
  Storey's Gate 31, 32, 35
  Union Street 82, 83, 86
  Westminster 63
  Westminster Underground Station 49
braided river see Thames
Bramcote Green, Bermondsey 14
  Bronze Age 120
  lake 14
  Late Glacial deposits 119
  trackway 65
  vegetation 18, 19, 106
  Windermere interstadial 106
Brentford, Pleistocene strata 13
brick and tile
  Roman, Westminster 22
  Tudor, St Stephen's East 49
Bricklayers Arms, Bermondsey 65
bridges, Thorney Island 22
Broad Sanctuary, Westminster 18
  pollen 19, 116
Broadness, sea level 16
Bronze Age 12, 120–1
  agriculture 19, 60, 64–5, 76, 77, 113, 114, 117, 121, 122, 124
  ard marks 21, 63, 64–5, 117, 121, 122
  brackish-water conditions 113, 115
  climatic change 113
  dune systems 92
  erosive event (St Stephen's East) 60
  estuarine system, change to 44, 45
  halophytes 113, 115
  lime (*Tilia*) declines 33, 77, 98, 113–15, 117
  lime (*Tilia*) woodland 111, 113
  organic muds 27, 30, 34, 48
  peats 11, 93
  plough marks 65, 124
  pollen 27, 43, 46, 47, 60, 115, 116
  pottery 21, 89
  retrogressive hydrosere 113, 115
  revetments 21
  sea and water-level rise 78, 113, 122
  Thames 110
  tidal inundation 87, 97, 98
  tidal river 48, 60, 110, 122
  tidal surge 122
  trackways 19, 65, 122
  woodland and clearances 19, 45, 47, 60, 77, 98, 112, 113–15, 117
  Canada Water 93, 97, 98, 99, 114
  Canning Town 89
  Joan Street 76, 77
  Palace Chambers South 38, 39, 40, 41, 42, 43, 44, 45, 46, 47, 121
  St Stephen's East 60, 114

Storey's Gate, organic muds 27, 30, 34
Thorney Island 21
Union Street 78, 86, 114
Westminster 63, 122
Westminster Underground Station 48
Bryan Road, Rotherhithe 18, 19, 89, 90, 113
Burghal Hidage 66

Canada Docks 89, 92, 93
Canada Water (CAW91) **2**, 3, 89, 92–9, 100, 101, 104
  agriculture 96, 98, 114, 115
  brackish-water conditions 95, 97
  Bronze Age 93, 97, 98, 99, 114
  channel marginal processes 92, 93, 98
  channel migration 95
  charcoal 93
  deer antlers 3, 93
  diatoms 95, 97–8, 101
  estuarine environment 93, 95, 97, 98, 101
  fen 96–7
  flint 93, 95
  flooding 93, 95, 96, 97, 98
  floodplain 93, 95, 96, 97
  freshwater conditions 94, 95, 97
  Iron Age 97, 115, 116–17
  lithostratigraphy 93–4
  marshes 92, 93, 94, 95, 98
  molluscs 94
  monolith sampling 93
  mudflats 101
  Neolithic 93, 99
  organic muds 93, 95, 96, 98
  overbank flooding 93, 95
  peat 93, 94, 95, 96, 98, 101, 104, 109
  Pleistocene gravels 93, 98, 106
  pollen 94, 95–8, **96–8**, 99, 112, 114, 115, 116–17, 127
  pottery 94
  pre-Quaternary palynomorphs 95
  radiocarbon 93, 95, 101, **129**
  reclamation 97, 98
  river migration 93
  RSL 93, 94
  salinity 94, 95, 101
  samples **7**
  sands 93, 95, 98, 107
  silt/clays 93, 94, 95, 97
  thermoluminescence date 123, 128
  tidal processes 93, 95, 97
Canary Wharf station **2**, 7
Canning Town **2**, 3, 4, 89–101
  brackish-water conditions 100
  Bronze Age 89
  dune systems 99
  flooding 100
  land snails 100
  Limmo 99
    coring 6
    samples assessed 6
  lithostratigraphy 99–100
  marshes 90, 99, 100
  meandering river 99, 101
  Mesolithic 120
  mudflats 101
  organic muds 99–100
  palaeosol 100
  peats 100–1
  Pleistocene gravels 106
  post-medieval 90
  RSL 100
  sands 99, 101
  Saxon 90
  silt/clays 100
  Station site 99, 100
canons' house, Palace Chambers South **7**
cemetery, Bronze Age 89
cereal pollen 19, 112, 114, 116–17
  Canada Water 95, 96, 97
  Joan Street 69, 70, 71, 75, 76

Palace Chambers South 43, 46, 47
St Stephen's East 54, 55, 56, 59, 61, 63
Storey's Gate 28, 29, 33, 36, 37, 63
Union Street 79, 81, 84, 85
Westminster Underground Station 48, 49
cesspits, medieval 23
channel bars **104**, 120
channel junction bars 107
channel marginal position 37, 48, 50, 52, 53, 63, 78, 79, 92, 93, 98, 106, 119
channel margin bar 44
channel migration 11, 15, 16, 119
  Canada Water 95
  Canning Town 101
  Culling Road 92
  Joan Street 67–8, 69, 74
  Palace Chambers South 40, 43, 47
  Parliament Square 36
  St Stephen's East, Westminster 50, 52, 60
  Westminster 63, 108
channels (palaeochannels) 11, 13, 14, 106, 107
  abandoned 14, 15, 26, 40, 43, 50, 106, 119
  buried (Pleistocene) 14
  organic fills 14, 106, 107, 119
  Culling Road 91, 92
  Palace Chambers South 39, 40, 42, 43, 44
  Parliament Square 36, 37
  St Stephen's East 49, 50, 52–3, 60
  Storey's Gate (palaeochannel) 26
  Westminster 23
  Westminster Underground Station 48, 49
  see also channel marginal position; channel migration; Tyburn
charcoal
  Canada Water 93
  Culling Road 91
  Palace Chambers South 40, 41, 42, 45, 47
  Parliament Square 36
  St Stephen's East 50, 51, 52
  Union Street 79
  Westminster 63
  Westminster Underground Station 48
charlocks (Brassicaceae, Sinapis type) 37, 54, 56, 71
Chenopodiaceae 46, 49, 54, 55, 56, 59, 71, 86
Cherry Gardens 89
Chiswick Eyot 92, 120
chronological chart **12**
chronostratigraphy 5, 7, 10
Clapton 14
climate 12, 13, 15, 103, 107, 113
college of St Stephen's Chapel 48
colluviation, Culling Road 92
Colne river 119, 122
Copthall Avenue 18, 19
Corbets Tey Gravel 13, **13**
coring 5–6, **6**
Cornus see dogwood
Corylus avellana see hazel
Courage Brewery site 64, 65
Crayford **13**, 14
cremations, Bronze/Iron Age 65
Cromwell Green, pollen 116
cross-bedding 7, 15, **104**, 106, 107
Crossness 16, 17, 109
Culling Road, Rotherhithe 3, 89, 90–2, 101, 104, 107
  bar features 119
  channel (palaeochannel) 91, 92
    migration 92
  charcoal 91
  colluviation 92
  diagenesis 92
  dune development 92, 101, 107
  flint 91

lithostratigraphy 91–2, 104, 107
magnetic susceptibility 91, 92
Mesolithic 91
monolith tins 91
Neolithic 91, 92, 101, 104, 120
palaeosols 92
pedogenesis 92
Pleistocene gravels 91, 106
post-medieval 90, 91
pottery 91
radiocarbon dating 123
Roman/Romano-British 92, 101, 104
RSL 92
samples assessed 6
sands (eyot) 91–2, 107
sedimentology 91–2, 104, 107
silt/clays 92
Cyperaceae (sedges) 28, 29, 115
  Canada Water 96
  Joan Street 71, 72, 77
  Palace Chambers South 43
  Parliament Square 37
  St Stephen's East 55, 59
  Storey's Gate 35
  Union Street 85

Dagenham 16, 17
Dartford, sea level 16
Dartford Heath Gravel 13
deer antlers see antlers
deer park (St James's Park) 25
dendrochronology 10, 17
Devensian Late Glacial 11, 12, **12**, 14, 15, 106–7
  channel fills 14, 106, 107, 119
  Early 14
  gravels 14, 99, 101, 107
  Middle 14
  freshwater fluvial systems 14–15
  sands (Westminster) 33
  Thames development 103–10
  vegetation 18–19
  see also Thames, braided river
diagenesis 106
  Culling Road 92
  Palace Chambers South 39
  St Stephen's East 50, 51
  Westminster Underground Station 48
diatoms 6, **88**, **99**, 104, 108, 109, 110, 123, 125, 126, **126**
  analysis 9, **10**
  brackish 9, **10**, 17, 31, 32, 35, 37, 43, 49, 57, 58, 72, 73–4, 82, 83, 86, 95, 109
  estuarine 9, 18, 30, 31, 32, 43, 49, 56, 57, 58, 60, 72, 81, 82, 86, 95, 97–8
  freshwater 9, **10**, 17, **17**, 30, 31–2, 34, 37, 44, 49, 56, 57, 58, 61, 63, 72, 73, 81, 82, 83, 84, 86, 95, 109
  halobian groups 9, **10**, 128
  marine 9, **10**, 17, 31, 35, 37, 44, 49, 57, 58, 60, 61, 72, 73, 74, 82, 86, 110
  planktonic 9, 17, 18, 56, 57, 73, 82
  previous studies 17–18
  salinity 9, **10**, 17–18, 128 (and see separate entry)
  Canada Water 95, 97–8, 101
  Joan Street 67, 72–4, **74–7**
  Palace Chambers South 43–4, 47
  Parliament Square 37
  St Stephen's East 49, 56–8, **58**, 60, 61
  Storey's Gate 30–2, **32–5**, 33, 34, 35
  Union Street 77, 79, 81–3, 84, **84–7**, 85–6, 109, 110
  Westminster 61, 63, 106, 108, 109, 110
  Westminster Underground Station 49
  see also algae
Dimlington stadial **12**
docks
  Palace Chambers South, timber 38, 41
  Rotherhithe, post-medieval 90
  Thorney Island 23
dogwood (Cornus) 29, 116
Downing Street, Neolithic axe 120
drainage channels, Westminster

Underground Station 48
dune systems 15, 92, 107, 124
  Canning Town 99
  Culling Road 92, 101, 107
  Westminster 61, 107
Durands Wharf, Rotherhithe 7, 89

Elizabeth Fry School, Newham 18
elm (Ulmus) 19, 29, 34, 71, 75, 84, 95, 111, 112
elm decline 19, 74, 84, 111, 112, 114, 115
Enfield Lock 18, 19
Epping Forest, Neolithic lime declines 33
Erith
  'brickearth spread' 14
  Bronze Age 120
  Mesolithic 107, 119, 120, 124
  sand systems 15, 99, 107, 108
  see also Spine Road
estuarine habitats (systems) 14, 15–16, 103, 108, 109, **110**
  clays 11, 16
  diatoms 9, 109
  Roman and post-Roman 115
  three-stage model of development 16
  Canada Water 95, 97, 98, 101
  Joan Street 72
  Palace Chambers South 43, 44
  Rotherhithe 109
  St Stephen's East 56, 57, 58, 60, 61
  Southwark 109
  Storey's Gate 30, 31, 32
  Union Street 81, 82, 86, 109
  Westminster 63, 106, 108, 109
  Westminster Underground Station 49
eyots 16, 65, 120, 124
  Culling Eyot 91, 92

facies (facies-based modelling) 3, 6, 16, 60, 104, **104**, **105**, 107, 108, 123
  St Stephen's East Facies Associations 50–2, 60
Fagus see beech
Falcon House, pollen 115
Fennings Wharf 65
fens (fen carr; fen marsh) 111, 112, 114
  Canada Water 96–7
  Joan Street 69, 75, 76, 77, 115
  Parliament Square 37
  Union Street 85, 115
  poor fen 113
  shrubs 115
Ferndale Street 19, 113
ferns (Polypodium, Dryopteris) 28, 37, 43, 55, 56, 59, 71, 72
fieldwork 5–6
fir (Abies) 29, 34, 37, 115, 116
fish bone, St Stephen's East 52
Flandrian Chronozones I and II **12**, 19, 111, 113
Fleet river, pollution 18
flint (worked)
  Palaeolithic 121
  Mesolithic 21, 64, 91, 107, 119–20, 121, 124
  Neolithic 21, 91, 120
  Canada Water 93, 95
  Culling Road 91
  Palace Chambers South, prehistoric 38, 42, 44
  Parliament Square 36
  Rotherhithe 89
  Storey's Gate, prehistoric and burnt 26
  Westminster Underground Station, undated 48
flooding (flood deposits, events; inundation)
  short-lived 8
  Canada Water 93, 95, 96
  Canning Town 100
  Joan Street 68, 69, 73, 74, 77, 88
  Palace Chambers South 40, 41, 42, 44, 106
  Parliament Square 37
  St Stephen's East, Westminster 50, 54,

58, 106
  Southwark 87, 88
  Storey's Gate 26, 31, 35–6
  Thorney Island, 11th century 22
  Union Street 78, 79, 83–4, 88, 109
  Westminster Underground Station 49
  see also overbank deposits
floodplain 11, 13, 14, 15, 16, 19, 117, 121, 122
  vegetation 111, 112
  Canada Water 93, 95, 96, 97
  Joan Street 68, 69, 75, 76, 77
  Palace Chambers South 41, 45–6, 47
  St Stephen's East (floodplain marginal) 50, 52, 58–9, 60
  Storey's Gate 37
  Union Street 79, 83, 85, 87
foraminiferal analysis 123
Frangula alnus 29, 112
Fraxinus see ash
freshwater habitats 14–15, 104, 107, 108, 109, 110, 113, 115
  Pleistocene 14
  Canada Water 94, 95, 97
  Culling Road 92
  Joan Street 69, 71, 72, 73, 77, 109
  Palace Chambers South 41, 42, 43, 44, 46, 47
  St Stephen's East, Westminster 56, 57, 58, 59, 61, 63
  Storey's Gate 30, 31, 32, 34, 35
  Union Street 81–2, 83, 84, 86
  Westminster 61, 63, 108

Gatcombe Withy Bed, Isle of Wight 113
Geographic Information System (GIS) 123
geology, Late Quaternary 11–18
geomorphology 4, 11–18
'Goring gap' 12
Grand Surrey Canal 89
grasses 35, 85, 112, 113, 115
gravel terraces see Pleistocene
Grays 13, **13**
Grays Thurrock **13**, 14
Green Park, Palaeolithic **2**, 119
Green Yard 23

Hackney 14
halophytes 17, 46, 113, 115, 116
Hame 90
Hampstead Heath 18
  lime 113
  pollen 19, 113, 116
  vegetation 111, 112
Hampton Court, pollen 116
hazel (Corylus avellana) 9, 19, 28, 29, 30, 34, 35, 37, 43, 45, 46, 47, 48, 54, 55, 58, 59, 63, 84, 85, 98, 111, 112–13, 114, 115, 116
  Canada Water 94, 95, 96
  Joan Street 69, 70, 71, 75, 77
  Union Street 80
Hedera see ivy
hemp (Cannabis type) 56
herb pollen 9, 19, 28, 29, 37, 43, 48, 49, 54, 55, 56, 59, 60, 106, 112, 113, 114, 117
  Canada Water 94, 95, 96
  Joan Street 69, 70, 71, 75, 76
  Union Street 79, 80, 81
high-resolution sedimentary analysis 6
Highbury 14
Hockham Mere, pollen 113
holly (Ilex) 29, 34, 37, 59, 85, 111, 115, 116
hop pollen 75
Hopton Street 122, 64, 65
Hoxnian 13
hypocaust pila, Roman 22
Hystrichospheres 43, 46, 55, 56, 59, 76, 86, 97, 116

Ilex see holly
Ilford 13, 14
infra-red stimulated luminescence (IRSL)

123, 128
inn, late 13th-century, Westminster 23, **25**
Ipswichian periods 14, 119
Iron Age **12**, 121
  agriculture 46, 76, 108, 117
  inundation 69, 74
  lime 34
  lithostratigraphy 104
  marine transgression 76
  peats 11
  pollen (palynology) and vegetation 19, 34, 41, 43, 46, 76, 115, 117
  pottery 21
  research questions 124
  revetments 21
  tidal head 122
  Canada Water 97, 115, 116–17
  Joan Street 69, 74, 76, 115, 121
  Palace Chambers South 41, 43, 46
  Southwark 65
  Thorney Island 21
  Union Street 83, 84, 85, 115, 116–17, 121
  Westminster **62**, 108
  Westminster Underground Station, organic muds 48
Isle of Dogs **2**, 109, 120
  Bronze Age 120
  Iron Age 121
  see also Masthouse Terrace
Isle of Grain 16
Isle of Wight, lime 113
Isleworth 14
ivy (Hedera) 80, 111

Jewel Tower 23
Joan Street, Southwark (JOA90) 3, 66–77, 87, 88
  agriculture 75, 76, 77, 88, 112, 114
  brackish-water conditions 69, 72, 73–4, 76, 77
  Bronze Age 76, 77
  channel (migration) 67–8, 69, 74
  deer antlers 3
  diatoms 67, 72–4, **74–7**
  estuarine environment 72
  fen 69, 75, 76, 77
  flooding 68, 69, 73, 74, 77, 88
  floodplain 68, 69, 74, 75, 76, 77
  freshwater 69, 71, 72, 73, 77, 109
  gravel 67
  Iron Age 69, 74, 76, 115, 121
  lime decline 33, 77, 114
  lithostratigraphy 67–9, **67–8**, 72
  marine conditions 72, 73, 74
  marsh 70, 71, 72
  mineral magnetic data 66, 67
  molluscs 69
  monolith sampling 66, 72
  Neolithic 33, 75, 77, 112–13, 114
  organic carbon content (LOI) 66, 68, 69
  organic muds 66, 68, 69, 72, 73, 74, 109
  particle-size analysis 66, 69, 127, **127**
  peat 66–7, 68–9, 72, 74, 86, 87, 104, 106, 109, 112
  pollen 67, 69–72, **70–3**, 74–6, 77, 88, 111, 112–13, 114, 115, 116, 127
  pottery 66
  radiocarbon dating 66, 67, 69, 76, 88, 113, **129**
  Roman and post-Roman 115
  RSL rise 69, 76, 77
  salinity 72, 73, 74
  samples 5, **7**
  sedimentology 67–9
  silt/clays 66, 67, 68, 69, 72, 73

Kempton Park, Sunbury 18
Kempton Park Gravel 13, 14
Kesgrave Sands and Gravels 13
King Street 23

Lafone Street 65
Lambeth, Mesolithic 119

Langley Silt Complex 14
Late Glacial see Devensian Late Glacial
Late Quaternary see Quaternary
Lea river 99, 101, 122
    Late Upper Palaeolithic sites 119
lime (Tilia) 9, 19, 111, 112–13, 115–16
    Canada Water 94, 96, 97, 98
    Joan Street 69, 70, 71, 75, 77
    Palace Chambers South 43, 45, 47
    Parliament Square 37
    St Stephen's East 54, 55, 58, 59
    Storey's Gate 28, 29, 33–4, 35
    Union Street 80, 84, 85
    Westminster Underground Station 48
lime declines 33–4, 48, 49, 59, 63, 77, 85,
    95, 98, 113–15, 117
lithofacies 16, and see facies
lithostratigraphy 4, 5, 7–8, 16, 122–3
    methodology 125–6
    Thames sequences 104–6
    wetland sites 16
    Canada Water 93–4
    Canning Town 99–100
    Culling Road 91–2, 104, 107
    Joan Street 67–9, 67–8, 72
    Palace Chambers South 39–43, 42
    Parliament Square 36
    St Stephen's East, Westminster 50–2,
        51, 58
    Storey's Gate 26–7, 27
    Union Street 77–9, 78, 109
    Westminster 61, 107–8, 122
    Westminster Underground Station
        48, 106, 115
Loch Lomond stadial 12, 14, 15, 106,
    107
LOCUS 10
LOI (loss-on-ignition) see organic
    carbon content
London Bridge 2, 17
    bridge constructed 110
    Bronze Age ring-ditch near 120
    pollen 115
    Roman buildings 65
    samples (LBE95) 7
London Bridge Station, Neolithic 120
'Long Ditch' (the Tyburn) see Tyburn
loss-on-ignition (LOI) 126, 127, and see
    organic carbon content
Lottbridge Drove (E Sussex) 116
luminescence-dating 14, 123, 128
Lynch Hill Gravel 13

Maas river 15, 107
magnetic susceptibility (MS) analysis
    (mineral magnetic data) 8, 126–7, 126
    Culling Road 92
    Joan Street 66
    Palace Chambers South 45
    St Stephen's East, Westminster 49, 50,
        51
    Storey's Gate 26
    Union Street 79
Maidenhead formation 61
Malus (apple) 69, 116
Mar Dyke (Essex) 18
marine transgression 14, 15
marshes (marshland) 16, 19, 106, 110,
    114, 117, 122
    Canada Water 92, 93, 94, 95
    Canning Town 90, 99
    Joan Street 70, 71, 72
    Palace Chambers South 43
    Parliament Square 37
    St Stephen's East 55
    Storey's Gate 25, 28, 29
    Union Street 78, 79, 80, 81, 85
    Westminster 63, 106
    channel marginal
        Canada Water 92
        Union Street 78, 79
        Westminster 106
Masthouse Terrace, Isle of Dogs 14, 99,
    106, 107, 119
Maudit family 25
meandering river see Thames

mean sea level (MSL) 109
medieval 12
    agriculture 35, 36
    building (14th-century) 38
    diatoms 43–4
    pollen 46, 47
    pottery 38, 42, 43, 115
    river levels 37
    rubbish in the Thames 79
    samples 11–12
    sediments 38, 41
    storms 79
    Thames 103, 110
    tidal influence 86
    Tyburn tributary 53
    Rotherhithe 90
    St Stephen's East 51, 52, 53, 54, 60, 61
    Southwark 66, 87
    Storey's Gate 25, 26, 27, 31, 35
        channel 26, 34, 35, 36
    Thorney Island 22–3, 25
    Union Street 79, 86
    Westminster Underground Station
        48, 49
Meridian Point 19
Mesolithic 12, 119–20
    and effects of the Thames 121–2
    flint 21, 64, 107, 121, 124
    hearths 64
    maps of 122–3
    meander 107, 108
    pollen 112
    Southwark 64
    Thames 121, 122
    vegetation 112
    vegetation and environment 19
    Culling Road, flint blades 91
    Thorney Island 21
    Westminster 62, 123
mineral magnetic data see magnetic
    susceptibility
molluscs 6, 107, 126, 128
    Pleistocene 14
    land snails 100
    Canada Water 94
    Joan Street 69
    Palace Chambers South 42
    Parliament Square 36
    St Stephen's East, Westminster 49, 50,
        51, 52–4, 53, 128
    Union Street 79
monolith sampling 5–6, 6, 7–8, 125, 126
    Canada Water 93
    Joan Street 72
    Palace Chambers South 38, 45
    Parliament Square 36, 37
    St Stephen's East 49
    Storey's Gate 26
    Union Street 77
    Westminster Underground Station 48
monolith tins 5, 125, 126
Mucking Gravel 13, 13, 14
mudflats 17, 98, 101, 104, 121, 124

Neolithic 12, 120
    agriculture 64–5, 84, 112, 113
    ard marks 64–5
    axes 38, 42
    and effects of the Thames 122
    elm decline 84, 112
    flints 21, 91
    lime declines 33–4, 114
    lithostratigraphy 104
    peats 11, 83, 93, 95, 112, 113
    pollen (vegetation) 19, 84, 95, 111,
        112–13, 114
    pottery 21, 64
    sampling 38
    trackway 112, 120
    woodland and clearances 19, 45, 75,
        77
    Canada Water 93, 99
    Culling Road 91, 92, 101, 104, 120
    Joan Street 112–13, 114
    Palace Chambers South 38, 39, 40, 42,
        44, 45, 47, 120

Rotherhithe 89
    St Stephen's East 60
    Southwark 64
    Thorney Island 21
    Union Street 33, 83, 84, 112–13, 114
    Westminster 62, 120
New Fresh Wharf 18
New Palace Yard, Westminster 24
    drains and well 25
    gates 23
    peats 19
    timber dock 23
Newham, Elizabeth Fry School 18
Northern Line Ticket Hall site 65
Northfleet 13, 14
North Greenwich station 7, 89, 90

oak (Quercus) 10, 19, 111, 113, 115
    Canada Water 94, 95, 98
    Joan Street 69, 70, 71, 76, 77
    Palace Chambers South 43, 45, 46, 47
    Parliament Square 37
    St Stephen's East 54, 55, 58, 59
    Storey's Gate 28, 29, 30, 34
    Union Street 80, 84, 85
    Westminster 63
    Westminster Underground Station 48
oats 115, 116–17
optically stimulated luminescence (OSL)
    123
opus signinum, Roman 22
organic carbon content (loss-on-
    ignition analysis) 127
    of soils 8
    Joan Street 66, 68, 69
    Palace Chambers South 39, 40, 41, 42,
        45
    St Stephen's East 49, 50, 51
    Storey's Gate 26
    Union Street 77, 78, 78, 79, 85
organic muds 9, 15, 104, 104, 107, 109
    Canada Water 93, 95, 96, 98
    Canning Town 99–100
    Joan Street 66, 68, 69, 72, 73, 74, 109
    Palace Chambers South 38, 40–1, 43,
        45, 46, 47
    Parliament Square 37
    St Stephen's East 50, 52, 55
    Southwark 87
    Storey's Gate 26, 27, 28, 30, 31, 33, 34
    Union Street 77, 78, 79, 81, 85, 109
    Westminster 63, 106
    Westminster Underground Station
        48, 49, 48
Orsett Heath Gravel 13, 13
ostracod
    Pleistocene 14
    St Stephen's East 52
overbank (flood) deposits/processes
    104, 108
    Canada Water 93, 95
    Palace Chambers South 40, 45, 63
    St Stephen's East 104
    Storey's Gate 26
    Westminster 63
    Westminster Underground Station
        48, 49

palace of the bishops of Winchester 66
Palace Chambers South (WSS94)
    37–47, 61, 63, 107
    agriculture 46, 47
    AMS 39
    brackish-water 43, 46
    Bronze Age 38, 39, 40, 41, 42, 43, 44,
        45, 46, 47, 121
    canons' house, late 14th-century 7
        39, 40, 42, 43, 44
    charcoal 40, 41, 42, 45, 47
    diatoms 43–4, 47
    estuarine system 41, 43, 44
    flint, prehistoric 38, 42, 44
    flood deposits 40, 41, 42, 44, 63, 106
    freshwater 41, 42, 43, 44, 46, 47
    Iron Age 41, 43, 46
    lithostratigraphy 39–43, 42

magnetic susceptibility 40, 41, 45
marine influence 44
meandering river 44, 107
medieval
    building 7, 38
    diatoms 43–4
    pollen 46, 47
    pottery 38, 42, 43
    sediments 38, 41, 47
    wall and dock 38, 41–2
molluscs 42
monolith samples 38, 45
Neolithic 38, 39, 40, 42, 44, 45, 47,
    120
organic carbon contents 39, 40, 41,
    42, 43, 45
organic muds 38, 40–1, 43, 45, 46, 47
overbank deposits 40, 45, 47, 63
particle-size analysis 39, 41, 127, 127
peat 115
pedogenesis 45
pollen 38, 43, 44, 45–6, 47, 115, 116,
    127
pottery 38, 41, 42, 43, 44, 120
radiocarbon dating 38, 39, 40, 124
reclamation 38
retrogressive hydrosere 43
river wall, 12th-century 38, 41, 42
RSL 41, 43, 44, 45, 47
samples 6, 7
sands 38, 39–40, 41, 42, 43, 44, 107,
    124
sedimentology 39–43
silt/clays 38, 39, 40, 41, 42, 43, 44, 45,
    46, 47, 63, 106
Site 1 east 37, 38, 44
Site 1 west 37, 38, 43, 44
Site [2] 38, 42, 43, 44
Site [6] 38
tidal waters 44, 45, 46
palaeochannels see channels
palaeoecology 3; and see diatoms; pollen
palaeoenvironmental project 2–3, 4, 7,
    11–19
Palaeolithic 118–19
    evidence of activity 121
    flint 121
    stone tools 118–19
    Thames 119, 121
    Upper Palaeolithic 12, 119
palaeosols 92, 126
    Canning Town 100
    Culling Road 92
    Storey's Gate 28, 33, 35
    Union Street 77
paludification (inundation) 97, 114; see
    also flooding
palynology see pollen
parasite ovum, St Stephen's East 56
Park Street see Courage Brewery site
Parliament Square (PSQ94),
    Westminster 22, 36–7, 63, 114
    brackish-water conditions 37
    channel 36, 37
    channel migration 36
    charcoal 36
    diatoms 37
    flint 36
    flooding 37
    freshwater 37
    lithostratigraphy 36
    marine environment 37
    medieval 36, 37
    molluscs 36
    monolith samples 36, 37
    organic muds 37
    pollen 37, 38–9, 115, 116
    pottery, Early Iron Age 21
    retrogressive hydrosere 37
    samples 7
    sands 36
    silt/clays 36, 37
particle-size analysis 8, 125, 127, 127
    Joan Street 66, 69, 127, 127
    Palace Chambers South 39, 41, 127,
        127

St Stephen's East, Westminster **41**, 49, 50, 51, 127, **127**
Union Street 79, 127, **127**
peat 11, 16, 19, 59, 104, 106, 108, 109
 analysis (palynology) 8, 9, 18, 19
 Holocene formation 10, 16
 organic carbon content 8
 vegetation 111
  Canada Water 93, 94, 95, 96, 98, 101, 104, 109
  Canning Town 100–1
  Joan Street 66–7, 68–9, 72, 74, 86, 104, 106, 109, 112
  Palace Chambers South 115
  Rotherhithe and Canning Town 89, 101
  Southwark 86–8, 106
  Storey's Gate 26, 35–6
  Union Street 77–8, 79, 81, 83–4, 85, 86–7, 104, 106, 109, 112
pedogenesis 8
 Culling Road 92
 Palace Chambers South 45
 St Stephen's East 50, 60
 Storey's Gate 26
Peninsula House 19
Phoenix Wharf 64, 65, 122
pine (*Pinus*) 9, 14, 18, 19, 29, 30, 37, 43, 46, 47, 70, 71–2, 75, 80, 85, 114, 115, 116
Platform Wharf 66, 90
Pleistocene 12–14, **12**, **13**, 15, 118, 119
 environments 106
 gravels/gravel terraces 3, 10, 11, 12–14, 124
  Canada Water 93, 98, 106
  Canning Town 99, 106
  Culling Road 106
  Union Street 106
 pollen 116
plough marks, Bronze Age 65, 124
Plough Way 90
point bars 107
Point Pleasant, Wandsworth 18, 19
pollen (palynology) 8–9, 106, 107, 123, 125, 126, **126**, 127–8
 anemophily 9
 assessment 6
 entomophily 9
 research questions 124
 Early Holocene 14, 18–19
 Pleistocene 14
 Late Devensian 18
 Mesolithic 19, 112
 Neolithic 19
 Iron Age 19
 Romano-British 19
  Canada Water 94, 95–8, **96–8**, 99, 112, 114, 115, 116–17, 127
  Joan Street 67, 69–72, **70–3**, 74–6, 77, 111, 112–13, 114, 115, 127
  Palace Chambers South 38, 43, **44**, 45–6, 47, 115, 116, 127
  Parliament Square 37, **38–9**, 115
  St Stephen's East 49, 54–6, **54–7**, 58–60, 61, 112, 114, 115, 116, 127
  Southwark 88
  Storey's Gate 27–30, 33–4, 35–6, 114, 115, 116, 127
  Union Street 77, 79–81, **80–3**, 84–6, 111, 112–13, 114, 115, 116–17, 127
  Westminster 63
  Westminster Underground Station 48–9, 116
 see also by name
Poole Harbour, pollen 116
post-medieval 12, **12**
 vegetation (pollen) 116
 Culling Road 90, 91
 Rotherhithe 90
 Southwark 66
 Storey's Gate 25–6, 35
 Union Street 77
 Westminster Underground Station 48
Potamogeton (pondweed) 43, 46, 86
pottery 8

prehistoric 89, 93
 Late Neolithic 21
  Peterborough ware 91
 Beaker 64
 Early Bronze Age 21
 Bronze Age urns 89
 Iron Age 21
 Roman 79, 87
  Grey ware 91
  Verulamium ware 78
 medieval and post-medieval 48, 49, 93
  delftware bottle 25
  green-glazed 79
  Kingston ware 49, 51
  Storey's Gate 26, 27, 34
  Tudor 49
  Tudor Brown ware 79
  watering cans, 16th-century 48
 Canada Water 93
 Culling Road 91
 Joan Street 66
 Palace Chambers South 38, 41, 42, 43, 44, 120
 Thorney Island 21
 Union Street 78, 79, 87
pre-Quaternary palynomorphs 46, 55, 56, 59, 72, 76, 81, 95, 116
Prunus 116
Pteridium aquilinum (bracken) 28, 30, 43, 48, 55, 71, 72, 86
Pudding Lane, diatom studies 17
Purfleet 13, **13**, 14

Quaternary (Late), geology and geomorphology 11–18, **15**
quays, Roman 17, 110
Quercus see oak

radiocarbon dating 6, 10, 113, 114, 123, 125, **126**, 128, **129**
 Early Holocene 15
 pollen 18, 19
 Thames 108, 109
 Canada Water 93, 95, 101, **129**
 Joan Street 66, 67, 69, 76, 88, 113, **129**
 Palace Chambers South 38, 39, 40, 124
 St Stephen's East, Westminster 52, 60
 Thorney Island 22
 Union Street 77, 78, 114, **129**
 Westminster Underground Station 48
Rainham, lime 113
Rainham Marshes 19
reclamation 110
 Canada Water 97, 98
 Palace Chambers South 38
 St Stephen's East, Westminster 61
 Southwark 65, 86, 87
 Storey's Gate 35
 Thorney Island 23
 Union Street 86
 Westminster Underground Station 48, 49
Redcross Way, Southwark 1, 6
Redriff 90
reeds and reed fen/swamp 29, 35, 36, 85, 96, 113, 115
Regis House, Roman quays 17
relative sea level (RSL) 11, 14, 15–17, 103, 104, 108, 109, 112, 113, 115, 118, 120
 Pleistocene 14
 Bronze Age/Iron Age 121
 Roman 17
 medieval 17
 Canada Water 93, 94
 Canning Town 100
 Culling Road 92
 Joan Street 69, 76, 77
 Palace Chambers South 43, 44, 45, 47
 Union Street 84, 85, 86
 Westminster 108
 Westminster Underground Station 49
research priorities in the future 123–4
retrogressive hydrosere
 Bronze Age 113, 115

Palace Chambers South 43
Parliament Square 37
Roman 115
revetments
 late medieval/Tudor, St Stephen's East 61
 Thorney Island, Bronze Age/Iron Age 21
 Thames Court, 12th-century 17
Rhamnus catharticus 43, 112, 116
Richmond 107
ring-ditch, Bronze Age 120
river defences 35, 49, 103, 110
river wall, Palace Chambers South, 12th-century 38, 41, 42
Roman **12**
 cultivation (pollen) 116–17
 floodplain silt/clays 104
 Londinium 51, 65, 110
 pollen (Romano-British) 18, 19
 pottery 78, 79, 87, 91
 quays 17, 110
 research questions 124
 retrogressive hydrosere 115
 sea and river levels 17
 tidal head migration 17, 77, 110, 122
 tile (Romano-British) 26
 vegetation 59, 115, 17
 Culling Road 92, 101, 104
 Joan Street 115
 Rotherhithe 89–90
 Southwark 65
 Storey's Gate 26
 Thorney Island 22, 25
 Union Street 78, 79, 87, 115
 Westminster Underground Station 115
Rosary, Edward II's residence 66
Rotherhithe 4, 89–101
 prehistoric 89
 Iron Age 121
 Roman 89–90
 Saxon 90
 medieval 90
 post-medieval 90
 tidal waters 109
RSL *see* relative sea level
Runnymede Bridge 18, 19, 111, 113
Rupack Street 89

Saalian/Wolstonian 13
St James's Park
 as a deer park 25
 Iron Age coin hoard 121
 see also Storey's Gate
St James's Square, Palaeolithic artefacts 119
St Saviour's Abbey, Bermondsey 66
St Stephen's Chapel
 canons' houses 23, **24**
 college of 48
St Stephen's East, Westminster (SSE94) 49–61, 104
 agriculture, late prehistoric 59, 60
 brackish-water conditions 57, 58, 114
 brick and tile, Tudor 49
 Bronze Age 60, 114
 channel migration 50, 52, 60
 channels 49, 50, 52–3, 60
 charcoal 50, 51, 52
 diagenesis 50, 51
 diatoms 49, 56–8, **58**, 60, 61
 estuarine environment 56, 57, 58, 60, 61
 fish bone 52
 flooding 50, 54, 58, 106, 114
 floodplain marginal 50, 52, 58–9, 60
 freshwater 56, 57, 58, 59, 61, 63
 lithostratigraphy 50–2, **51**, 58
 magnetic susceptibility analysis 49, 50, 51
 marine influence 57, 60, 61
 medieval 51, 52, 53, 54, 60, 61
 molluscs 49, 50, 51, 52–4, **53**, 128
 monolith samples 49
 Neolithic (Late) 60

organic carbon content (LOI) 49, 50, 51
organic muds 50, 52, 55
overbank flooding 53, 104
parasite ovum 56
particle-size analysis 41, 49, 50, 51, 127, **127**
pedogenesis 50, 60
pollen 49, 54–6, **54–7**, 58–60, 61, 112, 114, 115, 116, 127
pottery 49, 51, 52
radiocarbon dating 52, 60
reclamation 61
revetment, late medieval/Tudor 61
saline water 56, 57
salt marshes 59
samples **7**
sands 49, 50, 51, 52
sedimentology 50–2
silt/clays 49, 50, 51–2, 106
tidal influences 57, 58, 59, 60, 114
Tudor period 49, 52, 54, 61
Tyburn tributary 52, 53, 61, 63, 106
salinity (saline conditions) 9, **10**, 17–18, 115, 128
 Canada Water 95, 101
 Joan Street 72, 73, 74
 Palace Chambers South 46, 47
 St Stephen's East 56, 57
 Storey's Gate 30, 31, 32, 34, 35
 Union Street 81, 82, 83
Salix see willow
salt marshes 113, 121
 pollen and diatoms 116
 St Stephen's East 59
 Westminster Underground Station 49
sampling 2, 5–6; *see also* monolith sampling; trench sampling
sand bars 44, 52, 120
sand islands 65, 120, 124
sands (sand strata; sand facies) 10, 11, 15, 44, 104, 106, 107–8, **108**, 124
 Canada Water 93, 95, 98, 107
 Canning Town 99, 101
 Culling Road 91–2, 107
 Palace Chambers South 38, 39–40, 41, 42, 43, 44, 107, 124
 Parliament Square 36
 St Stephen's East 49, 50, 51, 52
 Storey's Gate 26, 27, 32–3, 35
 Westminster 107–8, 109, 120
 Westminster Underground Station 48, 49
Sandy Lane 14
sarcophagus, stone, Roman 22
Saxon **12**, 110, 113–14, 124
 Lundenwic 110
 pollen (vegetation) 19, 116
 sea levels 17
 Rotherhithe 90
 Southwark 65–6
 Thorney Island (Middle Saxon) 22
 Westminster (Middle Saxon) 22
sea level *see* relative sea level
sedge fen 37, 97, 112
sedges *see* Cyperaceae
Sedigraph techniques 8
sedimentology 3, 7–8, 125–7
 Culling Road 91–2, 104, 107
 Joan Street 67–9
 Palace Chambers South 39–43
 Rotherhithe and Canning Town 101
 St Stephen's East, Westminster 50–2
 Storey's Gate 26–7
 Union Street 77–9, **78**, 109
sediments, assessment 6
seeds 8
Shacklewell 14
Shepperton Gravel **13**, 14, 67, 91, 99, 106, 107, 119
ship timbers, from a cog 23
shrubs 9, 29, 34, 37, 43, 59, 69, 70, 75, 94, 111, 112, 116; *and see by name*
silt/clays 16, 104, **104**, 108, 109, 110
 Canada Water 93, 94, 95, 97
 Canning Town 100

Culling Road 92
Joan Street 66, 67, 68, 69, 72, 73
Palace Chambers South 38, 39, 40, 41, 42, 44, 45, 46, 47, 106
Parliament Square 36, 37
St Stephen's East 49, 50, 51–2, 106
Storey's Gate 26, 27, 30, 31, 35
Union Street 77, 79, 81, 86
Westminster 61, 63, 106, 108
Westminster Underground Station 48, 115
Silvertown
    abandoned channels 14
    Bronze Age trackways 19
    channel fills 106
    dune sequence (Early Holocene) 92
    Late Glacial deposits 106, 119
    lime 113
    Neolithic trackway 112, 120
    organic muds 107
    peat strata 101
    pollen 18, 19, 37, 106
    sand systems 15, 99
    sea level 109, **110**
    vegetation 18
    see also West Silvertown Urban Village
South Kensington Ismaili Centre 14
Southwark 1, **2**, 4, **65**
    Mesolithic 64, 119, 120, 122, 123
    Neolithic 64, 120
    Bronze Age 110, 121
        ard marks 64–5, 117, 122
        tidal inundation 87
    Iron Age 65, 121
    Roman 64, 65, 87
    Saxon 65–6
    medieval 66, 87
    post-medieval 66
    estuary 87, 106, 109
    flooding 87, 88
    organic mud 87
    peat 86–8, 106, 120
    pollen 18, 88
    reclamation 86, 87
    sedimentation and environment 86–8, 104, 110, 124
    silt/clays 124
    south bank tributary 123
    three-stage model 87
    tidal waters 88, 109, 110
    see also Joan Street; Union Street
Southwark Park 90
Spine Road, Erith 119, 122
spring tides 41, 109
spruce (Picea) 28, 34, 37, 43, 55, 59, 63, 116
Stoke Newington 14
Storey, Edward 25
Storey organic mud bed 63, **63**, 104, 106, 109
Storey's Gate, Westminster (SGT94) 25–36, 61, 104, 106
    agriculture, medieval 35, 36
    brackish-water conditions 31, 32, 35
    Bronze Age 27, 30, 34, 116
    channel, Tyburn (palaeo)channel 25, 26, 32–3, 34, 35, 36
    diatoms 30–2, **32–5**, 33, 34, 35
    estuarine environment 30, 31, 32
    flint, prehistoric and burnt 26
    flood events 26, 27, 31, 35–6
    freshwater 30, 31, 32, 34, 35
    lithostratigraphy 26–7
    magnetic susceptibility 26
    marine species 31, 34, 35
    marshes 25, 28, 29
    medieval 25, 26, 27, 31, 35, 115
        channel 26–7, 34, 35, 36
    monolith sampling 26
    organic carbon content 26
    organic muds 26, 27, 28, 30, 31, 33, 34, 114
    overbank deposits 26
    palaeosol 28, 33, 35
    peat 26, 35

pedogenesis 26
pollen 27–30, 33–4, 35–6, 114, 115, 116, 127
post-medieval 25–6, 35
pottery 26, 27
    medieval 26, 27, 34
    reclamation 35
    river defences 35
    Romano-British tile 26
    samples **7**
    sands 26, 27, 32–3, 35, 108
    sedimentology 26–7
    silt/clays 26, 27, 30, 31, 35
    tidal environment 32, 34, 35
    storm event 41
    Union Street 79, 86
Strand, Palaeolithic 119
Stratford 1, **2**
    Palaeolithic artefacts 119
    Mesolithic 119
    Neolithic 120
    Saxon 90
Strathville Road 18, 19
Swanscombe Gravels 13, **13**, 119
Swanscombe skull 13

Taplow Gravel 13, **13**, 14, 119
Temple of Mithras 18
    peats 19
    pollen 116
Thames 4, 11–12, **15**
    development 14–15, 103–10
        Pleistocene 12–14
        braided river, Late Devensian 13, 14, 15, 103, 106–7, 119, 121
        meandering (freshwater) river, Early and Middle Holocene 14, 15, 92, 101, 104, 107–9, 119, 121–2, 124
        Canning Town 99, 101
        Palace Chambers South 44, 107
        Westminster 61, 110
        transition to tidal river 109–10, 122
        tidal river in the Late Holocene 110, 124
    ceramics in clastic content 79
    confluence with Tyburn 35, 106, 107, 110
    diatom studies 17–18
    lithostratigraphic sequences 104–6
    sea-level change (Middle Holocene to later) 15–17
    tributaries 3, 14, 42, 43
    see also tidal environment; tidal head
Thames Court
    chronology 10
    river levels 17
Thames Foreshore Survey 120
'Thames-Tilbury' model 16
Thamesmead 16
Thatcham (Berks), Mesolithic 119
thermoluminescence (TL) date, Canada Water 123, 128
Thorney Island, Westminster 21–5, **24**, 122, 123
    dune systems 107
    flooding, 11th-century 22, 110
    hiatus 110, 122
    meander bend 110
    pollen 115
    pottery 21
    radiocarbon 22
    reclamation 23
    sand bed **63**
    tidal river 110
    Mesolithic 21
    Neolithic 21
    Bronze Age 21
        farming 63, 124
    Iron Age 21
    Roman 22, 25
    Middle Saxon 22
    medieval 22–3, 25
        river defences 110
Three Ways Wharf, Uxbridge 18, 19, 119, 121, 122

tidal environment (tidal river/waters) 3, 17
    transition to 109
    in the Late Holocene 110
    medieval 63
    Joan Street 69
    Palace Chambers South 44, 45, 46
    St Stephen's East 57, 58, 59, 60, 114
    Westminster Underground Station 48, 49
tidal head
    Iron Age 122
    location 110, 124
    St Stephen's East 52
tidal head migrations 110, 124
    Bronze Age 34, 35, 36, 122
    Roman period 17, 77, 110, 122
    Joan Street 77
    Southwark 110
    Storey's Gate 34, 35, 36
    Union Street 110
tidal islands 17
Tilbury 15, 16, 109
Tilbury Marshes Gravel **13**, 14
Tilia see lime
topographic modelling 10, 122, 123, 129
Tower of London, pollen 115, 116
trackways
    Neolithic 112, 120
    Bronze Age 19, 65, 120, 122
Trafalgar Square
    Palaeolithic 119
    Pleistocene strata **13**, 14, 118
trees (pollen) 9; see also by name
Tregaron Bog, pollen 113
trench sampling 5
Tudor
    Parliament Square 36
    pollen 18, 19, 116
    St Stephen's East 49, 52, 54, 61
Tudor Street 18
Tyburn river 110
    confluence with Thames 35, 106, 107, 110
    as 'Long Ditch' 25, 36
    St Stephen's East, tributary 52, 53, 61, 63, 106
    Storey's Gate, (palaeo)channel 25, 26–7, 32–3, 34, 35, 36
    Thorney Island 21
    Westminster, dry-land topography **62**
    Westminster Underground Station 49, 106

Ulmus see elm
Union Street, Southwark (UNS91) 3, 77–86, 87–8
    agriculture 77, 79, 84, 86, 112, 114
    brackish-water conditions 82, 83, 86
    Bronze Age (Late) 78, 86, 114
    charcoal 79
    diatoms 77, 79, 81–3, 84, **84–7**, 85–6, 109, 110
    estuarine environment 81, 82, 86, 109
    floodplain 79, 83, 85, 87
    floods 78, 79, 83–4, 88, 109
    freshwater 81–2, 83, 84, 86
    Iron Age 83, 84, 85, 115, 116–17, 121
    lithostratigraphy 77–9, **78**, 109
    magnetic susceptibility 79
    marsh 78, 79, 80, 81, 85
    medieval 79, 86
    molluscs 79
    monolith sampling 77
    Neolithic 33, 83, 84, 112–13, 114
    organic carbon contents (LOI) 77, 78, **78**, 79, 85
    organic muds 77, 78, 79, 81, 85, 109
    palaeosols 77
    particle-size analysis 79, 127, **127**
    peat 77–8, 79, 81, 83–4, 85, 86–7, 104, 106, 109, 112
    Pleistocene gravels 106
    ploughsoils, post-medieval 77, 79
    pollen 77, 79–81, **80–3**, 84–6, 111, 112, 113, 114, 115, 116–17, 127

post-medieval 77
pottery 78, 79, 87
radiocarbon dating 77, 78, 109, 114, **129**
reclamation 86
Roman 78, 79, 87, 115
RSL rise 84, 85, 86
salinity 81–2, 83
samples **7**
sedimentology 77–9, **78**, 109
semi-permanent pools 78
silt/clays 77, 79, 81, 83, 86
storm event 79, 86
terrestrial deposits 12
tidal head migrations 82, 110
tidal processes 82, 84, 86, 87, 88, 109
Upper Palaeolithic see Palaeolithic
Uxbridge 18; see also Three Ways Wharf

vegetation 2, 4, 12
    autochthonous 9
    natural 111–12
    Holocene 3, 12, 18–19, 111–17
    Late Devensian 18–19
    Mesolithic 112
    Neolithic 111, 112–13, 114
    Bronze Age 111, 112, 113–15, 117
    Iron Age 115, 117
    Roman 115–17
    post-Roman 115–17
    see also pollen; shrub; trees
Viburnum 112, 116
Vistula river 15

walnut (Juglans) 19, 56, 59, 63, 116
Warta river 107
Waterloo, Mesolithic **2**, 119
Watling Street 65
weeds (pollen) 36, 46, 47, 48, 55, 85, 113, 114
wells, 16th-century 48
West Drayton
    abandoned channels 14
    Palaeolithic artefacts 119
West Drayton Marshes 18
Westhamme 90
Westminster 1, 2, **2**, 4, 12, 21–63, **23**, 124
    agriculture 1, 63, 108
    bar features 119
    brackish-water conditions 63, 110, 124
    Bronze Age 63, 121, 122
    channel migration 40, 43, 47, 50, 52, 60, 63, 108
    charcoal 63
    dendrochronology 10, 17
    diatoms 61, 63, 106, 108, 109, 110
    dune systems 61, 107
    estuarine environment 63, 106, 108, 109, 110
    freshwater 61, 63, 108, 110
    Iron Age 21, **62**, 108, 124
    lithostratigraphy 61, **63**, 107–8, 122
    marsh 63, 106
    meandering river 61, 107, 110
    medieval 41, 63, 110, 124
    Mesolithic **62**, 119–20, 123
    Neolithic 1, **62**, 120
    organic muds 63, 106
    overbank deposits 63
    pollen 63
    project assessment 6
    radiocarbon dating 123
    RSL 17, 108, 110
    sands (sand facies) 32–3, 48, 61, 107–8, 109, 120
    sedimentation and environment 61–3, 104–5, 110, 124
    silt/clays 41, 61, 63, 106, 108
    tidal head 124
    topographic modelling 10
    see also Palace Chambers South; St Stephen's East; Westminster Underground Station
Westminster Abbey 22, **24**, 63

Precinct, foreshore deposits 18
precinct walls and drain 23
Roman activity 22
Westminster Bridge 120
Bronze Age 120
Westminster Hall (Great Hall) 22, 23
Westminster Palace 22–3
Westminster Underground Station
(WUS90) 47–9, 106
brackish-water conditions 49
Bronze Age 48
channels 48, 49
charcoal 48
diatoms 49

drainage channels 48
estuarine 49
flint, undated 48
flooding (tidal) 49
freshwater marsh 49
Iron Age, organic muds 48
Late Bronze Age/Early Iron Age 48
lithostratigraphy 48, 106, 115
medieval 48, 49
monolith samples 48
organic muds 48, 49
overbank processes 48, 49
pollen 48–9, 116
post-medieval 48

pottery 48
radiocarbon dating 48
reclamation 48, 49
river defences, medieval 49
Roman and post-Roman 115
RSL rise 49
salt marsh taxa 49
samples 7
sands 26, 33, 48, 49
silt/clays 48, 115
tidal influences 48, 49
Tyburn 49, 106
well, 16th-century 48
West Silvertown Urban Village, sea level

16
West Thurrock 13, 14
Whitehall, Palaeolithic 119
'Wideflet' 66
William Street 77
willow (Salix) 36, 43, 55, 69, 70, 75, 112
Windermere interstadial 12, 14, 15, 18,
106, 107, 119
Wolseley Street 65
Wolstonian see Saalian/Wolstonian
Woolstaple 23
WSS see Palace Chambers South

yew (Taxus) 111, 112